Native Lordship in Medieval Scotland

For Grant G. Simpson

Native Lordship in Medieval Scotland

The Earldoms of Strathearn and Lennox, c.1140–1365

CYNTHIA J. NEVILLE

FOUR COURTS PRESS

Set in 10.5 pt on 12 pt Bembo for
FOUR COURTS PRESS LTD
7 Malpas Street, Dublin 8, Ireland
e-mail: info@four-courts-press.ie
http://www.four-courts-press.ie
and in North America by
FOUR COURTS PRESS
c/o ISBS, 920 N.E. 58th Avenue, Suite 300, Portland, OR 97213.

© Cynthia J. Neville 2005

A catalogue record for this title
is available from the British Library.

ISBN 1–85182–890–7

All rights reserved. No part of this publication may be
reproduced, stored in or introduced into a retrieval system, or transmitted, in
any form or by any means (electronic, mechanical, photocopying, recording
or otherwise), without the prior written permission of both the copyright
owner and publisher of this book.

Printed in England
by Antony Rowe Ltd, Chippenham, Wilts.

Contents

LIST OF MAPS AND TABLES	vi
LIST OF ABBREVIATIONS	vii
ACKNOWLEDGMENTS	ix
INTRODUCTION	1
1 The earls of Strathearn and the earls of Lennox, *c.*1140–1365	13
2 Lay tenants and household officials	39
3 Lords of property and lords of men: authority, power, and revenues	79
4 Relations with the church	131
5 Gaelic lordship in 'Anglo-Norman era' Scotland	185
CONCLUSION	222
BIBLIOGRAPHY	227
INDEX	241

Maps and tables

MAPS

1. Settlement in Strathearn, c.1170–1350 — xii
2. Settlement in Lennox, c.1170–1365 — xiv

TABLES

1. Genealogical table of Strathearn family, c.1140–1350 — 11
2. Genealogical table of Lennox family, c.1185–1365 — 12

Abbreviations

APS	*Acts of the parliaments of Scotland* (11 vols, Edinburgh, 1814–44).
Barrow, *Kingdom*	G.W.S. Barrow, *The kingdom of the Scots: government, church and society from the eleventh to the fourteenth century* (2nd edn. Edinburgh, 2003)
BL	British Library
CDS	*Calendar of documents relating to Scotland preserved in Her Majesty's Public Record Office, London*, ed. J. Bain (4 vols, Edinburgh, 1881–8)
CDS, v	*Calendar of documents relating to Scotland preserved in the Public Record Office and the British Library, vol. V (Supplementary)* (Edinburgh, 1986)
ER	*Rotuli scaccarii regum Scotorum: the Exchequer Rolls of Scotland*, ed. J. Stuart et al. (23 vols, Edinburgh, 1878–1908)
Duncan, *Making*	A.A.M. Duncan, *Scotland: the making of the kingdom* (Edinburgh, 1975)
Chron. Fordun	*Johannis de Fordun, Chronica gentis Scotorum*, ed. W.F. Skene (2 vols, Edinburgh, 1871–2)
Fraser, *Lennox*	W. Fraser (ed.), *The Lennox* (2 vols, Edinburgh 1874)
Glasgow Reg.	*Registrum episcopatus Glasguensis*, ed. C. Innes (2 vols, Bannatyne Club, 1843)
Inchaff. Chrs.	*Charters, bulls and other documents relating to the abbey of Inchaffray*, ed. W.A. Lindsay, J. Dowden and J.M. Thomson (Scottish History Society, 1908)
Inchaff. Liber	*Liber Insule Missarum*, ed. C. Innes (Bannatyne Club, 1847)
Lennox Cart.	*Cartularium comitatus de Levenax ab initio seculi decimi tertii usque ad annum* MCCCXCVIII, ed. J. Dennistoun (Maitland Club, 1833)
Lind. Cart.	*Chartulary of the abbey of Lindores, 1195–1479*, ed. J. Dowden (Scottish History Society, 1903)

Moray Reg.	Registrum episcopatus Moraviensis, e pluribus codicibus consarcinatum circa A.D. MCCCC, ed. C. Innes (Bannatyne Club, 1837)
MRHS	I.B. Cowan and D.E. Easson (eds), Medieval religious houses: Scotland with an appendix on the houses in the Isle of Man (2nd edn, London, 1976)
NAS	National Archives of Scotland
NLS	National Library of Scotland
Neville, 'Earls of Strathearn'	C.J. Neville, 'The earls of Strathearn from the twelfth to the mid-fourteenth century, with an edition of their written acts' (PhD thesis, 2 vols, University of Aberdeen, 1983)
NMRS	National Monuments Record of Scotland
Origines	Origines parochiales Scotiae, ed. C. Innes et al. (2 vols in 3, Bannatyne Club, 1850–5)
Paisley Reg.	Registrum monasterii de Passelet, ed. C. Innes (Maitland Club, 1832)
PSAS	Proceedings of the Society of Antiquaries of Scotland
RCHAMS	Royal Commission on the Ancient and Historical Monuments of Scotland
RMS	Registrum magni sigilli regum Scotorum: the register of the great seal of Scotland, ed. J.M. Thomson et al. (11 vols, Edinburgh, 1882–1914)
RRS, i	Acts of Malcolm IV, king of Scots, 1153–1165, ed. G.W.S. Barrow (Edinburgh, 1960)
RRS, ii	Acts of William I, king of Scots, 1165–1214, ed. G.W.S. Barrow (Edinburgh, 1971)
RRS, v	Acts of Robert I, king of Scots, 1306–29, ed. A.A.M. Duncan (Edinburgh, 1987)
RRS, vi	Acts of David II, king of Scots, 1329–1371, ed. B. Webster (Edinburgh, 1982)
SAS	Society of Antiquaries of Scotland
Scotichronicon	Scotichronicon by Walter Bower, ed. D.E.R. Watt et al. (9 vols, 1987–98)
SHR	Scottish Historical Review
SHS	Scottish History Society
SP	J. Balfour Paul, The Scots peerage (9 vols, Edinburgh, 1904–14)
TA	Accounts of the lord high treasurer of Scotland: compota thesaurarioru regum Scotorum (13 vols, Edinburgh, 1877–1978)
TRHS	Transactions of the Royal Historical Society

Acknowledgments

My interest in the study of native lordship in medieval Scotland began several years ago, when I was a doctoral candidate. This book has therefore had a long gestation, and its completion would not have been possible without the assistance of a number of organizations and persons. I must acknowledge first the generous financial support of the Social Sciences and Humanities Research Council of Canada and its fine officers, especially Laurent Messier. In the fall term of 1999 I had the good fortune to spend a term at the University of Edinburgh, where I was made welcome and given full access to the resources of the university library. The Carnegie Trust for the Universities of Scotland provided much appreciated funding for extended stays in Scotland. In 2003 I benefited from a release from undergraduate teaching funded in part by the Burgess Research Award of the Faculty of Arts and Social Sciences at Dalhousie University. I am also indebted to members of the staff of several English and Scottish archives, who were ever ready and willing to assist me, in particular those of the National Library of Scotland, the National Archives of Scotland, the National Monuments Record of Scotland, and the National Archives at Kew. To the following individuals or corporations I owe thanks for permission to consult and cite manuscripts in their possession or custody: the Keeper of the Records of Scotland, the Office of the Lord Lyon of Scotland, the earl of Dalhousie, and the earl of Morton. The staff at the Document Delivery office of the Killam Library at Dalhousie University deserve a warm thanks for their unstinting and always cheerful responses to my requests for interlibrary loan materials.

Over the years, I have read with great interest the work of historians engaged in the challenging and sometimes provocative 'new' British history, and my debt to them is apparent in the footnotes and bibliography of this book. Of all my intellectual debts, however, none is greater than that I owe to Grant Simpson, who was my doctoral supervisor and has remained a good friend and careful critic for upwards of two decades. No student could hope for a finer mentor. Keith Stringer, Alexander Grant, Hector MacQueen and Geoffrey Barrow offered valuable advice during my visits to Edinburgh. At regular intervals aspects of my work on native Scottish lordship were the subject of presentations in the weekly Faculty–Graduate Student Colloquium held in the Department of History at Dalhousie University, and at various international conferences. The comments and queries of several of my colleagues, especially Jack Crowley, Phil Zachernuk, and Paul Hyams helped me to identify, but also to resolve, problems in my research. If I have not always agreed with these friends and fellow workers, discussions with them have nevertheless been cordial and fruitful. Thanks also to Misty De Meo, for her help with the maps. Finally, I wish to thank sincerely my husband Stephen who never fails to demonstrate genuine interest in my work.

Halifax, Nova Scotia

MAPS

xii   *Native Lordship in Medieval Scotland*

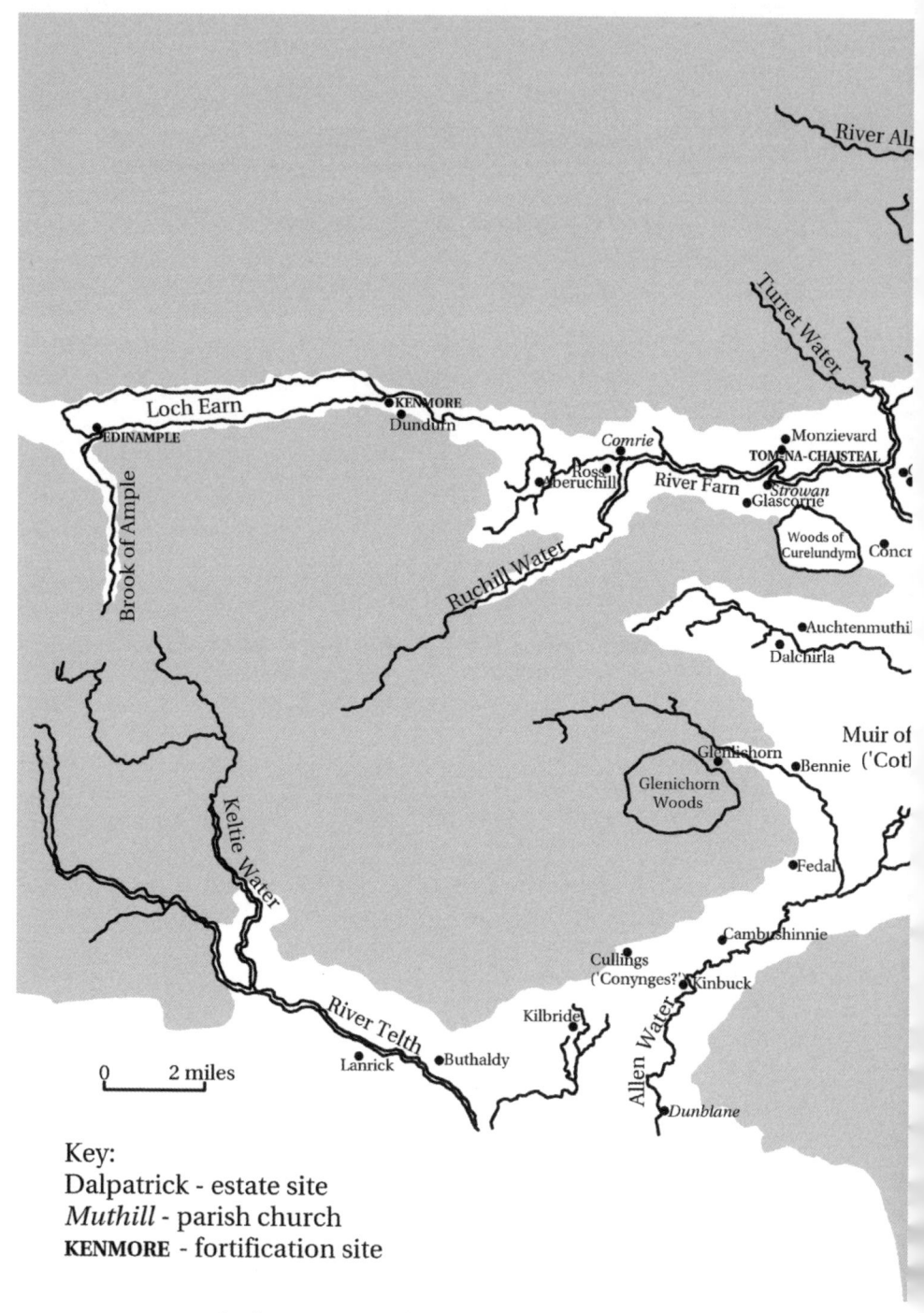

Key:
Dalpatrick - estate site
Muthill - parish church
KENMORE - fortification site

Settlement in Strathearn, *c.*1170–1350

Maps xiii

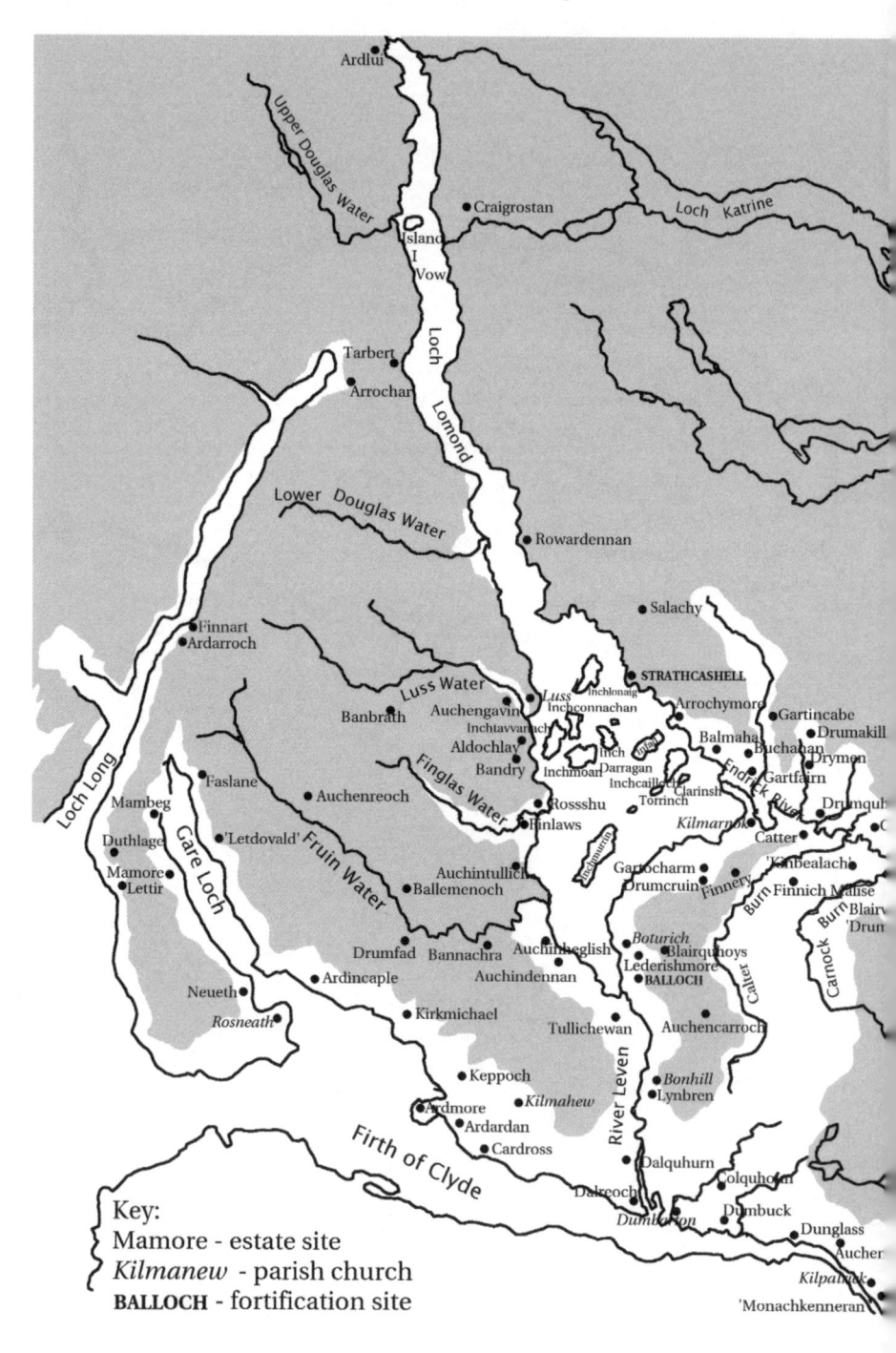

Settement in Lennox, c.1170–1365

Maps xv

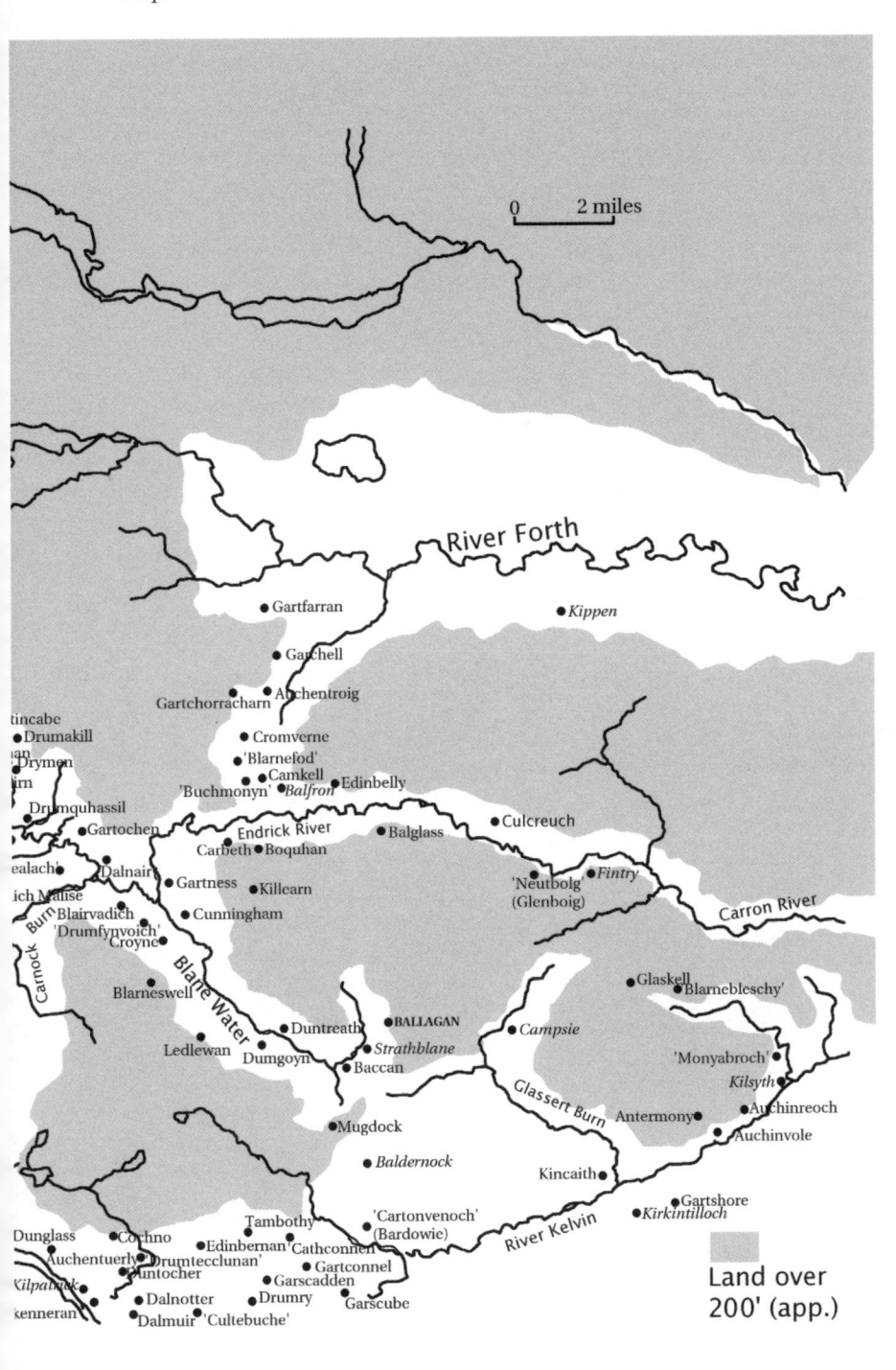

Introduction

In 1333, among the dead left lying on the field of Halidon Hill was a nobleman who represented one of the oldest families in Scotland, Malcolm earl of Lennox. Only slightly more fortunate was his fellow, Malise of Strathearn, who managed to flee the field alive, but who, within months, lost his title to the lands that his family had held in an unbroken line for seven generations. The battle fought between the armies of the Bruce and Balliol factions represented but one episode in Scotland's long war for independence from English rule, but it marked an important moment in the personal histories of the Strathearn and Lennox families. A few years later, when in 1346 King David II mustered his forces afresh at Perth, neither Malise nor Malcolm's son Donald thought it wise to join the Scottish army. From the modern perspective, to repeat, it is possible to see the early years of David II's reign as something of a watershed for both families, a period in which, by circumstance or choice, each took stock of its position within the Scottish aristocracy and reassessed its personal and political interests.

The families of Strathearn and Lennox were not the only ones to be deeply affected by the events of the early fourteenth century. The period has been widely characterized as one of profound change within the structure of Scottish royal government, a consequence of Robert I's seizure of the throne in 1306. It witnessed also important transformations within the noble order of the kingdom, especially among its highest ranks. The creation of new 'honorific' earldoms brought to a close the exclusive dominance of old lordships like those of Strathearn, Lennox, Fife, Atholl, and Buchan, based on territorial divisions that dated back to the pre-twelfth century. The reordering of the Scottish nobility and the rise to prominence of new families whose members had few links with the Galiec past of the kingdom may have been as yet 'incoherent' in the 1330s, but it has also been called 'inevitable', and 'a chapter in the general disintegration of land-based relationships which took place throughout most of western Europe during the late middle ages'.[1] For these and other reasons, the rules of Malise V of Strathearn, who died around 1350, and Donald earl of Lennox (died c.1365) constitute a natural end point for a study of the native nobility of medieval Scotland.

In many respects, the use of the term 'native' to describe Malise and Donald is anachronistic, for by the early fourteenth century both shared a system of cul-

[1] A. Grant, 'Earls and earldoms in late medieval Scotland (c.1310–1460)' (1976), 39–40.

tural beliefs and practices common to aristocrats throughout Europe. The chivalric ethos, with its emphasis on the knightly qualities of prowess, largesse, and courage, was a powerfully cohesive force, one that stressed characteristics common to all noblemen, irrespective of their national background. The seals of the early fourteenth-century earls of Strathearn and Lennox, for example, stamped on the obverse with the universal depiction of the mounted knight and, on the obverse, with motifs of chevronells and roses, respectively, attest the degree to which both men had absorbed and internalized the chivalric conventions of their day.[2] In Scotland, as elsewhere, the choice of heraldic devices from among an array of common European armorial symbols reflected the collective aspirations of family members; the seal itself was a 'semiotic trope' through which a kinship group at once articulated and asserted its identity.[3] The language and practice of heraldry simultaneously promoted the idea of membership within an exclusive pan-European order and the effacement of ethnic and national identity. Throughout most of mainland Scotland, too, the social preoccupations of the period left little opportunity – or reason – for the earls of Strathearn and Lennox to champion their native Gaelic past.

Much the same might be said of the earls' place within the political world of their day. The fourteenth century in Scotland, it has aptly been said, 'begins early', with the death in 1290 of the last of the descendants of King Mael Coluim III.[4] The long conflict with England that originated soon thereafter had a crucial influence on the forging of a distinct Scottish identity among the noble families of the realm, transforming it into 'something far more concrete and enduring' than had been the case under Alexander III.[5] The long struggle for independence and nationhood compelled noblemen to develop new ways of expressing their relationship with the Scottish crown. From the upheavals of Robert I's reign in particular there emerged a new emphasis on the integrity of the Bruce dynasty and the sovereign status of the realm, both of which focused the prospects of the kingdom and its noble subjects away from their past toward their collective future. If the vicissitudes of war created a new Scottish identity, they did so in part at least at the expense of cultural distinctions that had featured prominently in the thirteenth century, chief among them appreciation of the importance of the native Gaelic past to the making of a hybrid Scottish nobility.

In the years before 1290, however, recognition of the place of Gaelic customs and practices was widespread, especially in the great territorial lordships north of the Forth-Clyde line. The enthronement of Alexander III at Scone in 1249 celebrated in the most public of forums the cultural and political debt that the new

---

2 J.H. Stevenson and M. Wood, *Scottish heraldic seals* (1940), ii, 454, 625. **3** B.M. Bedos-Rezak, 'Medieval identity: a sign and a concept' (2000), 1491–2. Early Scottish seals are discussed in J.H. Stevenson, *Heraldry in Scotland* (1914), i, 10, 19–20, 134; ii, 257–74. **4** A. Grant, 'Fourteenth-century Scotland' (2000), 345. **5** F. Watson, 'The enigmatic lion: Scotland, kingship and national identity in the wars of independence' (1998), 20; R. Frame, 'Aristocracies and the political configuration of the British Isles' (1988), 152; A. Grant, 'The development of the Scottish peerage' (1978), 1–8.

king owed to both his Gaelic and Anglo-Saxon ancestors. Before the bishops and noblemen assembled there, 'a highland Scot (*quidam Scotus montanus*) suddenly went down on his knees before the throne and, bowing his head, hailed the king in his native tongue'.[6] Open acknowledgment of the Gaelic antecedents of the royal house were, admittedly, few and far between, but the ceremony of 1249 demonstrated that the earls who claimed native descent were a force to be reckoned with at the Scottish court; like the royal family itself, it has been remarked, they 'formed a link between the Gaelic past and the Anglo-Norman present'.[7] Moreover, in contrast to the English crown in its dealings with the natives of Wales and Ireland, the Scottish kings never created conditions under which a sense of 'Celtic inferiority' might develop or flourish.[8] The efforts of the noble families of Strathearn and Lennox to champion this past and to preserve the unique features of Gaelic lordship with which it endowed them are the focus of this study.

Recognition of the central importance of native culture to the making of medieval Scotland has long been a feature of the scholarship relating to the literary history of the period. Until the sixteenth century Gaelic was the language of half the kingdom's population, and the study of the poetry, song, secular and religious prose that its speakers produced has uncovered a rich and varied vernacular tradition that was second to none in Britain or Europe.[9] In the social, political, and legal fields, however, historians have only very recently, and very selectively, been prepared to acknowledge the enduring influence of native culture. In the 1950s, R.L. Graeme Ritchie's work on the unusual 'Norman Conquest' of Scotland initiated a flurry of interest among scholars in the similarities and differences that distinguished the experience of England from that of its northern neighbour in the period after 1066.[10] For many years thereafter, the field of Scottish historical enquiry was dominated by an historiographical debate that centred on the extent to which the kingdom was 'feudalized' to the same extent as was England. G.W.S. Barrow, famously, dubbed the century and a half or so after 1125 the 'Anglo-Norman era in Scottish history',[11] and in his voluminous and erudite body of writings argued that the reign of David I witnessed the opening stages in the thorough 'feudalization' of the kingdom, 'a process', he maintains, that 'continued unabated under Malcolm IV and William the Lion'.[12] Barrow's model of a wholly new social and military order imported from England and the continent and imposed on a heretofore 'unfeudalized' Scotland in turn informed the work of a generation of scholars. A recent study of matri-

---

[6] *Chron. Fordun*, i, 294. [7] R. Nicholson, *Scotland: the later Middle Ages* (1984), 25. [8] A. Grant, 'Scotland's "Celtic fringe" in the late middle ages: the Macdonald lords of the Isles and the kingdom of Scotland' (1988), 119. [9] M. MacGregor, 'The genealogical histories of Gaelic Scotland' (2002); D.E. Meek, 'The Scots-Gaelic scribes of late medieval Perthshire: an overview of the orthography and contents of the book of the Dean of Lismore' (1996); D. Murison, 'The historical background' (1979), 2–13; T.O. Clancy (ed.), *The triumph tree: Scotland's earliest poetry, 550–1350* (1998). [10] R.L.G. Ritchie, *The Normans in Scotland* (1954). [11] G.W.S. Barrow, *The Anglo-Norman era in Scottish history* (1981). [12] G.W.S. Barrow, *David I of Scotland (1124–1153)* (1985), 10.

monial alliances in the late twelfth century can thus still refer to the penetration of 'Anglo-Norman' lords, with their 'attendant institutions, feudalism among them',[13] while another, which examines the political development of the kingdom, remarks on the impact of the 'new feudalism' on the twelfth century.[14]

Barrow's paradigm, it is true, has not gone unchallenged. Archibald Duncan long ago agued that the royal policy of 'feudalization' was in some regions significantly less intrusive than David I and his successors might have wished, and warned that '[i]n our preoccupation with the new men of David I and Malcolm IV we must not lose sight of the native landowners whom they left undisturbed ... who were neither submerged nor depressed in their own or the king's eyes as a local gentry and even aristocracy'.[15] Other historians have taken up Duncan's lead, and shown that the feudal model, with its emphasis on mounted military service and its concomitant, the conditional tenure of land, does not adequately reflect the structure of native society in the great Gaelic lordships of the period.[16] Scholars now also eschew the label 'Anglo-Norman' to identify the aristocrats who settled in Scotland in significant numbers in response to the royal invitation. As Barrow himself showed in his meticulous study of the incomers, they counted among them not only younger sons and adventurers from England, but from Normandy, Picardy, Brittany, Flanders, and further afield as well.[17]

If the 'tyranny' of the construct of feudalism has begun to loosen its hold on the historiography of medieval Scotland,[18] scholars have none the less proved reluctant to abandon the paradigm altogether. The proponents of the 'new' British history, which claims to have restored their respective pasts to the different realms that comprised the British Isles, still tend to conceive in monolithic terms of a process of 'Normanization' (now an all encompassing term), 'anglicization' or, most recently, 'Europeanization' that influenced Ireland, Wales, and Scotland in the years after 1066. With few exceptions, their focus, in short, remains centred either on the degree to which the newcomers were able successfully to impose a foreign set of ideas and values over the Gaelic populations of the British Isles, or the extent to which native notions of lordship and social organization survived the cultural onslaught of the newcomers. Studies of the impact of the settlers on the political relations between each of the Celtic realms and England, for example, inevitably (and appropriately) note the unusual degree of independence that characterized the Scottish crown,[19] but many echo

---

13 R.A. McDonald, 'Matrimonial politics and core-periphery interactions in twelfth- and early thirteenth-century Scotland' (1995), 238; see also idem, 'Rebels without a cause? The relations of Fergus of Galloway and Somerled of Argyll with the Scottish kings, 1153–1164' (2000), 180–1. **14** K.J. Stringer and A. Grant, 'Scottish foundations' (1995), 92–3. **15** Duncan, *Making*, 141; see also his comments on 'static concepts such as "feudalism"', in his *The kingship of the Scots, 842–1292* (2002), 76. **16** C.J. Neville, 'Charter writing in thirteenth century Celtic Scotland' (2001); R. Oram, *The lordship of Galloway* (2000), esp. 191–217; more recently still, see S. Reynolds, 'Fiefs and vassals in Scotland: a view from outside' (2003). **17** Barrow, *Anglo-Norman era*, passim. **18** E.A.R. Brown, 'The tyranny of a construct: feudalism and the historians of medieval Europe' (1974), 1063–88 **19** See, for example, R. Bartlett, 'The Celtic lands of the British Isles' (1999),

Keith Stringer's observation that the relative autonomy of the kingdom was achieved *in spite* of 'considerable interaction between Gaelic tradition and "modernization"'.[20] For Rees Davies, likewise, the century between 1066 and 1166 saw the transformation of the Scottish crown into 'a monarchy of a contemporary northern European character', but one whose authority reflected ultimately the success of the kings in imitating 'English practices of governance and tenure' and spearheading an effective colonization of the realm by continental settlers.[21] Champions of the Gaelic 'cause' in this debate have only recently begun to recover a history for the native nobility of medieval Scotland that projects neither an overtly 'anti-feudal' nor an ideologically 'pro-Celtic' perspective. Richard Oram's study of medieval Galloway, for example, has made cogent use of the theoretical and methodological approaches of cultural sociologists to argue against interpreting baronial opposition to the twelfth- and early thirteenth-century crown as either a manifestation of 'Gaelic conservatism' or 'violent "anti-feudal" sentiment'. He portrays that resistance instead as a 'backlash' directed specifically against 'Scottish – royal – domination'.[22] For Andrew McDonald, similarly, the prolonged opposition to the rule of the Canmore kings of rebels as widely separated in time and place as Feargus of Galloway, Somhairle of Argyll, and the kindreds of Mac Uilleim and Mac Aeda represented something much more than a blind, inchoate reaction of native leaders against the introduction into their territories of new-fangled ideas about political and social organization. Such oversimplification, he shows, obscures the complexity of the motives that drove each of these men to oppose their king.[23]

The Scotland in which foreigners from England and the continent set down new roots was already in the twelfth century a cultural mosaic, exemplified in royal charters that addressed 'French and English, Scots and Galwegians'.[24] While the crown's new tenants received rich and extensive estates in the lowland portions of the realm, north of Forth in particular (with the notable exception of Moray) the native nobility was not displaced, and the testing clauses of royal *acta* offer abundant and altogether compelling evidence for seeing the courts of David I, Malcolm IV, and William I as a rich admixture of French-, English- and Gaelic-speaking lords, with all accorded some voice at least in the business of governing the realm. The loyalty of the newcomers to the dynasty that David represented has long been apparent to scholars familiar with the language of 'feudalism'. Bruces, Balliols, Stewarts and other new settlers owed the crown 'fealty' and 'homage', and subscribed to the notion that they held their estates on condition that they respect their oaths of allegiance. The native lords' ties to the king were of a different, but no less binding, sort. As Alexander Grant

---

822; D. Carpenter, *The struggle for mastery, Britain 1066–1284* (2003), 11–14, 118–19, 256; R. Frame, *The political development of the British Isles, 1100–1400* (1990), 10–11, 89–91. **20** Stringer and Grant, 'Scottish foundations', 91 (my emphasis). **21** R.R. Davies, *The first English empire: power and identities in the British Isles, 1093–1343* (2000), 73. **22** Oram, *Lordship of Galloway*, 192–3. **23** R.A. McDonald, *Outlaws of medieval Scotland: challenges to the Canmore kings, 1058–1266* (2003), 119–22. **24** G.W.S. Barrow (ed.), *The charters of King David I* (1999), nos. 68, 205.

has observed, the mormaers of the early twelfth century conceived of themselves as 'great stewards' of the crown, and understood fully that the term 'automatically [implied] subordination to some superior authority, in this case, obviously, the king'.[25]

The reigns of David I and his successors Malcolm IV and William I witnessed the beginnings of the transformation of the mormaers of Strathearn, Lennox, and other native regions into the *comites* familiar to modern readers of twelfth- and thirteenth-century charters. Yet, scholars have only just begun to examine in detail the specific ways in which this transformation occurred. Richard Oram's impressive survey of the native rulers of Galloway has shed much light on the slow but steady integration of the lordship into the later medieval Scottish polity,[26] and a recent collection of essays explores the interaction between Gaelic lords and French- and English-speaking newcomers in several different settings.[27] Drawing on a common set of theoretical assumptions, these studies have demonstrated the richness of an approach that privileges notions of cultural pluralism, rather than stressing the dominance of a European aristocracy over a passive and submissive native population. The portrait of medieval Scottish society that emerges from this fresh approach is one in which themes of continuity now claim pride of place, that is, a 'continuity in aristocratic and noble power', reaching across and beyond 'the apparent watershed represented by the appearance of a Frankish nobility in the twelfth century'.[28]

The work of these historians has gone some way toward according the native magnates of Galloway, Mar, Angus, and elsewhere a real and significant share in the making of the later medieval Scottish nation. There are, however, dangers and pitfalls inherent in portraying the process of acculturation as leading somehow inevitably to the emergence of a hybrid aristocracy. Chief among these is the tendency to minimize the antagonism that cultural encounters might generate. Oram's attempt to understand the fierceness with which the lords of Galloway resisted royal authority in the twelfth and early thirteenth centuries has led him to conclude that rebellion was only one feature, albeit well documented, of 'the unspectacular processes of cultural assimilation ... and the progressive integration of the lordly dynasty into the ranks of the emergent Anglo-Scottish nobility'.[29] Keith Stringer, likewise, has warned that 'Galloway's separateness from the rest of Scotland, while in some senses very real, must not be overstated'.[30] Other historians, working either on the theme of disaffection against the crown or on the 'survival' of native families and their 'success' in achieving rank and status in the multicultural world of post-Davidian Scotland, have similarly tended to stress the unity of the aristocracy in the later medieval

25 A. Grant, 'Aspects of national consciousness in medieval Scotland' (1994), 91. **26** Oram, *Lordship of Galloway*, passim. **27** S. Boardman and A. Ross (eds), *The exercise of power in medieval Scotland, c.1200–1500* (2003). **28** S. Boardman and A. Ross, 'Editors' introduction', in Boardman and Ross (eds), *The exercise of power* (2003), 18. **29** Oram, *Lordship of Galloway*, 192. **30** K.J. Stringer, 'Periphery and core in thirteenth-century Scotland: Alan, son of Roland, lord of Galloway and constable of Scotland' (1993), 100.

Introduction

period, and to read back into the years between 1125 and 1290 the gradual, but still inevitable, integration of the customs and mores of Gaels and Europeans, despite moments of rebellion and resistance.[31]

The history of the earldoms of Strathearn and Lennox belies this view of a gradual, occasionally uneven, but none the less steady 'progression' towards accommodation, assimilation, and unity. It is all too rarely admitted that the twelfth century was 'a time of tension between a native tradition and the expectations of incomers';[32] much less that the same might be said of the thirteenth. The Gaelic rulers of Strathearn and Lennox, however, had very good reasons to resent the intrusion of Bruces, Balliols, Stewarts, and others into the privileged ranks of Scottish royal government. The newcomers brought with them two unfamiliar languages, a system of land ownership that favoured written evidence (and, in so doing, still a third unfamiliar language), new ways of measuring wealth and status, and a host of followers as determined as their masters to benefit from a windfall in royal grants of land. A culture that celebrated customs, practices, values, social ties, and political relationships that were alien to the indigenous hierarchy could hardly have caused anything other than tension. In some regions of the kingdom the native sense of dislocation and displacement found expression in prolonged rebellion and resistance, as occurred in Galloway under Feargus and his sons, in the far north among the Mac Uilleim and Mac Aeda kindred dispossessed by the descendants of Mael Coluim III, and in Argyll, under the leadership of Somhairle, his family, and his allies.[33]

Overt rebellion, however, represented only one end of a wide spectrum of native reaction to foreign influence, and it is in the context of such a spectrum of opposition that the chapters that follow assess the response of the Gaelic earls of Strathearn and Lennox to the arrival in their midst of English and continental newcomers. At the opposite end of the range from the rulers of Galloway, Moray, and Argyll stood the native dynasty of Fife. Earls Donnchad III, Donnchad IV, and Mael Coluim (c.1136–1228) are often held up as examples of a native family able successfully to integrate itself into the polyglot environment of the twelfth and thirteenth centuries. For Geoffrey Barrow, these men were 'internal colonists' very much in the style of the Stewarts, Morvilles, Bruces, and Comyns. In agreeing to base their tenure of land on possession of written charters, they were 'able to hold their own beside Anglo-Norman newcomers'.[34] Yet the earls of Fife chose the path of accommodation only after they had secured formal recognition of their unique and close relationship with the royal house.[35] Quietude, in short, had its price. Somewhere in between these

---

31 H.L. MacQueen, 'Survival and success: the Kennedys of Dunure'; R.D. Oram, 'Continuity, adaptation and integration: the earls and earldom of Mar, c.1150–c.1300'; and M. Brown, 'Earldom and kindred: the Lennox and its earls, 120–1458', all in Boardman and Ross (eds), *The exercise of power*. **32** A.A.M. Duncan, *The kingship of the Scots, 842–1292* (2002), 333. **33** McDonald, *Outlaws*, 61–123. **34** Barrow, *Anglo-Norman era*, 87; see also McDonald, *Outlaws*, 121; Oram, 'Continuity, adaptation and integration', 48. **35** J. Bannerman, 'MacDuff of Fife' (1993), 20–38.

extremes lay the great majority of the native lords who ruled the other territorial earldoms that made up the 'land of earls' north of Forth.[36]

The chapters that follow explore aspects of the cultural encounter between the Gaels and the foreigners in the specific settings of the earldoms of Strathearn and Lennox. Several themes inform this work. The first is the importance of the century or so after 1140 to an understanding of the ways in which the Gaelic-speaking earls, their kinsmen, and their followers interacted with the newcomers to the kingdom. In 1290 the imperial ambitions of Edward I of England compelled the rulers of Strathearn and Lennox, and indeed land holders throughout the northern kingdom, to address the issue of Scottish identity from a new perspective. A century and more before this, native lords great and small confronted a different, but equally fundamental series of questions relating to identity and place. The first phase of their process of self-identification began towards the end of the twelfth century and lasted for several generations, and that period is given considerable emphasis in this book. During these years relations between the native rulers and the crown were generally cordial, and the rulers of both regions moved with some ease at the courts of William I and Alexander II as well as on the national stage more generally. At first glance, indeed, the years that spanned the tenure of Earls Maol Iosa I, Fearchar, Gille Brigte, and Robert of Strathearn (c.1140–1245), and of Ailin II and Maoldomhnaich of Lennox (c.1185–1250) saw the smooth assimilation of the Gaelic magnates into the 'money-striking, castle-building, charter-issuing' world of the Europeans.[37] In both regions, that is to say, there is compelling evidence of shifts in the agricultural economy, of a new emphasis on the siting of lordly power centres and, above all, of a ready recognition of the value of written deeds in the construction and expression of magnate authority. All these changes were the consequences of the native earls' contacts with the European newcomers. Close study of the records generated in both lordships during this period, however, suggests another narrative, one on which passive resistance to the influence of the foreigners and, occasionally, the dogged championing of native practices and beliefs in the face of change feature prominently. In some contexts, Gaelic custom proved so resilient that newer practices themselves changed in order to accommodate older custom. Surviving evidence, then, reveals a two-way process of transculturation, rather than the unidirectional flow of ideas associated with the use of the term 'acculturation', with a blend of native and European cultural constructs producing uniquely hybrid praxis. The accommodation of the two systems of belief is apparent above all in notions relating to property, but it may be traced also in the context of social relations between the earls and the people who populated their lands, lay and religious, men and women, free and unfree.

The study is based on an examination of almost three hundred charters relating to the earldoms of Strathearn and Lennox dating from the last decade of the

---

36 Duncan, *Making*, 164.   **37** Bartlett, 'Celtic lands', 822.

twelfth century to *c*.1400. Some three quarters of these deeds survive either as full texts, or as well documented notitiae, with only a handful extant as mere fragments or in vague notices of once extant *acta*. Roughly sixty percent of the documents were issued under the seals of the medieval earls themselves, with the remainder consisting of royal confirmations or records of grants made by their kinsmen or tenants. Almost forty percent of the records survive as single-sheet originals, far more as cartulary copies. The written records of the earls of Strathearn are scattered among several archives, chief among them those relating to the family's religious foundation at Inchaffray. For Lennox, by contrast, there survives a rare example of a lay cartulary. The original copy of this compilation has long been lost, but an early modern version includes several dozen of the earls' *acta*.[38] Several more records survive in the sixteenth-century cartulary relating to Paisley abbey, and still others in the archives of the dukes of Montrose, descendants of the David de Graham who features prominently in this work. Although manuscript sources were consulted exclusively in the research undertaken for this study, the notes to the chapters that follow direct readers, wherever possible, to published versions of charters, brieves, and other written sources.[39]

The book is divided into several distinct sections. Chapter One reviews briefly the history of the families of Strathearn and Lennox over the long period between the reigns of David I and David II. It examines in particular the relative successes and failures of the Scottish kings in engaging the earls in the governance of the realm and in drawing them onto the national stage, and the consequences of the choices that each of the families made when its members became involved in national politics. Chapters Two, Three, and Four, by contrast, focus on the specific environments of the lordships of Strathearn and Lennox. Studies of the tenurial structure of each community, of the ways in which the earls expressed their authority as provincial rulers, and of the effects of the teachings of the reforming church on the people who lived in each of the territories reveal striking patterns in the social, political, and religious transformation of these lands between 1140 and the later thirteenth century. In Strathearn, the initial period of encounter between the cultures of the Gaels and the Europeans ended around 1245, with Malise II's assumption of the title of earl. In Lennox, the process of accommodation was slower and its results not readily apparent until around 1270, when Malcolm I, the grandson of Earl Maoldomhnaich, reached the age of majority and took control of his inheritance. In both lordships, the period before 1250/70 was marked by profound tension between natives and newcomers, and by a notable (if mostly passive) resistance to the influence of new ideas. Thereafter, opposition to foreign ideas faded. Charter materials reveal, in later thirteenth-century Strathearn and

---

38 NAS, GD 220/2/202.   **39** Whenever possible, moreover, preference has been given to charters that survive as single sheet originals rather than cartulary copies. Several deeds relating to Inchaffray abbey, for example, survive both as originals and copies.

Lennox, new tenurial structures, new forms of lordly prerogative, and new ecclesiastical and confessional practices, which reflect both Gaelic and European influences. The importance of the divide that occurred in both earldoms around the middle years of the thirteenth century is underlined throughout this work in the use of the Gaelic form of personal names before *c.*1250 in respect of Strathearn and *c.*1270 in Lennox, and of the more familiar English forms thereafter.[40] Exceptions there are to this general rule. Fergus son of Earl Gille Brigte of Strathearn, for example, actively sought to emulate the chivalric conventions of the 1230s and 1240s in accepting knighthood and the title 'Sir' (*Dominus*). His territorial and social ambitions show clearly that he looked for advancement and promotion to the European aristocratic world of his day, and considered himself a member of that cosmopolitan milieu. Other kinsmen of the earls of Strathearn and Lennox, however, were more comfortable in the traditional Gaelic setting of their lordships; thus, Mael Coluim son of Maoldomhnaich of Lennox was quite overtly hostile to newcomers within in his lands.

While landowners and tenants in both lordships accepted some of the innovations brought into their midst by English and continental settlers, notably written charters, they also preserved much of the Gaelic past in their social, cultural and tenurial practices. By the late thirteenth century, the communities of Strathearn and Lennox were hybrids in the true sense of that term, neither wholly 'native' nor genuinely 'European'. The final chapter in the book explores specific aspects of this hybrid culture in both regions. It argues that the process of transculturation and accommodation that occurred in the course of the several decades after 1140 cannot be characterized either as conservative or reactionary. Gaelic-speaking land holders, great and small, absorbed and internalized the influences of the newcomers in their midst. The foreigners, for their part, found much of value in the kin based society of their native fellows.

The lordships of Strathearn and Lennox in the years between 1140 and 1365 reveal the great variety of experience that members of the Gaelic aristocracy encountered during the 'Anglo-Norman era' of Scottish history. At one extreme there was the example of Galloway and rebellion, at the other an open welcome for the newcomers by the rulers of Fife. For the great majority of the other great families living north of Forth, cultural transformation was a more markedly nuanced process, with the abandonment of old traditions and the acceptance of new ideas reflecting individual hopes and aspirations.

---

40 A.A.M. Duncan makes a similar differentiation, and for much the same reason, in *Kingship of the Scots*, 78.

Table 1: The Earls of Strathearn, c.1140–1350

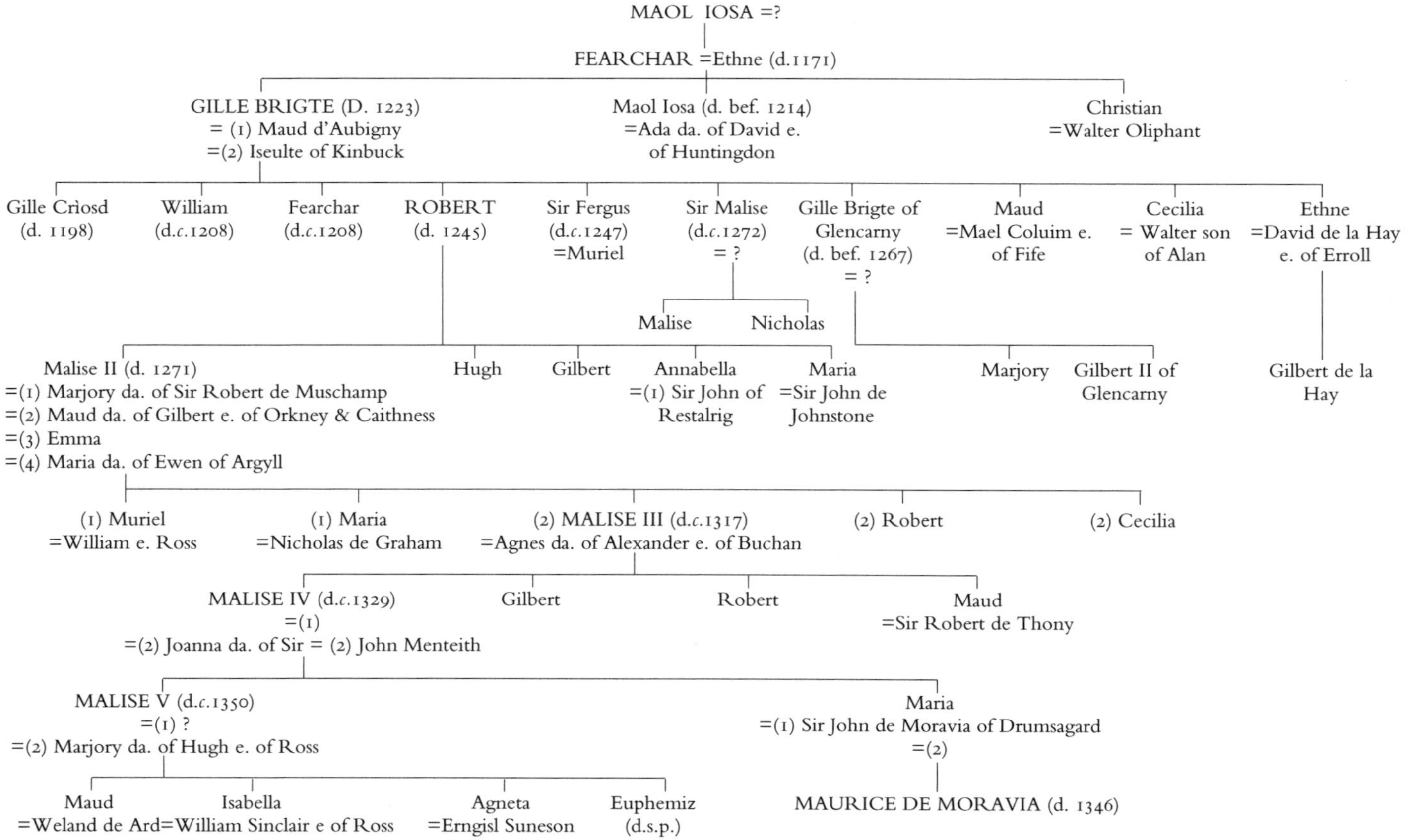

```
MAOL IOSA = ?
    |
    FEARCHAR = Ethne (d.1171)
        |
    ┌───────────────────────────────────────────────────────────┬──────────────┐
    │                                                           │              │
GILLE BRIGTE (D. 1223)          Maol Iosa (d. bef. 1214)    Christian      
= (1) Maud d'Aubigny            = Ada da. of David e.       = Walter Oliphant
= (2) Iseulte of Kinbuck          of Huntingdon
    │                               │
    │                   ┌───────────┼──────────────┬──────────┬──────────────┐
    │                   │           │              │          │              │
    │               Sir Malise   Gille Brigte of  Maud     Cecilia          Ethne
    │               (d.c.1272)   Glencarny        = Mael Coluim e.  = Walter son  = David de la Hay
    │               = ?          (d. bef. 1267)     of Fife         of Alan       e. of Erroll
    │                            = ?                                              │
    │                   ┌────────┬──────────┐      Marjory  Gilbert II of      Gilbert de la
    │                   │        │          │               Glencarny           Hay
    │                 Malise  Nicholas   Annabella
    │                                    = (1) Sir John of
    │                                      Restalrig
    │                                    Maria
    │                                    = Sir John de
    │                                      Johnstone
    │
┌───────┬────────┬────────┬─────────┐
│       │        │        │         │
Gille  William  Fearchar  ROBERT  Sir Fergus
Criosd (d.c.1208)(d.c.1208)(d. 1245)(d.c.1247)
(d. 1198)                          = Muriel
                              │
                    ┌─────────┼────────┐
                    │         │        │
                   Hugh    Gilbert   Malise II (d. 1271)
                                    = (1) Marjory da. of Sir Robert de Muschamp
                                    = (2) Maud da. of Gilbert e. of Orkney & Caithness
                                    = (3) Emma
                                    = (4) Maria da. of Ewen of Argyll
                                        │
                            ┌───────────┼──────────────┐
                            │           │              │
                        (1) Muriel   (1) Maria      (2) MALISE III (d.c.1317)
                        = William e. = Nicholas     = Agnes da. of Alexander e. of Buchan
                          of Ross      de Graham         │
                                                ┌────────┼────────┬─────────┐
                                                │        │        │         │
                                            MALISE IV Gilbert  Robert   (2) Cecilia
                                            (d.c.1329)                   Robert
                                            = (1) Joanna da. of Sir = (2) John Menteith
                                                │                    Maud
                                                │                    = Sir Robert de Thony
                                        ┌───────┴────────┐
                                        │                │
                                    MALISE V (d.c.1350)  Maria
                                    = (1) ?              = (1) Sir John de Moravia of Drumsagard
                                    = (2) Marjory da. of Hugh e. of Ross
                                                         = (2)
                                                         MAURICE DE MORAVIA (d. 1346)
        ┌───────────┬─────────────┐
        │           │             │
      Maud       Isabella      Agneta       Euphemiz
      = Weland de Ard = William Sinclair  = Erngisl Suneson  (d.s.p.)
                      e of Ross
```

Table 2: The Earls of Lennox c.1185–1365

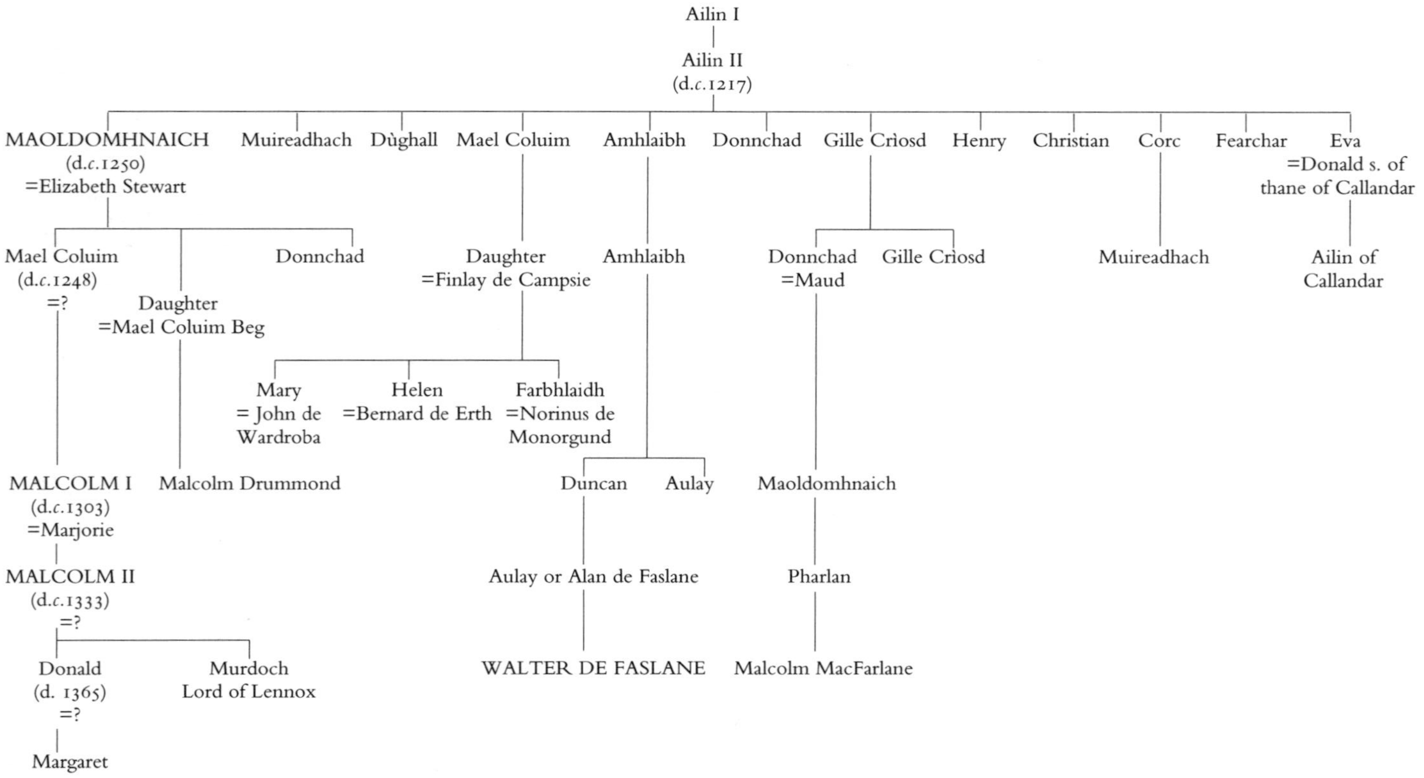

```
                              Ailín I
                                │
                             Ailín II
                             (d.c.1217)
                                │
    ┌──────┬──────┬────────┬───────┬─────────┬──────────┬────────┬──────────┬──────────┬──────────┬──────────┬────────┐
MAOLDOMHNAICH  Muireadhach  Dúghall  Mael Coluim  Amhlaíbh  Donnchad  Gille Críosd  Henry  Christian  Corc  Fearchar  Eva
(d.c.1250)                                                   =Maud                                        =Donald, s. of
=Elizabeth Stewart                                                                                        thane of Callandar
    │                                              │          │
    │                                   Daughter   │     ┌────┴────┐              Muireadhach    Ailín of
    │                                   =Finlay    │  Donnchad  Gille Críosd                      Callandar
    │                                    de Campsie│
    │
    ├──────────────┬──────────────┐
Mael Coluim     Donnchad      Daughter
(d.c.1248)                    =Mael Coluim Beg
=?
    │
    ├──────────────┬──────────────┬──────────────┐
MALCOLM I      Malcolm Drummond   Mary        Farbhlaidh
(d.c.1303)                      =John de    =Nornius de
=Marjorie                        Wardroba    Monorgund
    │                              Helen
    │                           =Bernard de Erth
    │
    ├──────────────┬──────────────┐
MALCOLM II                    Duncan    Aulay
(d.c.1333)
=?                            Aulay or Alan de Faslane
    │                                │
    │                            Phatán
    │
    ├──────────────┐            WALTER DE FASLANE    Malcolm MacFarlane
Donald         Murdoch                              Maoldomhnaich
(d. 1365)     Lord of Lennox
=?
    │
Margaret
```

CHAPTER I

The earls of Strathearn and the earls of Lennox, c.1140–1365

The early histories of the native rulers of Strathearn and Lennox belong to a period about which historians know lamentably little. The genealogists who so enthusiastically launched the 'Scottish family history-writing industry' in the eighteenth century wove fascinating tales for each of the lordships.[1] In a detailed and wholly fanciful account of the Scottish aristocracy published in 1716, for example, George Crawfurd found for the earls of Strathearn an ancestor in the Anglo-Saxon nobleman Walenus, who fled England in the company of Mael Coluim III, and for the earls of Lennox an equally illustrious Northumbrian baron, Arkill, who likewise threw in his fortune with the young prince.[2] Early in the twentieth century the Historiographer Royal, William Forbes Skene, excoriated the efforts of such 'Saxonizing antiquaries'.[3] While his critical treatment of a range of Gaelic texts is still today acknowledged as 'impressive', 'bold', and 'durable',[4] Skene's attempts to establish the unimpeachably 'Celtic' origins of the native nobility were, unfortunately, not much more accurate.

In recent years the paucity of early record materials has discouraged historians from trying to impart improbable beginnings to native families. Scholars have arrived, instead, at a cautious consensus in dating the origins of the great provincial lordships north of Forth to the turbulent period following the intensification of Norse raiding, when the mormaers or 'great stewards' assumed responsibility for leading the armies of their territories in the defence of the several regions of the kingdom.[5] Still elusive, however, is a clear understanding of the role that the mormaers played in the period following the accession of Mael Coluim III in 1058. The king's avowed aim of extending his southern frontier generated a flurry of comment and criticism from chroniclers resident in northern England, which for long kept the gaze of historians fixed firmly on the theme of Anglo-Scottish relations rather than on developments in the internal history of Scotland. Recent examinations of early king lists and of eleventh-century rebellions against the Canmore dynasty, however, offer compelling evi-

---

1 M. MacGregor, 'The genealogical histories of Gaelic Scotland' (2002), 202–3. 2 G. Crawfurd, *The peerage of Scotland* (1716), ii, 256, 466. 3 W.F. Skene, *The highlanders of Scotland* (1902), 271; see also idem, *Celtic Scotland: a history of ancient Alban* (1886–90), iii, 349, 359–61. 4 W.D.H. Sellar, 'William Forbes Skene (1909–92): historian of Celtic Scotland' (2001), 17. See also E.J. Cowan, 'The invention of Celtic Scotland' (2000), 1–4. 5 A.P. Smyth, *Warlords and holy men: Scotland AD 80–1000* (1994), 219–20; Duncan, *Making,* 110–11.

dence for regarding Mael Coluim's reign as a period deeply troubled by discontent and dissent in the north.[6] Together, the focus of the king's ambitions in England and political instability in the far reaches of his realm help to account for the survival of the territorial mormaerships well into the second half of the eleventh century, with mobilization of the territorial armies remaining among the earls' most pressing responsibilities. Certainly, the great lordships are still recognizable as distinct political units by the reign of David I. The clerics who drafted the earliest royal charters referred to these magnates by the familiar Latin term *comites*, and associated the holders of these exalted titles with the provinces that recreated in their extents much older divisions.

Prominent among these lordships were the lands of Strathearn, part of the ancient kingdom of Fortriu, and those of Lennox, closely identified with a subdivision of the old kingdom of Strathclyde.[7] It is thus as witnesses to several *acta* of David I and Malcolm IV that *Malis comes* and *Ferteth comes* first appear in formal record in their capacities as powerful provincial rulers of Strathearn and native magnates of the highest rank.[8] Whether or not these men were direct descendants of the mormaers of old no longer mattered. Of greater importance to contemporary observers was the antiquity of their association with Strathearn and the crown's readiness to acknowledge their role in its governance.

In the early sixteenth century Hector Boece claimed that at his coronation in 1061 Mael Coluim III gathered around him all the great nobles of the realm. 'Mony of þame', he wrote, 'quhilkis were thanys afoir war maid erlis, as Fyfe, Menteth, Atholl, Levenax, Murray, Caithenes, Rosfs and Angus. þir war þe first erlis amanges Scottes, as our cronikillis beris'.[9] The 'extreme credulity' that is said to have flawed Boece's *History of Scotland* nevertheless contained more than a grain of truth in this instance,[10] for over the course of the twelfth century the crown accorded several other Gaelic magnates formal recognition as rulers of large territorial blocs, and thereby created a 'chain of earldoms stretching from the Clyde to the Moray Firth'.[11] The names of many of the newly minted earls begin to appear with increasing frequency in the witness lists of royal charters and in the earliest chronicle narratives as major political figures on the Scottish political stage.

Despite Boece's claims, however, the process of delineating the provinces was still ongoing in the reign of William I, and the rich prize that was the lordship of Lennox had yet to be finally awarded. A charter dated 1208 x 1214 identifies the

---

6 R.A. McDonald, *Outlaws of medieval Scotland: challenges to the Canmore kings, 1058–1266* (2003), 16–23; B.T. Hudson, *Kings of Celtic Scotland* (Westport, 1994), 143–6.   **7** Smyth, *Warlords*, 43–4; Barrow, *Kingdom*, 18–19; K.J. Stringer, *Earl David of Huntingdon, 1152–1219: a study in Anglo-Scottish history* (Edinburgh, 1985), 15.   **8** G.W.S. Barrow (ed.), *The charters of King David I* (1999), nos. 33, 44, 51, 86, 87; *RRS*, i, nos. 118, 130, 138, 157, 159, 173, 176, 226, 227, 254; C. Innes (ed.), *Liber sancte Marie de Melros* (1837), i, nos. 29, 39.   **9** E.C. Batho and H.W. Husbands (eds), *Hector Boece, The chronicles of Scotland* (1936–41), ii, 164–5.   **10** G. Donaldson and R. Morpeth, *A dictionary of Scottish history* (1977), 23.   **11** M. Brown, 'Earldom and kindred: the Lennox and its earls, 120–1458' (2003), 202; Duncan, *Making*, 199.

grantor as *Alewinus Comes de Leuenax' filius et heres Alewini comitis de Leuen'*,[12] but a single Melrose deed constitutes the only written reference to this otherwise elusive Ailin,[13] and the witness lists of the written acts of David I and Malcolm IV make no mention of the lordship as a distinct entity. While Ailin I may well have enjoyed a local reputation as a chief land holder in the region, he almost certainly did not have the formal recognition of the crown as its ruler. The earliest mention of a 'lord' of Lennox, in fact, dates from the 1170s, when these lands were in the possession of William's younger brother, David. The chronicler Jordan Fantosme, whose testimony is generally considered sound, noted that David received 'the gift of Lennox for life' from the king,[14] and a royal charter dated *c*.1178 bestowing the earldom in return for an unspecified number of knights confirms his account.[15] By the mid 1190s, however, the title of earl had been granted or restored to Ailin, son of the native magnate Ailin,[16] in whose lineage it descended in undisputed succession until the fifteenth century.

The crown's treatment of the lordship of Lennox has much vexed scholars, and various explanations have been adduced in explanation of its unusual history. An old claim that David controlled it only during the minority of a rightful native heir has quite justifiably been rejected as unfounded.[17] The suggestion that William assigned the earldom to his younger brother as an appanage, in the tradition of the Scottish royal house, is more convincing,[18] especially when such a grant is placed in the context of William's designs to secure a vulnerable, and hitherto only lightly colonized, part of the realm against incursions from the aggressive and fiercely independent Somhairle, ruler of Argyll and the western isles.[19] The latter's death in 1164, however, brought to a close an important chapter in the politics of the Irish Sea world. For some fifty years thereafter the crown adopted a 'non-interventionist attitude' towards the region, and largely ignored the internecine conflicts that erupted among the sons of Somhairle.[20] With the royal attention instead firmly fixed on its southern neighbours the lordship of Lennox lost much of its identity as a frontier region separating the inner core of the kingdom from the hostile west, and acquired instead the more benign character of a buffer zone. The crown's change of attitude in respect of the western seaboard, while not destined to endure, nevertheless made the need for David's presence in Lennox less compelling, and in turn vastly improved the circumstances of the family of the native ruler Ailin I. From the 1180s the king's brother was deployed elsewhere in the realm; a decade later, Ailin's son and namesake was back in control of the lordship. Suitably chastened, Ailin II and his successors may well have accepted that they would henceforth be secure in their title only 'by accepting a tighter alliance with the king than had previously been the case'.[21]

12 *Glasgow Reg.*, i, no. 101. **13** Innes (ed.), *Melrose Liber*, ii, no. 22. **14** R. Howell (ed.), *Chronicles of the reigns of Stephen, Henry II, and Richard I* (4 vols, London, 1884–89), iii, 297. **15** *RRS*, ii, no. 205; Stringer, *Earl David*, 14. **16** *Paisley Reg.*, 157. **17** Stringer, *Earl David*, 17. **18** Ibid., 17. **19** Ibid., 16–17; R.A. McDonald, *The kingdom of the isles: Scotland's western seaboard, c.1190–c.1336* (1997), 61–6. **20** Ibid., 69–80. **21** Stringer, *Earl David*, 18; Brown, 'Earldom and kindred', 203.

The closing decades of the twelfth century, then, saw the consolidation on the western front of the 'chain of earldoms' that remained the chief territorial lordships of the highland zone for years to come. Therafter, the earls of Menteith, Strathearn, Fife, Angus, Atholl, Mar, Buchan, Moray, Ross, Sutherland, and Caithness are readily identifiable in royal records and contemporary chronicles, even if succession to their titles is not always clear. The thirteenth century, moreover, proved of great significance in the internal politics of each of these lordships. Some, like Buchan and Menteith, passed into the hands of new families who had settled in the realm at the invitation of the sons of Mael Coluim III and his queen, Margaret. Over others, notably Moray and the Norse dominated lands lying beyond the Dornoch Firth, the crown maintained only tenuous and hard won control. Strathearn, Lennox, and Fife, situated across the central belt of the kingdom, now came firmly within the orbit of royal government. Nevertheless, each developed a distinct identity. Implicit in the chapters that follow is the central argument that patterns of lordship in medieval Scotland cannot easily be reduced to generalizations. Simply put, there was no such thing as a 'typical' native lordship. That said, the period between roughly 1150 and 1300 reveals a striking uniformity in the autonomy with which the descendants of the mormaers of old were left to govern their territories. There was, famously, no wholesale disenfranchisement of the native rulers under David I, Malcolm IV, or William I, and recent studies of twelfth-century lordships great and small demonstrate that in Scotland, as indeed in Ireland and Wales, Gaelic land holders adopted a wide variety of strategies designed to accommodate, marginalise, or dominate the foreigners who settled in their midst.[22] The crown's unwillingness, or inability, to effect a total reordering of the Scottish aristocracy on the scale and order of the changes that occurred, most obviously, in England after 1066, had important consequences for the evolution of the institutions of central government, but more tellingly still for the development of a series of distinctive identities among the provinces. The histories of the earldoms of Strathearn and Lennox and of the families whose members controlled them in the period between 1140 and 1365 represent two models among many of the

---

[22] The literature here is now considerable, but for a small sampling, see, for Scotland, R. Oram, 'Continuity, adaptation and integration: the earls and earldom of Mar, *c*.1150–*c*.1300' (2003); idem, 'David I and the Scottish conquest and colonization of Moray' (1999); idem, 'A family business?: colonization and settlement in twelfth- and thirteenth-century Galloway' (1993); R.A. McDonald, 'Rebels without a cause? The relations of Fergus of Galloway and Somerled of Argyll with the Scottish kings, 1153–1164' (2000); idem, 'Matrimonial politics and core-periphery interactions in twelfth- and early thirteenth-century Scotland' (1995); K.J. Stringer, 'Periphery and core in thirteenth-century Scotland: Alan, son of Roland, lord of Galloway and constable of Scotland' (1993); G.W.S. Barrow, 'Badenoch and Strathspey, 1130–1312. 1. Secular and political' (1988); idem, 'Badenoch and Strathspey, 1130–1312: 2. The church' (1989). For Ireland, see, for example, M.-T. Flanagan, 'Strategies of lordship in pre-Norman and post-Norman Leinster' (1997), 107–26 and, more generally, the essays collected in B. Smith (ed.), *Britain and Ireland, 900–1300* (1999). For Wales, see, R.R. Davies, *The age of conquest: Wales, 1063–1415* (Oxford, 1991); idem, *Lordship and society in the march of Wales, 1282–1400* (1978).

experience of crown-magnate relations in medieval Scotland, and two examples among several of the consequences of thirteenth-century developments in particular on the nature of aristocratic lordship in the later medieval polity.

THE FIRST PHASE: c.1140–c.1290

The association between the family of Fearchar of Strathearn and the lands that comprised his earldom was already well established in the reign of Malcolm IV. While historians remain uncertain about the extent to which the earliest king lists and chronicle fragments circulated freely among both the Gaelic learned orders and the *literati* of the king's court in this period,[23] the dating and provenance of several exemplars of such materials are firm enough to suggest that written texts must have served to authenticate the claims of Fearchar, Ailin II, and other provincial rulers that their authority rested on stronger foundations than the royal pleasure alone. Like his predecessor, Fearchar attended the king, if not assiduously, then with some diligence on those occasions when royal progresses brought Malcolm into the environs of Strathearn.[24] Likewise, he was surely among those who, 'as is the custom of that nation [the Scots]' inaugurated the boy king at Scone in 1153.[25]

Neither Maol Iosa nor Fearchar of Strathearn, however, was especially prominent in the royal entourage in the twelfth century. The witness lists of the kings' deeds convey a vivid impression that among the native nobility, close contact with the foreign aristocracy now settling in the kingdom fell, instead, to other families, notably those of Fife and Dunbar.[26] Other contemporary or near contemporary evidence, moreover, points more compellingly to a sense of disenchantment and alienation from developments taking place in and around the royal court on the part of the earls of Strathearn. The sources are, admittedly, largely impressionistic. But collectively, they speak to an undercurrent of profound ethnic and cultural tension between natives and newcomers, and a political environment in which Maol Iosa and Fearchar used their status as chief representatives of the mormaers of old to position themselves as champions of Gaelic interests.

In August 1138 Maol Iosa joined forces with David I to fight the English at Northallerton, one of three invasions that the king undertook in support of his niece's claim to the throne.[27] The English monk Aelred of Rievaulx provided a detailed account of the events leading up to the battle of the Standard.[28] According to him, on the eve of the encounter bitter disagreement erupted

---

[23] M.O. Anderson, *Kings and kingship in early Scotland* (1973), esp. 1–118; B. Hudson, 'The Scottish chronicle' (1998), 133–8; D.N. Dumville, 'The chronicle of the kings of Alba' (2000), 73–86; T.O. Clancy, 'Scotland, the "Nennian" rescension of the *Historia Brittonum*, and the *Lebor Bretnach*', in ibid., 87–107. [24] *RRS*, i nos. 119, 131,138, 157, 159, 173, 176, 226, 227, 254. [25] Ibid., i, 7; T. Arnold (ed.), *Symeonis monachi opera onmia* (2 vols, London, 1882–5), ii, 331. [26] *RRS*, i, 7, 12. [27] Duncan, *Making*, 219–20. [28] Howlett (ed.), *Chron. Stephen*, iii, 185–95.

within the Scottish camp regarding the most effective deployment of the king's forces. At issue, more particularly, were the competing claims of the Gaelic soldiers and David's Anglo-Norman knights to pride of place in the van. Explicit in Aelred's account was the sound condemnation not merely of King Stephen, but of many of the native Scottish troops themselves. He wrote derisively of the barbarity of the native troops, with their 'half naked butts', and in appalled fascination of their record of atrocities, which he contrasted sharply with the finery and the style of 'civilized' warfare of the mounted knights. The words that Aelred put into the mouth of Walter Espec represented, on one level, little more than the kind of rhetoric typical of all medieval chronicle accounts of battle.[29] But Espec's critique of the native fighters must have resonated deeply with noble audiences in both England and Scotland irrespective of their allegiance, for the appalling deeds of the Galwegians in particular were said to be symptomatic of the savagery of Gaelic soldiers more generally. In Aelred's account the personification of such barbarity becomes Maol Iosa of Strathearn, who in a brief speech reminded King David of the precedence that Gaelic fighters had traditionally enjoyed in the royal army, and reprimanded him for failing to appreciate the loyalty of his native Scots.[30] The outcome of the battle, predictably for Aelred, was the defeat of David's forces and, more significantly, victory of the chivalric order over Gaelic barbarity.

Scottish chroniclers were as aware as were their English counterparts of cultural tensions between natives and foreigners at the royal court. In 1160, eager for adventure and above all hoping to achieve the coveted status of knighthood, Malcolm IV joined Henry II of England on an expedition to France.[31] Although he was not out of the kingdom for long, he returned to find several of his great native subjects in open rebellion against him. The Melrose chronicler reported the rising as follows:

> Malcolm king of Scots came from the army at Toulouse. And when he had come to the city that is called Perth, Earl Ferteth and five other earls, enraged against the king for going to Toulouse, besieged the city and wished to take the king prisoner, but their presumption did not prevail at all.[32]

The chronicler's trenchant remarks about the reasons for the revolt, and his reticence in identifying clearly the other conspirators suggest that he considered the incident distasteful and best forgotten. John of Fordun, writing towards the end of fourteenth century, was less sanguine. He emphasized that the earls' disquiet sprang from 'their king's too great intimacy and friendship with Henry, king of England', and that Fearchar and his fellows 'feared [that] this intimacy

---

29 See here J.R.E. Bliese, 'Aelred of Rievaulx's rhetoric and morale at the battle of the Standard, 1138' (1988). **30** Howlett (ed.), *Chron. Stephen*, iii, 189–90. **31** H.T. Riley (ed.), *The annals of Roger de Hoveden* (1853), i, 217. **32** A.O. Anderson and M.O. Anderson (eds), *The Chronicle of Melrose from the Cottonian Manuscript, Faustina B. IX, in the British Museum* (London, 1936), 36.

would bring them shame and disgrace'.[33] Fordun's account, although more expansive than that of the Melrose chronicler, is not really much clearer about the nature of the earls' discontent, though he hinted at ethnic tension when he defended their actions by claiming that the culprits sought only to 'safeguard the common weal' of the kingdom. It is tempting to read into both narratives the voice of a Gaelic aristocracy struggling to come to terms with perceived challenges to its standing in contemporary society, though the identity of the five earls who supported Fearchar precludes the drawing of firm conclusions.[34] Significantly, however, the king appears to have given some credence to the earls' complaints. Retribution was neither swift nor harsh, and the names of several native magnates in the witness lists of royal charters datable to the period 1160–2 offer strong evidence that amicable relations were soon restored.[35]

The source materials that survive from the period of Maol Iosa's and Fearchar's tenure of the earldom of Strathearn, while admittedly scanty, speak to an uneven record of integration and accommodation between native and European aristocrats, of cautious attendance by the Gaelic provincial lords on the king interspersed with episodes of vocal opposition to the perceived influence of newcomers to the royal court. A similar admixture of compromise and watchfulness is apparent in another aspect of the earls' relations with their king. In the aftermath of the Scottish defeat at Northallerton, David surrendered the sons of several prominent noblemen as guarantors of his oath to maintain the peace with King Stephen. Among them was the son of Maol Iosa of Strathearn.[36] Status as a royal hostage was at once honourable and dangerous; honourable because only the sons of the most prestigious aristocrats had any value as political pawns; dangerous, too, though, because angry kings sometimes targeted political enemies by threatening or harming their heirs.[37] David's choice of Maol Iosa's son represented both tacit recognition of the earl's status as one of the most influential noblemen in the realm and a warning of the king's displeasure with one of his greatest Gaelic subjects.

With the succession of Gille Brigte to the title of earl in 1171 written sources become considerably more plentiful, and a close study of relations between natives and incomers better informed. Immediately apparent is the continued ambivalence on the part of the native ruler of Strathearn towards the new aristocracy now comfortably ensconced at the royal court and looking to establish a more forceful presence north of Forth. Gille Brigte's name is found prominently placed in the witness lists or royal *acta* datable to the years between 1173 and 1200, more frequently indeed, than are the names of several other Gaelic magnates.[38] Yet, closer scrutiny of these deeds reveals that the vast majority were

---

33 *Chron. Fordun*, 256. **34** But see Barrow's tentative identification of the conspirators in *RRS*, i, 12. **35** See, for example, *RRS*, i, nos. 226, 267. **36** Howlett (ed.), *Chron. Stephen*, iii, 177–8. **37** See here King Stephen's infamous threat in 1152 to kill the young William Marshal by hanging him outside the walls of Newbury castle in punishment for his father's rebellion, and John Marshal's equally infamous reply, in D. Crouch, *William Marshal: court, career and chivalry in the Angevin empire, 1147–1219* (1990), 16–17. **38** *RRS*, ii, nos. 128, 137, 138, 149–53, 159, 171, 188,

issued from sites situated close to the lands of the earldom: Perth, Stirling, Scone, Clackmannan, Dunfermline. The earl acted as justiciar of Scotia on at least one occasion and attested a royal charter under this designation on another,[39] but these slim references do not, in fact, add up to a record of regular service in the recently created office, as has been claimed.[40] Gille Brigte's obligations as a provincial ruler included responsibility for leading the common army of Strathearn on royal expeditions, and it was probably in this capacity that he is found in the company of William I in 1196–7, when the king launched punitive campaigns against Harold Maddadsson of Orkney and Caithness.[41] The suggestion that Gille Brigte's presence in the north was intended to demonstrate his loyalty to the house of Canmore has much to commend it.[42] On the other hand, contemporary observers were unanimous in portraying Harold as an avowed enemy of the crown,[43] and Gille Brigte's shrewd decision to back the king rather than a notorious rebel speaks more to the earl's pragmatism than it does his steadfastness.

Some of the earl's appearances in written record are predictable. In 1174, for example, he was one of several noblemen who, following William's humiliating capture at York, were shipped off with their king into imprisonment at Falaise.[44] His choice as a guarantor of William's good behaviour is hardly surprising. Henry II wanted the treatment of his royal prisoner to be both humiliating and comprehensive. He accomplished the former when he had William delivered to him initially at Northampton with his feet 'ignominiously shackled beneath the belly of his horse',[45] the latter by stripping the king of the Scots of his highest ranking servants. Likewise, Gille Brigte was present at both the inauguration ceremonies of the young king Alexander II at Scone in Decmber 1214 and, a few days later, at the magnificent obsequies that marked the death of William I.[46] Even more than had been the case in 1174, however, the absence of the representative of one of the kingdom's most ancient families from such solemn and politically significant ceremonies would have been most remarkable. In 1249 another earl of Strathearn would figure prominently at the enthronement of the seventh of the direct descendants of Mael Coluim III;[47] their presence on both occasions offered visual testimony to the statement of a later chronicler that by 'ancestral' custom the magnates of Scotland – by which he meant the great Gaelic lords – 'made' their kings.[48] Still again, in 1213 Gille

---

190, 197, 198, 203–5, 207–10, 214, 223, 236, 242, 251, 261, 271–4, 278, 281–4, 295, 302, 321–4, 327, 328, 333–9, 344–6, 350, 355, 356, 359–62, 364, 373, 375, 388, 391, 392, 394, 405, 421; *Lind. Cart.*, no. 2, App., 284; *Inchaff. Chrs.*, no. 7; C. Innes (ed.), *Registrum de Dunfermline* (1842), nos. 147, 148; *APS*, i, 387; T. Thomson (ed.), *Liber cartarum prioratus Sancti Andree in Scotia* (1841), 147. **39** Barrow, *Kingdom*, 60, 66–7, 110; *RRS*, ii, no. 337. **40** Ibid., 85, 98; C.J. Neville, 'A Celtic enclave in Norman Scotland: earl Gilbert and the earldom of Strathearn, 1171–1223' (2000); Duncan, *Making*, 203. **41** *RRS*, ii, nos. 388, 391–2, 394; McDonald, *Outlaws*, 156–7. **42** McDonald, *Outlaws*, 157. **43** Ibid., 98–100. **44** A.C. Lawrie (ed.), *Annals of the reigns of Malcolm and William, kings of Scotland* (1910), 194, 196. **45** Duncan, *Making*, 230. **46** *Chron. Fordun*, 280. **47** See p. 213, below. **48** *Chron. Fordun*, 294.

Brigte acted as one of several arbitrators in a dispute over title to the earldom of Menteith.[49] This lordship, like Strathearn, was one of the ancient provinces of Scotland, and the adjudication of its succession was a business eminently suitable to the deliberations of noble peers.

Collectively, the evidence concerning Gille Brigte of Strathearn's integration or assimilation into the new political and cultural world of late twelfth-century Scotland may be more apparent than real. Source materials surviving from the part of his rule that falls after 1200 go some way towards reinforcing this impression. From then until his death in 1223, Gille Brigte in fact withdrew almost entirely from the national scene into his own territories. He confined his infrequent attendance on the king to occasions when the court visited burghs situated close to his own lands; during this period, moreover, he attested only seventeen royal and baronial *acta*, more than half of these relating to lands within his own earldom. Such appearances were hardly enough to qualify him as a person of influence in the political circles of his day. It is perhaps no coincidence that the year 1200 marked the establishment of a small priory of Austin canons at Inchaffray, hard by one of his residences, in commemoration of his eldest son's death.[50]

Gille Brigte's withdrawal into the relative insularity of Strathearn may also, however, have signalled a deliberate rejection of the pace of cultural change to which he had been exposed at the royal court, and an equally conscious decision to limit the spread of similar change at home. Evidence relating to the organization of the earl's household, to tenurial patterns both within and beyond Strathearn, and to his relations with the church, all discussed in some detail in this work, speaks to a thoughtfully conceived strategy designed to preserve the prerogatives of Gaelic lordship. Such a response should not cause surprise, nor should it necessarily be interpreted as a manifestation of some kind of inarticulate conservatism. The native magnates who ruled territories in the 'land of earls'[51] north of Forth based their extensive authority on a long and distinguished tradition that, in a host of ways, legitimized their claims to exalted social and political status. The profound changes that followed hard on the heels of the 'Norman' settlement all over the British Isles can hardly have failed to provoke disquiet, discontent, or, as in Strathearn, resistance to the newcomers and their foreign influence. To interpret such sentiments as 'reactionary' or 'conservative' is to underestimate the degree to which native lords like Gille Brigte of Strathearn consciously set about controlling the extent and the nature of change within their own territories. Other noble families adopted equally well articulated strategies. In Mar, for example, the native rulers used their ancestral lands 'as a springboard for the projection of authority on a national level'.[52] In Moray and Galloway, by contrast, native lords resorted to rebellion and resistance as a means of giving voice to their discontent.[53] The family of Fife, more than any

49 *RRS*, ii, no. 519. **50** See pp 132–4, below. **51** *Making*, 164. **52** Oram, 'Continuity, adaptation and integration', 65. **53** McDonald, *Outlaws*, 61–124; R. Oram, *The lordship of Galloway*

others, chose the path of accommodation, skillfully cultivating its kinship with the royal house to position its members at the forefront of the new aristocracy.[54] However different each of these responses to change may have been, all were designed ultimately to ensure the survival of distinctively Gaelic forms of lordship in a period when such notions were under threat throughout the realm.

Gille Brigte's efforts to protect his status and authority are apparent, finally, in the ambiguous tenurial relationship that he cultivated, then carefully maintained, with the crown. There is no evidence to suggest that he was ever formally infeft with the lands of Strathearn, nor that he owed any kind of knight service for them. William I and Alexander II, for their part, proved remarkably reluctant to challenge openly the earl's claims to virtual autonomy within his lands. In the course of the late twelfth and early thirteenth centuries, a series of circumstances permitted the kings of Scotland to intervene directly in the succession, the disposition, or the governance of several of the great provincial lordships, and on each of these occasions the crown was quick to assert its rights and prerogatives. In return for recognition of their special status as royal kinsmen, for example, the earls of Fife agreed to hold their lands by royal charter, and thereafter rapidly became the most 'feudalized' of the Gaelic lords of realm.[55] Buchan fell to an heiress after the death of the native ruler Feargus, and around the year 1212 William granted both heiress and earldom to William Comyn.[56] Not long thereafter, the crown assumed a leading role in adjudicating competing claims to the lordship of Menteith.[57] Towards the end of his reign William gained sufficient control over Ross and Atholl to have a hand in their disposition;[58] the crown also guided, if from a distance, the settlement of the earldom of Mar on one of two claimants.[59] Alexander II successfully engineered the marriage of the heiress of Menteith to another of the Comyns in 1234,[60] and oversaw the division of the rich and powerful lordship of Galloway among the three heiresses of the last of its native rulers.[61]

No such accidents of personal or political fortune befell the earldom of Strathearn. Fearchar emerged unscathed from the uprising of 1160 and passed his lands without consequence to his heir, Gille Brigte. Thereafter, chance, political wisdom, and good genes ensured the succession to the title of no fewer than five generations of Strathearn sons. Unable to intervene directly in the disposition of the earldom, the late twelfth-century crown sought other strategies to establish a clear tenurial relationship with these native lords.

Chief among these were grants of estates beyond the lands of Strathearn. After the defeat of Domnall Mac Uilleim in 1187, the lands of several forfeited rebels came into King William's hands, some of which he distributed among

(2000), esp. 51–14; D. Brooke, 'Fergus of Galloway: miscellaneous notes for a revised portrait' (1991), 47–58. **54** G.W.S. Barrow, *The Anglo-Norman era in Scottish history* (Oxford, 1981), 84–9. **55** Duncan, *Making*, 167–8; J. Bannerman, 'MacDuff of Fife', 20–38. **56** A. Young, *Robert the Bruce's rivals: the Comyns, 1212–1314* (1997), 22–3. **57** Duncan, *Making*, 199–200. **58** Ibid., 178–9, 196–8. **59** Oram, 'Continuity, adaptation and integration', 50–3. **60** Young, *Robert the Bruce's rivals*, 34. **61** Oram, *Lordship*, 142.

noblemen who had remained loyal to him throughout the turmoil of the previous decade.[62] One such beneficiary was Earl Gille Brigte, who received the lands of Kinveachy in Inverness-shire, probably the possession of one of a disgraced northern lord; around the same time, he was give the lands of Madderty, closer to home, which had more certainly belonged to another of the rebels.[63] The king's readiness to acknowledge the status of the lord of Strathearn is apparent in the remarkably favourable terms by which he was to hold the lands. The first charter required no specific military service, the second only a single knight. Yet the tenurial bond that the grants established was clear to both parties. Such ties were in turn enhanced and strengthened by recourse to more subtle strategies, notably the forging of social ties between the native kindred and the recently established aristocracy. William was acutely aware of the importance of marriage alliances to the creation of a network of social obligations and relationships among noble families of both Gaelic and European background, and he exercised his prerogatives to reinforce the ties he had already forged with Strathearn. Gille Brigte's marriage to Maud d'Aubigny accomplished this aim in highly satisfactory fashion, as did the marriage of the earl's brother, Maol Iosa son of Fearchar, with Ada, the natural daughter of David of Huntingdon.[64] Gille Brigte's subsequent actions ultimately compromised William's hopes that the earls of Strathearn would be drawn more firmly within the orbit of royal influence when he alienated both Kinveachy and Madderty[65] and, after the death of Maud d'Aubigny, retired to his estates. But in the 1180s the king must have regarded his success in initiating strong tenurial and social relations with one of his most independent native magnates as an important political victory.

Gille Brigte's successor, his fourth son Robert, followed his father's pattern of cautious and limited exposure to the national scene, and of strict control over the pace of cultural change at home. His name appears only very rarely in the witness lists of royal *acta*,[66] though he traveled with other great noblemen of the kingdom to York in the autumn of 1237 to attend the negotiations that culminated in the Anglo-Scottish treaty of that year.[67] The earl's public appearances were in fact so few that he can hardly have been known personally to many of his contemporaries.

Robert's death in 1245 marked a watershed of profound significance in Strathearn. The careers of his successors, Malise II through Malise V, show a conscious effort to abandon the insularity that had characterized the first half of the thirteenth century. From the early years of Alexander III's reign they became active, and important, participants on the national political stage. The sea change apparent in the earls' political lives is apparent at the local level, too. As the fol-

62 W. Stubbs (ed.), *Gesta Regis Henrici Secundi Benedicti abbatis* (1867), ii, 7–9; *Chron. Melrose, sub 1187*; McDonald, *Outlaws*, 35–9. **63** *RRS*, ii, nos. 206, 258. Both grants are discussed in Neville, 'A Celtic enclave', 77–8; see also McDonald, *Outlaws*, 156–7. **64** *SP*, viii, 241–2. **65** See chapters 2 and 4. **66** NAS, RH 6/29; W.B. D.D. Turnbull (ed.), *Liber sancte Marie de Balmorinach* (1841), App., no. 2 **67** *Foedera*, I, i, 131. See also *CDS*, i, no. 1654, dated 1244, a formal undertaking by Alexander II to observe the terms of the Anglo-Scottish truce.

lowing chapters demonstrate, the structure of the household and the retinues of the later lords of Strathearn became vehicles through which the sons and grandsons of English and continental lords who had been newcomers in the twelfth and early thirteenth centuries gained access to land and office within the earldom. The witness lists of Strathearn deeds dated after 1250 reveal personal entourages whose members now counted significant numbers of French- and English-speakers, and whose ties to the earls were almost entirely tenurial and official, rather than purely personal. The written charter itself as an artifact of lordship changed visibly in the middle years of the century.[68] An examination of the internal and external features of the written *acta* reveals that the restricted number of *clausulae* and the inexperienced scribal hands of the period of Gille Brigte and Robert gave way to markedly greater technical sophistication. The variety and form of the later deeds attest the scribes' familiarity with the distinctions among the writ charter, the letter patent, the brieve, the notification. These men accompanied their lords on their travels within Scotland, to England, and occasionally abroad as well.

If the changes apparent in so many aspects of the internal history of Strathearn were the consequence of Malise II's adoption of a new policy of involvement in national affairs, they were also a reflection of the increasingly complex political world of mid thirteenth-century Scotland. Members of the aristocracy were bound closely to the crown by social convention as well as by myriad tenurial and military obligations. The transformation of the realm into 'a force to be reckoned with in the community of North Sea kingdoms and principalities',[69] its relations with the papacy, and its contacts with England all drew numbers of the Scots nobility, irrespective of their backgrounds, into a new kind of relationship with the crown, one in which the insularity of Strathearn was no longer either workable nor advisable. It is, then, as a figure prominent in national affairs that Malise II appears in surviving source materials: at York for the renewal of the peace with England,[70] at Scone in 1249 for the magnificent inauguration of Alexander III,[71] as a member of the council appointed by Henry III to govern the kingdom during the minority of the king,[72] and as one of five earls mentioned in connection with arrangements for the birth of the queen's first child.[73] From 1249, immediately after Alexander III's enthronement, the native lords of Strathearn began actively to trade on their political currency as representative of one of the most ancient and prestigious families in the realm. Malise II profitably cultivated the patronage of King Henry III of England, and managed to steer a successful middle course through the bitter wrangling that marked the

---

[68] For much of what follows, see Neville, 'Earls of Strathearn', i, 300–40; idem, 'A Celtic enclave', 91–2. [69] G.W.S. Barrow, *Kingship and unity: Scotland, 1000–1306* (1981), 146. [70] H.R. Luard (ed.), *Matthaei Parisiensis monachi Sancti Albani chronica majora* (1972–3), iv, 381–3; *CDS*, i, nos. 1654, 1655. [71] *Chron. Fordun*, 294; see also below, p. 213. [72] *Foedera*, I, ii, 2, 5; *CDS*, i, nos. 1986–8, 2013, 2015; D.E.R. Watt, 'The minority of Alexander III of Scotland' (1971); Neville 'Earls of Strathearn', i, 101–5. [73] *CDS*, i, no. 2229.

first years of Alexander's reign,[74] and although associated with the Durward faction, negotiated an advantageous marriage between his heir Malise and Agnes, daughter of Alexander Comyn earl of Buchan.[75] That alliance in turn had important repercussions on the course of Malise III's career.

Like the earls of Strathearn, the early rulers of Lennox proved remarkably determined to control the intrusion of foreign influences within their lands. The experience of the 1180s, when William I awarded the title of earl to his younger brother, taught the native family a forceful lesson in the political realities of Canmore kingship, and brought home to its members the crown's determination to extend effective control to this portion of the realm. The lesson did not go unheeded, but neither did William's actions succeed in drawing the earls into the direct orbit of the court. Unlike their contemporary, Gille Brigte of Strathearn, neither Ailin II nor Maoldomhnaich sought royal appointments as justiciars or sheriffs, and neither witnessed royal *acta* on a regular basis. Retreat and isolation became very much the pattern of political and cultural life within Lennox for much of the thirteenth century. As the following chapters demonstrate, the earls settled only a handful of new families within their territories, and confined the few incomers they did introduce to the peripheries of their lands. Instead, they created a tenurial structure based almost entirely on native foundations. Maoldomhnaich proved particularly adept in this process, deploying his ten brothers across the full extent of the lordship and promoting to the ranks of major land holders families whose ties to him he further strengthened by appointment to offices within the comital household. Most of Maoldomhnaich's brothers and his chief tenants, moreover, chose Gaelic women as wives. Such marriage strategies perpetuated the cultural insularity of the region; more significantly, within just a few years they generated a kin based social and political organization in Lennox that was unique in Scotland outside the lordship of the isles. Close study of Maoldomhnaich's tenurial and household structures, indeed, belies a recent observation that '[f]rom the thirteenth century the Lennox was a community which combined upland pastoral, Gaelic-speaking areas with Anglicized agricultural districts'.[76] Instead, well after 1250, the lords of Lennox actively and, for the most part, successfully, resisted the intrusion of new men and the influence of European ideas. In his relations with the reforming church of his day, Maoldomhnaich demonstrated a similar ability to control the extent and the pace of change. He and his brother Amhlaibh became dutiful patrons of the reformed monastic orders when they made gifts of lands and privileges to the Cluniac house established by the neighbouring Stewart family at Paisley. But almost alone among their contemporaries, the native lords of Lennox chose not to imitate magnates elsewhere in the realm by endowing a religious house of their own.[77] The enduring vitality of local

---

[74] Young, *Robert the Bruce's rivals*, 53; idem, 'Noble families and political factions in the reign of Alexander III' (1990), 1–30: 220. [75] *SP*, viii, 235. [76] Brown, 'Earldom and kindred', 203. [77] R.A. McDonald, 'Scoto-Norse kings and the reformed religious orders: patterns of monastic

shrines and the measured rate of parish creation in the upland regions of the lordship reveal, rather, the limited impact of religious and confessional reform. Maoldomhnaich's long rule coincided almost exactly with that of his king, Alexander III, but the momentous changes that occurred in the political, social and cultural spheres within the wider realm of Scotland in this period are not apparent in Lennox.

The crown was not unaware of the enduring strength of native lordship in Lennox, nor of the implicit challenge to its authority that the native rulers' independence represented, and for a time the relationship between king and magnate was accordingly ambivalent. On the one hand, neither William I nor Alexander II ever had reason to doubt the loyalty of the native earls, and Maoldomhnaich remained utterly steadfast in his allegiance through several political crises. In 1215, for example, he showed no inclination to support the insurrection that the rebels Domnall Ban and Cinaed Mac Aeda with assistance from Ireland, launched against the young king.[78] Nor is there any evidence that he participated in the Mac Uilleim rising of 1229–30, or the rebellion of Thomas of Galloway in 1235, the latter an attack that also drew support from Ireland and, closer to home, the isle of Man.[79] When, early in the 1220s, then again in 1249, the crown set out to quell disturbances in Argyll, Alexander II and Alexander III may well have marched some of their troops through Maoldomhnaich's territories (and no doubt had them consume the stones of cheese that constituted the region's traditional contribution to the Scottish army).[80] More certainly, on the latter occasion the king's ships sailed Lennox waters en route to Kintyre.[81] On the other hand, Maoldomhnaich's success in maintaining a firm distance from the royal court and its influence evidently continued to be a source of some concern to the crown. Alexander II's removal of the castle of Dumbarton from the earl's control in 1238 and his appointment of a trusted royal servant as sheriff there represented the preliminary stages of a royal strategy designed to secure control of the western isles,[82] but these actions also struck directly at the independence that the earls of Lennox had championed to date. Well into the fourteenth century the stronghold at Dumbarton served as a potent symbol of the king's presence within the lordship, and a powerful reminder that the native rulers did not exercise exclusive authority in the region.

Another aspect of the crown's designs to assert its dominance over the Gaelic province was the issue of deeds under the royal seal to successive lords. Although there has survived no charter of infeftment marking Ailin II's restoration to Lennox after the promotion of William's brother to the earldom of Huntingdon,

---

patronage in twelfth-century Galloway and Argyll' (995), 187–219; idem, 'The foundation and patronage of nunneries by native elites in twelfth- and early thirteenth-century Scotland' (1999), 5–15; K. Stringer, 'Reform monasticism and Celtic Scotland: Galloway *c.*1140–*c.*1240' (2000), 127–65. **78** McDonald, *Outlaws*, 43–4. **79** Ibid., 48; Barrow, 'Badenoch and Strathspey, 1. secular and political', 5–6; Oram, *Lordship*, 143–5. **80** See pp 57, 104, below. **81** *Chron. Fordun*, 288–9; McDonald, *Kingdom of the isles*, 83–5, 99–101. **82** *Lennox Cart.*, 1–2; *Paisley Reg.*, 218; Barrow, *Kingship and unity*, 115.

it is tempting to conjecture the existence of such a document at one time. David, certainly, held the lands by royal charter.[83] The king must surely have appreciated the rare opportunity to confirm his authority over a traditionally independent lordship that David's departure represented. A second such chance did not present itself until 1238. On this occasion, Alexander II was quick to take advantage of his seizure of Dumbarton to define afresh his relationship with the ruler of Lennox. The royal charter issued in this year formally bestowed the earldom on Maoldomhnaich and his heirs, specifying in return the obligation to render military service. Malcolm II received a similar charter in 1321.[84] After 1238, moreover, Malcolm I and his successors held other lands and offices within Lennox by royal grant.[85] By 1300, the need for such overt reminders of subjection had faded, as had the insularity of Lennox itself, but in the thirteenth century each of these acts served to underscore the status of the Gaelic lords in relation to their king. Some time before 1238, indeed, Maoldomhnaich may have sensed the crown's unease with his reputation for independence and his poor record of welcoming foreign families into his lordship. It is perhaps in this light that his decision in 1232 to send his young son north to join the royal entourage in Moray should be interpreted. Mael Coluim of Lennox's presence on this expedition was both a symbol of his father's loyalty to the house of Canmore and security for his continued allegiance.

If charter materials from thirteenth century Lennox reveal much about Maoldomhnaich's efforts to limit the introduction of new people and foreign ideas into the lordship, they have disappointing little to say about the earl's perceptions of his place within the social and political hierarchy of the Gàidhealtachd. Fordun's detailed account of the ceremonies that accompanied the enthronement of Alexander II at Scone in December 1215 omits specific reference to Ailin II, though it states clearly that the earls of Fife, Strathearn, Atholl, Angus, Menteith, Buchan and Dunbar were present.[86] Distance may well have prevented the earls of Orkney-Caithness and Sutherland from attending the clebrations,[87] but Lennox can hardly have claimed similar hardship. Equally intriguing is Maoldomhnaich's absence from the inauguration of Alexander III, a ceremony that openly celebrated the new king's Gaelic heritage. It has been suggested that the earl had died by December 1249, leaving his grandson and heir Malcolm I a minor,[88] but a charter reliably dated more than a year later shows that this was not the case.[89] Maoldomhnaich's presence at other important events, notably the sealing of treaties of friendship with England in 1237 and 1244,[90] suggests that on these occasions, at least, the earl had assumed a public profile appropriate to his rank and status.

Champions of Gaelic tradition they certainly were, but a series of seemingly intriguing allusions (and equally telling silences) in surviving record materials sug-

---

83 *RRS*, ii, no. 205 84 *Lennox Cart.*, 1–2; *RRS*, v, no. 194. 85 *RRS*, v, nos. 11, 194, 408; *RMS*, i, no. 90; *RRS*, vi, nos. 128, 258; *APS*, i, 113. 86 *Chron. Fordun*, i, 280. 87 Duncan, *Making*, 116n. 88 Ibid., 139. 89 *Paisley Reg.*, 171–2. 90 E.L.G. Stones (ed.), *Anglo-Scottish relations, 1174–1328: some selected documents* (Oxford, 1965), 52–3; *CDS*, i, no. 1655.

gests that the early thirteenth-century earls of Lennox may still have been finding their place within the political context of the Scottish Gàidhealtachd. In 1281, for example, the announcement of wedding plans for the king's heir was the occasion for the issue of a solemn letter in which the crown set out the 'customs and uses' governing succession to the Scottish royal title.[91] Among the barons whose advice and expertise Alexander III claimed to have consulted in this extraordinary statement of political identity were six representatives of the ancient provincial lordships. Included in the list was Malise III of Strathearn, who may in fact have been a minor at this time. Conspicuous by his absence, by contrast, was Malcolm I of Lennox, although he was by then well past his age of majority. There are other indications, moreover, that until the crisis of the 1290s, the political community of Scotland did not consider the earls of Lennox among the very top ranks of the kingdom's native magnates. Of particular interest in this context is the anonymous tract entitled the 'Appeal of the Seven Earls'. Scholars have long known that the document was a carefully crafted pieced of propaganda intended to promote the Bruce claim to the throne at the time of the Great Cause; accordingly, few have explored the value of its several recensions as sources of information about the nature of Gaelic identity.[92] The implication that, Fife apart, none of the other Scottish earls was specifically required to make up the other six may, however, be inaccurate, and a remark made many years ago, that there existed a 'distinction between the old earldoms of Celtic origin and those of later feudal creation' may in fact echo the vestiges of ethnic and political beliefs current in the later thirteenth-century kingdom.[93] The seven earls made their fist appearance in Alexander I's foundation charter of Scone abbey.[94] Even if this document is not genuine, but a later twelfth century forgery, its importance lies in its early identification of the place of the seven lords within the context of the political community. In this charter, all seven purported to represent the old provinces of Scotia. The precedence specifically accorded to Fife later on in the inauguration ceremonies of Alexander II and Alexander III arose from the family's already venerable association with the royal lineage of Cinaed Mac Duib, Kenneth III of Scotland.[95] Already in 1214, Strathearn had also become, by implication if not explicitly, one of the 'seven', hence the prominent role given to Malise II in the prose and pictorial versions of the inauguration of 1249.[96] So, too, had Atholl, Angus, Menteith and Buchan, the status of which as ancient provinces was further reinforced in the treatise entitled *De situ Albanie*, which was circulating among the Gaelic-speaking elite of the kingdom towards the end of William I's reign.[97]

---

91 E.L.G. Stones and G G. Simpson (eds), *Edward I and the throne of Scotland, 1290–1296* (2 vols, Oxford, 1978), ii, 188–90. **92** Stones (ed.), *Anglo-Scottish relations*, 89n; G.W.S. Barrow, *Feudal Britain* (London, 1956), 391–2; idem, *Robert Bruce and the community of the realm of Scotland* (3rd edn., Edinburgh, 1988), 44–6; A.A.M. Duncan, *The kingship of the Scots, 842–1292* (Edinburgh, 2002), 123, 139, 200–5. **93** J. Ferguson, 'The seven earls of Scotland' (1913), 193. **94** A.C. Lawrie (ed.), *Early Scottish charters to A.D. 1153* (Glasgow, 1905), no. 36. **95** Bannerman, 'MacDuff of Fife', 21. **96** J. Bannerman, 'The king's poet and the inauguration of Alexander III' (1989), Duncan, *Kingship of the Scots*, 116. **97** D. Broun, 'The seven kingdoms in *De situ Albanie*: a record

Lennox, of course, had not been part of the old kingdom of Alba. Its rulers, moreover, could not lay claim to the impeccably ancient pedigree of their contemporaries from north of Forth. The antecedents of Scottish Cumbria were still widely remembered in 1250; only a century earlier Alexander I had assigned it as an appanage to his son David.[98] Like some of his contemporaries, Ailin II was conscious of the Brittonic origins of his lands, and in 1200 he was actively working to promote a thoroughly Gaelic history for his lineage.[99] Ailin's awareness of the distinctions between the provinces of ancient Alba and the domains that made up the kingdom of the Scots was echoed elsewhere in the realm, most obviously in the making and remaking of king lists which privileged the Gaelic past, and which sought to link the greatest families of the provinces north of Forth to the royal family.[1] Widely shared, but as yet unarticulated concepts about the distant past of the kingdom, then, may explain why the earls of Lennox were not offered as prominent a role as were other native lords in the making of the kings of Scots in 1214 and 1249.

As in Strathearn, the second half of the thirteenth century nevertheless proved a turning point within the lordship of Lennox. The death, around 1248, of Maoldomhnaich's heir, Mael Coluim, ushered in a period of minority rule for the latter's son. Malcolm I's status as the grandson of an earl entailed a period of royal wardship; unfortunately, all record of this early association with the court has perished, presumably as did so much else when Edward I later plundered the Scottish royal archives. Malcolm had reached his majority, however, by July 1272, when Alexander III granted him lands in free forest.[2] The texts of the earl's first deeds reveal the important effect that his exposure to the thoroughly Europeanized influence of the royal entourage exerted on the social, economic, and political landscape of Lennox. As the following chapters show, Malcolm settled a host of English-speaking tenants in his territories, many of whom claimed pride of place in the earl's household and in his baronial courts, side by side with his native kinsmen. The scribes who penned his charters were a highly sophisticated group, attuned to the latest diplomatic conventions of the day, and familiar with the distinctions among document types (writ charters, brieves, letters patent) then in use in the chanceries of the king and other barons. The marriages of Malcolm's grandfather Maoldomhnaich to Elizabeth Stewart, and those of Lennox kinsmen, bore important fruit in the social world of Malcolm's time. He was related by marriage to the Stewart earls of Menteith, who in turn had close ties with most of the major noble families of the realm.[3] Unlike his predecessors, Malcolm used such connections to move freely between

---

of Pictish political geography or imaginary map of ancient *Alba*?' (2000), 26–7. **98** Duncan, *Kingship of the Scots*, 60–2; Barrow, *Kingdom*, 204–5; K. Stringer, 'State-building in twelfth-century Britain: David I, king of Scots, and northern England' (1997), 40–62. **99** See pp 210–12, below. **1** D. Broun, 'The birth of Scottish history' (1997), 6–7; idem, 'Defining Scotland and the Scots before the wars of independence' (1988). **2** *RRS*, vi, no. 258. **3** Young, 'Noble families', 10, 14–15, 22; idem, *Robert the Bruce's rivals*, 72–3; E.J. Cowan, 'Norwegian sunset – Scottish dawn: Hakon IV and Alexander III' (1990), 121–2.

Lennox and the royal court. Frequent association with the king and his circle accounts also for the earl's open support of Alexander III's efforts to secure control of the western isles. That support earned Malcolm the enmity of King Hakon IV of Norway and his allies, who in 1263, after being refused shelter for their longboats in Loch Lomond, laid waste to several of its islands, and 'burned also all the dwellings all around the lake'.[4] But it also provided an invaluable demonstration to the crown that the lords of Lennox had become fully committed members of the kingdom of the Scots, prepared to aid in its defence and to promote royal aims on the western seaboard.

If there did exist, in the thirteenth century, a tendency for the Gaelic political community to define a family's status according to the antiquity of its title, such fine distinctions disappeared in the closing years of the same century. When Robert Bruce laid claim to the throne in 1291, he rallied to his cause as many earls as he could muster, irrespective of their backgrounds (or age).[5] In the course of the several decades that spanned the reign of Alexander III, the Scottish political community developed an identity all its own as an important arm of the royal government in the localities. The competition for the throne and the upheavals that shook the kingdom in the years after the death of the king inaugurated a whole new phase in the history of the nobility, just as it did in the development of the national consciousness of the kingdom itself. The long struggle for independence that began in 1296 generated the need for a new kind of national rhetoric, one that retreated from the earlier emphasis on the ethnic complexity of the kingdom and stressed instead its coherent and unified past. While such rhetoric could not ultimately preempt the fissures that came to divide the ranks of the nobility, it abandoned as largely irrelevant the distinctions that had once distinguished families of Gaelic and European descent. By the time that the wars of independence had ended in the fourteenth century, ethnic distinctions had been all but forgotten.

THE SECOND PHASE: c.1290–c.1365

In the later years of the thirteenth century the lordships of Strathearn and Lennox were caught up in a process that saw the full integration of the cultures of the Gàidhealtachd, England and the continent, and the genesis of a uniquely Scottish nobility. Alexander III' s success in consolidating royal authority over the full extent of the kingdom and his skilful handling of diplomatic relations with his powerful neighbours to the south have been aptly credited with providing ideal conditions for the development of a powerful sense of coherence among his noble subjects, irrespective of their ethnic background.[6] One measure of the

---

4 A.O. Anderson (ed.), *Early sources of Scottish history, A.D. 500–1286* (1990), *sub* 1263. 5 Stones and Simpson (eds), *Edward I*, ii, 82; Duncan, *Kingship of the Scots*, 201. 6 See, for example, Barrow, *Robert Bruce* (1st edn., 1965), xx–xxi; N. Reid, 'The kingless kingdom: the Scottish guardianships

stability that his reign offered was the unanimity with which thirteen earls and some twenty-four barons swore to accept the king's baby daughter, the 'Maid of Norway', as his heir in February 1284.[7] Another was the rapidity with which the Scots nobility, Gaelic-, English- and Scots-speaking alike, set about making arrangements for the governance of the realm following the king's sudden death in 1286. In place of the factionalism that might have marred the political scene, a parliament assembled at Scone established a provisional government that has been called both 'constitutionally impeccable' and 'politically prudent',[8] which set about competently conducting the business of managing the kingdom. It was probably in response to a general order issued by the Guardians, for example, that in 1287 Malise III raised an extraordinary levy from among the tenants of Inchaffray abbey, 'to assist in upholding peace and tranquility in the realm after the death of our fondly remembered lord, King Alexander'.[9]

The solidarity that united the political community during the early years of the guardianship could not, however, survive the circumstances that befell the kingdom after the death of the Maid of Norway in 1290. However firm thereafter in their avowed commitment to an independent Scotland, few noblemen could disentangle the myriad ties that bound them directly or indirectly, by marriage, tenure, or personal allegiance to one or the other of the factions now vying for the Scottish throne. Professor Duncan long ago noted that 'there can be no simple analysis of baronial loyalties in Robert I's Scotland'.[10] Neither can the alliances that were initially forged in 1291–2 be summarized easily. Political allegiances, moreover, shifted as the conflict intensified, sometimes with an alacrity that took even contemporaries by surprise. The consequences of the Anglo-Scottish war proved markedly different for the noble families of Strathearn and Lennox. The former ultimately lost its fortune, while the latter greatly enhanced its standing within the political community of the early fourteenth century. The experience of neither can be said to have been in any way typical, for there was no such experience. Each family's story, none the less, serves to underscore the extent to which notions of Gaelic identity, language, and custom, which had once served to distinguish the kingdom's native families from the newcomers, were subsumed within a broader and more compelling struggle for independence.

In the months leading up to the initial stages of the Great Cause, the Bruce and Balliol factions set about rallying support for their respective claims to the throne of Scotland. The elite status of the earls made these men particularly valuable allies. The lists of auditors presented to Edward I at Norham in June 1291 reveal the extent to which both parties had exploited personal, political and tenurial ties. Malise III of Strathearn's marriage to Agnes Comyn, probably in the earlier 1280s, had drawn him firmly within the orbit of the Comyn

of 1286–1306' (1982); Duncan, *Making*, 611–15. **7** *Foedera*, I, ii, 228. **8** Barrow, *Robert Bruce*,15; Reid, 'Kingless kingdom', 106. **9** *Inchaff. Chrs.*, no. 117; Barrow, *Robert Bruce*, 17. **10** A.A.M. Duncan, *The nation of the Scots and the Declaration of Arbroath (1320)* (1970), 29.

family during the last years of Alexander III's reign,[11] and it was as a member of the Comyn-dominated faction that he appeared at Norham as an auditor for John Balliol.[12] He swore fealty to the English king at Stirling in July,[13] and attended in person the final stages of the proceedings held at Berwick in the autumn of 1292.[14] Malcolm I of Lennox, on the other hand, sided with Bruce. Lack of information about the identity of the earl's wife, known only as Marjorie, makes it impossible to know if it was a marriage connection that linked him to the Bruce cause. The earl's long association with his Stewart neighbours, who in turn supported the Bruce claim, must also have influenced Malcolm's leanings. In November 1292 he appeared before Edward I, again as a member of the Bruce entourage.[15]

The experiences of the Strathearn and Lennox families in the first phase of the wars of independence reveal clearly how difficult it was for the magnates of Scotland to balance personal and family obligations against political interests. Initially, at least, Malise III's choices were dictated largely by his Comyn affiliations. He was one of four earls appointed to govern the kingdom following the deposition of John Balliol at the Stirling parliament that also negotiated a treaty of alliance with France in 1295,[16] and was one of the leaders of the expedition that ravaged Carlisle and its environs in the spring of 1296.[17] Both Strathearn and Lennox submitted to Edward I at Berwick in August 1296,[18] but the king signalled his particular displeasure with the former by taking two of his sons as guarantors of their father's good behaviour and sending them to confinement in the Tower.[19] In 1297 both Malise III of Strathearn and Malcolm I of Lennox received curt instructions to 'keep the peace',[20] and although Malise rebelled again, Edward once again pardoned him.[21] Until Bruce's murder of John Comyn and his seizure of the throne in 1306, in fact, both magnates attempted to steer a middle course between personal and political interests. In the midst of the revolt initiated by William Wallace and Andrew Murray in the summer of 1297, for example, Malise was active as an agent of King Edward I, capturing the 'traitor' Macduff and his sons, but within just a few weeks had joined Wallace in a savage raid into Northumberland.[22] Malcolm of Lennox and his wife, similarly, remained at once outwardly obedient to Edward I and defiant of his designs. Thus, in 1303, just after her husband's death, Countess

---

11 Young, 'Noble families', 17, 22.   12 Stones and Simpson (eds), *Edward I*, ii, 84, 220.   13 Ibid., ii, 120, 367.   14 Ibid., ii, 211, 227, 240, 249, 253.   15 Ibid., ii, 220.   16 *Chron. Fordun*, 327; H. Rothwell (ed.), *The chronicle of Walter of Guisborough* (1957), 264.   17 H.T. Riley (ed.), *Willelmi Rishanger ... chronica et annales* (1865), 156; Barrow, *Robert Bruce*, 66–7. See also *Reg. Morav.*, App., no, 17, a deed concerning the military aid that Sir William de Moravia offered the earl on the occasion of this campaign.   18 T. Thomson (ed.), *Instrumenta publica sive processus super fidelitatibus et homagiis Scotorum domino regi Angliae factis A.D. MCCXCI–MCCXCVI* (Bannatyne Club, 1834), 119.   19 *CDS*, ii, nos. 853; Neville, 'Earls of Strathearn', i, 120–1.   20 D. Macpherson et al. (eds), *Rotuli Scotiae in turri Londoniensi et in domo capitulari Westmonasteriensi asservati* (2 vols, 1814–19), i, 50.   21 For much of what follows, see C.J. Neville, 'The political allegiance of the earls of Strathearn during the war of independence' (1986).   22 PRO, SC 1/20/190; J. Stevenson (ed.), *Documents illustrative of the history of Scotland, 1286–1306* (1870), ii, 215, 217.

Marjorie duly wrote to the king informing him of the movements of the Scottish rebel army in and around the lands of Lennox.[23] Malcolm I of Lennox, however, had actively supported the rising of Wallace and Murray, and had played a prominent part in the Scottish defeat of the earl of Warenne's forces at the battle of Stirling Bridge.[24] His son, Malcolm II, was permitted to succeed to the earldom, but only after submitting formally to the English crown at the parliament convened in St Andrews in 1304, and only after spending some time at the English court as a political hostage.[25]

For the earls of Strathearn and Lennox, as for so many other noble families, even more than the decade between 1296 and 1306, the years after Bruce's seizure of the throne proved a troubled and tumultuous testing ground. As one scholar has noted: 'To support the patriotic cause meant supporting a usurper against the legitimate king, to support the legitimate king meant supporting the allies of the English against those who were fighting for independence'.[26] Initially, at least, Malise III of Strathearn's choices were once again dictated by his Comyn connections, but his attempts to avoid open confrontation with Bruce proved disastrous. Besieged on the one had at his stronghold of Kenmore by Bruce's forces, he later suffered the indignity of a prolonged period of imprisonment under the watchful eye of the English king who mistrusted his loyalty as much as had Robert I. He lost effective control over his vast Strathearn estates, and it was only the fierce loyalty of his son and heir, Malise, that spared the family its landed possessions, and probably the old earl his very life.[27]

The chequered career of Malise III reveals how the events of the years after 1306 bedeviled the political community in Scotland, and the gravity of the consequences of war among even the greatest families in the realm. But it attests also the enduring importance that the contending parties attached to the support of the kingdom's ancient families. Malise III repeatedly foreswore his oath of allegiance to the English crown, yet neither Edward I nor Edward II could afford to reject his support entirely. The earl's refusal openly to support Bruce in the weeks immediately after the latter's enthronement made it apparent that the patriotic cause would have to manage without Strathearn assistance, yet he was permitted to return to Scotland, if suitably chastened, in 1310.[28] A still more treasonable rejection of Bruce's authority occurred in 1313, when Malise III joined the English garrison at Perth and helped to hold the town against the assault of King Robert.[29] Taken prisoner by his own son, Malise was deprived of his lands, though his heir was permitted to succeed to them without penalty.[30]

There can be little doubt that it was the loyalty of Malise III's son and heir, Malise IV, that saved the family from total forfeiture in 1313; but the new earl

---

23 Stevenson (ed.), *Documents*, ii, 486. **24** Rothwell (ed.), *Chron. Guisborough*, 299–300. **25** *CDS*, iv, no. 375. **26** A. Grant, *Independence and nationhood: Scotland, 1306–1469* (London, 1984), 4. **27** Bruce granted Malise IV son of Malise III control of his father's estates in 1313, though the latter did not succeed to the title until 1317. Neville, 'Political allegiance', 143–9. **28** Macpherson et al. (eds), *Rot. Scot.*, i, 93, 94; Neville, 'Earls of Strathearn', i, 130–1. **29** A.A.M. Duncan (ed.), *John Barbour, The Bruce* (1997), 336–7. **30** Ibid., 342–3; Neville, 'Political allegiance', 151.

remained a firm adherent of the Bruce cause for the remainder of the reign. Quite apart from such considerations, however, Robert I had good reason to foster the friendship of Malise IV. Although the years after 1309 saw him make steady gains in securing control of the major strongholds of the kingdom and, more important still, in winning the allegiance of 'every province from Galloway to Caithness, from the Outer Isles to Buchan', [31] the manner of his accession to the Scots throne was still the stuff of deep dissension at home. The murder of John Comyn earned Bruce the enduring enmity of the family, and initiated a long period of conflict within Scotland that has been described as nothing less than a civil war.[32] Winning to his cause the heir to the earldom of Strathearn, whose Comyn connections were still close, represented a signal victory. Although in hindsight scholars have identified Bruce's defeat of the English forces at Bannockburn as a watershed in the declining fortunes of the Comyns,[33] the family's chief representatives were by no means prepared to cede political ground in 1314, and the Soules conspiracy of 1320 showed clearly that hopes for the return of a Balliol king had by no means been extinguished.[34] Bruce's decision to spare the life of the treacherous Malise III in 1313, then of his equally faithless wife Agnes, his kinsman Gilbert of Glencarnie, and his ward John de Logie, in 1320[35] reflected the hard political realities of the early years of the reign and the new king's understanding of the need to bolster his title with a semblance of the consensus that his predecessors had enjoyed.

The place of the ancient native families within the political community of the realm remained of pressing importance in Bruce's conception of kingship. Such considerations were apparent, most obviously, in the careful (if hurried) arrangements he made for his enthronement at Scone in March 1306, to which three earls representing the ancient Gaelic provinces of Fife, Atholl and Menteith, were invited.[36] The king's readiness to accord a leading role in the ceremonies to Isabel of Fife was unprecedented, but the countess represented the link between the new ruler and his Gaelic past that was an essential feature of Scottish inauguration ceremonies. Improvisation was all the more necessary, given the absence from Scone of men standing in for the other 'ancient' earldoms, notably Malise III of Strathearn, whose predecessors had played symbolic roles in previous enthronements, including that of John Balliol.[37] Malcolm II of Lennox, however, was also invited, and attended. His presence there spoke not only of his personal loyalty to the Bruce cause, but of the allegiance of his family to the new dynasty.

Ongoing consideration for the stature of the Strathearn family accounts in large part for Robert Bruce's cultivation of Malise IV's friendship in the remaining years of his rule. The earl remained close to the royal court throughout the

[31] Barrow, *Robert Bruce*, 202. [32] Grant, *Independence and nationhood*, 4–5. [33] Young, *Robert the Bruce's rivals*, 208–9. [34] M. Penman, '*A fell coniuracioun again Robert the doughty king*: the Soules conspiracy of 1318–20' (1999). [35] *Chron. Fordun*, 348–9. For Agnes Comyn's role in the Soules conspiracy, see Penman, '*A fell coniuracioun*', 40–3. [36] Barrow, *Robert Bruce*, 151–2. [37] Duncan, *Kingship of the Scots*, 138; *Rot. Scot.*, i, 12.

years between 1317 and 1328,[38] and he survived unscathed the condemnation of his mother, Agnes Comyn, in 1320.[39] The name of his first wife is not known, but his choice of a second wife was significant, for she was the daughter of Sir John Menteith who, although he spent the first years of the war in the allegiance of England, was won over to the Bruce cause in 1309. In a small but important way, Malise's marriage marked a healing of the rift between the factions.

Bruce's willingness to overlook the conduct of Malise III of Strathearn secured him the loyalty of Malise IV of Strathearn throughout his reign. The fragility of the bond between the new dynasty and the family, however, became apparent soon after the deaths of both men. In 1329 Malise V succeeded to the earldom of Strathearn and, a year later, to the earldom of Caithness and Orkney, through his great grandmother Maud, the second wife of Malise II.[40] The resurgence of Balliol fortunes in Scotland saw a return to the factionalism of the early fourteenth century, a rekindling of profound enmities and, for Malise V of Strathearn, a personal dilemma strongly reminiscent of that which his grandfather had confronted in 1306. In March 1333 the earl apparently allied himself once again with the Balliol faction, among whose ranks he fought at Halidon Hill. The English chronicler, Henry Knighton, mistakenly reported the earl's death on the battlefield,[41] but he was very much alive when he fled Perthshire for his northern estates in 1334.[42] From there, Malise launched a campaign in which he aimed simultaneously to project a show of support for Edward Balliol and to protect his landed interests, though the lukewarm nature of the former and his withdrawal from his Strathearn lands compromised both. In February 1334 a parliament convened at Holyrood set about forfeiting a number of Scots as traitors, and re-inheriting the 'disinherited' Englishmen who had fought on behalf of a Balliol kingship during the first phase of the wars of independence.[43] Its proceedings had a dramatic effect on the fortunes of the earl of Strathearn.

At some time between his flight to the north in the winter of 1334, Malise V had apparently resigned, or consented to resign, the title of Strathearn into Balliol's hands. His expectations of regaining the earldom, however, were met with stony disapproval. The parliament of 1334 branded him a 'notorious rebel and enemy' of the new crown, and awarded the title and the lands of Strathearn to Edward III's 'beloved and faithful kinsman', John de Warenne earl of Surrey, 'in reward for his efforts and his work' in supporting the overthrow of Bruce's regime.[44] Malise spent the remainder of his life vainly attempting to recover his Perthshire possessions. On two separate occasions he was brought to trial on charges of treason for surrendering his title to Balliol, and although the government of David II proved willing to interpret his actions in supporting Balliol

---

38 *RRS*, vi, nos. 112, 116, 140, 141, 167, 191, 239, 240, 267, 275, 281, 288, 295, 353. **39** *Chron. Fordun*, 348. **40** *SP*, viii, 252; see also Table 1. **41** J.R. Lumby (ed.), *Chronicon Henrici Knighton, vel Cnithon, monachi Leycestrensis* (2 vols, 1889–95), i, 468. **42** Neville 'Earls of Strathearn', i, 148. **43** R. Nicholson, *Edward III and the Scots* (Oxford, 1965), 129. **44** PRO, C 54/155 mm 33, 33d; calendared in *CDS*, iii, nos. 1118–19. See also *Foedera*, II, iii, 108.

in a more lenient light, it refused to reverse the forfeiture. The earldom of Strathearn passed first to Sir Maurice de Moravia, and eventually to Robert Stewart.[45] Although he lived until 1350, Malise's influence in Strathearn effectively ended in 1333. His flight to the north brought to an end almost two centuries of Gaelic rule in the earldom,[46] and signalled the demise of the political significance that its native rulers had cultivated so assiduously and so successfully in the past.

Lennox family fortunes followed a very different path in the course of the Anglo-Scottish conflict. Edward I not did quickly forget the support that Malcolm I gave to the patriotic cause in the years immediately after 1296, nor did he set much store by Countess Marjorie's attempts to reassure him of the loyalty of the Lennox family. Their son, Malcolm II, was compelled to submit formally to the English crown at the St Andrews parliament held in March 1304, and to petition formally for permission to succeed to his father's title.[47] Edward was prepared to relent, but not before placing one of his firmest adherents, Sir John Menteith, in control of the castle, town and sheriffdom of Dumbarton.[48] Together with Malise III of Strathearn, moreover, Malcolm was made to demonstrate his allegiance by raising men from his lands to assist the king to guard the area around Stirling from the activities of rebels.[49] Edward's doubts about the loyalty of the new earl of Lennox were soon confirmed. In March 1306 Malcolm II joined the handful of magnates who assembled at Scone to witness Bruce's enthronement as Robert I.[50] Thereafter, the earl remained a firm adherent of the Scottish king and the cause of independence.

Loyalty to Bruce was no easy feat in the troubled years after the battle of Methven, and Malcolm's actions earned him both immediate retribution from Edward I and the admiration of later chroniclers. John Barbour claimed that he 'wes put to full hard assay',[51] an oblique reference to the forfeiture of the earl's title, the loss of his lands to Sir John Menteith, and his near capture in August 1306.[52] John of Fordun, however, was a great deal more effusive in his praise. 'The earl of Lennox and Gilbert of Haya', he claimed became Bruce's 'inseparable companions in all his troubles ... they never departed from fealty and love towards him'.[53] His reward was restoration to his inheritance in 1309 when Menteith changed sides, as well as an hereditary appointment to the sheriffdom of Clackmannan and, after Bannockburn, grants of valuable estates in Banffshire

---

45 Neville, 'Earls of Strathearn', i, 148–54; *RRS*, vi, no. 77; Nicholson, *Edward III and the Scots*, 141, 156; M. Penman, *David II, 1329–71* (2004), 68, 106, 200. **46** Four of Malise V's five daughters married Norwegian noblemen, the fifth Sir William Sinclair, a member of an influential family in the region. Neville, 'Earls of Strathearn', i, 150, 155. **47** *CDS*, iv, no. 1815; H.G. Richardson and G. Sayles, 'The Scottish parliaments of Edward I' (1925), 311. **48** F. Palgrave (ed.), *Documents and records illustrating the history of Scotland* (1837), 305; Stevenson (ed.), *Documents illustrative of the history of Scotland*, ii, 474. **49** *CDS*, ii, nos. 1471, 1489. **50** Barrow, *Robert Bruce*, 151. **51** Duncan (ed.), *The Bruce*, 105, 134–44. **52** Palgrave (ed.), *Documents and records*, 305. **53** *Chron. Fordun*, i, 342.

and the long coveted sheriffdom of Dumbarton.[54] It was, perhaps, in partial recognition of the role that Malcolm II had played in the difficult early years of his reign that when Bruce made plans late in his life to build an elaborate retreat, he chose as a site the toun of Cardross, deep within Lennox territory.[55] Although one scholar has commented on the 'reluctance' of Malcolm II to 'play an active role in national politics outwith his province',[56] surviving evidence suggests more than a minimal commitment to the new dynasty. The earl's name was conspicuously absent from the list of conspirators who sought to overthrow Bruce in 1320, despite the fact that the plot had 'a potentially large basis of support among significant Scots',[57] nor did he have close links with any of the disaffected parties. Malcolm expressed his commitment to the crown more openly still in 1333, when he perished at the battle of Halidon Hill, fighting English attempts to place Edward Balliol on the Scottish throne.[58] A recent biography of David II more aptly describes Lennox's involvement in the earliest years of the reign of Bruce's heir as 'stalwart';[59] certainly, Donald earl of Lennox could not have laid the elaborate plans he did for the succession to his earldom in the absence of a direct male heir without the approval of the crown.[60] As has duly been noted, the marriage, around 1344, of Margaret of Lennox to her kinsman, Walter of Faslane, represented a 'clear exception' to other inheritance trends in fourteenth century Scotland.[61] Earl Donald's designs for the successful preservation of the integrity of his family's lands speak to his ability to use his predecessors' record of loyalty to the Bruce crown to good advantage.

The so-called 'Stewartization' of Strathearn and Lennox[62] in the 1340s and 1350s coincided not merely with the final stages of the Bruce-Balliol factionalism that had played such a formative role in Scottish politics since the 1290s,[63] but also with a change in the nature and expression of lordly power north of Forth. Recent scholarship has framed internal developments in the later fourteenth century in terms of the disintegration and decay of the once close association between the old provinces and the men who governed them. According to Alexander Grant, already by 1330 'the lordship of an earldom seems to have been thought of as something separate from the earldom itself'.[64] The fragmentation of magnate power in a part of the kingdom that had once been dominated by a handful of Gaelic rulers had important repercussions on the nobility as a body. Not least among these was a change in the significance of Gaelic heritage as a mark of social and political distinction. In 1400, the Scottish

54 *APS*, i, 459; *RRS*, v, nos. 11, 194; W. Robertson, *An index, drawn up about the year 1629, of many records of charters, granted by the different sovereigns of Scotland between the years 1309 and 1413* (1798), 17, no. 41. The Banffshire lands, far distant from Lennox, were disposed of quickly. 55 Barrow, *Robert Bruce*, 319. 56 Brown, 'Earldom and kindred', 205. 57 Penman, '*A fell coniuracioun*', 28. 58 F.W.D. Brie (ed.), *The Brut or The chronicles of England* (1906), 284; *SP*, v, 336. 59 Penman, *David II*, 89. 60 *SP*, viii, 337. Walter was the descendant of Maoldomhnaich's brother, Amhlaibh. 61 Brown, 'Earldom and kindred', 206. 62 Ibid., 213. 63 Grant, *Independence and nationhood*, 23–4. 64 A.H. Grant, 'Earls and earldoms in late medieval Scotland (*c*.1310–1460) (1976), 27; idem, *Independence and nationhood*, 123; S. Boardman, *The early Stewart kings: Robert II and Robert III, 1371–1406* (1996), 12–13.

Gàidhealtachd remained a vital aspect of the cultural landscapes of Strathearn and Lennox. Thus, it was undoubtedly pride in her ancestry that led the granddaughter of Robert Stewart, Euphemia countess palatine of Strathearn, to christen her son and heir Malise. A similar sense of respect for the antiquity of his lineage led Earl Duncan of Lennox to commission a new genealogy of his family.[65] In 1400, however, neither Gaelic ancestry nor a direct link with the ancient provinces of Alba was sufficiently weighty to secure an ambitious nobleman membership among the political elite of the realm. In the later years of the thirteenth century the native earls of Strathearn and Lennox had worked consciously, and for the most part, successfully, to parlay the native identity that their predecessors had striven so hard to preserve into a place on the national stage. A hundred years later, the stakes had changed, and with them importance of a close link with the Gaelic past.

---

[65] *SP*, viii, 260; K.A. Steer and J.W.M. Bannerman, *Late medieval monumental sculpture in the west highlands* (1977), 203.

CHAPTER 2

Lay tenants and household officials

In 1233, a suit launched by the abbot of Paisley to recover possession of the church of Kilpatrick and its lands brought together in the parish churches of Irvine and Ayr fifteen recognitors from the lordships of Lennox and Carrick. Almost all were native tenants: they included Earl Maoldomhnaich of Lennox's son Dùghall, his steward Mael Coluim Beg, and several lesser sorts, among them Anecol, Gille Beathag, Gille Moire, and Rotheric Beg.[1] A decade earlier, in the church of Strageath, Robert of Strathearn, son and heir of Earl Gille Brigte, had summoned another kind of assembly, this one a formal and public declaration of his wish to extend into a new generation the generosity and protection that had been the hallmarks of his father's relationship with the priory of Inchaffray. The men who gathered on this occasion included, among others, Donnchad son of Adam, Maol Iosa the steward of Strathearn, Maol Iosa son of Brice the parson of Crieff, and Macbeatha the *judex*.[2] The clerks who drafted the written deeds generated on both occasions struggled to render into Latinate forms the Gaelic names of the witnesses, but they had no problem conceiving of the native men as the acknowledged 'trustworthies' (*fidedigni*) of the earls of Lennox and Strathearn.

The records of formal assemblies and, more obviously still, the texts and witness lists of charters that survive from the two lordships make it possible to reconstruct profiles of the lay tenantry there in different periods, as well as to chart shifts in the pattern and intensity of settlement within the earls' territories. Such shifts are immediately apparent in the mid-thirteenth century, when there occurred a change in the sorts of men to whom the native earls granted landed property, and in the size, location, and value of the estates that tenants received. It began in earnest in Srathearn under Earl Malise II and became more marked under his successor, Malise III. In Lennox the shift began towards the end of Maoldomhnaich's rule in the third quarter of the thirteenth century. Noteworthy especially in Strathearn was the gradual but steady disappearance from written record of some old native families. In Lennox, Gaelic-speaking men were still important components of the tenurial landscape in 1270, when Malcolm I succeeded his grandfather, but within a generation their names, too, were giving way in charter witness lists to men of English and European descent recently settled in the lordship.

[1] *Paisley Reg.*, 166–8. [2] *Inchaff. Liber*, no. 16; *Inchaff. Chrs.*, no. 47.

Charter texts are also valuable in helping to reconstruct the households of the native earls of Strathearn and Lennox and to trace the elaboration there of administrative, judicial and fiscal offices. Previous studies of the Scots medieval baronage have demonstrated some of the difficulties inherent in attempting to identify a recognizable body of office holders, and few scholars have been able to resist contrasting the often informal structure of the thirteenth-century Scottish baronial household with its more sophisticated English counterpart. Thus, Earl David of Huntingdon's entourage in England is known to have included not merely an array of senior ministers appropriate to a great lord, such as stewards, constables, chaplains and clerics, but also a host of minor officials: a butler, a falconer, a porter. But of the household he maintained in Scotland, only his chamberlain, chaplains, and clerks appear prominently in surviving charters, and in some cases the identity and origins of these men remain uncertain.[3] Similarly, the English households of the great cross border lords Roger de Quincy and William Comyn appear to have been more complex in their organization and more clearly defined in their structure than those they established in Scotland.[4] Yet, all great lords, native or newcomer, drew heavily on the expertise and advice of friends and senior tenants, however formally or informally. An examination of the changing nature of the households of the earls of Strathearn and Lennox in the course of the thirteenth century reveals, as with respect to the tenantry, the interplay of old and new and the persistence of native tradition alongside foreign innovation.

One of the more striking aspects of the period of intensive colonization by families of Anglo-Norman and continental descent that King David I inaugurated in the mid-twelfth century was the creation, by royal fiat, of a new aristocracy. The estates that formed the basis of the great lordships of Renfrew, Cunningham, Kyle, Nithsdale, Liddesdale and, perhaps most famously, Annandale, saw, in most cases, a deliberate redrawing of the boundaries of long-existing blocs of land which were now invested with new territorial integrity and identity. In like fashion, other lands were shaped into endowments for newcomers of slightly less exalted, though still noble rank, such as David de Lindsay, Gervase Riddel, Walter de Berkeley, and Ranulph de Soules.[5] By contrast, the territories over which the native earls ruled remained, in the thirteenth century, remarkably ill-defined. In an oft-cited (if now lost) charter of the early twelfth century King David I granted the lands of the earldom of Fife to its native lord, Donnchad, in return for specified service.[6] But as has often been noted, the text of the charter in which the gift is recorded reveals very little about the precise boundaries of the lands that comprised the grant, or about the kind of service that the earl owed the crown.[7] For none of the other native lordships is there

---

[3] K.J. Stringer, *Earl David of Huntingdon* (1985), 149–53, 176. [4] G.G. Simpson, 'The *familia* of Roger de Quincy, earl of Winchester and constable of Scotland' (1985), 102–29; A. Young, 'The earls and earldom of Buchan in the thirteenth century' (1993), 180–1. [5] G.W.S. Barrow, *The Anglo-Norman era in Scottish history* (1981), 62; idem, *Kingdom*, 284–7; Duncan, *Making*, 136–40. [6] G.W.S. Barrow (ed.), *The charters of King David I* (1999), no. 16. [7] Barrow, *Kingdom*, 253.

a charter of any kind until well after David I's death, and even those which fell into royal hands relatively early in the thirteenth century, Buchan and Menteith, were granted to incoming lords with little attempt on the part of the crown to delineate their boundaries or to define precisely the terms under which they would be held. William Comyn's elevation to the earldom of Buchan by right of his wife around 1212 has been shown conclusively to have been a careful strategy of King William, intended to establish a firm royal presence in the north. But the obligations that he owed the crown in respect of the honour were never clearly specified, and a recent historian of Buchan is able to reconstruct the extent of the thirteenth-century earldom only from later sources. The tenurial conditions under which the lands that comprised the earldom of Menteith passed to William's son Walter in 1234 were similarly ambiguous.[8]

The native lords of Strathearn were never brought into a close tenurial relationship with the crown for the vast territories they governed. Strong links with the centre of government there certainly were: Earl Gille Brigte was a frequent witness to royal acts in the years between 1171 and 1200 in places as far apart as Elgin, Perth, Edinburgh and Lanark,[9] and in 1174 he was one of a number of magnates who travelled to Normandy as hostages for King William's observance of the treaty of Falaise.[10] More important still, his appointment to the very senior office of justiciar of Scotia at various times in the last two decades of the twelfth century[11] makes it clear that the lord of Strathearn was neither impervious to royal pressure to assume a position of responsibility in the government, nor reluctant to partake of the prestige and opportunity for advancement that access to the royal court promised. Yet, the period between 1171 and 1200 was an unusual one in the history of native Strathearn.[12] The second part of Gille Brigte's rule saw the earl retreat from the public stage back to his lands and into a period of marked insularity. After 1200 he ventured only seldom beyond the confines of his territories, and his focus (as well as that of his successor, Robert) remained firmly fixed on his estates, his tenants, and his spiritual affairs. A comparison between patterns of land holding and the structure of Gille Brigte's household in the period 1200–23, and those of his grandson Malise II later in the same century, undertaken below, is highly instructive. It shows, first, that Gille Brigte worked deliberately to preserve the status and rank of an overwhelmingly native tenantry, and second, that he fashioned a household organization designed above all to complement his status as a great native lord. A study of Gille Brigte's policies, moreover, reveals clear evidence of the careful management of the influence of newcomers within his territories.

8 Young, 'Earls and earldom of Buchan', 174–99: 176–8; idem, *Robert the Bruce's rivals: the Comyns, 1212–1314* (1997), 22–3, 34–5. **9** *RRS*, ii, nos. 128, 137–8, 149–53, 159, 171, 188, 190, 198, 203–5, 207–10, 214, 223, 236, 242, 251, 271–4, 278, 281–4, 294, 302, 321–4, 327–8, 333–6, 338–9, 344–6, 350, 355–62, 364, 373, 375, 388, 391–2, 394, 405, 421. **10** E.L.G. Stones (ed.), *Anglo-Scottish relations 1174–1328: some selected documents* (Oxford, 1965), no. 1. **11** *RRS*, ii, no. 337; Barrow, *Kingdom*, 85; NLS, Adv. MS. 34.4.2, fo. lxv. **12** See p. 21, above.

The earldom of Lennox was, if anything, more insular in the early thirteenth century than was Strathearn. The crown's temporary acquisition of the honour in the 1170s, surprisingly, made little difference to the status of the native earls when they were restored in the 1190s, or to patterns of settlement and demesne exploitation there. During his brief tenure of the earldom the king's brother David certainly 'acted *sicut dominus*', and his grant of the churches of Antermony and Campsie to Kelso abbey suggest that he 'plainly regarded himself as more than a mere custodian' of the lordship.[13] Yet, soon after he regained control of the earldom, the native magnate Ailin II made an equally bold statement of his own authority when he issued a new grant of both benefices to Bishop Walter of Glasgow.[14] David's presence in the lands of Lennox, moreover, left hardly a mark on the tenurial structure of the lordship. Despite the obligation, stated clearly in his charter of infeftment, to render the service of ten knights,[15] he created no new fees for his English or continental followers, and the witness list of his grant to Kelso abbey, comprised entirely of newcomers to the kingdom,[16] suggests strongly that he forged no close ties with the native aristocracy of Lennox.

Ailin II's restoration in the 1190s appears to have been accomplished without recourse to a royal charter of infeftment, and the relationship between the crown and the native lord of Lennox reverted to the ambiguous status that had characterized it from a very early stage. Even in 1238, when Alexander II succeeded in convincing Maoldomhnaich to accept a royal charter of infeftment for the lordship, the terms used to define the earl's obligations were remarkably imprecise. Although Maoldomhnaich had to relinquish control of the castle of Dumbarton, the charter demanded no knight service, merely the duty to render the forinsec service for which all great native lords were responsible.[17] Nor did the king attempt to define precisely what he intended when he stated that the earl should hold the lands 'as free and quit as any of our other earls hold their earldoms'. In fact, the inclusion within the terms of the charter of the lordly prerogatives of sake and soke, toll, team, infangentheof, pit and gallows provided a unique opportunity for Maoldomhnaich to secure unambiguous royal acknowledgment of the power and authority he meant to exercise within his territories. In 1238, then, the region of Lennox was still a long way from shedding its character as an 'exposed frontier lordship'.[18] From the late 1190s and well into the third quarter of the thirteenth century the region remained, like Strathearn, overwhelmingly a land of Gaelic-speaking lords and tenants. Here, native customs, traditions, and practices influenced the lives of English and continental incomers as much, if not more, than the latter did the former. As in Strathearn, too, the preservation of Gaelic culture was a deliberate policy of the native ruling family. The ways in which the early earls privileged native culture are recurring themes in this chapter.

13 Stringer, *Earl David*, 17. **14** *Glasgow Reg.*, i, n. 101. **15** *RRS*, ii, no. 205. **16** Stringer, *Earl David*, 238–9. **17** Ibid., 17. The royal charter survives only in a late cartulary copy, printed in *Lennox Cart.*, 1–2. **18** Stringer, *Earl David*, 18.

Just as the native earls of Strathearn and Lennox held their territories of the crown by the ambiguous force of custom, so, too, do almost all their native tenants appear to have held their estates according to unwritten terms. One of the most intractable problems in the reconstruction of the history of medieval Strathearn and Lennox is the poor representation of charters to lay persons among surviving record materials. In the former, the only text of a grant by Earl Gille Brigte in favour of a lay beneficiary is the record of a gift of land he made to his daughter Cecilia when she married Walter II son of Alan, a grant that survives, moreover, only in confirmations dating from the time of Earl Robert.[19] Although historians have long appreciated that private *acta* from the medieval period survive only haphazardly, the paucity of Strathearn material is none the less remarkable. Dauvit Broun has argued that the virtual absence of charters to lay persons in the Strathearn of Gille Brigte's time attests, more than anything else, a lack of interest in deeds of conveyance as evidence of claims to property.[20] Here, as in many other native lordships, a form of kindly tenancy based firmly on ties of kinship was the norm, and remained common and widely accepted until the middle of the thirteenth century. The earls' foreign tenants, very few in number, must have found the casual attitude to written deeds among native Strathearn tenants highly unusual. Yet, they, too, appear to have 'gone native' in this respect, and several of them held their lands without written record of their enfeftments.

In Lennox, interestingly, written charters to lay tenants became common in Earl Maoldomhnaich's time, not merely among foreign tenants newly settled in the region but among a handful of long-established native land holders. In fact, no fewer than 18 of the 25 charters to lay persons extant from the first half of the thirteenth century were issued to native men.[21] It would appear that different factors were at work in Lennox than in Strathearn. Yet, a review of patterns of settlement and of the creation of new feus under Earls Gille Brigte of Strathearn and Maoldomhnaich of Lennox reveals a remarkable similarity, as well as an indication about why the practice of charter writing in the two native lordships differed.

The chartered tenants of Earls Gille Brigte and Robert of Strathearn consisted almost entirely of the religious of Inchaffray priory and, later, abbey. This is hardly surprising, given the importance that monastic establishments attached

---

19 *Inchaff. Liber*, App., no. 8. The marriage took place around 1223. These confirmation charters, moreover, are the only complete texts of acts in favour of lay persons from the period of Robert's rule. **20** D. Broun, *The charters of Gaelic Scotland and Ireland in the early and central middle ages* (1995); esp. 34–42; W. Davies, 'Charter-writing and its uses in early medieval Celtic societies' (1996), 99–112; idem, 'The Latin charter-tradition in western Britain, Brittany and Ireland in the early medieval period' (1982); M. Herbert, 'Charter material from Kells' (1994), 63–7. **21** These numbers include full and partial texts, as well as reliable notitiae of grants, the texts of which have subsequently been lost. They include also grants for which two distinct texts have survived, for example NAS, GD 1/88/2, 3, charters of Earl Maoldomhnaich in favour of Mael Coluim of Fife and his wife, Eva, the earl's sister, printed in Fraser, *Lennox*, ii, nos. 202, 203.

to the written word, not only in Scotland, but throughout the Christian west. But as a new foundation, it was especially pressing for the Augustinian canons recently planted at Inchaffray to create a sound evidentiary basis for the great variety of endowments that a native magnate of Earl Gille Brigte's stature bestowed on them. Thus, the early records relating to Inchaffray are in many respects as rich, proportionately speaking, as are those of the great monastic houses of Melrose, St Andrews and Kelso.

Few lay tenants, however, shared the preoccupation of Inchaffray clerics for amassing written deeds. That Earl Gille Brigte infeft lay tenants and required sometimes onerous services and customary renders of them can hardly be doubted: these are implicit, for example, in the obligations to produce the cain that he regularly granted to the priory, and in his own duty to assemble and lead the fighting men of the common army of Strathearn when the crown required him to do so. But among the lay tenants known to have held lands directly of him, only two or three were of non-Gaelic origin. One of these was Nigel 'de Dalpatrick', a man who also used the surname of Luvetot.[22] Almost certainly Nigel belonged to a family that traced its roots to Normandy, and to the same family whose members held the lands of Worksop and Hallam in England of Earl David of Huntingdon. The Luvetots came to Scotland in the train of Gille Brigte's first wife, Maud D'Aubigny.[23] Nigel de Luvetot's close links with the countess of Strathearn are revealed in the choice location in which he secured his lands. The toun of Dalpatrick, in the middle reaches of the Earn valley, lay in the most fertile and agriculturally productive portion of the comital territories, and just a few miles from its spiritual centre at Inchaffray. The conditions under which Nigel held these lands, however, are unknown, for no charter of infeftment has survived, if indeed there ever was one. Nigel's brother or son, Sir Roger, also came to Strathearn in the following of Countess Maud. He appears as a witness in locally issued charters from the late 1220s and early 1230s, but he was the man not of Earls Gille Brigte or Robert, but of Fergus son of Earl Gille Brigte, from whom he held a portion of the estate of Bennie in south-western Strathearn.[24] Roger's designation as *dominus* in surviving charter materials suggests that he owed knight service of some sort for his estates, but whether this included a formal commitment to provide the fully armed, mounted warriors normally associated with Anglo-Norman military obligations is by no means clear.

In the early years of the thirteenth century lay tenants also included a man who bore the fanciful name of Tristram, the son of a Breton woman named Avicia.[25] He, too, may have come to Scotland as a follower of Countess Maud and, like Nigel de Luvetot, was shown special favour when he received as a feu the centrally located lands of Gorthy, just north of the Pow Burn, adjacent to the priory of Inchaffray. Tristram, in fact, appears to have taken advantage of

---

22 *Inchaff. Chrs.*, nos. 9, 27.   **23** Barrow, *Anglo-Norman era*, 124–5 and n. 44 assembles the evidence discussed here for the origins of the Luvetots; see also Stringer, *Earl David*, 130, 143.   **24** Neville, 'Earls of Strathearn', i, 274; *Lind. Cart.*, nos. 24, 26.   **25** Duncan, *Making*, 449.

the dismantling of the community of hermits on the Isle of Masses and its reestablishment as a community of Austin canons to try to stake a claim to priory lands. Around 1208 he gave to Inchaffray a croft in his territory of 'Edardoennech', located hard by the mill he had built at Gorthy, the marches of which were 'those by which Maol Iosa the prior held [the croft] in his lifetime'.[26] The Gorthy family remained prominent in Strathearn for many years to come.[27] Tristram's son and namesake, Tristram, inherited his father's lands soon after the succession of Earl Robert; another son, Henry, held a feu centred on the nearby toun of Kintocher.[28] Yet, Tristram I's attempts to expand his family's lands at the expense of Inchaffray ultimately failed. In 1265, with the support of Earl Malise II of Strathearn, Abbot Alan successfully sued Tristram's grandson for recovery of the lands of 'Cambinch' and of other estates reclaimed from what had been marshland on which the canons had built an infirmary and chapel.[29]

Nigel and Tristram set down deep roots under the influence of Earl Gille Brigte's first wife, but as French- or English-speaking incomers they nevertheless represented a very small minority among Strathearn land holders, and one which written record would suggest was augmented by only one more family in Earl Robert's time. In the later 1220s Theobald son of William son of Clement acquired the lands of Pitlandy, and Theobald's son Luke was still lord of an estate centred there in Earl Malise II's time.[30] Surviving charter materials offer occasional glimpses of the men who numbered among the dependents of these newcomers, such as Alan de Kintocher, perhaps a tenant of Henry son of Tristram, and the 'Richard' who worked tofts on the Dalpatrick estates.[31] But charter witness lists reveal unmistakably that the vast majority of significant Strathearn land holders were men of native stock, and their tenant population Gaelic-speaking.[32] When Gille Brigte and Robert assembled the elites of their entourages to bear witness to ceremonial acts such as the granting of land, the ranks of such land holders were comprised overwhelmingly of men who bore Gaelic names such as Gille Crìosd, Gille Brigte, Gille Naomh, Donnchad, Maol Iosa, Causantin, Brice and Anecol (to name only a few).[33] If the Scottish kings who counted Gille Brigte and Robert among their most important magnates hoped that the earls would emulate royal practice in settling foreign families within their territories, they must have been sorely disappointed with the performance of this native family. Until well after the middle of the thirteenth century foreign penetration into Strathearn was only superficial, and limited geo-

---

26 *Inchaff. Chrs.*, no. 26.   **27** W.J. Watson, *The surnames of Scotland* (1929, repr. 1986), 320.   **28** Neville, 'Earls of Strathearn', i, 271–2; *Inchaff. Chrs.*, no. 57; *Inchaff. Liber*, no. 59.   **29** *Inchaff. Liber*, nos. 47, 48.   **30** Neville 'Earls of Strathearn', i, 274–5; *Inchaff. Chrs.*, nos. 56, 103.   **31** *Inchaff. Chrs.*, no. 57.   **32** Thus, one of Richard's near neighbours in Dalpatrick was a native man by the name of Máel Snechtai. Ibid., no. 57.   **33** C.J. Neville, 'A Celtic enclave in Norman Scotland: Earl Gilbert and the earldom of Strathearn, 1171–1223' (2000), 87, and the witness lists of Strathearn charters edited in Neville, 'Earls of Strathearn', ii, passim.

graphically to a small enclave in the environs of the Isle of Masses. Anglo-Norman and European tenants remained for many years exotic rarities.

As Gaelic lords of high standing, the earls of Strathearn stood at the apex of a large group of kinsmen and kinswomen.[34] Good lordship was expressed above all in a magnate's ability to ensure the prosperity of his extended family. Earl Gille Brigte's unwillingness to encourage wholesale colonization of his lands by French- and English-speaking newcomers was a reflection of a carefully designed strategy intended both to marshal his landed resources and to balance the aspirations of his kinspeople against the traditional obligations he owed them. It was equally clearly designed to preserve the native social structure of the earldom. With very few exceptions, Gille Brigte's most important lay tenants were close blood relatives. Chief among these were his brother Maol Iosa, who held a valuable feu made up of a number of scattered estates located in the heartland of the earldom in the parishes of Comrie, Muthill, Blackford, and Dunning.[35] Significantly, Maol Iosa held these lands for the very meagre service of one knight, and the extensive jurisdiction that he exercised within them bore eloquent witness to his status as a lord of high standing.[36]

Gille Brigte and Maud D'Aubigny had a large family, consisting of eight sons and three daughters. The three eldest sons were dead by 1210, and in a charter of that year Gille Brigte designated his fourth son, Robert, *filius et heres meus*.[37] Three of the remaining sons, Fergus, Malise and Gille Brigte, outlived their father by many years. Two established families that dominated the comital household and, more generally, landed Scottish society, for a good part of the thirteenth century. The descendants of the last, Gille Brigte, who was endowed with his father's Inverness-shire properties, controlled the lordship of Glencarnie for several generations to come. Earl Gille Brigte's various endowments in favour of his male kinsmen offer a particularly apt example of the ways in which native lords fulfilled simultaneously the obligations incumbent on them as fathers and heads of large kinship groups.

Fergus son of Gille Brigte first occurs in the testing clause of a charter of his father dated early in the thirteenth century, together with several other comital children. Between these years and the late 1240s he witnessed a further twenty-four deeds, all but one concerning the monasteries of Inchaffray and Lindores with which Gille Brigte had been so closely involved.[38] When Gille Brigte's brother Maol Iosa son of Fearchar died childless before 1214, the earl designated Fergus as his heir, thus ensuring that a valuable feu should not be

---

[34] R. Davies, 'Kinsmen, neighbours and communities in Wales and the western British Isles, *c.*1100–*c.*1400' (2001), 173–9. For the Scottish context, see especially H.L. MacQueen, 'The kin of Kennedy, "kenkynnol" and the common law' (1993). [35] No original charter of infeftment survives, but in 1172 or 1173 King William confirmed Gille Brigte's grant of these lands to Maol Iosa son of Fearchar; *RRS*, ii, no. 136. [36] Maol Iosa's career in the later twelfth and the early thirteenth centuries is reviewed in C.J. Neville, 'Native lords and the church in thirteenth-century Strathearn, Scotland' (2002), 459–61. [37] *Inchaff. Chrs.*, no. 28; Neville, 'Earls of Strathearn', i, 72. [38] Neville, 'Earls of Strathearn', 72–3.

dismantled. Fergus succeeded also to Maol Iosa's estates in Strathtay, which the latter had held of the crown,[39] a further indication of Gille Brigte's intention to keep these properties under watchful comital control. Fergus proved himself an equally careful steward of ancestral lands. Childless in turn, he granted the estate of Rossie, which he had inherited from his uncle, to his nephew Malise son of Gille Brigte.[40] The land thus stayed within the immediate comital family for most of the thirteenth century; in the 1260s Nicholas son of Malise son of Gille Brigte was still drawing revenues from the lands of Rossie as rector of the parish church of Crieff and chamberlain to his cousin, Earl Malise II.[41]

Earl Gille Brigte demonstrated equally careful planning in disposing of the lands of Kinveachie and Glencarnie in Inverness-shire that he acquired as part of an extensive royal grant from King William I following the suppression of the Mac Uilleim rebellion in 1187: these he set aside as an endowment for a younger son, Gille Criosd.[42] The latter secured two successive royal confirmations of his possessions; first, from William I in 1206, then from Alexander II soon after 1214.[43] When Gille Criosd died without heirs the earl transferred the lands of Kinveachie and Glencarnie, as well as others in Duthil parish, together with the patronage of the church there, to his youngest son, Gille Brigte.[44] Gille Brigte son of Gille Brigte in turn used them to good account as a basis for further aggrandizement in the north and east. By 1257 he had added to his already substantial interests in the region lands in the earldom of Mar, secured from Alan Durward, and an interest in at least one full davach in the toun of Abernethy.[45] The family of Gille Brigte of Glencarnie remained influential in Moray for another full century, and eventually in 1363 King David II erected the honour into a barony of the same name.[46] Earl Gille Brigte's judicious disposition of a valuable but distant portion of his landed holdings demonstrates a level of shrewdness that has often been characterized as a feature of Anglo-Norman estate management, but one that has only recently been noted among native magnates as well.[47] The crown, for its part, found much to welcome in the earl's efforts to manage his far flung possessions, for Gille Brigte of Glencarnie's establishment in the north and the firm allegiance to the king that he and his heirs subsequently demonstrated represented much needed support in a dangerous and unstable part of the realm.

Among the more substantial of the native tenant families in Strathearn were the sons of the Gaelic lord Luguen who, in the time of Earl Fearchar, secured

---

39 *RRS*, ii, no. 524; Neville, 'Native lords', 467. **40** *Inchaff. Liber*, no. 63. Fergus's other lands reverted, on his death in the later 1240s, to Earl Malise II. **41** Neville, 'Earls of Strathearn', i, 75. **42** Gille Criosd was perhaps the son of the earl's second wife; almost certainly he was named in memory of the earl's first son of the same name, who had died in 1198. **43** *RRS*, ii, no. 474; NAS, GD 248/4/3. **44** *Moray Reg.*, no. 80; G.W.S. Barrow, 'Badenoch and Strathspey, 1130–1312' (1988), 5. **45** W. Fraser (ed.), *The chiefs of Grant* (1883), iii, nos. 6, 11; D.C. Murray, 'Notes on the parish of Duthil' (1960–3), 24. **46** Ibid., i, xlv–lviii; *RRS*, v, no. 284. **47** Barrow, *Anglo-Norman era*, 12 and the works cited there; A.D.M. Barrell, *Medieval Scotland* (2000), 29; R. Oram, *The lordship of Galloway* (2000), 211–12.

control of a feu based in Kinbuck on the southern edges of the earldom. Richard son of Luguen appears as the 'knight of Kinbuck' in the first decade of the thirteenth century, and thereafter witnessed other charters of Earls Gille Brigte and Robert, sometimes simply as 'Richard the knight', or as 'Richard son of Luguen the knight'.[48] He may well have spent time in the comital household as a 'gentleman retainer', as one scholar has suggested;[49] more likely, given the Gaelic flavour of the entourage that Gille Brigte deliberately cultivated, he may have been fostered there before achieving the rank of a Strathearn land holder. Richard's feu included also the touns of Wester, Mid, and Nether Cambushinnie, for a late fourteenth-century charter confirmed to the abbey of Cambuskenneth gifts made to its monks from some of these lands by Richard and his heir, Joachim.[50] Luguen also controlled the lands of Abercairney, situated deep within Strathearn territory on the north bank of the River Earn. The estate formed part of the tocher that Luguen's daughter, Iseulte, brought to Earl Gille Brigte when she became his second wife, probably soon after 1210.[51] A third of Luguen's children, identified in charter witness lists as Geoffrey 'de Gask' hovered on the fringes of the comital entourage, but disappears from record after Earl Gille Brigte's time.[52] He probably died without male heirs, and the lands of Gask, together with a handsome fortified residence later passed into the hands of the powerful Oliphant family.[53]

In the thirteenth century marriage conventions among the Gaelic and European aristocracy alike created a vigorous market in tocher and dower lands, and the native lords of Strathearn made judicious use of the opportunities for good estate management that marriage agreements offered. Gille Brigte of Strathearn himself received (or recovered) title to the lands of Abercairny when he married Iseulte daughter of Luguen. She in turn gifted part of the estate to the canons of Inchaffray towards the end of her husband's lifetime,[54] but the bulk of these valuable lands stayed within the firm control of the earls of Strathearn until well into the fourteenth century, when they passed to Sir John de Moravia of Drumsagard as part of the tocher of Maria, the daughter of Earl Malise IV.[55] Territorial gains achieved through advantageous marriages in one generation, however, were offset by losses incurred in providing adequate tochers for marriageable daughters in the next. Earl Gille Brigte had three daughters. In the arrangements he made for each one's marriage he demonstrated the same concern to balance the interests of his native kindred against the expectations of his sons-in-law and their families as he showed in providing for his male children.

The eldest daughter, Maud, married Mael Coluim, son and heir of Donnchad earl of Fife. It was fitting that her marriage portion reflect not only her status as the child of one of the most important native magnates in the realm,

---

48 *Inchaff. Chrs.*, nos. 27, 30, 31, 55, 56, 58; *Lind. Cart.*, nos. 30, 31. **49** Barrow, *Anglo-Norman era*, 125. **50** W. Fraser (ed.), *Registrum monasterii S. Marie de Cambuskenneth A.D. 1147–1535* (1872), no. 68. **51** *Inchaff. Chrs.*, no. 46. **52** Ibid., nos. 27, 46. **53** NLS, Ch. B.1760. For reference to the residence near Gask, see *CDS*, iv. 475. **54** Ibid., no. 46. **55** *Inchaff. Liber*, App., no. 24; see also the much mutilated NAS, GD 24/5/1/3.

but also that of her husband's family, for the close connections between the earls of Fife and the royal house had long secured them pride of place among the Scots nobility. Gille Brigte created for the couple a large and compact feu made up of several substantial estates in the parishes of Glendevon and Fossoway.[56] It is none the less noteworthy that the grant brought together a series of farm touns located in the furthermost south-eastern reaches of the Earl's Brigte's territories. As has been noted, these lands were 'easily accessible' to other Fife estates,[57] but, situated on the far slope of the Ochill Hills, they also lay a considerable distance from the heartland of Gille Brigte's earldom. In effect, the creation of a tocher endowment for Maud merely involved the detachment from direct Strathearn control of a distant corner of comital territory. A second marriage portion, this one assigned to Cecilia of Strathearn and her Stewart husband Walter II son of Alan consisted of the lands of Coulgask,[58] on the northern side of the River Earn along the route of the old Roman road running between Strageath and Ardoch.[59] The choice location of these estates was an acknowledgment of the influence and prestige of the Stewart family.

The youngest daughter, Ethne, married Sir David de la Hay.[60] The tocher she brought with her was carved out of lands in Strathtay (Meikleour) and Fossoway that had once been part of the feu of Gille Brigte's brother, Maol Iosa son of Fearchar.[61] Both estates have in common their location in the eastern reaches of Strathearn. Like the marriage portion assigned to Maud, these were peripheral lands, and their removal from direct comital control was accomplished with relatively small impact on the territorial integrity of the earldom. As it transpired, Gille Brigte's revenues were not seriously diminished as a consequence of his daughters' marriages. Cecilia and Ethne eventually produced heirs, and Coulgask and Meikleour passed to the new families they created, but the most generously endowed daughter, Maud, had no surviving children with Mael Coluim of Fife, and the valuable tocher lands they had enjoyed eventually reverted to the earl of Strathearn. Peripheral they may have been, but well into the thirteenth century some of these estates were still producing revenues for the earl's coffers.[62]

When Earl Robert of Strathearn died in 1245 patterns of land holding in the lordship were in many respects hardly different from what they had been under his grandfather Fearchar. Robert himself is an enigmatic figure, who appears only rarely in a public capacity or at the royal court. His focus, like that of his father, was firmly fixed on his own territories. Very few written deeds to lay beneficiaries survive from his twenty-odd years as earl, but the overwhelming

---

56 Barrow, 'Earls of Fife', 60–1. The original charter is now lost; Professor Barrow's text is based on Sir John Skene's manuscript notebook, but see also the photographic negative of a text among Scottish charter transcripts belonging to John Maitland Thomson, Edinburgh University Library, no. 26.   57 Barrow, 'Earls of Fife', 58.   58 *Inchaff. Liber*, App., no. 8.   59 P.G.B. McNeill and H.L. MacQueen (eds), *Atlas of Scottish history to 1707* (2000), 46.   60 *SP*, viii, 244.   61 Muniments of the Earl of Moray, Moray Charters, Box 32, Bundle 1, no. 21; D.E. Easson (ed.), *Charters of the abbey of Coupar Angus* (1947), i, no. 35.   62 Barrow, 'Earls of Fife', 59.

silence of the scanty records that have come down to the present point to a policy of infeftment consciously modeled on that of Earl Gille Brigte. The witness lists of his charters attest a comital entourage still populated chiefly by men of native stock.[63] The marriages of his two daughters, Annabelle and Maria, and the allocation of tocher lands to their husbands, did not occur until after his death.[64] Robert's infeft tenants were hardly more numerous than those who had held land of his father, and indeed, he appears to have increased his mesne tenantry by only a handful of new men. A deed of King Alexander II of 1234 confirmed to Conghal son of Donnchad the lands of Tullibardine originally granted by Earl Robert.[65] Robert de Methven became a comital tenant soon after Gille Brigte's death when he acquired the feu of Dalpatrick in right of his wife, Soliva de Luvetot.[66] Her brother, Roger, expanded his holdings in Strathearn to include a small estate close to Bennie, along the Knaik Water, but he was the man of Robert's brother Fergus rather than a tenant of the earl himself.[67] Sometime early in his rule Robert assigned the lands of Pitlandy in the parish of Fowlis Wester to Theobald son of William son of Clement.[68] This man's origins are wholly obscure, but his patronymic suggests a foreign, rather than a native, background. He may, in fact, have migrated to Strathearn from Anglian Lothian, for in one of his written deeds he referred to a field by the decidedly English name of 'Fitheleres Flat'.[69] Theobald's infeftment constitutes the only known example of the settlement of a non-Gaelic tenant in Robert's Strathearn. Robert de Methven's feu was not a new creation. Nor was that held by Conghal, who was a direct descendant of the native lord who had served Earl Gille Brigte as steward in the last decade of the twelfth century and the early years of the thirteenth, and whose family had lived in the lordship for four generations already.[70]

The location of the estates that Robert chose to alienate displays the same deliberate thought which had characterized his father's pattern of enfeftment. He granted away no large or well developed blocs of land. In the first half of the thirteenth century Tullibardine, still known by its older Gaelic name of Catherlavenach, was little more than an underdeveloped estate situated on the edge of the moor of Cathermothel (see Map 1). Like his father, then, Robert passed on to his son and heir a lordship that had hardly been diminished.

The presence of officials known as thanes within Strathearn reinforces the impression of the profound resilience of the region in the face of foreign influence. A recent study of the distinct nature of the office in medieval Scotland

---

63 *Inchaff. Chrs.*, nos. 51,52, 55, 58; *Inchaff. Liber*, nos. 12, 59, 60, App., no. 8; *Lind. Cart.*, nos. 25, 31, 44. **64** Annabelle married first Sir John de Restalrig, who was dead by 1260. Her second husband was Sir David de Graham. Their tocher lands consisted of the estates of Kincardine, Coul, Cloan, Foswell, Pairney and Bardrill. Maria married the Dumfriesshire lord, Sir John de Johnstone, and brought with her lands in Strathy and Pairney. Neville, 'Earls of Strathearn', i, 84; NAS, GD 220/1/A1/3/2–4; *Inchaff. Liber*, no. 55; *Inchaff. Chrs.*, App., no. 5. **65** *Inchaff. Liber*, App., no. 10. **66** Ibid., no. 12; *Inchaff. Chrs.*, no. 57. **67** *Inchaff. Chrs.*, no. 57; *Lind. Cart.*, no. 24. **68** *Inchaff. Chrs.*, no. 56. **69** Ibid., no. 56. **70** See above, p. 41.

emphasizes the close links between the crown and its thanes throughout the thirteenth and fourteenth centuries,[71] but notes only in passing the existence of a handful of comital thanages. The lordship of Strathearn was one of a very few to include both royal and comital officials. If, as this study implies, the existence of thanages should be read as evidence of a strong royal presence north of Forth, then the Scots kings' anxiety to maintain firm control over Auchterarder and Forteviot is understandable. The former, situated deep inside the earldom, provided a rare opportunity for the crown to make its presence felt in an otherwise independent territory; the latter, located on the periphery of Strathearn, overlooked the earls' eastern lands. Surviving records confirm that the appointment of officials to both these thanages and the allocation of revenues arising from them were closely controlled from the royal court.[72] The thanes of Dunning and Strowan, however, held their lands of the earls of Strathearn, and already by the year 1200 they were deeply entrenched among the elites of the lordship. They performed important functions within native society as agents of lordly authority, and served as constant reminders to all and sundry of pre-twelfth-century power structures. Anecol of Dunning, whom Earl Gille Brigte called 'my thane', was a frequent witness to comital *acta* in the years between 1199 and 1214.[73] His name suggests a Hebridean background rarely found in Strathearn, but by the late twelfth century he had established firm roots in central Scotland. Donnchad thane of Strowan appears in charters of a slightly earlier period.[74] For much of the thirteenth century both offices were uniquely the preserve of men of native stock and, for a while at least, they passed from father to son. One of Anecol's sons, Brice, succeeded him in office and served a long career under Earls Robert and Malise II.[75]

Like their royal counterparts, the thanes of Strowan and Dunning were primarily fiscal agents, responsible for delivering to the earls' household rents in kind and, by the mid-thirteenth century, money, but they were also important instruments of lordly power and authority. In early Strathearn deeds they appear frequently in charters that assigned cain, conveth, and teinds from Gille Brigte's demesne lands. The thane of Strowan is a shadowy figure after Gille Brigte's time, but two generations later, when Malise II assigned twenty marks of his annual rent from Dunning to the religious of Inchaffray, he issued a brieve to Brice the thane commanding him to pay this sum to the abbot's agent.[76] Malise made a further grant to the canons in 1283, this one to be derived from the thanage of Dunning and the neighbouring demesne estate of Pitcairns, specifying that the revenues derived from income he was accustomed to receive *pro fretellis*.[77] This term, which refers to a tenant's duty to attend his lord, and thus

---

[71] A. Grant, 'Thanes and thanages, from the eleventh to the fourteenth centuries' (1993), 46, 49–51. See also S.T. Driscoll, 'Formalising the mechanisms of state power: early Scottish lordship from the ninth to the thirteenth centuries' (1998), 35–6.   [72] Ibid., 80.   [73] *Inchaff. Chrs.*, nos. 4, 9, 11, 12, 14, 15, 17, 19; *Lind. Cart.*, no. 43.   [74] *Inchaff. Chrs.*, nos. 15, 19; *Inchaff. Liber*, App. No. 2.   [75] *Inchaff. Liber*, App., no. 8; *Inchaff. Chrs.*, nos. 74, 76, 77; *Lind. Cart.*, no. 28.   [76] *Inchaff. Chrs.*, nos. 76, 77.   [77] *Inchaff. Chrs.*, no. 113; *Inchaff. Liber*, no. 14.

to a form of conveth, was an unusual one. Found also in near-contemporary charters from Buchan and Stirling,[78] it attests the longevity of traditional forms of obligation in Strathearn and the association of its payment with the office of the thane. The income that accrued to the earls from the lands of Dunning, moreover, was considerable, and the generous rents that the earls assigned to Inchaffray abbey in 1247 and again in 1283 represented only a portion of its overall value. In 1274 and 1275 the vicarage alone was worth £6 per annum,[79] and in the mid-fourteenth century Robert Stewart earl of Strathearn considered it worth his while to try to reclaim the annual revenues from Dunning that his predecessors had alienated.[80] When Christian Clerk, mair of the shire of Dunning, submitted his accounts to the earl's auditors in 1380, the estates were yielding well over £55 annually.[81] Control over royal thanage lands, moreover, remained a mark of status and prestige; thus, in 1290 Earl Malise III had secured the ferme of a small but lucrative new sheriffdom erected from the thanage of Auchterarder located deep within Strathearn territory.[82]

In many of the ancient lordships north of Forth the term 'thane' was translated into Gaelic as *toísech*, although the word had there 'a rather looser concept', in that it might refer both 'to the head of a kindred and to the subordinate officer of a king or mormaer'.[83] Both the *toísech* and the office to which it refers, *toíseachdeor*, are found in significant numbers in the Gaelic-speaking regions of the kingdom, including Lennox;[84] it is rather surprising, then, that the terms should not appear in any records from Strathearn, where a native land holding tenantry was deeply entrenched. The key to understanding this curious lacuna, however, may lie in the nature of the surviving charter materials themselves. From the earliest years of the thirteenth century the earls of Strathearn called on canons from the reformed religious establishment at Inchaffray to act as scribes for their written *acta*, men who, after 1200, were almost certainly of English and continental, rather than native, background.[85] These clerics, perhaps interested in promoting the reformed status of their house, may simply have replaced the native term *toísech* with the more appropriate Latinate form of 'thane'. In fact, the practice of designating household officials by alternating Gaelic and Latin terms is a marked feature of Strathearn documents well into the thirteenth century,[86] as is the preference for the Latinate version of the legal office of the *breitheamh*, the *judex*.[87] Absence of the Gaelic term *toísech* from Strathearn record, then, need not be understood as evidence of the absence of Gaelic-style heads of kindred.

Like thanages, the term 'shire' attests the survival of ancient land division in Strathearn. Documents of the first half of the thirteenth century refer occa-

---

[78] C.N. Innes (ed.), *Registrum Episcopatus Aberdonensis* (1845), i, 32; *ER*, i, 47. See also ibid., i, 12–13, 20. [79] A.I. Dunlop (ed.), 'Bagimond's roll: statement of the tenths of the kingdom of Scotland' (1939), 54, 71. [80] *Inchaff. Chrs.*, nos. 133, 134. [81] *ER*, iii, 33–4. [82] Ibid., i, 51. [83] Grant, 'Thanes and thanages', 42; W.D.H. Sellar, 'Celtic law and Scots law: survival and integration' (1989), 8–9. [84] W.C. Dickinson, 'The *toschederach*' (1941), 85–6; *Lennox Cart.*, 49. [85] Neville, 'Earls of Strathearn', i, 322–30; idem, 'Celtic enclave', 84. [86] Ibid., 81–2; Duncan, *Making*, 432. [87] Neville, 'Celtic enclave', 81; Sellar, 'Celtic law', 3.

sionally to the *syro of Foul'* (Fowlis Wester),[88] and scholars have posited the existence within the lordship of the remnants of several other very early shires, centred on Catherlevenach (Carlownie), Cathermothel (Muthill), Dunning, Abernethy, and Forteviot, each associated with common pasture and an early church.[89] The shires, he argues, represented fiscal units owing rents in kind to the crown, but in Strathearn, the lands of Catherlavenach and Cathermothel, like the thanages of Dunning and Strowan, were under the firm control of the earls and their immediate family. Robert granted the former to a descendant of family that had long served as comital stewards,[90] while several fermtouns within the latter were the stuff of grants effected by Earls Gille Brigte and Robert.[91]

Several observations arise from this survey of the land holding elite in the earldom of Strathearn during the first half of the thirteenth century. First, it is apparent that neither Gille Brigte nor Robert rejected outright a policy of formally infefting tenants within their territories. Neither would have enjoyed the prestige and respect he did in his capacity as a mormaer if he had not been ready and willing to allocate land, revenues, and rights over peasant farmers to his native kinsmen and supporters. Equally evident, however, is the fact that neither could insulate himself altogether from the steady infiltration into Scotland north of Forth of the *fitz pusnes* whom, one chronicler noted, King William I encouraged to settle after his release from imprisonment at Falaise.[92] The encroachment of land-hungry incomers and obligations arising from the provision of suitable marriage portions for comital children represented challenges to estate planning. Yet, there was nothing haphazard about the estate management of the earls of Strathearn. There is good reason to argue that Gille Brigte and Robert were aware of these challenges and that they developed policies carefully designed to safeguard patrimonial lands for future generations. The estates they granted to younger sons and to sons-in-law were, almost without exception, chosen from the eastern peripheries of the earldom, some consisting wholly of lands that they had acquired by accident and good fortune rather than by inheritance. In vast stretches of the earldom there was nary a French-speaking tenant to be found until well into the thirteenth century, and scarcely an estate exploited directly by the canons of Inchaffray. In a pattern similar to that found in Galloway, moreover, the earls maintained firm control over the extensive upland regions of their territories.[93] The pattern of castle construction illustrated in Map 1 confirms this observation, with many fortified sites strategically scattered across the entire extent of the earldom. In the first half of the thirteenth century cash rents and money rev-

---

88 *Inchaff. Chrs.*, no. 37. **89** Barrow, *Kingdom*, 43, 54, and Maps 10, 11; S.T. Driscoll, 'The archaeology of state formation in Scotland' (1991), 101–7. **90** *Inchaff. Liber*, App., no. 10. **91** *Lind. Cart.*, nos. 24, 25, 28; Neville, 'Native lords and the church', 468–9. **92** J. Stevenson (ed.), *Scalacronica by Sir Thomas Gray of Heton, knight* (1836), 41. **93** Oram, *Lordship of Galloway*, 212; idem, 'A family business? Colonization and settlement in twelfth- and thirteenth-century Galloway' (1993), 121, 135.

enues, which begin to appear in considerable numbers in the lowland, agrarian-based estates of the eastern Earn valley, are nowhere in evidence in the upland region. Under Gille Brigte and Robert a substantial portion of the earldom remained a bastion of Gaelic power, largely untouched by the social and cultural changes that were taking place in the easternmost regions of Strathearn. This pattern of land exploitation, in fact, endured until well into the later medieval period. Accounts rendered at the Exchequer in 1380 reveal that a century and more after Robert's death the majority of the earl's great tenants remained firmly ensconced in the east.[94] In this respect at least, the patterns of enfeftment first established by Earl Gille Brigte at the very beginning of the thirteenth century proved remarkably impervious to the influence of English and continental incomers.

The tenacity of Gaelic customs and practices in early thirteenth-century Strathearn had its counterpart in the lordship of Lennox. Just as foreign colonists were able to establish footholds only on the periphery of Strathearn, so, too, did they encounter similar difficulties in penetrating the intensely Gaelic environment of the Loch Lomond region under Earls Ailin II and Maoldomhnaich. Surviving charter evidence, it is true, reveals that the latter at least was familiar with the practice of issuing written deeds authenticated with waxen seals to ecclesiastical and lay beneficiaries alike. The eighteen charters that Maoldomhnaich drafted in favour of lay persons are much more numerous than in contemporary Strathearn, and a close study of the texts reveals that Maoldomhnaich used written deeds in a carefully articulated strategy designed to achieve specific goals.[95] Until the end of his rule, none the less, Lennox otherwise remained strikingly – and deliberately – resistant to foreign influence.

As noted above, the period during which David of Huntingdon held the earldom of Lennox saw little alteration to the tenurial structure of the lordship. Although Ailin II thought it appropriate to record in writing gifts to the parish church of Kilpatrick and the cathedral of Glasgow,[96] there survives from his period no charter in favour of a lay person, and no indication that his lay tenants owed him any kind of service other than the customary obligations that everywhere north of Forth bound native tenants to their Gaelic lords. Tenants there undoubtedly were: Ailin's grants in free alms to Kilpatrick and Glasgow included the usual dispensation from performing the forinsec military service incumbent on the estates they named, and which, by implication, other lay tenants owed him. The only clearly identified comital tenants were the native men Maoldomhnaich and Gille Moire, for whom Ailin created a considerable feu centred on Luss, on the western shores of Loch Lomond and extending to a considerable distance both north and west.[97] The earliest lords of Luss established something of a dynasty within Lennox as a consequence of this grant: Maoldomhnaich of Luss and his son served Earl Maoldomhnaich, and their

---

94 *ER*, iii, 33–8.   **95** See pp 192–3, below.   **96** *Paisley Reg.*, 157; *Glasgow Reg.*, i, no. 101.   **97** Ailin's grant is noted in a charter of his son Maoldomhnaich; Fraser, *Lennox*, ii, no. 207.

descendants maintained very close relations with the comital family throughout the medieval period and well beyond.[98]

The attestors of Ailin's few extant deeds were men whose counsel the earl valued and who almost certainly held lands of him. The persons so named were, without exception, of native stock. Among them were men who, at a slightly later date, are known to have been comital tenants, such as Ailin's son Dùghall, Gilleasbuig Galbraith, Mael Coluim son of Gilleasbuig, and Gille Brigte de Cathcart.[99] Scanty record materials from the time of Ailin II make generalizations about the tenurial profile of Lennox largely conjectural, but incidental references and *notitiae* in deeds that survive from his son's governance of the lordship suggest a region of Scotland still at the time of Ailin's death around 1217 largely traditional in its outlook and impervious to the influence of Anglo-Norman or continental newcomers.

The abundant charter evidence surviving from the period of Maoldomhnaich's rule allows a more confident reconstruction of the pattern of settlement and land exploitation in Lennox in the central decades of the thirteenth century. A significant portion of the earl's territories lay hard by regions of the country that had been most densely populated by foreign colonizers under the careful guidance of the sons of King Mael Coluim III, an area that is often sharply contrasted with the 'land of earls' that lay north of a line running from the Forth westward to the Clyde River.[1] The southernmost Lennox parishes of Kilpatrick, Baldernock, and Kirkintilloch, in particular, shared land-based boundaries with the large Stewart lordship of Strathgryfe, ranging over Renfrewshire and Lanarkshire, to which royal and baronial tenants of English, Norman, Flemish and other continental origins imported a so-called 'ready to wear' form of feudalism, complete with homage and fealty, knight service, and written deeds of infeftment.[2] It is hardly surprising, then, that from this same region the native rulers of Lennox should have been exposed to, and perhaps felt the pressure of, new ideas and new forms of land tenure. And indeed, it was in this part of the earldom that comital tenants, lay and ecclesiastical, most frequently sought written charters, and in which Maoldomhnaich created the bulk of new feus for French- and English-speaking tenants.

The foreign families who secured lands within Lennox in the early thirteenth century were almost all followers of Walter II son of Alan. Walter himself did not become a land holder within the lordship, but he forged important social and familial links with his Gaelic neighbour when Earl Maoldomhnaich married his daughter, Elizabeth.[3] In her train came Simon son of Robert Croc, already a tenant in the Stewart lordship, and the Flemish adventurer Simon son of Bertolf.[4] The former secured a scattered feu made up of lands in Carbeth and

---

[98] 'Families of the Lennox: a survey' (1975), 33; D. McRoberts, 'Rossdhu church and its book of hours' (1965), 16; Mackinlay, (ed.), *Origines*, i, 30. [99] *Glasgow Reg.*, i, no. 101. [1] Duncan, *Making*, 164; more generally, see 160–7, and Barrell, *Medieval Scotland*, 24–5. [2] Barrow, *Anglo-Norman era*, 139. [3] *SP*, v, 332; *Paisley Reg.*, 158. [4] Barrow, *Kingdom*, 327; idem, *Anglo-Norman*

Killermont; the latter an estate at Letter, at the opposite end of the southern reaches of Lennox, on the Loch Long coast of Rosneath parish.[5] Maoldomhnaich also settled Stephen of Blantyre, whose name suggests an import from Stewart lands, in a half a carucate in Killearn parish, and favoured him with substantial judicial powers within his lands.[6]

By far the most important of the earl's foreign tenants, however, was Sir David de Graham of Dundaff, already in the 1240s embarking on a career as a rapacious speculator. He secured from Maoldomhnaich valuable feus in Stathblane and Mugdock, as well as an annual rent formerly rendered to the earl himself.[7] Graham's move into Lennox witnessed the displacement of two native tenants. Fearchar Mac Gille Mhartainn gave up his tenancy in Strathblane in exchange for lands in the more rugged hill country of Fintry parish, while Luke, a native man of some social standing, renounced a choice site in Mugdock, possibly in exchange for others in Luss parish.[8] Graham's ambitions, however, did not go unopposed.[9] While, by 1250, he had managed to establish a firm foothold in Lennox, his sphere of influence never extended beyond the confines of the parish of Strathblane. Like his fellows, Simon Croc and Simon son of Bertolf, David de Graham had to content himself with a feu situated on the periphery the heartland of Maoldomhnaich's lordship.

Earl Maoldomhnaich's status as a great lord and, with no fewer than ten brothers a sister and three children, head of an extensive kin group imposed on him onerous obligations to endow family members with estates appropriate to their rank, and other men with grants commensurate with their levels of service to his household and person. Among the Gaelic-speaking lay persons who held land directly of him were his brothers Dùghall, Amhlaibh, Gille Crìosd, Muireadhach, and Corc; his son and heir Mael Coluim; his steward Mael Coluim Beg; his son-in-law Donnchad thane of Callendar; Dùghall son of his *judex* Cristin; and more than twenty other men of standing.[10] This group of lay tenants is noteworthy in several respects. The overwhelming preponderance of native land holders in comparison with foreign newcomers reinforces the impression of a lordship still largely untouched by the French- and English-speaking aristocracy that had been established south of Forth for almost a century already.

era, 126. **5** Fraser, *Lennox*, ii, no. 3; Blair Castle, Athole Muniments, volume of inlaid charters, no. 4. **6** Fraser, *Lennox*, ii, no. 11 **7** Ibid., ii, nos. 6, 7, 10. For a list of Graham's acquisitions to 1253, see a charter of confirmation of King Alexander III, ibid., no. 12. **8** Luke had been dean of Lennox, though he was also a lay person. He may have been related to the native Luss family. **9** In 1248 Mael Coluim son of Maoldomhnaich sought to overturn his father's grant of lands and revenues in Strathblane to Graham. The dispute was brought before the king himself for resolution. Fraser, *Lennox*, ii, no. 9. **10** These men included Mael Coluim son of Donnchad thane of Callander, Maoldomhnaich and Gille Moire of Luss, Absolon son of Macbeatha, Gille Brigte son of Samuel, Maurice and Arthur sons of Gilleasbuig and Arthur's son William, Cessóc MacCessóc, Adam son of Edolf, Humfrey de Kilpatrick, Fearchar Mac Gille Mhartainn, Feargus son of Cunningham and his son Mael Coluim, Farbhlaidh daughter of Kerald, Gille Mícheil, Gille Mhartainn and Gillecondad (Gille Chomghain?) the sons of Gille Mícheil, Domnall MacYvel (MacIomhair?), Maol Muire son of Niall, and Gilleasbuig MacGille Crìosd; *SP*, v, 328–31.

Professor Barrow may be correct in stating that Maoldomhnaich 'was recruiting, evidently from the Stewart's circle of vassals, knights of a type which could not yet be provided locally',[11] but in limiting severely the number of foreign newcomers into his lordship, he made it clear that he had little interest in a wholesale importation of the new style of military tenure. Knight service did come to Lennox: three of the earl's tenants held their estates for one thirty-second, one seventh, and one twentieth part of a knight respectively.[12] Such obligations were by no means merely nominal, but as in Strathearn, where Maol Iosa son of Fearchar was responsible for rendering the service of a single knight to his brother Earl Gille Brigte,[13] their rarity in Lennox underscores their exotic nature in this part of the realm.

By contrast, in both Lennox and Strathearn, charters of infeftment to native and incoming lay tenants refer almost without exception only to forinsec service in the king's common army. Like the other descendants of the mormaers north of Forth, Maoldomhnaich of Lennox and Gille Brigte and Robert of Strathearn had an obligation to lead their provincial armies whenever the king required. The unit of assessment in both regions, again as elsewhere, was the amount of arable land in each lordship, measured in Lennox in carucates and arachors, though not in *quarteria* until the end of the century.[14] In Strathearn, forinsec service was rendered in person by the earl's tenants,[15] but Lennox was unique in that in Maoldomhnaich's day, and well beyond, land holders fulfilled their obligations by providing cheeses to the royal host, normally 'two cheeses from every house in which cheese is made'.[16] It has been suggested that this food service may have harkened back to renders once customary in the kingdom of Strathclyde or, on the other hand, that it reflected the lack of arable in much of the Lennox region.[17] Surviving evidence would seem to favour the latter. Collectively, the range of specific military services demanded of English and continental newcomers that scholars still sometimes refer to as 'feudalism' touched the lordship of Lennox only lightly in the first fifty years of the thirteenth century.

Noteworthy also in this brief survey of Maoldomhnaich's native tenants is the geographical distribution of the feus they held. While he confined newcomers like Stephen of Blantyre and David de Graham to the southern reaches of his considerable territories, the earl encouraged his Gaelic tenants to acquire landed interests the length and breadth of Lennox, in places ranging from Arrochar in the heavily forested north (an honour created for his nephew Donnchad son of Gille Criosd),[18] south to Gartconnel, and from Mambeg in the west to Auchinreoch in the east. Unlike his Stewart neighbours, moreover, the earl was willing to share with his more important Gaelic tenants the rich hunting grounds of some of the islands of Loch Lomond and the fertile arable

11 Barrow, *Anglo-Norman era*, 126. 12 *Lennox Cart.*, 26–7, 58; NLS, Adv. MS 34.3.25, fos. 58–9. 13 *RRS*, ii, no. 136. 14 E.g. Fraser, *Lennox*, ii, no. 10; *RMS*, ii, no. 187. 15 Forinsec service was normally known as 'Scottish' service in Strathearn. 16 E.g. Fraser, *Lennox*, ii, nos. 204, 207; *Lennox Cart.*, 20; *RMS*, ii, no. 187. 17 Duncan, *Making*, 358, 382. 18 Royal Faculty of Procurators, Glasgow, Hill Collection of MSS, Macfarlane Muniments, ii, no. 73.

lands of others.[19] Although he reserved Inchmurrin, the largest of these, as a site for one of his fortified residences, he gave to Absolon son of Macbeatha the island of Clarinch, and to the Luss family several others (Inchtavannach, Inchconnachan, Inchmoan and Inchcruin) lying a little further north.[20] Family members held feus made up of estates located both in the highland zone of the lordship as well as the more limited – and so more valuable – lands of the lower southern and eastern reaches of the earldom. Amhlaibh son of Ailin II, for example, controlled a small but valuable honour made up of lands on the peninsula that lay between the Gare Loch and Loch Long, as well as Glenfruin, and Kilmahew,[21] while his brother Dùghall's landed interests consisted of estates in the southernmost tip of Loch Lomond around Balloch, as well as in Kilpatrick in Bonhill parish.[22] Gille Crìosd obtained from his brother the lordship of Luss and Arrochar. When this valuable feu passed (or was restored) to the Luss family the earl moved Gille Crìosd further north, into the hilly country at the tip of Loch Lomond.[23] For his son Mael Coluim, Maoldomhnaich took particular care to fashion an endowment appropriate to the heir of a great magnate, a rich feu consisting of estates in Dalnotter and elsewhere in Kilpatrick parish, as well, apparently, of a significant portion of the parish of Strathblane, near those of David de Graham.[24] A second son, Donnchad, was alive in 1248 when he witnessed one of Maoldomhnaich's written deeds,[25] but the location of his lands, if indeed he held any, is unknown.

In contrast with Earls Fearchar, Gille Brigte and Robert of Strathearn, Ailin II and Maoldomhnaich of Lennox did not have to make extensive provision for marriageable daughters. Following Ailin's death in 1217, it fell to his son and heir to assemble a tocher for his sister Eva and her husband, the native lord Donnchad son of Mael Coluim thane of Callendar. Their marriage portion consisted of several estates on the Keltie Water, all in the easternmost reaches of the earldom, and all within comfortable reach of the Callendar family's Strathblane lands.[26] Donnchad's connections with the royal court through his father made him a valuable political and personal ally, and in the years after Eva's marriage, although he surrendered a sizeable portion of the thanage of Callendar to King Alexander II, Mael Coluim became a wealthy and influential baron in neighbouring Stirlingshire,[27] and Donnchad himself eventually lord of an even larger barony.[28]

Other important native land holders included the earl's steward Mael Coluim Beg, Mael Muire son of Niall, and early representatives of the families of

---

19 Some of Walter II son of Alan's grants to Paisley abbey excluded the birds and beasts of his forest. See, for example, *Paisley Reg.*, 48. **20** Fraser, *Lennox*, ii, no. 4; *Lennox Cart.*, 25–6. Absolon was also lord of Buchanan, on the opposite shore of Loch Lomond; *Paisley Reg.*, 217. **21** *Paisley Reg.*, 209–11; *Lennox Cart.*, 91–2. **22** *Paisley Reg.*, 171–2, 217. **23** Royal Faculty of Procurators, Glasgow, Macfarlane Muniments, ii, no. 73. **24** Fraser, *Lennox*, ii, nos. 8, 9, 206; *Paisley Reg.*, 161–2. **25** Fraser, *Lennox*, ii, no. 11. **26** Ibid., ii, no. 202. **27** Grant, 'Thanes and thanages', 56–8, 61, 81; Barrow, *Kingdom of the Scots*, 37–8. **28** A. Nisbet, *A system of heraldry* (1722), ii, *History and critical notes on the Ragman Roll*, 17–18.

Colquhoun and Galbraith, the latter perhaps an import, some time previously, from Brittonic Strathclyde.[29] Their estates were in Drymen parish and the southwestern shore of Loch Lomond; Mamore and Mambeg (Rosneath parish); Colquhoun, near Ardoch; Tambowie; Gartconnel; Bardenock (Strathblane parish); and Auchencloich in the Stewart lordship of Renfrew, perhaps a portion of the lands that Maoldomhnaich had acquired when he married Elizabeth Stewart.[30] Viewed collectively, the feus created for family members and native tenants attest a well conceived strategy on the part of Earls Ailin II and, especially, Maoldomhnaich. The introduction of foreign families to the earldom was a very gradual process. In a conscious effort to offset their influence over the native population, moreover, their settlement in the lordship was to a marked extent accompanied by the establishment hard by their new estates of older Gaelic families. Such, for example, were the grants issued in favour of William son of Arthur Galbraith at Bardenock next to the new Graham feu at Mugdock, and of Mael Muire son of Niall in the western portion of Rosneath parish near the lands assigned to Stephen of Blantyre. Maoldomhnaich's marital connections with the Stewart lordship to his south, and through his in-laws, with the world of the foreign aristocracy made it next to impossible for him to resist altogether pressure from English and continental tenants for admission to his territories. But careful estate planning ensured that he maintained firm control over the extent of their influence. The successful integration of the foreign and native cultures is nicely illustrated in a charter of Maoldomhnaich's great-grandson Malcolm II, which granted to Patrick de Lindsay of Bonhill the offices of *toíseachdeor* and forester of Lennox.[31]

Although Malcolm's grant of the toíseachdeorship of Lennox is of relatively late date, there is significant evidence to suggest that the office was already rooted in some antiquity there. The charter itself referred to 'all the easements pertaining to the said office or that ought to pertain to it *de jure*'. The ambiguity of the phrase implies a general understanding on the part of Malcolm II's tenants of a variety of privileges and perquisites associated with *toíseachean* and thanes. Like other native magnates, moreover, the thirteenth-century earls of Lennox drew their revenues, and based much of their wealth, on myriad agricultural and pastoral goods rendered to them under the guise of cain and conveth. The collection of these payments from the distant reaches of their territories necessitated the same administrative expertise that in other lordships from Moray to Fife fell to the *toíseachean* and thanes.[32] Finally, onomastic evidence, though limited, may be adduced here: the toun of Auchentoshan, located in the spiritual heartland of Lennox in the parish of Kilpatrick, may preserve in its name an estate once controlled by the medieval *toíseachean*.

29 'Families of the Lennox', 32. Both Gille Críosd Mac an Bhreatnaigh and his son Gillescop appear in early Lennox documents; Gille Críosd Bretnach, 'the Breton', appears as a witness in an early charter to Melrose abbey; C. Innes (ed.), *Liber sancte Marie de Melros* (1837), i, no. 29. **30** *Lennox Cart.*, 25, 26–7, 30–1, 97–8; Fraser, *Lennox*, ii, no. 205. **31** *Lennox Cart.*, 49. **32** Grant, 'Thanes and thanages', 48–9.

In Strathearn, the office of thane was hereditary on a native family throughout most of the thirteenth century. This may also have been the case in neighbouring Lennox, as indeed it was elsewhere, as well as in the royal thanage of Callendar,[33] but the evidence is too scanty to permit firm conclusions. Patrick de Lindsay's elevation to the offices of *toíseach* and forester was short-lived. Before long Malcolm II's kinsman, Walter lord of Faslane, had purchased both, and sought confirmation of his new status from Malcolm's successor, Earl Donald.[34] Whether he did so merely in expectation of financial profit, or because he resented the grant of such an important office to a man who had no close blood tie with the comital family cannot now be ascertained. Whatever the reason, Walter's eventual succession to the lands of the earldom in right of his wife had the effect of merging the toíseachdeorship and the office of forester with that of the comital title, a situation that endured well into the fifteenth century. Already by Walter's time, however, the place of Scottish thanes in the fiscal and legal administration of the great lordships had become vestigial and purely honourary.

The resilience of native tradition in medieval Strathearn and Lennox down to the middle years of the thirteenth century is as apparent within the earls' households as it is in their patterns of infeftment. In both lordships the transition from a relatively simple body of comital officials to a more sophisticated system of household and estate management was gradual, with adaptations made as required, rather than in response to external, foreign influence. Changes did occur over time: as early as 1247, for example, Earl Malise II of Strathearn had created the office of chamberlain, a reflection of the intensified exploitation of the landed resources of the earldom.[35] But in both regions there is considerable evidence to suggest that until mid-century the governance of the lordships remained a family concern and their adminsitration the exclusive business of men of native origin.

The official most frequently mentioned in early Strathearn and Lennox charters is the steward. In the former the term *dapifer* was used until 1200 to describe the steward; between then and 1223 it appears to have been interchangeable with the Latin *senescallus*. It has been argued that in Anglo-Norman England the second designation coincided with a separation of the household duties from those concerned with the administration of the lord's demesne lands.[36] There is no evidence to support such a level of sophistication in Strathearn. Gille Naomh and his successor Maol Iosa were both referred to as *dapifer* and *senescallus* in earl Gille Brigte's written deeds, even during a brief period when they held office simultaneously. If the scribes who drafted comital charters intended to infer a difference between the duties assigned to each office, such a nuance is now lost. More likely is that the reformed canons who acted as Gille Brigte's secretaries slowly but steadily replaced the older word *dapifer* with a more famil-

---

[33] Ibid., 57.   [34] NLS, Adv. MS. 34.3.25, fo. 62.   [35] *Inchaff. Chrs.*, no. 76.   [36] N. Denholm-Young, *Seignorial administration in England* (1937), 67.

Lay tenants and household officials 61

iar term, much as their designations of Inchaffray abbey itself by the Gaelic name *Innis Aiffrean* gave way, after Gille Brigte's death to the Latinate *Insula Missarum*.[37] Earl Robert's clerks, some of them second or third generation inmates of Inchaffray, always called the steward *senescallus*. In early thirteenth-century Lennox, where Earls Ailin II and Maoldomhnaich likewise called on the scribal services of a nearby religious house (in their case Paisley abbey), only the Latin term occurs.

Surviving records attest the central role of the steward in both lordships until about 1250; thereafter, there occurred a decline in the status of this official, though the trend was especially marked in Strathearn. Unusual here, too, is the rapidity with which the steward was superseded as the chief minister in the earls' household. Of 26 full-text charters surviving from the time of Gille Brigte, Gille Naomh witnessed some 15 and his son and successor 16; their names almost always appear at the head of lists of household officials.[38] The steward remained an important man in Robert's time. Maol Iosa, who continued in office after Earl Gille Brigte's death, witnessed 7 of Robert's 11 surviving *acta*, and maintained his precedence over other ministers in witness lists. But Brice thane of Dunning, who became steward to Earl Malise III in the early 1270s, attested no comital charters in his official capacity; in fact, his tenure of the position of steward is known only thanks to the survival of a handful of non-baronial deeds, and in them his name is relegated to the bottom of the list of witnesses.[39] By then, too, the office had ceased to be hereditary in Strathearn.[40] In more markedly traditional Lennox the early thirteenth-century earls likewise reserved the office to Gaelic-speaking natives, though there is little indication that it was hereditary. Maoldomhnaich's first recorded steward was Mael Coluim Beg, though the office subsequently passed to Absolon of Lennox and thence to a native man by the name of Kerald.[41] As in contemporary Strathearn, the names of the men who held the office appear high in the witness lists of comital and other *acta*, but here until the very end of the thirteenth century. In Lennox, moreover, the office was assigned briefly towards the end of his rule to one of Earl Malcolm I's new European tenants, but otherwise remained in the hands of native aristocrats.[42]

If the steward claimed precedence in the households of the Gaelic earls of Strathearn and Lennox, second place must undoubtedly have fallen to the *judex*. Some years ago, Professor Barrow noted the association of the office (Gaelic *breitheamh*) with traditional territorial divisions north of Forth as well as in

---

37 Compare, for example, *Inchaff. Chrs.*, nos. 5, 27 and 39, all from Gille Brigte's time, with charters dating from that of Malise II, e.g. ibid., nos. 76, 95 and 97. The transition period was clearly the rule of Earl Robert (1223–45). See also p. 217, below.. **38** Neville, 'Celtic enclave', Table 1, 87. **39** *Inchaff. Chrs.*, nos. 99, 100, 103. **40** For a review of the descent of the office in the thirteenth century, see Neville, 'Earls of Strathearn', i, 174–7. **41** Keraldus was the Latinized form of the Irish Gaelic name Cairell; J. Bannerman, 'The king's poet and the inauguration of Alexander III' (1989), 139. **42** Walter Sproull: *Lennox Cart.*, 24, 80–1; *Paisley Reg.*, 201; Patrick Galbraith: *Lennox Cart.*, 48–9; Donald son of Anecol: ibid., 86–7.

Galloway, and its status as 'a survival from pre-twelfth-century Scotland ... part of the older, Celtic order of society'.[43] Charter evidence from Strathearn and Lennox attests the importance attached to the office of the *judex*, not merely in the first half of the thirteenth century, but well beyond and, more tellingly, its identification with men of exclusively native origin. In the former, the office was held in succession by Brice, Causantin, Macbeatha, and, after disappearing from written record for several years, surfaces anew in the time of Earl Malise II and his successor, Malise III, still in the hands of Gaelic lords.[44] Successive *judices* of Lennox were also men of Gaelic, and almost certainly local, extraction, notably Gille Criosd, Gille Brigte, Cristin and Kerald (witnesses to charters of Earl Maoldomhnaich) and, in the time of Malcolm I, Gillecolman son of Domnall 'MacBref'.[45] The *judex* is among the most visible officials in thirteenth-century charter materials from both regions, and while the Latin-trained clerks in the employ of the native earls preferred to use the Latinate term rather than its Gaelic counterpart to designate them, their functions were clearly those of other *breitheamhnan* throughout Gaelic Britain.[46] Responsible for the administration of law and justice, and keepers of the legal customs of their provinces, the *judices* were actively involved in the formal attestation of acts of enfeftment and quitclaim, the perambulation of new or disputed estate boundaries, and as justices in the earls' courts. Causantin of Strathearn, for example, witnessed no fewer than thirteen of his lord's grants of sasine,[47] and when Countess Iseulte gifted a portion of her estate of Abercairny to the religious of Inchaffray, the land was perambulated by a group of local worthies, including *Macbet judex*.[48] Gille Criosd and Kerald, *judices* of Lennox, witnessed charters issued in similarly solemn circumstances.[49] Although there is no firm evidence to suggest that the office was hereditary in either lordship, this may have been the case in Lennox, at least in the early thirteenth century. Gille Criosd, perhaps the same man as the Gille Criosd son of Bede who was at the centre of the Kilpatrick inquiry of 1233, was succeeded in office by the *judex* Cristin, who was more definitely one of Bede's sons.[50] But Cristin's son Dùghall never held the office; indeed, in 1234 reduced circumstances led him to sell his lands in Cochno to Paisley abbey.[51]

At the heart of all medieval lordships, Scottish, English, and European, was the baronial court. Here, the lords made manifest their will and negotiated with their major tenants the social, political, and economic contours of their community. Although Strathearn and Lennox documents only seldom make explicit

---

43 Barrow, *Kingdom*, 57; see also Sellar, 'Celtic law', 3–7; McNeill and MacQueen (eds), *Atlas of Scottish history*, 189.   **44** Neville, 'Earls of Strathearn', i, 179–83.   **45** Fraser, *Lennox*, ii, nos. 203, 204; C. Innes (ed.), *Liber S. Marie de Calchou* (1946), i, no. 222; C. Innes and P. Chalmers (eds), *Liber S. Thome de Aberbrothoc* (2 vols, 1848–56), i, no. 133; *Paisley Reg.*, 178–80, 203.   **46** Barrow, *Kingdom*, 57–60; Sellar, 'Celtic law', 3.   **47** *Inchaff. Chrs.*, nos. 3–5, 9, 11–13, 15, 16, 25; *Inchaff. Liber*, nos. 5, 27, 69.   **48** *Inchaff. Chrs.*, no. 46.   **49** Fraser, *Lennox*, ii, nos. 203, 204; C. Innes (ed.), *Kelso Liber*, i, no. 222 (where Gille Criosd is mistakenly named *Gilbertus*); *Arbroath Liber*, i, no. 133.   **50** *Paisley Reg.*, 166–7, 175–6, 178–80.   **51** Ibid., 178–80.

reference to meetings of the baronial court, the presence of the *judices* in their legal capacity may be inferred in charter witness lists, such as that found in a deed which describes the formal assembly held in the parish church of Strageath, in which Robert son and heir of Gille Brigte of Strathearn swore to protect and promote the interests of Inchaffray abbey,[52] in glimpses of the comital court in action in both Strathearn and Lennox,[53] and in the lengthy dispute between the earls of Lennox and Paisley abbey with respect to the lands of Kilpatrick.[54] Yet, there is reason to wonder just how suited were the native *judices* and their dooms to the legal problems associated with incoming, foreign settlers, or how trustworthy their authority in the eyes of clerics well versed in the reform ideology of their day. In 1235 a formal agreement between Earl Maoldomhnaich and one of his brother's tenants brought to a conclusion the first phase of the dispute concerning the same kirk of Kilpatrick.[55] The presiding dignitaries included only one man of native standing (the earl's own son) among a panel of more than six. The rest were all French-speakers drawn largely from the Stewart lordship that lay to the south. Once again, with a single exception, foreigners stood as pledges for Maoldomhnaich's solemn oath to observe the agreement.[56] The abbot of Paisley's unwillingness to acknowledge the weight of native law and native testimony may have been intended as a deliberate snub in what had by then become a vexatious dispute. The earl's readiness to acquiesce with the appointment of a panel made up almost exclusively of foreign judges and pledges, moreover, may have reflected his own uncertainty about the strength of native opinion in the matter. On the other hand, the inclusion of his heir Mael Coluim, suggests that even in the face of defeat, Maoldomhnaich was able to secure a Gaelic voice in the business of dispute settlement.

Professor Barrow's statement that the dempster 'was not merely a survival, but a somewhat remarkable survival, from Celtic Scotland' is particularly relevant to the native lordships of Strathearn and Lennox.[57] While other traditional offices, notably those of the *rannaire* and the dispenser, had lapsed in both regions by the middle years of the thirteenth century, the later earls chose to retain that of the *judex*. At one level, they recognized that the keeper of laws performed much more than merely a vestigial role within their lands; at another, they saw in the office a valuable opportunity to preserve the legitimacy and integrity of the native legal tradition in the face of foreign change and innovation. Some occasions warranted an appeal to jurors familiar with common-law notions they had brought with them from England; such, for example, was the gathering in

---

52 *Inchaff. Liber*, no. 16. For other Strathearn examples, see Neville, 'Earls of Strathearn', i, 181–2. **53** See, for example, *Inchaff. Chrs.*, nos. 43, 44, in which Gille Brigte directs his *judex* to preside over sessions of the court of Inchaffray priory, and *Kelso Liber*, i, no. 22, when Earl Maoldomhnaich formally acknowledged his father's removal of the patronage of Campsie church from the see of Glasgow and its regrant to Kelso abbey. **54** *Paisley Reg.*, 203, dated 1294. **55** *Paisley Reg.*, 170–1. The dispute is discussed below at pp 145–8. **56** The others were Walter Stewart, justiciar of Scotia, William abbot of Paisley, Thomas Croc, Hugh son of Simon, and Simon son of Bertolf. **57** Barrow, *Kingdom*, 57.

which Robert de Croc acknowledged that he had assigned dower lands to his mother in violation of another (Anglo-Norman) tenant's claim over them. At this inquest only one of the suitors was of native origin.[58] Similarly, it was probably at the insistence of Sir David de Graham that the ceremony in which Earl Maoldomhnaich displaced a sitting tenant in Graham's favour was attended almost exclusively by non-native witnesses.[59]

A host of other ministers, lay and ecclesiastical, are also well attested in the native households of Strathearn and Lennox. Some were foreign imports but, as elsewhere in Gaelic Scotland, most others represented offices that had long been features of magnatial entourages, native or newcomer. Household clerks and chaplains constituted the largest collective body in service to the native earls. They are, for the most part, shadowy figures whose careers are difficult to track in surviving record materials. Occasionally, however, some left a mark upon their locality. A chaplain by the name of Abraham began modestly enough in the household of Earl Gille Brigte of Strathearn, then in 1214 went on to election and consecration as bishop of Dunblane. Abraham was noteworthy, too, for fathering a son, and for this offence drew the ire of the formidable Pope Innocent III.[60] In Lennox, Earl Maoldomhnaich rewarded the household work of his clerk Robert Hertford with the modest but still valuable estate of Dalmanno in Bonhill parish.[61] Again in Strathearn, Master Cristin first honed his skills as a scribe for Earl Gille Brigte's heir Robert, then was attracted to the service of Mael Coluim earl of Fife in the early 1220s; from there he moved into the employ of the abbot of Paisley. In the course of his career he earned a university degree, then chose to return to Strathearn in the early 1230s, perhaps with a view to gaining advancement under the rigorous leadership of Bishop Clement of Dunblane. He does not appear to have secured a regular position in the episcopal household, but for his services to Earl Robert as a scribe he secured the benefice of Monzie parish church.[62]

Clerics like Robert and Cristin performed essential tasks in the earls' households, acting as scribes for their lords, performing vital confessional services and, more generally, representing 'a reserve of literate and perhaps even educated men', who boasted skills in administrative and financial matters.[63] The Scottish kings employed clerics as keepers of royal seals and assistants to the chancellor,[64] and David earl of Huntingdon employed a more or less permanent clerical staff, which travelled with him, not merely in Scotland, but across the border to his English estates as well. Some, indeed, specialized in the redaction of specific

---

58 NAS, RH 5/21. **59** Fraser, *Lennox*, ii, no. 7. **60** *Inchaff. Chrs.*, nos. 3–5, 11–13, 15, 25, 27; *Inchaff. Liber*, no. 69; A. Theiner (ed.), *Vetera monumenta Hibernorum et Scotorum illustrantia* (1864), no. 6; J.H. Cockburn, *The medieval bishops of Dunblane and their church* (1959), 37. **61** *Paisley Reg.*, 217. **62** *Inchaff. Liber*, no. 16; *Inchaff. Chrs.*, no. 56; C. Innes (ed.), *Registrum de Dunfermelyn* (1842), nos. 213, 214; *Paisley Reg.*, 86, 114–15, 319, 323–7; *Glasgow Reg.*, i, no. 143; D.E.R. Watt, *A biographical dictionary of Scottish graduates to A.D. 1410* (1977), 522; Neville, 'Earls of Strathearn', i, 328–9. **63** W.E. Wightman, *The Lacy family in England and Normandy, 1066–1194* (1966), 106. **64** *RRS*, ii, 31.

kinds of document.[65] No such level of sophistication is discernible in the native lordships of Strathearn and Lennox, nor was it needed. Charter witness lists there reveal that clerks there were in abundance in both households throughout the thirteenth century, some perhaps semi-permanent residents, but the greater majority by far only birds of passage, called upon to fill the ranks of witnesses at formal ceremonies, then to record such business on parchment, or to handle the correspondence that passed between the earls and their local bishops. It is, however, a striking feature of the lists of clerics that it is possible to compile for both regions that men identified as 'clerks' should all have borne non-Gaelic personal names. Earls Ailin II and Maoldomhnaich of Lennox, as well as Gille Brigte and Robert of Strathearn, depended above all on residents of the abbeys of Paisley and Inchaffray respectively for scribal expertise in the drafting of legal instruments. The growing complexity of the laws and customs governing the tenure and conveyance of land in the thirteenth century required a level of knowledge that appears to have been largely beyond the competence of their native clerics.

Chaplains, too, appear in Strathearn and Lennox records only fleetingly. Studies of Scottish royal charters have shown that in the early thirteenth century 'a firm distinction seems to have been drawn between clerks and chaplains, the former being presumably concerned with administrative, secretarial work, the latter with the spiritual life of the royal household and with celebrating daily mass for the king to hear'.[66] This distinction may well hold true for the native lordships, but surviving evidence here is at best inconclusive. Still, chaplains were essential members of the earls' households. Daily or weekly masses required the presence of priests, and plentiful supplies of such men were available from Inchaffray and Paisley, whose abbots were responsible for the patronage of many local parish churches. Taken as a group, however, there is evident a notable difference between the background of clerks and those of chaplains, one that was more marked in Lennox than in Strathearn. The chaplains who served Earl Gille Brigte of Strathearn, for example, were a mixed group, consisting of two men with the French names of John and Richard, another who bore the Gaelic-sounding name of Cungi, and a fourth, whose Hebrew name, Abraham, conceals an English provenance.[67] This eclectic gathering reflected the greater exposure to foreign elements beyond the territories of the earldom that Gille Brigte had forged early in his career, and which is apparent in other aspects of his rule. Lennox, by contrast, was still in the first half of the thirteenth century largely – albeit not wholly – immune to such influences. Ailin II's named chaplains, Gille Crìosd, Absolon, and (probably) Adam, were sons of Gaelic men of local extraction.[68] Despite his marriage to a Stewart woman Earl Maoldomhnaich, too, preferred the ministrations of native chaplains, including Gille Brigte, Muireadhach,

---

65 Stringer, *Earl David*, 151–2; idem, 'The charters of David earl of Huntingdon and lord of Garioch: a study in Anglo-Scottish diplomatic' (1985), 95–6. See also Simpson, '*Familia* of Roger de Quincy', 110. **66** *RRS*, ii, 31. **67** *Inchaff. Chrs.*, nos. 1, 3–5, 10–13, 15, 25, 27, 30, 31, 34, 43, 44; *Inchaff. Liber*, nos. 18, 69. **68** *Paisley Reg.*, 157; *Glasgow Reg.*, i, nos. 101, 108.

Absolon, and Thomas de Carrick, calling much less frequently on the service of men whose names imply a non-native origin.[69] Chaplains offered the most intimate of spiritual services in the masses they sang and in their confessional roles. The near monopoly of this important office by native incumbents bears witness to the entrenchment of Gaelic culture and language within the intimate surroundings of Maoldomhnaich's family.

Parsons, rectors, and vicars of the parish churches of Strathearn and Lennox abound in charter witness lists until well into the fourteenth century. It is not likely that they played an important role in the administrative or spiritual affairs of the earls, for most were merely occasional visitors to their households. Some were canons or dignitaries of the cathedral churches of Dunblane or Glasgow, and as *familiares* of the bishops accompanied their masters to meetings in which comital deeds were authenticated and attested. Their names served as useful fillers in charter witness lists, adding weight and dignity to the earls' grants. Whatever their functions, this varied body of clerics – clerks, chaplains and parish priests – constituted the largest single group in the entourages of the earls of Strathearn and Lennox throughout the period between the mid-twelfth and the early fourteenth centuries. If the nature of surviving record materials makes it difficult to trace the precise nature of their duties in the business of family and estate management, their involvement in matters secretarial, administrative and spiritual was of crucial importance.

The households of the thirteenth-century native earls included several other named officials, as well as the 'hosts of minions' who attached themselves to the entourages of all great magnates.[70] Maoldomhnaich of Lennox appears to have adopted the practice of assigning specific duties relating to household finance to a native man described as 'my chamberlain',[71] but the single reference to this office during the period of his rule occurs in a document written by a cleric resident in Kelso abbey, and probably represents the scribe's imposition of a foreign term to a native minister whose duties resembled those found in the households of the English and continental newcomers. The chamberlain is otherwise unrecorded in Lennox down to the fifteenth century, but in Strathearn, Malise II introduced the office in the early 1250s, assigning it for some years to clerics, and thereafter to lay men.[72] The precise function of the chamberlain in the earl's household remains unclear, but it has been noted that elsewhere in Scotland by the mid-thirteenth century such officials had assumed the management of their lords' finances, superseding the steward in this capacity.[73] This observation is not

---

69 Fraser, *Lennox*, ii, nos. 7, 10, 203–5, 207; *Paisley Reg.*, 87–8, 158–61, 211, 216–17; *Glasgow Reg.*, i, nos. 108, 141; *Lennox Cart.*, 19–20, 26–7; NLS, Adv. MS. 34.3.25, fos. 58–9; *Arbroath Liber*, i, no. 133; Maurice the chaplain: *Lennox Cart.*, 19–20, 27; Fraser, *Lennox*, ii, nos. 207; *Paisley Reg.*, 171–2 ('my' chaplain). Germanus the chaplain: ibid., 159–60.   **70** Stringer, *Earl David*, 151.   **71** *Kelso Liber*, i, no. 222. Duibhne son of Croscrach, whose name suggests an Irish import, served both Ailin II and his son; *Glasgow Reg.*, i, nos. 101, 102; Fraser, *Lennox*, ii, no. 207; *Lennox Cart.*, 25–6.   **72** *Inchaff. Chrs.*, nos. 87, 95; *Inchaff, Liber*, nos. 52, 58, App., no., 12; *Lind. Cart.*, no. 35; Neville, 'Earls of Strathearn', i, 189.   **73** Duncan, *Making*, 432.

inconsistent with the evidence of Malise II's grants in the same period. The number of lay tenants holding directly of him in 1271 was considerably larger than those who had been infeft by Gille Brigte or Robert. In the earlier period, when grants of land in free alms to the church had predominated and lay persons held their estates in return for food rents, there was little need for a refined machinery of fiscal administration. The changes apparent in the tenurial structure of the earldom from the second half of the thirteenth century, discussed below, together with an increasing trend toward the payment of traditional renders such as cain and conveth in cash rather than in kind, necessitated a more sophisticated system of revenue collection and accounting. It is difficult, for this reason, to explain the absence of reference to chamberlains in surviving Lennox documents. While generally more resistant to innovation along foreign models than Strathearn, there is no doubt that the profound changes occurring in the economy of the earldom in the later part of the century must have required the attention of a fiscal officer well versed in the minutiae of estate management. The apportioning of money payments to lay and ecclesiastical beneficiaries increased in both lordships in this same period, and attest the influence there of a general trend in Scotland toward a money economy. The likelihood is that by the time of Earl Malcolm I of Lennox, an official charged with the specific task of managing comital revenues was indeed a feature of the household, and that absence of references to him are merely accidental.

The early thirteenth-century native earls drew on the services of several other officials, some of them permanent fixtures, others more transient. Gille Brigte and Robert of Strathearn, for example, hosted a servant of Inchaffray whose sole duty was the collection of a teind of all the food and drink brought to the comital kitchens.[74] Especially during Countess Maud D'Aubigny's time, daily life in the household was marked by a blend of two distinct linguistic cultures, but the vitality there of native custom has not escaped the notice of historians.[75] Two men, one designated by the Latin term *dispensarius*, the other by the Gaelic derived name of *rannaire*, held office simultaneously.[76] No clear distinction between their responsibilities is apparent, and both seem to have been charged with the division and distribution of foodstuffs within the household. Perhaps one served the countess and her French- and English-speaking circle, the other the earl and his native followers. Alternatively, the *rannaire* of the Latin-language Strathearn charters may in fact represent the official known elsewhere in Gaelic Scotland as the *rechtaire*, an official responsible for collecting cain, who resurfaces in later records as the mair.[77] Where the two offices appear together in charter witness lists precedence is accorded to the *rannaire*, which may suggest the authority of the Gaelic official over the newer man, the dispenser.[78] The presence of both in the household, however, serves as a reminder

---

[74] *Inchaff. Chrs.*, no. 16; *Inchaff. Liber*, no. 59. [75] Duncan, *Making*, 432. [76] *Inchaff. Chrs.*, nos. 5, 39. [77] J. Bannerman, 'The Scots language and the kin-based society' (1988), 8–9. The mair appears in later fourteenth-century Strathearn record, e.g. *ER*, iii, 33. [78] This was certainly the

of the enduring influence of older custom, for the *rannaire* had disappeared from the royal household as far back as the 1180s, and is not found among the domestic staff of the Anglo-Scottish earls of Winchester or Huntingdon.[79] There is no evidence to suggest that the office was hereditary, but neither was it merely honourary: the men who occupied it held modest estates of their lords, one in Pitlandy, the other in Kintocher.[80] The office of butler, referred to by the old-fashioned designation of *pincerna*, also appears in the early thirteenth-century Strathearn household. Causantin, clearly a man of native background, held the former. The lowly position of his name in charter witness lists argues for the subordination of this office to that of the *dapifer*, who was, like the *rannaire*, involved in the distribution of food. The duplication of some officials and the domination of Strathearn household offices by men of Gaelic origin amply demonstrate Professor Barrow's observation that the earls' retention of customary positions 'reminds us, in the midst of so much innovation and introduction of English and continental ways, of the traditional flavour and quality of the older royal household establishment'.[81] Their survival, moreover, did not reflect either lack of sophistication or resistance to change, but rather the enduring appeal of Gaelic culture within the intimate setting of the earl's household.

Charter texts from the period of Earls Ailin II and Maoldomhnaich of Lennox reveal little about the domestic arrangements that regulated daily life there. A solitary *hostiarius* lent his credence to a charter of Mael Coluim son of Maoldomhnaich,[82] though the Gaelic name of Maol Iosa shows that he was a native man rather than a newcomer. But in both Strathearn and Lennox, the earls' responsibility for assembling provincial armies necessitated the services of marshals who assisted them on these endeavours. The ongoing importance of these officials in Strathearn in particular is reflected in the steady number of references to the marshal in the written *acta* well into the fourteenth century.[83] Curiously, the marshal appears only once in a Lennox document of the early thirteenth century.[84] This may be a consequence of the earls' obligation to discharge their military duties to the crown in the form of food renders (cheese) rather than men. On the other hand, it may also reflect scribal accident or omission. Lack of attention to details, and especially the association of comital offices with specific individuals in charter witness lists, is, in fact, a feature of much of surviving Lennox source materials both in the thirteenth and the fourteenth centuries. And yet, collectively these documents convey the impression of a large, sophisticated and busy household, still in the 1360s, when Walter de Faslane succeeded as lord of Lennox in right of his wife Margaret, staffed largely by men with native backgrounds. In a milieu still at this late date strongly imbued with Gaelic cultural and linguistic features, the absence of formal ministerial titles familiar to Latin trained scribes should not overly concern historians.

case in the household of Donnchad earl of Carrick; see H.L. MacQueen, 'Survival and success: the Kennedys of Dunure' (2003), 73–4. **79** *RRS*, ii, 37. **80** *Inchaff. Chrs.*, nos. 26, 56; *Inchaff. Liber*, no. 59. **81** *RRS*, ii, 37. **82** Fraser, *Lennox*, ii, no. 205. **83** *Inchaff. Chrs.*, nos. 76, 86, 87; *Inchaff. Liber*, no. 58. **84** *Paisley Reg.*, 159.

The numerous estate and household officials who interacted on a regular basis with the native earls of Strathearn and Lennox, the *discreti viri* beloved of charter scribes, represent much more than merely names in the witness lists of comital *acta*. In addition to the specific administrative responsibilities that each performed, they acted collectively as counsellors to their lords, providing the kind of advice without which no magnate, native or newcomer, could operate effectively. To call the occasions when the early thirteenth-century earls summoned their *familiares* 'baronial councils' is to endow these assemblies with a formality that is neither accurate nor, in the Gaelic cultural context, wholly appropriate. Nevertheless, surviving documents leave no doubt that the native lords interacted frequently with kinsmen close and distant, tenants of varying degree, and clerics of all sorts in the complicated business of governing their territories. The conclusions reached in a recent study of Gille Brigte of Strathearn's *familiares* generally hold true also for the earldom of Lennox.[85] Gille Brigte surrounded himself with a small but, for the most part, unchanging group of favourites throughout the fifty years of his rule. His neighbours and contemporaries, Ailin II and Maoldomhnaich of Lennox, did much the same. The inner circle of *familiares* in both lordships stand in some contrast to the cosmopolitan nature of the councils that advised some of the great Anglo-Scottish barons of their time, notably David earl of Huntingdon, Roger de Quincy, and Walter Stewart.[86] In discussing and implementing matters of importance to their lands the native earls sought the advice and counsel above all of persons whose relationship was primarily personal rather than purely tenurial. The inner circles of Gille Brigte and Robert of Strathearn counted chiefly members of their own family: sons, brothers, nephews. More interesting still, Gille Brigte accorded the womenfolk of his household a prominent role in the attestation of comital *acta*.[87] Ailin II and Maoldomhnaich of Lennox similarly looked to their close relations in the business of governing their territories, the predominance of the latter's ten brothers in charter witness lists showing that he attached especial weight to the testimony of family members.[88] In both lordships, moreover, the early thirteenth-century earls held in high esteem and numbered among their inner circles of advisors men entrusted with important household or estate offices (sometimes also family members themselves), including stewards, *judices*, and thanes.[89] Hovering on the edge of the intimate circle were other officials and various clerics.

---

85 Neville, 'Celtic enclave', 86–8. **86** Discussed in Stringer, *Earl David*, 153–65; Simpson, '*Familia* of Roger de Quincy', 113–23; and the reconstruction of the Stewart tenantry presented in Barrow, *Kingdom*, 326–31. **87** *Inchaff. Chrs.*, nos. 11, 12 (daughter Maud); ibid., nos. 3, 4, 11–13, 25, 28; *Inchaff. Liber*, nos. 5, 18, 69, App., no. 2 (Countess Maud). Maud also appears as co-donor in the foundation charter of Inchaffray priory (*Inchaff. Chrs.*, no. 9). **88** *Glasgow Reg.*, i, nos 102, 108; Fraser, *Lennox*, ii, nos. 10, 11, 202–4, 207; *Paisley Reg.*, 158–61, 171–2, 211–13, 216–17; *Arbroath Liber*, I, no. 133; *Lennox Cart.*, 19–20, 25–7, 30–1; NLS, Adv. MS. 34.3.25, fos. 58–9. **89** For Strathearn, see Neville, 'Celtic enclave', 87; for Lennox, *Paisley Reg.*, 158–61, 209, 211, 217; Fraser, *Lennox*, ii, nos. 7, 9–11, 203, 204; *Glasgow Reg.*, i, nos. 102, 108, 144, 178; *Lennox Cart.*, 14, 25–7, 30–1; *Kelso Liber*, i, no. 222; *Arbroath Liber*, i, no. 133.

Both households also included many hangers-on, such as Gilbert, 'the earl's fellow' (*socius comitis*), who danced attendance on Gille Brigte of Strathearn,[90] and a more mysterious group of Gaelic men identified in Lennox documents as the earls' 'servants'. The former was almost certainly one of the sparsely documented 'household knights' found in the entourages of all thirteenth-century Scottish magnates,[91] one of hundreds whose names fill countless charter witness lists, and who 'followed the course taken by many landless younger sons by entering into service in the household of a major baron'.[92] The earl of Lennox's 'servants' are more intriguing still. They appear frequently in the attestation clauses of written *acta* during the period of Earls Ailin II and Maoldomhnaich, and all, without exception, bear Gaelic names. Landless they may have been, but they were not without prospects: Ailin's servant Duibhne son of Croscrach, for example, secured the office of chamberlain under Maoldohmnaich.[93] The key to understanding the place of these native men in the comital entrourage lies in an appreciation of the tenacious influence of Gaelic tradition apparent in all aspects of Lennox society. The custom of fosterage is well documented in Gaelic Scotland until the end of the Middle Ages and well beyond,[94] and a household as wealthy and influential as that of the earls of Lennox no doubt represented a choice opportunity for native fathers to advance the fortunes of their sons. One young Lennox man is almost certainly identifiable as a foster son: Ailin II referred to Gilleasbuig Galbraith as 'my nephew', though there was no blood connection between them.[95] The scribes who drafted the Lennox deeds, Benedictine monks of Paisley abbey, were a sophisticated group, strongly influenced by the reforming ideology of the early thirteenth-century church and trained in the Latin charter writing tradition. Cultural prejudice may have led them to eschew terminology identified closely with native customs that they considered barbarous, and to cloak irregular or unfamiliar relationships in formal records with the less offensive word 'servant'.

Strathearn and Lennox documents reveal clearly that, unlike their secular lords, ecclesiastical dignitaries generally accorded the opinion of native men significantly less weight and respect than that of Anglo-Norman or continental newcomers. Here again, the initial stages of the dispute over the lands of Kilpatrick that so deeply disturbed lay-ecclesiastical relations in thirteenth-century Lennox illustrate the subtle ways in which the church made known its views.[96] In his attempts to sort out the complex tenurial history of the lands attached to the parish church, the pursuer, Abbot William of Paisley, was compelled to call on the testimony of a dozen Gaelic men, but when the judges delegate required that Earl

---

90 *Inchaff. Chrs.*, nos. 4, 11, 12; *Inchaff. Liber*, no. 69. Another Gille Crìosd 'Gall' (the Gael?), who witnessed five of Gille Brigte's charters, may have been another of these household knights, but see also the discussion of fosterage below. **91** Barrow, *Anglo-Norman era*, 123–6; Stringer, *Earl David*, 166–7; Simpson, '*Familia* of Roger de Quincy', 116–18. **92** Simpson, '*Familia* of Roger de Quincy', 116. **93** *Glasgow Reg.*, i, no. 101; *Kelso Liber*, i, no. 222. **94** Sellar, 'Celtic law', 12; R. Nicholson, *Scotland: the later Middle Ages* (1974), 73. **95** *Glasgow Reg.*, i, no. 101. Gille Crìosd 'Gall', a frequent witness to the charters of Earl Gille Brigte of Strathearn, may also have been a foster son; *Inchaff. Chrs.*, nos. 3, 5, 9, 13; *Inchaff. Liber*, no. 27. **96** *Paisley Reg.*, 165–7, 170–1.

Maoldomhnaich provide pledges for his compliance with the decreet of award made in 1235, William directed that three of the four be chosen from among the knights and sworn tenants of the Anglo-Norman magnate Walter Stewart.[97] Lay persons newly settled in Lennox may have shared this prejudice, for charters that record the creation of new feus for incomers consistently include significantly more foreign than Gaelic names their witness lists.[98] The opinions of the native earls in respect of native testimony, however, were decidedly at variance with those of ecclesiastical lawyers. Local knowledge was vital in cases in which there were rival claims to property, and in the demarcation of new estates out of lands once held collectively by kin groups. In virtually all surviving charter texts relating to such business the names of Gaelic tenants and worthies predominate. More than a dozen of Maoldohmnaich of Lennox's written deeds include long clauses describing the marches of estates created for native tenants, and invariably the testing clauses of such *acta* reveal that the men who undertook the task of tramping the lands were native and local.[99] At the end of the thirteenth century Earl Malcolm I still entertained a profound respect for of such knowledge. An inquest summoned to determine succession to the lands of Blantyre was entrusted to a jury composed exclusively of native recognitors.[1] Earl Gille Brigte's confidence in the testimony of Gaelic relatives and tenants was even more marked: he permitted his wife Iseulte herself to lead a local group in the perambulation of a new estate that she intended to grant to Inchaffray abbey.[2]

The marked preference of the early thirteenth-century Gaelic earls of Strathearn and Lennox in matters concerning household and estate management for men (and sometimes women) who had constant and intimate contact with them represents another manifestation of the limited extent to which these magnates were prepared to abandon native custom in deference to novel European practices. Keith Stringer argued that in the Scottish estates controlled by David of Huntingdon, men who sought advancement and reward found that 'it was not an advantage to have been born a native Scot'.[3] The opposite was very much the case in the great native lordships of Lennox and Strathearn. Both regions serve as salutary reminders that, far from sweeping over the region north of Forth in what has been portrayed as an inevitable process of 'feudalization' in old Scotia,[4] by mid-century new families and their followings had secured only limited access to the riches of Strathearn and Lennox and to the inner circles of the great native households. Recent research has shown conclusively that the introduction of French- and English-speaking newcomers elsewhere in Gaelic Scotland was similarly gradual and piecemeal. In the lordship of Galloway, for example, incoming families were few in number well into the century;

---

97 T.M. Cooper (ed.), *Select Scottish cases of the thirteenth century* (1944), 37–9. The dispute is also discussed in I.D. Willock, *The origins and development of the jury in Scotland* (1966), 16–17. **98** See, for example, Fraser, *Lennox*, ii, nos. 6, 7 (grants to Sir David de Graham). **99** For two examples, see ibid., ii, no. 207 (lands in Luss), and *Lennox Cart.*, 34–5 (lands in Fintry parish). **1** APS, i, 102; NAS, RH 5/45. **2** *Inchaff. Chrs.*, no.46. **3** Stringer, *Earl David*, 161. **4** Barrow, *Anglo-Norman era*, passim; idem, *Kingdom*, esp. 250–784; R.L.G. Ritchie, *The Normans in Scotland* (1954), passim.

between 1160 and 1234, moreover, almost all were settled in areas that the lords of Galloway had acquired by grant rather than by inheritance.[5] In the earldom of Mar, it has been noted, 'despite the close family links of the native lineages with major Anglo-Norman families such as the de Warennes and the strong relationship between the earls and the crown there was no introduction of colonizing families', and the same appears to have been the case in Atholl until the late thirteenth century.[6] The earldom of Buchan remained strongly Gaelic in character well into the century, even after the succession to the title of the Comyn famly,[7] and, despite their well attested record as 'internal colonists', the earls of Fife still counted among his followers in 1250 noblemen who were overwhelmingly of native stock.[8] Collectively, these findings argue strongly in favour of an adjustment in the current understanding of the so called 'feudalization' of Scotland north of Forth for a century and more after the accession of King David I in 1124. The resilience of native traditions has not gone unnoticed by historians. Recent studies of the political development of the kingdom, for example, have stressed both the continuity in aristocratic and noble power structures across the 'apparent watershed' of David I's reign and the vitality of Gaelic culture well into the reign of Alexander III.[9] Few historians, however, have looked closely enough at any of the great native lordships to appreciate fully the extent to which some Gaelic magnates were committed to the preservation of their distinct culture, and the strategies that they adopted in order to accomplish their ends.[10] The thirteenth-century earls of Strathearn and Lennox were determined and enthusiastic champions of Gaelic style lordship, and their tenurial and household arrangements offer valuable insight into the ways that they negotiated, controlled and managed the influence of new ideas at home and on the ground.

The middle years of the century in fact proved to be a watershed in the process. The period saw the forging of a genuinely distinct aristocratic culture, one made up in equal, interrelated, and interdependent parts of European and Gaelic influences. The change, however, was gradual. Alexander III's elaborate inauguration ceremonies at Scone in 1249, which celebrated both the king's Gaelic heritage as well as his European descent, represented at the highest social level a process that on a smaller scale was under way in many parts of the kingdom north of Forth.[11] Evident within each of these lordships was a notable move away from a system of land tenure characterized as 'clan based' and 'pseudo tribal'[12] to one that included considerably more families of foreign descent. Arrangements were made for the governance of larger and more complex households. Gaelic-speakers no longer held a monopoly over positions of

---

[5] Oram, *Lordship of Galloway*, 211 and, more generally, 191–213. [6] Ibid., 211; Duncan, *Making*, 178, 180. [7] Young, 'Earls and earldom of Buchan', 180–1; Duncan, *Making*, 188. [8] Barrow, *Anglo-Norman era*, 84–99. [9] A.A.M. Duncan, *The kingship of the Scots, 842–1292* (2002), 335. See also idem, *Making*, 164–7; S. Boardman and A. Ross, 'Editors' introduction', in Boardman and Ross (eds), *Exercise of power*, 18. [10] The exception here is the work of Oram and Stringer on medieval Galloway. [11] Alexander's inauguration is most recently discussed in Duncan, *Kingship of the Scots*, 131–50. [12] R.A. Dodgshon, *Land and society in early Scotland* (1981), 113.

importance among the *familiares* of the great territorial lords. Changes are visible in Lennox beginning in the time of Earl Malcolm I, in the third quarter of the thirteenth century. They become apparent in the Strathearn of Malise II, who succeeded in 1245, and quickened under the influence of his son and successor, Malise III. In neither region did these changes entail the abandonment of Gaelic ways in favour of new fangled European practices. The cultural milieus forged over the course of the century were, rather, genuinely and uniquely hybrid, with old and new, native and non-native in constant interaction.

If the early earls of Lennox managed to stem the tide of foreign settlement and influence within their lands, their late thirteenth-century successors adopted a more open policy of infeftment. Malcolm I was not concerned to champion the independence of Lennox to the same extent as his grandfather had been. He became the sworn man of the king in July 1272, when he accepted from Alexander III a large bloc of territory around Glen Douglas in free forest. His son, Malcolm II, was ready and willing to accept from Robert I a deed granting him the earldom of Lennox itself.[13] The latter's close friendship with Bruce, moreover, ensured that further royal gifts should follow, and that in consequence, ties between the old native family and the new king should be strong.[14]

Families of Gaelic origin whose members had been endowed in the earlier part of the century continued to prosper. Galbraiths, Lusses, Carricks, Colquhouns, Drummonds, and others received new grants of land or consolidated their holdings,[15] with a few (notably the Galbraiths and Colquhouns) rising to prominence in Lennox noble society. Beginning in Malcolm I's time, however, native roots were no longer the main criteria for social and economic advancement. The best estates and the richest revenues now went to men who served the earl most loyally, at home, on the political stage, or in some combination of both, irrespective of their origins. The Grahams, first introduced to Lennox by Earl Maoldomhnaich, augmented their holdings hand over fist, acquiring estates from Gaelic land holders and Stewart tenants alike.[16] Newcomers to the earldom included Walter de Ros, John and Duncan Napier, Walter Sproull, Thomas de Cremannan, and Patrick de Lindsay, cadet of the family that served the Bruce cause so faithfully.[17] Some of these tenants dis-

---

13 Fraser, *Lennox*, ii, no. 25; *RRS*, v, no. 194. 14 *RRS*, v, no. 11, 468; *RMS*, i, 27; Fraser, *Lennox*, ii, no. 212; G.W.S. Barrow, *Robert Bruce and the community of the realm of Scotland* (3rd edn, 1988), 275–6. 15 Galbraith family: W. Fraser (ed.), *The Stirlings of Keir, and their family papers* (1858), 204–5; *Lennox Cart.*, 24, 28–33. Luss family: Royal Faculty of Procurators, Glasgow, Macfarlane Muniments, ii, no. 73; *Lennox Cart.*, 19–21, 23–4; *RRS*, v, no. 2. Carrick family: *Lennox Cart.*, 43–4. MacAulay family: NLS, Adv. MS. 34.3.35, fo. 62. Colquhoun family: *RRS*, v, no. 81. Michael son of Edulf: *Lennox Cart.*, 85–7. MacCessán the Younger: ibid., 43, 45–6. Gille Moire son of Maol Iosa 'Bane': ibid., 47–8. Donnchad brother of Gille Crìosd son of Gille Crìosd: *RMS*, ii, 41–2. 16 Fraser, *Lennox*, ii, nos. 13, 15; *Lennox Cart.*, 38–40, 88–9; *Lind. Cart.*, no. 78. 17 Fraser, *Lennox*, ii, no. 15 (Ros); *Lennox Cart.*, 69–71; NLS, Adv MS 35.2.4, ii, 401 (Napier); *Lennox Cart.*, 48–9 (Leny); ibid., 40–2 (Sproull); ibid., 79–83 (Cremannan); ibid., 49–50; Barrow, *Robert Bruce*,138, 279 (Lindsay).

placed native land holders,[18] but others, such as Alan de Leny, represented cadet offshoots of older families.[19] Surviving charters and other materials, moreover, reveal that at slightly lower levels of the social scale changes to the profile of elite land holders in Lennox did not effect a radical restructuring of the native population. In the later thirteenth century, in fact, there is still occasional evidence of two solitudes: in 1263, for example, it was to an all-Gaelic panel of recognitors that the earl entrusted an inquisition into the age of the Patrick, son and heir of Stephen de Blantyre.[20] On the other hand, there is increasing evidence of the merging of the cultures among men who were once distinguished as native or newcomers. Two of Thomas de Cremannan's daughters, for example, bore the European names of Maud and Elizabeth, but the third the decidedly (Irish) Gaelic name of Farbhlaidh.[21] Thomas' family in many ways typifies the integration of the cultures that characterized the later thirteenth century, not merely in Lennox, but throughout the region north of Forth, for he counted among his tenants and adherents Grahams and Galbraiths, as well as a kinsman of the earl, Muireadhach son of Corc.[22] The descendants of native land holders themselves attracted new followers and established close family links with them. In Malcolm I's time two of the granddaughters of Mael Coluim son of Ailin II married men of European background and eventually became, with a third, heiresses of their great-uncle Dùghall,[23] and the Napier family sought at least one marriage partner from among the MacAulays, descendants of Amhlaibh, another son of Ailin II.[24] Apparent in this process of change, too, was an end to the marginalization of new tenants in relation to their Gaelic fellows that had been so marked a feature of the earlier thirteenth century. Napiers, Cremannans, Sproulls and Grahams rubbed shoulders now with MacEdulfs, Lusses, Buchanans, and MacAulays in all parts of the lordship, sharing not merely the agriculturally rich estates of the lowlands, but pastoral lands based in the hills and glens of the highland zone of Lennox.

The cross fertilization apparent in the tenurial landscape of later thirteenth-century Lennox is apparent also in the cultural milieus of the comital household. The earls' estate stewards were as likely to be men with European names as they were native Gaels: the charters mention Patrick and Maurice de Galbraith as well as Donald son of Anecol in this capacity, but also Walter Sproull.[25] Malcolm II's steward was the Dumbarton burgess William Fleming.[26] Malcolm also chose to preserve both the dignity and the title of *toíseach* in Lennox, though he had no hesitation granting it to an up and coming man whose ties with the

---

18 The Napier family, for example, settled in Kilmahew, formerly under the control of the MacAulay family. Sir Patrick de Graham acquired lands in Killearn that belonged to Stephen of Blantyre, who nevertheless left a son. *Lennox Cart.*, 38. **19** W. Buchanan, *A historical and genealogical essay upon the family and surname of Buchanan* (1723), 96. **20** RH 5/45, calendared in *CDS*, i, no. 2338. **21** *Lennox Cart.*, 82–3. **22** *Lennox Cart.*, 79–81, 86–7. **23** J.G. Smith, *Strathendrick and its inhabitants from early times* (Glasgow, 1896), 244; idem, *The parish of Strathblane and its inhabitants from early times: a chapter of Lennox history* (Glasgow, 1886), 130, n. 5; *Paisley Reg.*, 180–98. **24** Smith, *Strathendrick*, 191, 193–4. **25** *Lennox Cart.*, 24, 28–30, 32–3, 43–4, 47–9, 80–1, 86–7; *CDS*, i, no. 2338. **26** *Lennox Cart.*, 83.

Gaelic tenantry of the region were tenuous at best.[27] A quickening economy and, especially in the decade between 1296 and 1306, the need to raise cash and men in support of the cause of Robert Bruce required a more sophisticated accounting system. While rents in cheese as contributions to the royal army did not disappear from Lennox,[28] charter texts reveal that in other respects the trend toward cash renders intensified.[29]

Charter witness lists in later thirteenth- and early fourteenth-century Lennox also point to a changing household profile. The close knit, cohesive comital entourage, made up largely of family members and long established native tenants characteristic of Maoldomhnaich's rule gave way under his two successors to a looser, more varied group. Gaelic families still attended the earl, including the families of Drummond, Galbraith, Colquhoun, Buchanan, and MacCessán, but with the exception of Malcolm de Drummond, none witnessed more than a handful of their lords' *acta*. The household became instead a larger but more ad hoc body, its membership consisting of men who happened to be in the earl's presence when he set his seal to a written deed, but a group of men that the earl sometimes designated confidently as 'my council'.[30] A significant majority of these were men who had no tenurial (or blood) relationship with either Malcolm I or Malcolm II.

Changes to the profile of the tenurial structure and the trend toward a more inchoate household environment are even more apparent in Strathearn. Here, the accession of Malise II in 1245 signalled an almost immediate broadening of tenurial relationships within the lordship. Gaelic landholders did not disappear here either, and the earl continued to make especially generous provision for his siblings. Thus, Gilbert son of Robert received an estate in Belnello, and his sister Maria held Strathy and Pairney in Auchterarder parish.[31] The descendants of Maol Iosa, the steward who had served Earls Gille Brigte and Robert, continued to prosper: by the end of the thirteenth century they had established a large kinship network, drawn into their circle several important native families, and built a rich and substantial honour.[32] Both Malise II and Malise III similarly maintained close ties with the lords of Kinbuck and with distant Glencarnie.[33] Most of the families originally infeft in the earldom in the time of Earl Gille Brigte are still found in the records of the later part of the century; some, indeed, expanded their holdings, such as the families of Gorthy, Luvetot, Pitlandy and Hay.[34] But charter evidence also reveals an unmistakable shift in the tenurial landscape within the earldom away from the insularity of the earlier period toward greater accommodation for incomers. Brice of Ardrossan, probably a cadet of the important Ayrshire family; Sir William de Moravia, son of Sir Malcolm; Thomas de Monymusk, a loyal

---

27 *Lennox Cart.*, 49–50. **28** Royal Faculty of Procurators, Glasgow, Macfarlane Muniments, ii, no. 73; *RMS*, i, 128–9. **29** *Lennox Cart.*, 83, 85–6. **30** Ibid., 49. **31** *Inchaff. Liber*, no. 35; *Inchaff. Chrs.*, App., no. 5. **32** Neville, 'Earls of Strathearn', i, 177. **33** Ibid., i, 276–82. **34** *Inchaff. Liber*, nos. 19, 44, 51, 52, 53; Moray Reg., App., nos. 13, 15; *Royal commission on historical manuscripts, 7th Report* (Edinburgh, 1879), App., 705, nos. 8, 9; *Facsimiles of the national manuscripts of Scotland* (3 vols, London, 1867–72), i, no. 66; NAS, GD 220/1/A1/3/7, GD 220/1/A1/4/5, 6; Barrow, *Robert Bruce*, 159, 328.

Aberdeenshire supporter of Robert Bruce; and Sir Patrick Graham, son of the rapacious Sir David: all were welcomed into Strathearn, all endowed with considerable property, and all settled not merely on the periphery of the earls' territories, but deep within them as well.[35] New infeftments continued apace under Earls Malise IV and Malise V, bringing to the lands of Srathearn from Lanarkshire Sir John de Moravia (later of Drumsagard), and the northerner Reginald More.[36]

By the time of Malise V's forfeiture in the earl 1330s, the tenurial landscape of a century earlier had altered dramatically. So, too, had the intimate governance of the household. The witness lists of Malise III's surviving charter texts show that the close knit setting of earlier times, consisting mainly of local men holding honourary positions, had given way to a household which counted more landed knights and tenants in ministerial positions than before. The trend is evident as early as the time of Malise II in mid-century. Anxious to assert himself as a national figure, he made a conscious effort to broaden his cultural and social horizons beyond the confines of his own territories. While maintaining a household which counted among its members old families and modest land holders, for example, the Kinbucks and Luvetots, he also sought actively to include among the witnesses listed in his written *acta* representatives of some of the most important influential families in the kingdom: Hays, Ruthvens, Grahams, Oliphants, de Moravias. In the later thirteenth and the fourteenth centuries there was still a steady stream of clerical men in and out of the household surroundings. But, especially from the time of Earl Malise III, who succeeded in 1271, there is visible a considerable shift in the profile of charter attestors.[37] Almost half of the witnesses to Gille Brigte's deeds were drawn from a close circle made up of family members, important household ministers, and old tenant families. In addition, more than half of the clerics in the lists served Gille Brigte as chaplains or scribes, or in other areas of household administration. The *discreti viri* who attended the sessions in which Earl Robert's deeds were sealed tended to be drawn from the same intimate circle. One again, half the clerics who witnessed were employed in some capacity in the household. Here, in short, were men well known to their Gaelic lords.

When Malise II succeeded as earl in 1245, the insular attitude of the earls of Strathearn toward affairs both within and beyond the earldom altered dramatically. Malise instigated a policy, continued by his son, of enfefting in Strathearn men who were influential landowners elsewhere in Scotland, and who were politically active in national events. The range and quality of evidence surviving from the time of the last native earls is, admittedly, deficient, but even this patchy material permits some generalizations.

The clerical element remained significant in the witness lists of Malise II's deeds. Family members and household ministers, too, are still included, but lay tenants

---

35 *Inchaff. Liber*, nos. 32, 47, 48, 66, App. No. 12; *Inchaff. Chrs.*, no. 103; Neville, 'Earls of Strathearn', i, 281. **36** Neville, 'Earls of Strathearn', i, 282–5. **37** See here the tables setting out the social positions of witnesses to Strathearn charters, c.1195–c.1333, in Neville, 'Earls of Strathearn', i 208–9.

were now equally represented. From the time of Malise III onward the balance of witnesses becomes notably more heavily weighted in favour of individuals who had no intimate ties whatsoever with the earl. The later earls, in fact, appear to have been concerned to ensure for their public *acta* the weighty testimony of men who were well known as important national figures and political sympathizers. Few individuals attested frequently. Instead, membership in the body of *discreti viri* who attended the ceremonies in which charters were authenticated changed continuously. It becomes very difficult, in short, to identify 'inner' and 'outer' circles of advisors for the later earls. Many of the men whose names are found in later Strathearn documents came into contact with the earls only briefly. Their connections were most often of the political kind. Sir William de Brechin, for example, who witnessed a charter of 1257, was one of a group of barons who, with Malise II, were appointed by King Henry III in 1255 as guardians of the young king and queen of Scots.[38] Three of the knights whose names are found in a deed of Earl Malise III, Ralph de Lasceles, Robert de Cameron, and William de Moravia stood with him as auditors for John Balliol at Norham in June 1291.[39] The intimacy of an earlier age was superseded in the thirteenth century by the demands of a society in which great lords forged political bonds that transcended (though they never excluded) linguistic and ethnic affiliations.

Like the Lennox of Earl Malcolm II, the Strathearn of the early 1330s was a region in which a mixed Gaelic and European aristocracy held lands side by side, intermarried freely, and shared common social and cultural values. At the level of tenant farmers, free and unfree, some Gaelic customs and practices remained little altered. Written deeds offer instructive, if rare, glimpses of lesser folk, for example, Earl Malise III of Strathearn's tenants Macbeatha son of Fearchar and Isaac MacElibarn, or Michael and Eòghann MacCessán, who held portions of Garchell and Balloch in the parish of Drymen of earl Malcolm II of Lennox.[40] The *nativi* whom Malise II granted to Inchaffray abbey in 1258 lived rigidly regimented lives that were not far removed from those that their twelfth-century ancestors had known.[41] But at the level of wealthy land holders the story was quite different. So successful was the integration of the Gaelic and continental cultures that it is no longer appropriate to distinguish between 'native' and 'incoming' families, and decidedly more accurate to speak in terms of a hybrid, uniquely Scottish nobility. The presence of a large number of men distinguished by the title of knight in the entourages of the fourteenth-century earls of Strathearn and Lennox bears eloquent testimony to the extent to which European social mores and cultural values had successfully penetrated remote enclaves of Gaelic Scotland. Neither Earl Gille Brigte nor his contemporary Maoldomhnaich of Lennox aspired to the dignity of knighthood, perhaps

---

38 Ibid., no. 86; Young, *Robert Bruce's rivals*, 71–2. **39** W. Fraser, (ed.), *The red book of Grandtully* (2 vols, Edinburgh, 1868), i, App., no. 69. E.L.G. Stones and G.G. Simpson (eds), *Edward I and the throne of Scotland 1290–1296: an edition of the record sources for the Great Cause* (1978), ii, 84–5. **40** *Inchaff. Liber*, no. 30; *Historical Manuscripts Commission, 7th Report*, App. 705, no. 9; *Lennox Cart.*, 43; Barrow, *Robert Bruce*, 159, 327. **41** *Inchaff. Chrs.*, nos. 87, 88.

because the rank was so obviously foreign, but perhaps also because they believed that their exalted status rendered it superfluous. The native magnates also insisted that when the king granted them new estates he include in his charters clear statements that these were to be held as 'freely and quit' as they held their earldom lands.[42] Such concerns speak clearly to thoughtful and well conceived strategies designed to emphasize the earls' unique tenurial status.

By the 1250s, by contrast, several of the earls' immediate kinsman and important tenants had come to regard the title of knight as an important symbol of rank and honour, and even as an essential designation for men of their kind. In Strathearn, Gille Brigte's brother Maol Iosa, then his sons Fergus and Malise, became knights around the same time as they received grants of land from the crown. In nearby Lennox, native kinsmen appear to have been equally receptive to the allure of continental-style honorific titles. Maoldomhnaich's brothers Donnchad, Amhlaibh, and Cristin all became knights, as did his son and heir Mael Coluim.[43] Noblemen aspiring for recognition in thirteenth-century Scotland found the many and varied perquisites of knighthood extremely attractive. Not least among these was the legitimacy that the title accorded their claims to exercise lordship over lesser tenants and kinsmen. In this respect, as in others, the ethos of European-style knighthood complemented the authority with which Gaelic culture endowed them.

The men who populated the entourages of the early fourteenth-century earls were collectively a cosmopolitan group, most of them able to move freely from one great comital household to another. Such, for example, were the de Moravias, Logies, and Oliphants in Strathearn, and the Lindsays and Grahams in Lennox. Some travelled back and forth from the Gaelic-speaking environments of their own estates into the larger world of the European nobility with ease, notably Malcolm Buchanan, Donald Galbraith, and Duncan MacAulay of Lennox, and Malcolm Kinbuck, Maurice de Auchterarder, and Monach Mac Alpin of Strathearn, all of whom, incidentally, swore oaths of fealty to Edward I together with their lords in August 1296.[44] Renders of silver pennies, exotic spices, wax, scarlet hose, and gloves symbolized the changed economic conditions that now obtained throughout the kingdom, but they were symptomatic, too, of the entrenchment of the heritable rights of landowners in Scottish law, the fundamental tenets of which were as familiar to men of native origin as they were to the descendants of English and continental settlers. References to such renders in written documents appear side by side with clauses referring to the ancient forinsec or 'Scottish' service with which Earls Maoldomhnaich and Gille Brigte had been so well acquainted. The Scotland of the Bruce and Stewart kings was very much a European realm, but it was one in which members of the landed ranks no longer felt the need to champion – or to deny – their Gaelic heritage.

---

42 See, for example, *RRS*, ii, no. 206; *Lennox Cart.*, 1.   **43** Fraser, *Lennox*, ii, no. 202.   **44** T. Thomson (ed.), *Instrumenta publica sive processus super fidelitatibus et homagiis Scotorum domino Regi Angliae factis AD MCCXCI–MCCXCVI* (Bannatyne Club, 1834), 128, 139, 145, 167.

CHAPTER 3

Lords of property and lords of men: authority, power, and revenues

In the summer of 1296, as he progressed around the kingdom that he had just claimed to conquer, Edward I came to the borders of the lordship of Strathearn, where he was met by seven women, 'who accompanied the king on the road between Gask and Ogilvie, singing to him, as was the custom in the time of the late Alexander king of Scots'.[1] The lands through which Edward passed were substantially different in appearance than those which Earl Gille Brigte had governed a hundred years earlier. The amount of land under the plough had grown considerably in the intervening century, and in 1296 Malise III drew on sources of revenue that his grandfather had not yet begun to exploit. In Lennox, the late thirteenth-century landscape had also undergone change, and the resources which Earl Malcolm I bequeathed to his son at his death around 1303 were much more varied than those his predecessor Maoldomhnaich had known. There survive for both lordships precious few records in the way of inquisitions, rentals, or extents, making the reconstruction of the physical setting and material resources of the two earldoms problematic at best. It is not until the thirteenth century that documents begin to yield reliable impressions about patterns of rural settlement in the hills and valleys of either lordship. When combined with place name evidence, however, charter texts offer valuable information about the ways in which the thirteenth- and fourteenth-century magnates exploited their lands, derived income from them, and in turn expended these resources as lordly consumers.

The charters afford occasional glimpses of quite substantial rents. A deed of Sir John de Moravia of Drumsagard dated c.1284, for example, granted to his brother Sir William the lands of Aldie in the parish of Fowlis Wester in return for an annual blench ferme, but also for the obligation of discharging to the earl of Strathearn ten pounds of silver every year.[2] The rents from the lands associated with the thanage of Dunning were sufficiently large in 1283 to permit Earl Malise III to increase one of his predecessors' gifts to Inchaffray abbey from twenty merks per annum to thirty.[3] In Lennox, the lands attached to the parish kirk of Campsie generated sufficient revenues in 1221 for the bishop of Glasgow to assign ten merks of silver annually from them to Kelso abbey. Ongoing disagreement in respect of this sum between the bishop and the abbot long after

---

[1] *CDS*, iv, 475. [2] Muniments of the Dean and Chapter, Durham, DCD Misc. Chrs., nos. 770, 771. [3] *Inchaff. Chrs.*, no. 113.

the death of both principals suggests that it represented only a fraction of an otherwise valuable yearly return.[4] Other grants of more modest amounts of six and four merks to Inchaffray from lands scattered throughout eastern Strathearn, and the bitterness of the contest between the family of the native earls of Lennox and Paisley abbey over the estates associated with the church of Kilpatrick reveal that in the early thirteenth century the rich, if limited, arable lands that lay within each of the lordships were subject to intense exploitation. Straddling as they did the geological highland-lowland divide, both regions included extensive grazing lands. They boasted also a host of natural resources the value of which the earls grasped from a very early date. A survey of the charter texts that survive from both earldoms for the period between roughly 1170 and 1365, then, goes some way towards offsetting the paucity of other source materials, and makes it possible to sketch broad patterns of change, development, and decay over the long term.

Gille Brigte of Strathearn and Maoldomhnaich of Lennox were lords of men as well as manors. They derived a significant portion of their annual incomes not merely from the exploitation of the natural resources of their lands, but also from the obligations, customary and of more recent vintage, that their kinsmen, tenants, and peasants owed them. In the early decades of the fourteenth century Malise V of Strathearn and Donald of Lennox interacted with all three groups in ways that were in many respects vastly different than had their predecessors. The language used to describe the obligations of tenants, currencies of social and economic exchange, and symbols of lordly authority had all changed after two hundred years of encounter and interaction between Gaelic and European cultures. But in the fourteenth century lordship was still the most important feature in the economy of lord-man relations, and ultimately lordship derived its strength from the readiness of men and women, free and unfree, to acknowledge, and to give, material expression to their obligations.

The rural economies of medieval Strathearn and Lennox were above all a reflection of the geography and topography of each of the regions. These presented a host of challenges, most obviously to lords and peasants who sought to make a living as agrarian farmers. Drainage throughout Strathearn was poor, for the River Earn and its numerous small tributaries lie in flat alluvial valleys with little or no slope to facilitate water run-off from their boggy floors. A considerable range of the low lying lands was covered with reeds, rushes, and other marshy plants, and subject to flooding during the spring months. In areas such as these human settlement was restricted to islets of high, dry ground; the best known of these was the Isle of Masses, where Céli Dé priests and, later, Augustinian canons built a religious house. In drier portions of the lowlands, in the eastern and southern portions of the earldom, heather covered most of the unwooded areas, providing a limited, but potentially rich region of arable land.

[4] C. Innes (ed.), *Liber S. Marie de Calchou* (1846), i, nos. 229, 230, 234, 279.

Long before the twelfth century Pictish farmers had learned to make judicious use of the limited arable of the landscape, situating their settlements on loamy slopes or under the shelter of ridges, and avoiding altogether the floors of the Pow and Earn valleys, which were prone to flooding and standing water.[5] The economy of Strathearn, however, was predominantly pastoral. Place name evidence, especially the distribution of names that include the Gaelic terms *airigh* and *ruighe*, shows that vast stretches of the uplands situated west and south of the Turret Water were devoted to transhumance.[6] The nature of surviving charter evidence itself goes some way towards illuminating the patterns of economic exploitation in medieval Strathearn, with a clear concentration of documents originating in the fertile eastern parts of the earldom where, in the first half of the thirteenth century, the earliest foreign families were settled and the chief ecclesiastical centre of the lordship was established. Strathearn records, moreover, include one of a very few references in medieval Scottish charters of the elusive term *fortir*, signifying 'upper land' or 'overland'.[7]

The economy of Lennox was equally firmly based on the physical landscape, and even more heavily geared to the raising of animals. Some two-thirds of the earls' territories lay well beyond the Highland line, and here again, place name evidence reveals an array of terms (though not all Gaelic) associated directly or by inference with transhumance. South of Loch Lomond, in the valleys of the Endrick, Leven and Blane Rivers, as well as the numerous tributaries of the Clyde, hills and heather gave way to arable land. Place names that include elements such as *ach*, *baile*, as well as Brittonic *gart*, testify to the antiquity of crop farming throughout this part of the earldom. Similarly, references in charters to cereal renders of oats, corn and bere are frequent, both as the stuff of gifts as well as components of the earls' annual incomes. As in Strathearn, though, the Lennox landscape offered only limited access to good arable ground.

The obstacles against which the medieval farmers of Strathearn and Lennox toiled were significant, but not insurmountable, and charter materials attest a gradual but steady process of intensified agricultural exploitation over the course of the period between 1170 and 1365. In the last years of the twelfth century, for example, the canons of Inchaffray priory held three acres of land on the edge of the marsh that surrounded their island community, to which they had access by means of a small channel cut for their boats. The steady clearing of wood and the reclamation of waste enabled them to build out of this unpromising ground a croft that was known as Brewland in the fifteenth century.[8] In 1200, Earl Gille Brigte's foundation charter further granted them license to take timber from nearby woods for the making of *utensilium*.[9] The place name Edardoennech, *eadar dà enach*, 'between two marshes', found in two charters of

5 G. Whittington and J.A. Soulsby, 'A preliminary report on an investigation into *Pit* place-names' (1968). 6 A. Bill, 'Transhumance place-names in Perthshire' (1992), 388–93. 7 W. Fraser, *The red book of Grandtully* (1868), i, App., no. 69; Barrow, *Kingdom*, 242. The place name Gorthy, similar to the Welsh *gorthir*, and with the same meaning of 'upper land', may represent another reference. 8 *Inchaff. Chrs.*, 317. 9 *Ibid.*, no. 9.

c.1208, testifies to the creation of a small patch of arable from previously infertile ground.[10] Scholars have argued, moreover, that 'clusters of crannogs', such as those found in both Loch Earn and Loch Lomond, once thought to be purely defensive, attest instead the well planned efforts of residents to 'maximise their use' of arable land by turning the valuable soil of the shore lines entirely to agriculture.[11] The building of one or more bridges across the Earn facilitated movement through and across the fertile portions of the lordship.[12]

By the mid-fourteenth century improved methods of drainage, the steady process of land reclamation, and the adoption by farmers of methods for the cultivation of dry sloping areas of land had much altered the appearance of, and yields from, the landscape of Strathearn and Lennox. There is evidence, moreover, that by this time the lords of both had begun to look to wooded lands as a new source of arable. Fermtouns scattered around the extensive uplands of both regions reveal that a growing tenant population challenged farmers to expand their fields into areas that in subsequent centuries were abandoned as being too marginal. In 1218 the canons on the Isle of Masses were already actively engaged in a programme the aim of which was to drain increasingly large tracts of the marshland situated close to their buildings.[13] Earl Malise II's grant of two serfs to the religious house in 1258 provided them with the manpower necessary to pursue other such projects.[14] Attempts to reclaim land from waste, however, were not always easily effected. The monks of Lindores abbey vigorously opposed the efforts of Fergus son of Gille Brigte to introduce the plough to a portion of the Muir of Orchill that, they claimed, had customarily been considered common pasture.[15] In Lennox, the transfer of tenants from one portion of the earldom to another, such as occurred around 1240 when Fearchar Mac Gille Mhartainn exchanged his lands in Strathblane for Dundaff in Fintry parish,[16] sometimes signalled the breaking of new agricultural ground or attempts to expand the arable beyond the confines of the lowland portions of the earldom. The splitting of fermtouns, signalled by placename prefixes such as 'Mid' or 'Nether', or suffixes such as 'Mor' and 'Beg', attests not merely the division of land among two or more tenants,[17] but the more intensive cultivation of patches of arable. Although pastoral farming remained the basis of the economy of both lordships well beyond the medieval period, it was by no means the only, or indeed the most important, of the earls' sources of wealth. If the harvest of oats, corn, and bere was probably too insignificant to be a source of real profit in the burgeoning markets of Perth and Glasgow, it was nevertheless sufficiently

---

10 W.J. Watson, *The Celtic placenames of Scotland* (1993, repr. of 1926 edn), 417; *Inchaff. Chrs.*, nos. 26, 27. **11** C.R. Wickahm-Jones, *The landscape of Scotland: a hidden history* (2001), 95–6. **12** F.W.D. Brie (ed.), *The Brut or The chronicles of England* (1906), 276–7. **13** *Inchaff. Chrs.*, no 37. **14** Ibid., nos. 87, 88. In 1265/6 still another small area in the environs of the abbey had been reclaimed from the marsh and marked off with a trench; see *Inchaff. Liber*, no. 48, and, more generally, G. Ewart, 'Inchaffray abbey, Perth & Kinross: excavation and research, 1987' (1996), 479, 513. **15** *Lind. Cart.*, no. 28. **16** Fraser, *Lennox*, ii, no. 7. **17** R.A. Dodgshon, 'Changes in Scottish township organization during the medieval and early modern periods' (1977), 53–60.

abundant to satisfy the local requirements of lord and peasant, and there were other commodities aplenty, especially cheese.

In the thirteenth and early fourteenth centuries large areas of forest still dominated the physical landscapes of Strathearn and Lennox,[18] and in the closing years of the former the crown was still deriving many of the annual renders of cain from the shires of Dumbarton and Stirling in kind, chiefly meat and hides.[19] But here, too, boundaries were by no means fixed and were yielding to the advance of the plough and the hungry animal. By the time of Earl Malise V of Strathearn, for example, the small estates of Ross and Aberuchill had been carved out of the hitherto wooded and undeveloped banks of Loch Earn;[20] encroachments had also begun on the woodlands of Glendevon, once the tocher of Earl Gille Brigte's daughter, Maud.[21] The area around Glen Lednock abounded in dykes that marked off small patches of arable land in the wooded northern reaches of the earldom;[22] they serve, incidentally, as reminders that native custom allowed comital tenants freer use of lands legally designated as forest than did the laws observed in areas of English or continental settlement.

In Lennox, the most significant and frequent reclamation projects occurred in forested, rather than marshy or waste, lands. Portions of the heavily wooded islands scattered around the southern part of Loch Lomond had long been under the plough in the later thirteenth century. Earls Maoldomhnaich and Malcolm I maintained a residence (perhaps on a site already occupied for some time) at Inchcailloch, a holy place long associated with St Mirren,[23] and in 1263 a force of Norwegian mercenaries plundered these 'well inhabited' islands while passing through Lennox.[24] A half a century later the three daughters of Sir Thomas de Cremannan were still able to derive an income from lands that their father had developed on another small island.[25]

Encroachments on wooded areas occurred at a relatively steady pace throughout the thirteenth century and well into the fourteenth elsewhere in the lordship. In a series of early charters to the Cluniac house at Paisley, for example, Maoldomhnaich permitted the monks to clear a portion of the forested lands of Bonhill, and lesser lords soon followed suit, granting access to woodlands in northern Lennox, as well as at Tarbert and on the slopes leading down to Loch Lomond around Luss.[26] Beginning in 1326, King Robert's construction of a sumptuous residence at Cardross on the Clyde saw the massive clearing of woodland to accommodate the house and its outbuildings, and the establishment of small, probably temporary settlements of trades- and craftsmen within

---

18 See M.L. Anderson, *A history of Scottish forestry* (1967), i, 113–15, 119–21, for references to named forests in both regions.   **19** *ER*, i, 30, 38–9, 47, 51.   **20** NAS, GD 24/5/1/4.   **21** *RRS*, vi, no. 482.   **22** E.C. Bain, *A short guide to deserted settlements in Glen Lednock* (1976). For evidence concerning assarting in the forests of the Anglo-Scottish border region, see P.J. Dixon, 'Settlement in the hunting forests of southern Scotland in the medieval and later periods' (1997), 345–54.   **23** See below, p. 122; *Origines*, i, 32–3; NMRS MS 993/1, Loch Lomond islands survey, 9.   **24** A.O. Anderson (ed.), *Early sources of Scottish history A.D. 500–1286* (1990), ii, *sub* 1263.   **25** *Lennox Cart.*, 81–3.   **26** *Paisley Reg.*, 157, 216, 220; *Glasgow Reg.*, i, no. 229.

the forest for the manufacture of materials associated with timber.[27] Members of the Buchanan family, who first appear in record early in the thirteenth century, slowly but steadily erected a sizeable lordship in the rough territory lying east of Loch Lomond on lands that they reclaimed in part from forest, as well as from moor. The retreat of Lennox woodlands before the plough in the period between 1250 and 1400 may in fact have been more extensive than it was in Strathearn. One scholar has even argued on the basis of charter evidence that 'instead of clearings in a more or less continuous woodland, there were now distinct, and therefore named, woods in an otherwise open landscape'.[28]

The Buchanan estates serve as a useful reminder that land reclamation projects in Lennox involved more than merely encroachments into tree-covered regions. Soon after the Graham family gained a foothold within the parish of Strathblane its members embarked on an ambitious plan to bring under the plough the rough moor and bog lands that covered large portions of their newly acquired estates around Mugdock, an effort not eventually completed until the early twentieth century.[29] When he granted Paisley abbey a lucrative fishery in the River Leven, Earl Maoldomhnaich encouraged the monks to develop the adjacent woodlands.[30] Expansion of the arable and intensification of its exploitation were very much the order of the day in thirteenth- and fourteenth-century Lennox, just as they were in Strathearn. For most of the period between 1170 and 1365, however, forested land continued to dominate much of the physical landscape of both regions. Arable estates remained largely confined to small portions of each lordship, and newly erected holdings were for the most part hardscrabble and hard won.

The medieval earls of Strathearn and Lennox prized their forests above all for the venison, boar, and other wild animals they sheltered. John Gilbert's comprehensive study of the forest law of medieval Scotland has done much to correct the notion that the settlement of English and continental lords in lowland regions of the kingdom brought dramatic change to the customs that governed hunting and hunting reserves throughout the realm. Scholars now widely acknowledge that while both the incomers, and above all the crown, designated vast tracts of land as legal 'forest', native magnates were left relatively undisturbed in the exercise of lordly authority over the woodlands of their own territories.[31] While royal theory held that no lord, Gaelic or European, might hunt or grant hunting privileges within his lands without royal license, early thirteenth-century records attest the almost total independence of the native lords of Strathearn and Lennox to do both. Thus, one of Earl Gille Brigte's earliest grants to the newly reconstituted Augustinian house at Inchaffray offered the

[27] G.W.S. Barrow, *Robert Bruce and the community of the realm of Scotland*, 319–20; ER, i, 53–7, 123–36; *Glasgow Reg.*, i, no. 229. [28] R.M. Tittensor, 'History of the Loch Lomond oakwoods' (1970), 103; more generally, see C. Smout, 'Woodland history before 1850' (1993). [29] RCAHMS, *Stirlingshire: an inventory of the ancient monuments* (1963), i, 249–54; J.G. Smith, *Strathblane and its inhabitants from early times* (1886), 17. [30] *Paisley Reg.*, 212. [31] J. Gilbert, *Hunting and hunting reserves in medieval Scotland* (1979), 10.

canons 'a teind of all our venison', a gift repeated in Lennox around the same time, when Maoldomhnaich issued written deeds in favour of two of his lay tenants, and gave to the monks of Paisley abbey unlimited access to timber and fuel for their needs.[32] Gilbert demonstrates, in fact, that Gille Brigte of Strathearn and Maoldomhnaich of Lennox in particular drew on both native and more recent customs in their treatment of forest land.[33] The first allowed them ample opportunity to give expression to the gift giving ethos of traditional Gaelic culture and perpetuated the notion, deeply engrained in native society, that game was *res nullius*, that is, available to all free men. Equally important, it afforded them nominal control over hunting even in lands that they alienated from their own hands. The English practices of the incomers they regarded as equally important, however, because implicit in firm lordly title over hunting grounds were potentially lucrative judicial rights arising from cases litigated at forest law.

The crown was uneasily aware of the subtle challenge to its authority that native rights in the forest represented. In his wide ranging study Gilbert looked in vain for documentary evidence which would confirm that in the thirteenth and early fourteenth centuries the earls of Strathearn exercised jurisdiction over their forests only with the permission of the crown. That such evidence should be lacking, however, is hardly surprising. The independence that the early earls enjoyed within their territories in forest related matters is equally well attested in virtually every other aspect of their lordly authority, most notably in the ambiguity of their tenurial relationship with the Scottish crown. It is small wonder that they should have resisted or merely ignored royal intrusion into their valuable forest lands, for recognition of the crown's right to meddle in this feature of their lordship would have undermined the strength of their traditional authority as native magnates. In Lennox, royal efforts to assert control were slightly more successful, though it remained nominal until well into the fifteenth century. Maoldomhnaich's willingness to accept a charter of King Alexander II for the earldom of Lennox may have signalled his implicit acknowledgment of the crown's claim to cognisance over matters relating to the forest. Nevertheless, like the earls of Strathearn, he, too, made grants of woodland pertinents and hunting rights throughout the years of his rule without reference to the king.[34] The royal charter of 1238 referred only in general terms to the authority he was to enjoy as a baronial vassal,[35] and it was not until 1272, in the time of his grandson and successor, Malcolm I, that the crown was able to assert unequivocally its concession of 'free' forest rights to the earls of Lennox.[36]

Malcolm I, however, belonged to a new generation of native lords, one whose members had less compelling reasons to fear royal encroachments on their traditional prerogatives than had their predecessors in the early days of English and continental settlement in Scotland. His deference to the royal will

---

32 *Inchaff. Chrs.*, no. 9; Fraser, *Lennox*, ii, no. 202; *Lennox Cart.*, 19–20; *Paisley Reg.*, 212. **33** Gilbert, *Hunting*, 198, 27. **34** See, for example, Fraser, *Lennox*, ii, no. 202 **35** *Lennox Cart.*, 1–2. **36** Fraser, *Lennox*, ii,. no. 25.

bore witness to the accommodation of Gaelic and foreign customs in Lennox, much as did that of his contemporary, Malise III of Strathearn, and well illustrates the blend of old and new ideas about forest law that Gilbert has traced throughout Scotland north of Forth in the thirteenth century.

There were, none the less, differences in the ways in which the earls of Strathearn and Lennox managed their forest lands. In the early years of the century Gille Brigte allowed the canons of Inchaffray and their servants common hunting and hawking rights throughout his lands, access to pannage, and the freedom to take timber and fuel 'wherever they want and for whatever purposes they deem necessary'.[37] His liberality was no doubt a reflection of his piety and his belief that acts of generosity to the church in this world would speed passage of his soul through purgatory in the next. But it echoed also Gaelic notions about the status of forest creatures as *res nullius* that, Gilbert has argued, operated in Scotland before the twelfth century.[38] Members of the earl's immediate family also exercised wide ranging rights in the woodlands of Strathearn,[39] though significantly neither Gille Brigte nor his successor, Robert, appears to have extended comparable privileges to the few French- and English-speaking tenants settled within their territories. Moreover, their liberality stands in some contrast to the restricted access that Gille Brigte's near contemporaries, the Stewarts, allowed in their forests. Walter son of Alan, for example, was generous in endowing his new foundation at Paisley with lands, but like many of the newcomers, he strictly controlled its share of the venison and wild birds that inhabited the wooded area of his estates. In like fashion, he made provision in another grant for the protection of his deer against the monks' encroachment on their habitat.[40]

Despite the royal grant of 1238, the long rule of Maoldomhnaich of Lennox saw little real change to lordly practice in respect of the forest. Like Gille Brigte of Strathearn in his first few years as earl, he, too, exercised the native prerogative of making grants of timber, fuel, and venison from his woodlands and, like Gille Brigte, he understood his traditional rights to include not merely beasts of the forest but also wild birds and their nesting grounds.[41] Senior members of the comital family likewise enjoyed extensive rights to make grants from the forest, as did an especially favoured handful of native tenants. In keeping with native custom, common folk enjoyed traditional, if limited, communal privileges in wooded areas for grazing, or collecting firewood or peat for domestic use.[42] Thus, Maoldomhnaich's grant of the 'superiority' of Arrochar to his nephew Donnchad son of Gille Crìosd included 'hunting and nesting grounds'.[43] Although it is of later date, Maurice de Luss' gift in 1277 to the bishop of Glasgow of a generous amount of timber for the construction of the bell tower

---

[37] *Inchaff. Liber*, no. 5. [38] Gilbert, *Hunting*, 8–10, 226. [39] *RRS*, ii, no. 136; *Lind. Cart.*, no. 28. [40] *Paisley Reg.*, 17, 409; Duncan, *Making*, 365. [41] See, for example, NAS, GD 1/88/2; Fraser, *Lennox*, ii, nos. 203, 204. [42] Anderson, *Scottish forestry*, i, 89. [43] Royal Faculty of Procurators, Glasgow, Hill Collection of MSS, Macfarlane Muniments, ii, no. 73.

and treasury suggests that this native family, too, freely disposed of woodland resources.[44] In Lennox, as in contemporary Strathearn, however, the earl reserved control over the alienation of forested lands to his native kinsmen and friends. For example, none of Maoldomhnaich's charters to Sir David de Graham, although they granted the new tenant a wide variety of pertinents, included references to woodlands or forest based resources – probably to the great annoyance of Sir David, who would have conceived of the exercise of such prerogatives as appropriate to his status.[45] As Gilbert has argued, continental ideas about lordly rights may have exerted a powerful influence on the shaping of Scottish forest law in the Middle Ages, but for several generations after the settlement of the newcomers in both Strathearn and Lennox, Gaelic custom in respect of the forest and its resources remained largely unaffected by foreign influence.

Yet, change there was, and it becomes apparent towards the end of the thirteenth century in both lordships. If the proliferation of named forests does indeed attest the spread of pasture or plough, as has been argued, then such evidence should be added to other signs of deforestation As early as mid- century, for example, charters begin to identify woodlands by name, including Fedale, Glenlichorn, 'Curelundyn', 'Rossmadirdyn' and, a little later, Crieff and Methven, all in Strathearn.[46] Alexander III's charter of 1272 to Earl Malcolm I designated a substantial portion of the northern reaches of the earldom as the 'free forest of Lennox'.[47] Named woodlands and coppices begin to appear in the written deeds of the lordship around the same time,[48] and with greater regularity by the early years of the fourteenth century.[49] Such designations suggest that already by 1250 areas cleared for settlement, grazing, or farming in both regions had begun to alter landscapes once extensively if not entirely given over to oak, alder, hazel and a variety of coniferous trees.[50] Although the extent of the encroachment north of Forth was not as marked as it was in the lowland south, the process was none the less significant enough to warrant changes to the ways in which the Gaelic lords controlled, managed, and exploited their woodland resources.

Evidence here is plentiful from the Lennox of Maoldomhnaich and his successor, whose combined rules spanned most of the thirteenth century. Maoldomhnaich made generous gifts of forested lands, lands, timber, and pannage to the religious of Paisley abbey, but also to several of his native tenants. The frequency with which such pertinents appear in his written deeds reveals that he was little influenced by continental ideas that strictly reserved such

---

44 *Glasgow Reg.*, i, no. 229. **45** Fraser, *Lennox*, ii, nos. 6, 7, 10. **46** *Lind. Cart.*, nos. 24, 111, 112; *Inchaff. Chrs.*, no. 108; *CDS*, ii, no. 1883; A.A.M. Duncan (ed.), *John Barbour, The Bruce* (1997), 97. **47** *Lennox Cart.*, 29–30. For the meaning of this term, see Gilbert, *Hunting*, 32–3, 191. **48** The earl referred to 'my woods of Bonhill' in a charter to the monks of Paisley; *Paisley Reg.*, 216. For other named woods, see ibid., 157 (Tarbert); *Glasgow Reg.*, i, no. 229 (Luss); Fraser, *Lennox*, ii, no. 25 (Ross Wood). **49** *ER*, i, 53–7, 123–36; *Glasgow Reg.*, i, no. 229. **50** Tittensor, 'Loch Lomond oakwoods', 103; Smout, 'Woodland history', 42–4.

resources to great lords alone, though, as noted above, he was not noticeably generous in granting access to the woodlands of Lennox to his French- and English-speaking tenants. Earl Malcolm I continued his grandfather's practice of including the produce of his forests to favoured lay and ecclesiastical tenants, but already in his time Gaelic tradition was giving way to English influence. Unlike Maoldomhnaich, Malcolm counted among such beneficiaries tenants who were not of native descent, including Grahams, Crocs, Lenys, and Sproulls. His closer contacts with the culture of the royal court had impressed on him the value to be gained by making formal grants of woodland pertinents, for each of these reinforced his ultimate control of these resources and his authority to alienate them as might a Stewart, a Comyn, a Bruce, or a Brechin. A similar way of thinking in turn informed the grants of Earls Malcolm II and Donald, and the charter in which Malcolm ceded to Walter Sproull control over timber, game, wild fowl, and the revenues arising from the sale of these in the lands of Dalquhurn was in many respects entirely typical of the period.[51] In Lennox, then, a host of favoured tenants enjoyed considerable perquisites in the forest from the time of the earliest earls. By Malcolm I's death in the early fourteenth century, however, the Gaelic notion of *res nullius* had begun to change, subsumed by more recent ideas about lordly authority and its exercise, and the number of such favoured tenants had increased substantially.

Changing notions about woodland resources, the steadily increasing value of such perquisites in an expanding economy, and the increasing commutation into cash of obligations once paid in kind all necessitated a more sophisticated system of forest administration. The thirteenth century, Gilbert has argued, saw a rise in the number of royal grants in free forest and a concomitant elaboration of forest law. Earl Malcolm II of Lennox appears to have grasped the potential for increased revenues from both his legally defined forest as well as from his woodlands more generally. One of his charters notes the existence of the office of forester for the first time in Lennox, and records the appointment to that position a well established tenant of Anglo-Norman descent, Sir Patrick de Lindsay.[52] Like those of baronial foresters elsewhere, the latter's duties included the protection of game from unlicensed hunters, the apprehension of persons caught stealing animals or wild birds, the protection of trees from illegal gleaning or cutting, and perhaps also the collection of tolls and other dues that the earl charged less favoured tenants for access to these resources.[53] Although Malcolm's grant made no specific mention of a forester's court, the existence of such a tribunal is implicit in the clause that granted to Lindsay 'all the profits arising from the said office'. These would have included at least a portion of the fines, escheats, and other money payments understood in Alexander III's grant of 1272 of a portion of the lordship in free forest, as well as in the traditional claims that Malcolm's predecessors had established over the forested lands of Lennox.

51 *Lennox Cart.*, 40–1.   52 Ibid., 49–50.   53 Gilbert, *Hunting*, 197.

Scholars have long been intrigued by Malcolm's linking of the new office of forester with that of the older Gaelic *toísech* in the grant to Lindsay. For Gilbert, it was a notable example of the combination of native and English custom; according to William Croft Dickinson, it signalled a linking of the *toísech*'s responsibility to regulate the movement of strangers with the dangers that woodlands represented as havens for suspicious persons.[54] Writing a century ago, the genealogist John Lindsay was also struck by Malcolm's unique association of the two offices, and noted aptly that the appointment of Patrick Lindsay, 'a person not of the native race, reflects the change that was passing over the social organisation of Scotland'.[55] In the closing years of the thirteenth century the cultural milieu of Lennox was in a state of profound change. Old notions about lordly rights in the forest had not disappeared, but in the time since Maoldomhnaich's death they had merged with English ideas about the ways in which noble authority in this region might be expressed most comprehensively. In the intervening years, moreover, the financial profits arising from the natural resources of forests and woodlands had probably increased significantly. Few lords could afford to adopt a casual attitude towards the income in ready money now available from the exercise of a near monopoly over game, timber, fuel, and new woodland settlements, and from jurisdiction over the business of the courts that were now in place to regulate movement in and out of the forest. Malcolm I's unique association of the offices of *toísech* and forester demonstrated a shrewd understanding of the conditions of his time, and an opportunity to blend the weight of Gaelic tradition with the promise of future profit. By the time Earl Donald succeeded to the lordship in 1333, the link between the offices had become firmly established, though neither was apparently hereditary. Thus, when Patrick de Lindsay died, the honours passed not to his son and heir, but to Earl Donald's kinsman, Walter de Faslane.[56]

Almost as valuable to the medieval earls of Strathearn and Lennox as their forests were the waters of the rivers, lochs, and streams found throughout their territories. Lordly rights in fishing have not attracted much scholarly attention from Scottish historians, yet there is reliable evidence to suggest, as John Gilbert has done tentatively, that the Gaelic notion of *res nullius* applied as widely to fish as it did to game.[57] Of particular interest here is the contrast apparent between early references to fisheries in Anglo-Saxon England, particularly Northumbria, and thirteenth-century Scottish sources. Charter materials reveal that many English fisheries included old personal name compounds, suggesting that from an early date lords successfully laid claim to rights in water borne resources, and equally successfully controlled access to them.[58] There is no comparable association of fisheries with specific personal names in either Strathearn

---

54 Ibid., 196; W.C. Dickinson, 'The *toschederach*' (1941), 101. **55** J. Lindsay, 'The heritable bailies of the Lennox' (1904), 8. **56** NLS, Adv. MS. 34.3.25, fo. 62; *Lennox Cart.*, 69–70. **57** Gilbert, *Hunting*, 186. **58** V.E. Watts, 'Medieval fisheries in the Wear, Tyne and Tweed: the place-name evidence' (1983), 37.

or Lennox in the early thirteenth century. The implication must be that native magnates north of Forth shared the natural resources of their waters with their tenants, much as they did those of their forests. It is significant, too, that early attempts to define the kinds of privileges that beneficiaries might exercise in the waters of each territory occur in charters granted in favour of monastic houses. By the time the earls began to write charters with some regularity, the influence of post-conquest English practice, which reserved fish, wears, and saltpans to lords, was already beginning to alter local custom. Thus, Gille Brigte of Strathearn's early grants to the brethren of Inchaffray included not merely a teind of the fish brought to his own kitchens, but more specifically leave to fish in the Pow Burn, 'as well as in other waters, wherever and whenever they wish'.[59] Maoldomhnaich of Lennox's charters to Paisley abbey similarly mention fish and fisheries, not merely as general pertinents, but often as valuable gifts in and of themselves; such, for example, was the grant of a half a new wear on the River Leven.[60] As they did in respect of woodland resources, the earls of Lennox also granted access to fisheries and wears to favoured native tenants,[61] and extended to their closest kinsmen the authority to erect saltpans and to exploit new ponds on the River Leven and the Gare Loch.[62] Generous both may have been, but there was no mistaking the authority that each claimed to allocate rights in these resources.

The value of such gifts was by no means negligible. Maoldomhnaich's wear on the Leven together with his brother's gift of a saltpan supplied the monks of Paisley abbey for generations with fresh and salted fish, the mainstay of the monastic diet, as well as with a steady income from the sale of surplus fish. The many islands in the waters of Strathearn and Lennox, natural and artificial, may have been exploited to expand access to valuable stocks of fish beyond the reach of river and lochside based wears, as they had for hundreds of years on the continent.[63] The king himself cast envious eyes on the riches available in the fresh and sea waters of western Lennox. In 1237 he commissioned an inquest into the course of the Leven near Dumbarton, and when, the following year, he drafted a formal grant of the earldom of Lennox in favour of Maoldomhnaich, he reserved to his own uses the portion of the river as far upstream as the Murroch Burn.[64] References to sites for the drying of fish and fishnets, to ponds, and to the most highly prized among the fruits of the water, salmon, all attest the vitality of the industry in the Lennox economy,[65] but also the firm proprietary right which the earls claimed over these resources. Those rights do not appear to have diminished significantly over the course of the thirteenth century. Thus, while Earl Donald was prepared to allow his brother Murdoch and two other kinsmen to collect revenues from the fish traps located within Lennox waters, he withheld the same courtesy from another of his tenants.[66]

59 *Inchaff. Chrs.*, nos. 5, 9, 11, 12, 16; *Inchaff. Liber*, no. 5.   **60** *Paisley Reg.*, 158, 160, 212–13.   **61** Fraser, *Lennox*, ii, nos. 202–4; *Lennox Cart.*, 19–20.   **62** *Paisley Reg.*, 210–13.   **63** P. Squatriti, *Water and society in early medieval Italy, AD 400–1000* (1998), 134.   **64** *Paisley Reg.*, 218; *Lennox Cart.*, 1–2.   **65** *Paisley Reg.*, 211, 212.   **66** NAS, GD 430/76; *Lennox Cart.*, 31, 55; Fraser, *Lennox*,

Like the king, the monks of Paisley abbey were well aware of the value of water based resources. They sought from Maoldomhnaich, as well as from the crown, formal charters of confirmation that listed the specific privileges in wears, salmon stocks, and salt that the earl and his kinsmen had gifted them and, when a later lord of Lennox challenged their rights in the waters of the River Leven, they compelled him to set his seal to a new confirmation of all the thirteenth-century grants.[67] These same documents, in fact, show that the monks valued possession of the fishery so highly that they were willing to surrender a long held title over a nearby patch of arable in order to secure access to the water and its fish. The jealous preservation of fisheries on the part of the church is readily explicable, given the dependence of monks on this commodity, and on the salt needed to preserve it as a staple of their diet, and their interest in controlling the market value of any surplus that rivers and streams might produce. Among the native rulers of Lennox, however, it stands in contrast to the considerable freedom allowed to some tenants to exercise authority over lands designated as forest, and the generous access that common folk enjoyed to woodland resources. It may be that the earls of Strathearn and Lennox sought merely to take advantage of the steady rise that affected the price of fish from the thirteenth through the fifteenth centuries,[68] for similar concerns helped to make fishing privileges one of the most coveted of prerogatives elsewhere in the realm.[69] It may equally well reflect the earls' awareness that their generosity to the church had already alienated from their control a substantial portion of an important natural resource, and that the rights that remained to them should be managed more carefully. But it is tempting also to see in the strict reservation of water based resources on the part of Earl Maoldomhnaich in particular something of a conservative reaction to developments that, in the course of his long rule, had begun to challenge his status as a great native lord. The culture of the Gaels accorded special significance to water, and the literature and legend of early Christian Scotland drew especially strong links between bodies of water on the one hand, and saints, spirits, and hermits on the other.[70] A praise poem in Gaelic composed in the early thirteenth century, moreover, celebrated the descent of Maoldomhnaich himself from the waters of the River Leven.[71] Such profound symbolic associations must have resonated deeply in the culture of medieval Lennox, and must have influenced the ways in which the earl conceived of his rights in the lochs, rivers, and other waterways of his lordship. They may have exerted a powerful, if now long obscured, effect over the ways in which he treated these most special natural resources.

In the thirteenth century, then, the native earls' expression of their authority over the fruits of the forests and the waters of their territories owed as much

---

ii, no. 21. **67** *Paisley Reg.*, 212–23. **68** E. Gemmill and N. Mayhew, *Changing values in medieval Scotland: a study of prices, money, and weights and measures* (1995), 11–15. **69** Duncan, *Making*, 471. **70** M. Low, *Celtic Christianity and nature: early Irish and Hebridean traditions* (1996), 57–78; P. Hopkins, 'The symbology of water in Irish pseudo-history' (1992), 80–6. **71** T.O. Clancy (ed.), *The triumph tree* (1998), 258. The poem is discussed at length below, at p. 210.

to Gaelic custom and tradition as it did to the influence of more recent English and European ideas. By the 1330s, when Earl Malise V of Strathearn forfeited his title, and Earl Malcolm II of Lennox perished at Halidon Hill, native and European practices in respect of these resources had ossified, and it is no longer possible to distinguish native from English influences in the administration of hunting and fishing rights. Thus, the later earls of Strathearn and Lennox still reserved to themselves control over the portions of their lands legally defined as forest, and they enjoyed annual revenues from the courts over which his forester and *toísech* presided. All, however, now normally granted some forest privileges to their more important tenants, including John de Moravia of Drumsagard and Reginald More in Strathearn, and Sir John Napier in Lennox.[72] Some of these men had only recently risen to prominence; others, such as Manach of Strathearn, Patrick Galbraith, and Maurice de Luss,[73] were members of Gaelic families which had long been associated with their lords. Just as both vied equally for favour in their lords' entourages, so did they seek privileged access to a share of their lords' natural resources. As was the case elsewhere in the realm, the earls' hold over their forests and fisheries remained strong, but whether this reflected the enduring appeal of native custom or simple lordly avarice no longer mattered. In the Strathearn and Lennox of the 1330s the 'Scottish custom' over the pertinents of forest and water that are mentioned so frequently in writs, inquests, charters, and other documents had assumed a hybrid form and a new identity, one now characteristic of the kingdom as a whole. Although each of the great earldoms north of Forth remained distinct in many respects ways, two centuries of accommodation between Gaelic natives and foreign incomers had done much to blur cultural differences. Even in regions where when Gaelic identity remained strong, practices specific to individual lordships and baronies now most often complemented, supplemented, and only occasionally conflicted with, an emerging common law of the realm.[74] A survey of the changing nature of lordly rights in the woodlands and waters of Strathearn and Lennox shows that the thirteenth century was a crucial period in the making and shaping of the physical and economic landscape.

There can be little doubt that the goods in kind and the revenues they derived annually from the rights they exercised in the forest and waters of their lands made up a significant proportion of the annual income of the medieval earls of Strathearn and Lennox. As one scholar has noted, the former may in fact have been 'rather more important for the maintenance of life' in the highlands than elsewhere in the kingdom.[75] In the course of the twelfth and early thirteenth centuries there took place throughout the realm a steady transformation of rents and other dues traditionally rendered in kind into money pay-

---

[72] *Inchaff. Liber*, App., no. 24; *RRS*, V, no. 482; NLS, Adv. MS. 35.2.4, ii, 401. [73] BL, Lord Frederick Campbell Charters, xxx, 13; *Lennox Cart.*, 19–20, 24, 31–2. [74] H.L. MacQueen, 'The laws of Galloway: a preliminary survey' (1991); idem, 'The kin of Kennedy, "kenkynnol" and the common law' (1993); W.D.H. Sellar, 'Custom in Scots law' (1990): 413; idem, 'Celtic law and Scots law: survival and integration' (1989). [75] G.W.S. Barrow, *Kingship and unity* (1981), 11.

ments. In some areas, however, that change was slow in coming. It has become commonplace for historians to refer to the cheese renders that made up the contribution of the medieval earls of Lennox to the common army of Scotland as something of a quaint 'holdover',[76] but in the late fourteenth century the crown, chronically short of cash, still depended heavily on food renders for the provisioning of its armies.[77] Thus, in the late 1360s, Earl Donald required in a charter of infeftment granted to Maurice de Buchanan that the latter provide the king's army with 'a cheese from every house in that land in which cheese is made'.[78] Loyalty to some cherished tradition had no place in such an arrangement; it was, rather, an eminently sensible way for a lord whose lands lay in a rough and largely infertile part of the realm to discharge his obligations to the crown. Food rents must also have gone some way towards supplying the households that the native magnates maintained in their chief residences. Charter witness lists are, for the most part, reliable indicators of the size of the retinues that surrounded great lords, and a glance at the deeds of earls such as Malise III and Malise IV of Strathearn, and Malcolm II and Donald of Lennox show that in the early fourteenth century the size of the comital entourages had increased substantially since the time of Gille Brigte and Maoldomhnaich. The lavish hospitality that noble retainers expected of these magnates required a steady flow into the earls' kitchens of vast quantities of drink, meat, fish, grain, and other foodstuffs from outlying estates, and sophisticated domestic arrangements intended to ensure their availability. Monastic houses also depended heavily on food, rather than money, rents, and excavations of middens on the site of Inchaffray abbey confirm that the canons consumed sufficient quantities of cattle (as well as wild and domestic fowl) to warrant maintaining a slaughterhouse on their premises.[79]

Lordship over the forests and waters of their territories provided the medieval earls of Strathearn and Lennox with substantial rents in kind and cash, but by far the most important sources of their annual incomes derived from their possession of vast stretches of moorland, pasture, and arable. The overwhelmingly pastoral nature of the economies of both regions did not diminish the importance of arable farming; indeed, it must have served to emphasize the value of good farm land. In both regions, moreover, the comparative scarcity of fields suitable for the cultivation of grain meant that already in the thirteenth century the arable was under considerable pressure. Evidence for such pressure is readily available, and not merely in the expansion of the arable at the expense of wood, island, waste, and marsh, discussed above. Aerial photographs of the modern day Parks of Aldie in Strathearn, it has been observed, reveal 'cottage sites, tofts, and lengthy curved ploughed rigs of a long-vanished peasant settlement,

---

[76] Duncan, *Making*, 382; Barrow, *Kingdom*, 273. [77] See other examples of food renders cited in G.W.S. Barrow, 'The army of Alexander III's Scotland' (1990), 141, and nn. 63, 64. [78] NAS, GD 220/1/D5/1/4. [79] Ewart, 'Inchaffray abbey', 509–11.

evidence of the determined efforts of a medieval tenant anxious to increase the income from his lands'.[80] Similarly, scholars have argued for a 'direct link' between expanding arable acreage and the notable increase in written references to mills and multures.[81] Simply put, mills would hardly have been constructed in the numbers that they were if there had not been a considerable increase in demand for this kind of technology. In Strathearn there were mills in the early thirteenth century at Bellyclone on the Pow Burn, Milton and Dunfallin on the Earn, and at Gorthy; in Lennox there are references to sites at Balloch on the Leven and 'Aschend' on a tributary of the River Blane, both lying within the rich but limited arable zone of the earldom.[82] Still another sign of efforts to increase yields and incomes from arable lands was the steady rise of litigation concerning teinds, described as becoming a 'stream of judgements and concords' over the course of the thirteenth century.[83] In their efforts to take advantage of the expanding demand for agricultural produce the earls of Strathearn and Lennox, like their fellows elsewhere in the realm, often found that sound fiscal management competed with spiritual obligations, and it is in this light that the disputes that deeply troubled relations between the lords of Strathearn on the one hand, and the bishop of Dunblane and the canons of Inchaffray on the other in the matter of teinds are best understood.[84]

In both regions, then, the heavy demand for grain to supply household and other needs had a critical influence on the ways in which the earls exploited their territories for fiscal profit. So, however, did ancient patterns of rural settlement that long predated the thirteenth century. One of the challenges that confronted the medieval earls and their estate managers, then, was to devise effective means for adapting the ancient rural landscape to the requirements of a rising population and a quickening, increasingly cash based economy.

Superimposed over the terrain of Strathearn and Lennox were territorial structures that were already old by the time that the earliest charters began to be written there. Recent research on the pre-twelfth-century landscape of northern England and portions of Scotland has done much to recover evidence of large scale multiple estates, many of which subsequently found new life as rural deaneries and parishes and as administrative units such as wards, townships, and thanages.[85] Some of the key features of these old divisions may be traced in Strathearn and, more obscurely, in Lennox, notably the inclusion within each of shares of pasture, rough upland, and lowland arable, and the association of a church with the larger territorial unit. Thus, in Strathearn portions of the Muir of Orchill have been posited as the common grazing of the 'vanished' shires of

---

[80] Barrow, *Kingship and unity*, 141. [81] Duncan, *Making*, 366. [82] *Inchaff. Liber*, no. 27; *Inchaff. Chrs.*, nos. 27, 34; *Lennox Cart.*, 66, 81; NLS, Adv. MS 35.2.4, fo. 403; *RRS*, vi, no. 155. [83] Duncan, *Making*, 366; [84] See pp 151–5, below. [85] G.R. Jones, 'Multiple estates and early settlement' (1976), 16–40; A.J.L. Winchester, 'The multiple estate: a framework for the evolution of settlement in Anglo-Saxon and Scandinavian Cumbria' (1985), 89–101: 90; Barrow, *Kingdom*, 7–56; R.A. Dodgshon, *Land and society in medieval Scotland* (1981), 58–67; A. Grant, 'The construction of the early Scottish state' (2000), 47–71.

Cathermothel and Catherlavenach, with the shire churches of each at Muthill and Strageath respectively.[86] A thirteenth-century charter refers also to the 'shire' of Fowlis Wester, a good portion of which must have included the upland portions of the parish of the same name.[87] In Lennox, the place name *cathair*, linked elsewhere in the kingdom with the existence of pre-feudal shires,[88] is found in Catter (Drymen parish), where the medieval earls are known to have built a fortified residence, where they erected their gallows, and where they occasionally convened their courts.[89] Although the word 'shire' does not appear in Lennox record in the period 1170–1365, the presence there of the offices of thane and *toíseach*, whose incumbents were responsible for managing estates and collecting renders from them, suggests a settlement pattern not unlike that found elsewhere in the kingdom, of secular lordship based on scattered holdings, organized around an administrative centre.[90] Of relevance here, too, are the locations of the several residences maintained by the earls of Strathearn and Lennox. Dispersed throughout their territories each was perhaps the centre of an organized network of comital estates.[91]

Ancient land divisions, it has been aptly noted, offer 'some indication of the underlying economic support mechanisms' upon which medieval lords depended.[92] The 'cultural complexity' and 'eclecticism'[93] that characterized rural settlement in thirteenth- and fourteenth-century Galloway were equally important features of contemporary Strathearn and, to an even greater extent, Lennox, where a similar blend of ancient custom and more recent practice shows how the earls and their estate managers sought to exploit lands in the most profitable ways possible. By the year 1200 in both regions, peasant and other obligations were assessed in large part, though not exclusively, on units of arable land. And yet, just as the historic and physical landscapes of these lordships differed, so, too, did the specific ways in which such units were measured and described. In the rapidly expanding economy of the period between 1170 and 1365 the earls shaped and adapted valuation methods to suit their changing needs. More striking than anything else in a survey of the rural landscapes of Strathearn and Lennox, however, are the resilience of Gaelic custom and the enduring hold of traditional ways of exploiting the land.

The Picts left their mark on Strathearn, ancient Fortriu, in an abundance of *pett-* place names such as Pitlandy, Pettincleroch, Pitcairns, and Pitmeadow, and in the use there of the davoch as a measure of arable land. The clerics whom the earls employed to write their charters may well have been 'chary' of using unfamiliar words for a large unit of cultivated land, preferring the Latin terms *villa* or *terra* over the 'uncouth and strongly vernacular' Gaelic terms davach or carucate.[94] But there is good reason to believe that the *terra* of Bellyclone

---

86 Barrow, *Kingdom*, 37, 40, 43. **87** *Inchaff. Chrs.*, no. 37. **88** Barrow, *Kingdom*, 54. **89** *RRS*, vi, no. 478. **90** Jones, 'Multiple estates'; Winchester, 'The multiple estate'; Grant, 'Construction', 55. **91** Below, pp 117–24. **92** R. Oram, *The lordship of Galloway* (2000), 247. **93** Ibid., 235. **94** Barrow, *Kingdom*, 240, 246.

'according to its right marches', or the *terra* associated with the church of St Ethernan of Madderty,[95] both of which Earl Gille Brigte granted to the priory of Inchaffray, represented fixed measures of land, the latter perhaps a half a davach typical of parish church endowments throughout Scotland north of Forth.[96] Firmer evidence for the existence of the davach in Strathearn comes from the place names Raith, in Trinity Gask parish, and Rottearns, in Ardoch parish, the Gaelic term *rath* signifying a quarter of a davach.[97] Davachs were also used, of course, as fiscal units, but here again, the clerks responsible for drafting Strathearn charters have made it very difficult to discover the area of land they represented. Earl Gille Brigte's readiness to account for 'all the king's forinsec service due from the *terra* of Bellyclone' and, towards the end of the thirteenth century, William de Moravia's obligation to perform 'all the king's forinsec service that pertains to the 'lands' of Drumdowan and Pitvar' confirm only the existence of measured and marched lands owing customary renders.[98] But the thirteen-acre bovate of cultivated land – and, by extension, the 104 acre carucate – is attested in charters like that of Roger de Berkeley to Lindores abbey of lands near Exmagirdle, and perhaps lurks under Nigel de Luvetot's gift in Gille Brigte's time of six acres in his 'territory' of (the davach of?) Dalpatrick.[99] Arable land was by necessity linked with the nearby pasture needed to feed the animals that worked it, and there are numerous references to such land, in the shape of 'common pasture' pertaining to church lands, pasture assessed on the basis of specific numbers of animals, and rights of pasturage associated with estates.[1] A deed that mentions pasture for a mixture of cattle, sheep and horses lends credence to the observation that in some parts of the earldom ploughs were powered by animals other than just oxen.[2]

Evidence relating to smaller units of arable land is more plentiful and permits more than merely a passing glimpse of how Strathearn peasants worked their lords' lands. An early charter to the religious men living on the Isle of Masses granted three 'measures' of land in Fowlis Wester, undoubtedly the 'three acres of land nearest to Inchaffray toward the north' of his foundation charter of 1200 and subsequent confirmations.[3] Portions of land described as *particula*, parcels of contiguous acres, were the stuff of occasional grants,[4] but more frequently charter scribes used the word 'acre' to refer to small units. In some cases they clearly referred to the scattered rigs found also throughout the rich arable zone of south eastern Scotland.[5] Written deeds usually describe such acres as lying within the 'territory' of a specific toun, such as the toft and three acres which Henry son of Tristram de Gorthy gave to Inchaffray *in villa sua de Kintocher*, Nigel de Luvetot's six acres in his *territorio de Dolpatric*, mentioned

---

95 *Inchaff. Liber*, nos. 34, 69. **96** Barrow, *Kingdom*, 244. **97** Ibid., 274; *Inchaff. Chrs.*, no. 52; Watson, *Celtic placenames*, 227. **98** *Inchaff. Liber*, no. 34, App., no. 19. **99** *Lind. Cart.*, no. 68; *Inchaff. Chrs.*, no. 59. **1** See, for example, *Inchaff. Chrs.*, nos. 3, 39, 41; *Inchaff. Liber*, no. 59. **2** *Inchaff. Liber*, no. 12; Duncan, *Making*, 310–11. **3** *Inchaff. Liber*, no. 18; *Inchaff. Chrs.*, nos. 9, 41 **4** E.g. *Inchaff. Chrs.*, nos. 103, 112; *Inchaff. Liber*, nos. 52, 66. **5** Duncan, *Making*, 311–13.

above, and Robert de Methven's four acres, also in Dalpatrick.[6] The canons of Inchaffray secured from another donor a toft of six perches square together with two acres in his toun of Pitlandy, 'that is, in the field that is called Fitheleres Flat';[7] another charter mentions a toft and the acre of land pertaining to it, as well as small portions of land needed to make up four acres;[8] still another sixteen acres 'in the field called Langflath'.[9] References to fermtouns (*villae*) and the tofts and crofts that comprised them are heavily concentrated in the eastern region of Strathearn, where common farming of arable ground was possible and where, as was the case elsewhere in Scotland, few peasant families were wealthy enough to own a complete plough team. But the charter evidence suggests also that references to 'acres' sometimes designated compact rather than scattered measures of land. The 'three acres' north of the Isle of Masses that Earl Gille Brigte mentioned in his foundation charter can hardly have been anything but contiguous; the same must have been true for the two acres of land that lay adjacent to Earl Malise II's quarry at Nethergask, and truer still for the occasional references to *particula* on which parish churches were erected.[10] Collectively, the evidence suggests that in the arable regions of the earls' territories there was considerable variety in the ways in which people settled and worked the land. This observation should come as no surprise, for in their discussions of rural settlement historians have always warned against generalizations and in favour of an appreciation of the myriad 'local modifications' that medieval farmers effected to what otherwise appear to be consistent patterns.[11]

Although limited in its extent and confined largely to the eastern end of the earldom, the arable land of Strathearn was the focus of lordly efforts at improvement throughout the thirteenth and fourteenth centuries. The efforts of the residents of Inchaffray to reclaim acreage from their marshy surroundings have been noted, as has the carving out of new estates on the shores of Loch Earn. The canons' efforts were unstinting. By 1218 they had arranged to surround their island community with a trench in order to increase and protect the area of habitable land upon which the house and its growing number of outbuildings had been erected.[12] Further projects designed to expand the abbey's demesne holdings continued apace thereafter, when a patch of arable on the south side of the island, later known by the unambiguous name of Bordland, was similarly brought under the plough, the name signifying 'table' or 'demesne' land.[13] In the early 1190s the lands of Aldie passed temporarily into the hands

---

6 *Inchaff. Chrs.*, nos. 12, 59. **7** Ibid., no. 56; Barrow, *Kingdom*, 246. **8** *Inchaff. Chrs.*, no. 57. **9** Ibid., no. 99. **10** Ibid., nos. 9, 95, 112. See also Muniments of the Earl of Moray, Darnaway Castle, Moray Charters, Box 32, Div. 32, Bundle 1, no. 22, an incomplete text of which is printed in D.E. Easson (ed.), *Charters of the abbey of Coupar Angus* (2 vols, SHS, 1947), i, no. 86. **11** Duncan, *Making*, 314; see also Barrow, *Kingdom*, 248–9; Oram, *Lordship of Galloway*, 234. **12** *Inchaff. Chrs.*, no. 37; Ewart, 'Inchaffray abbey', 469–516. **13** *Inchaff. Chrs.*, 318 and no. 146; see also the croft reclaimed from the marsh later known as Brewland, ibid., 317. For the significance of the term 'bordland', see A.L. Winchester, 'The distribution and significance of the place-name "bordland" in medieval Britain' (1986).

of Mael Coluim of Fife when he married Earl Gille Brigte's daughter Maud. Situated in hilly Kinross-shire, the estate probably consisted of little more than a small oasis of arable field within a much larger area of rough pasture. But only eighty years later, when Sir William de Moravia of Drumsagard obtained title to the estate, he had to render his superior £10 of silver in annual rent.[14] It has been observed that the grounds of the modern day Parks of Aldie still show evidence of medieval landowners' attempts to manage the land effectively.[15] Cropmarks and other settlement remains, often visible only in aerial photographs, reveal that marginal lands, long since abandoned, were strenuously exploited in the later medieval period in parts of the earldom such as Dunbarney, near present day Bridge of Earn and, further north, Glen Lednock.[16]

The steadily expanding economy of the thirteenth century, spurred in large part by the increased circulation of coin, stimulated among the upper ranks of the Scots nobility a pressing demand for new sources of revenue, and placed at a distinct disadvantage lords whose territories consisted of lands that were at best marginal, and at worst sub-marginal.[17] By the middle years of the century, in fact, some Strathearn lords were casting envious eyes on the large stretches of moorland that covered a substantial part of the southern reaches of the earldom. When these efforts threatened the interests of the church they were likely to meet with determined opposition. The debacle over lands in Cathermothel (the Muir of Orchill) aptly illustrates the tension that such attempts might engender. In the mid-1240s Fergus son of earl Gille Brigte tried to exert control over the part of the Muir known as 'Cotken' (*coitchionn*, 'common pasture') with the intention of initiating there a programme of reclamation. His plans were frustrated, however, when the monks of Lindores abbey raised strong objections. Eventually, Fergus was compelled to issue a formal declaration that the land in question 'was, in the time of his ancestors, free and common pasture to all the men who resided around there, so that no one might build on the land or plough it, or otherwise do anything to alter its use as pasture', and further to promise that it would remain thus in future.[18] Another effort to expand his arable holdings in nearby Fedale, a portion of which he had already granted to Lindores, also proved unsuccessful.[19]

Attempts by lords like Fergus and, on a grander scale still, monastic houses such as Inchaffray and Lindores, to increase their demesne lands through assarting necessarily entailed the risk of igniting disputes from neighbouring lords and of generating rival claims to waste land, and examples of such tensions are well

---

14 Durham, Muniments of the Dean and Chapter, Misc. Chrs., nos. 770, 771.   **15** Barrow, *Kingship and unity*, 141.   **16** D. Hall, 'The Middle Ages' (1999), 71–2; SAS Archaeological Field Survey, *The archaeological sites and monuments of Clackmannan District and Falkirk District, Central Region* (1999), 9–13.   **17** See here S.P. Halliday, 'Marginal agriculture in Scotland' (1993), 66, and M.L. Parry, 'Upland settlement and climatic change: the medieval evidence' (1985), 40, Map 2.3, 44.   **18** *Lind. Cart.*, no. 28. See also C.J. Neville, 'Native lords and the church in thirteenth-century Strathearn, Scotland' (2002), 469.   **19** *Lind. Cart.*, no. 23.

documented throughout thirteenth-century Scotland. Less often taken into account, however, is the extent to which custom must also have acted as a check against intrusion into waste or common land. The great mass of the labouring peasantry and even of 'middling sorts' of minor land holders appears only fleetingly and mostly by inference in the charters and other written deeds that survive from the thirteenth and early fourteenth centuries, but the presence of the latter in such everyday occurrences as perambulations and boundary marking ceremonies shows that local opinion was deeply valued. The weight of custom in the business of land exploitation must have been particularly onerous in regions – including Strathearn – where powerful native lords and lesser men alike shared an interest in preserving time tested and time honoured Gaelic practices in the face of cultural and economic change. The monks of Lindores skilfully harnessed this conservatism in support of their claims against Fergus son of Gille Brigte. So, too, must other lords, including the crown itself, have done so when, elsewhere in the realm, they set limits on encroachments into common moor and pasture land.

Another significant indication of assarting in Strathearn may be found in a notable increase in litigation concerning teinds, a link that has been well documented for the kingdom as a whole.[20] Such disputes increasingly troubled relations between the earls and Inchaffray abbey in the years after Gille Brigte's death in 1223. The canons learned through unhappy experience to extract from each of his three successors a solemn promise that the abbey's rights to a variety of teinds would be respected, but long before the end of the thirteenth century the abbot was writing in frustration to Rome seeking papal support to recover revenues allegedly poached by other lords, 'clerical and secular'.[21] Under Malise II, moreover, grants of teinds tended to be commuted into fixed annual payments drawn from a variety of rents. The abbey cannot have been wholly satisfied with this arrangement, for fixed rents did not take into account fluctuations in the value of the sources from which these were derived or, over the long term, the effects of inflation.

Lennox was, famously, 'the home of the arachor', a Gaelic term that described both a bounded area of arable land and its capacity.[22] But as was the case in Strathearn, clerical scribes were uncomfortable with such an obviously foreign term, and in every instance they expressed their unease by referring to the unit with the cautionary words 'which in Gaelic is called arachor'. The Lennox arachor, moreover, lay alongside other units of measurement and assessment typical of the region north and west of Forth, including carucates, acres, and, by the fourteenth century, fiscal merklands;[23] a testament to the piecemeal development of arable farming arrangements in a part of the kingdom where the economy was overwhelmingly pastoral. The evidence of written deeds, in some instances supplemented by the findings of archaeologists and by onomas-

20 Duncan, *Making*, 366. **21** *Inchaff. Chrs.*, nos. 78, 82, 84, 94. **22** Barrow, *Kingdom*, 246. **23** For the last, see, for example, NLS Adv. MS 35.2.4, ii, fo. 402; Fraser, *Lennox*, ii, no. 21.

tic evidence, offers intriguing clues about the processes of estate building and the exploitation of scant arable resources in Lennox in the period between the late twelfth and the mid-fourteenth centuries, and demonstrates patterns not found in neighbouring Strathearn.

That the arachor was the Lennox equivalent of the Scottish carucate is made clear in charters such as one of Maoldomhnaich, dated around 1240, in which the earl granted to Sir David de Graham 'the half carucate of Strathblane where the church is built, called in Gaelic Leth-arachor'.[24] Fractions of carucates and arachors were common in the lordship, and, before 1300 at least, few of the earls' tenants could boast holdings of the entire 104 acres estimated to have made up an entire Scots carucate.[25] Maoldomhnaich gifted a carucate and a half to Mael Coluim of Fife on the latter's marriage to Eva of Lennox,[26] and members of the family of Luss received formal grants of the two arachors and more that made up their sizeable lordship on the western shores of Loch Lomond.[27] But a significant number of the earls' tenants made do with half arachors, and the majority with quarters or even half quarters. The precise extent of such lands must have varied somewhat in different parts of Lennox, but fractions of half and less were still substantial endowments. Already by Maoldomhnaich's time the earl was calculating the fiscal obligation to perform forinsec service according to such measures. The precise boundaries described in deeds that transformed carucates and arachors into new estates sometimes covered extensive stretches of territory,[28] and many of the most substantial native tenants of the lordship built their family fortunes on the basis of half arachor holdings.

Small quantities of cultivatable terrain, moreover, were everywhere associated with pasture, and charter references to such lands reveal that Lennox farmers, great and small, were engaged in exploiting to the fullest the limited arable of the region and, wherever possible, in expanding the amount of land under the plough. The twelfth-century grants of Earl Ailin II made generous provision to the church of the grazing lands so essential to agriculture. Thus, the bishop of Glasgow enjoyed access to 'the common pasture of the whole parish of Campsie', while the monks of Paisley abbey had similar rights in the parish of Bonhill.[29] In Maoldomhnaich's time it became common for the earl's *acta* to associate specific stretches of pasture and moor with newly created estates. A grant of 1225 to Paisley abbey, for example, included pasture for eight cows and two horses.[30] Virtually all thirteenth-century deeds included pasture or moorland among the long list of pertinents attached to lands, and such references imply the intensification of agriculture in the earldom. Other evidence of the gradual but steady spread of arable fields and of the practice of assarting is evident in mentions of small parcels of land, such as the *'pecia* called Blarefad', near Drymen, that Maoldomhnaich gave to Gille Brigte of Carrick, or the three acres

---

[24] Fraser, *Lennox*, ii, no. 9; see also no. 11.   [25] G. Whittington, 'Field systems of Scotland' (1973), 543.   [26] Fraser, *Lennox*, ii, no. 202.   [27] Ibid., ii, no. 204.   [28] See, for example, *Lennox Cart.*, 34–5.   [29] *Glasgow Reg.*, i, no. 102; *Paisley Reg.*, 215–17, the latter a confirmation of earlier grants by Earl Maoldomhnaich.   [30] *Paisley Reg.*, 212–13.

carved out near the earls' mill at Balloch for grazing six cows which the abbot of Paisley secured in 1225.[31] Written references to rights granted in lands 'cultivated and uncultivated', a phrase included in charters relating to estates in Strathblane and Killearn, show that newly established tenants had a shrewd appreciation of the potential that their half- and quarter-carucate holdings might yield in future.[32] That arable land was at a premium, moreover, is apparent in the lengthy litigation that pitted Earl Maoldomhnaich and his brother Dùghall, and then the heirs of both, against Paisley abbey in 1233–35, again in 1271 and, finally, 1294–96.[33] Earl Ailin's II's original endowment of lands in 'Monachkenneran', Cochno and elsewhere in the parish of Kilpatrick alienated from the family's control valuable estates in the most fertile portions of the lordship, and the determined efforts of subsequent generations to regain title to them, even in the face of the most severe ecclesiastical censure, speak to the value that landowners placed on such lands. So, too, do the arrangements made by Paisley abbey in 1234 to buy out the rights that the son of the *judex* of Lennox enjoyed in the nearby moor lands of Knock (now Dumbarton Muir), which the abbey needed as it expanded its own arable.[34]

Reclamation from wood, waste, and marsh proceeded apace in the fourteenth century. In the years around 1350 Maurice de Buchanan began to develop the lands around Sallochy, once entirely covered by trees,[35] and members of the Graham family continued the process of extending the arable begun by Sir David in the time of Earl Maoldomhnaich. Some of the islands of Loch Lomond also came under the plough in the later fourteenth century, probably after their forest cover had been burned and wasted by an invading Norwegian army,[36] and a substantial estate at Finnick, near Croy, was split between two tenants, with each acquiring arable, meadow, and pasture.[37] By 1300, the Gaelic lords of Luss were already beginning to reap benefits from crops sown on the slopes leading down to the Loch.[38]

The distribution of Lennox place names containing the Gaelic terms *ach* (field) and *gart* (field, enclosure), many of them in the lowland portions of the lordship, illustrates that lands capable of sustaining cultivated crops had been occupied and farmed from a very early period. The terms *nuighe* and *righe*, which elsewhere in the kingdom identified the summer shielings that were so vital a feature of the pastoral economy, do not appear in Lennox, but other names, including those that include the prefix *craig-* (rock), *drum-* (ridge), and *ard-* (height), suggest that permanent settlements had never been confined to the gentle slopes of the southern and eastern reaches of the earldom. Named arachors and carucates such as Craigrostan, Druminnan, Drumgrew, Drumfad,

[31] *Lennox Cart.*, 43–4, 69. [32] Fraser, *Lennox*, ii, nos. 7, 10, 11. [33] *Paisley Reg.* 164–71, 173–6, 180–98, discussed below, at pp 145–8. [34] *Paisley Reg.*, 178–80; J.C. Lees, *The abbey of Paisley from its foundation till its dissolution* (1878), 51–2; [35] *Lennox Cart.*, 56–8. [36] Anderson (ed.), *Early sources, sub* 1263. [37] *Lennox Cart.*, 45–6, 81–3; J.G. Smith, *Strathendrick and its inhabitants from early times* (1896), 210–12. [38] RCAHMS, *The historical landscape of Loch Lomond and the Trossachs* (2000), 15–16, and Map 8.

Gortachorrans, and Gartbeg, moreover, must always have comprised upland as well as arable terrain. Place names associated with high ground and grazings (*Ard-*, *Ben-*, and *Blair-* or *Blar-* names) abound in the region north of the Endrick, Blane, and Leven valleys, and attest the importance of such lands to the inhabitants of the isolated fermtouns scattered across the northern Lennox countryside, as well as the close link between transhumance and the obligation of each and every household to render its forinsec service in the form of weighty stones of cheese. In a part of the kingdom so dependent on the regular movement of cattle, sheep, and goats to high ground, it is not surprising to find numbers of settlements in the hills and glens of the north evocative of four-legged creatures or their surroundings, including Ardoch ('high place'), Ardlui ('height of the calf'), Ardincaple ('house of the heath or hills'), Ben Chaorach ('hill of the sheep'), Ben Damhain (hill of the red deer'), Blairvaddick ('moor full of cottages'), Blairquhoise ('field at the foot of the hill'), and Glen Fruin ('glen of the place of shelter').

Precisely how the peasants of thirteenth- and fourteenth-century Lennox farmed their lands is difficult to know, in spite of the healthy survival of written deeds from the period. The frequency with which charters describe the boundaries of newly created estates suggests that here, as elsewhere north of Forth generally, arachors and carucates 'were not abstract units of measurements, but compact pieces of arable which [were] not and never [had been] composed of rigs or acres scattered across a large undifferentiated plain of cultivated ground'.[39] Such divisions of land were entirely appropriate to much of the rough terrain that made up highland Lennox. Here, the pertinents included in charters listed plains, moors, hunting grounds and nesting grounds for birds of prey as much as they did fields and meadows, and documents described the earls' annual renders in terms of hawks, deer, fish, butter and cheese as often as they did corn, malt and hay.[40] Occasional glimpses, however, are afforded of the agrarian way of life in the more fertile south. Archaeologists have uncovered traces of intensive rig cultivation in the areas around Mugdock, Campsie, Kilsyth and, further north, Gargunnock, Gartfarren, and Garchell,[41] where medieval improvers succeeded in growing hardy crops. Bovates were not uncommon in a region where arable farms were the exception rather than the norm and cultivated fields were sometimes very small; they appear in the upper reaches of the Leven River,[42] and in numerous grants of half quarters of a carucate or an arachor. Such small parcels of arable are found from Auchincarroch in Bonhill parish, through Gartconnel in Kilpatrick, and northward to Blairfad in Drymen. They show that, in the thirteenth century, even areas of marginal soil might be made to yield crops in the warmer months of the year.

---

39 Barrow, *Kingdom*, 240. **40** In 1496, the king, then resident a his hunting lodge, enjoyed a gift of butter from a 'wife' of a Glen Finglas man. *TA*, i, 274. **41** RCHAMS, *Stirlingshire*, i, 422–3.; see also J.F. Stevenson, 'How ancient is the woodland of Mugdock?' (1990), 164. **42** *Paisley Reg.*, 216, 220.

Irrespective of whether their peasants cultivated arable land collectively or as single families, in davachs, carucates or arachors, notional or measurable acres, the medieval earls of Strathearn and Lennox regularly collected from them a wide array of rents, originally in kind, but also, starting in the mid-thirteenth century, in coin. Foremost among these was the earls' cain, annual payment of which was made as a tribute to their lordship. In a charter of $c.$1199 Gille Brigte assigned to the religious of Inchaffray a tenth of his cain 'in wheat, meal, malt and cheese and in all the other things which I accept as cain'.[43] A subsequent deed enumerates further renders of grain, flour, fish, flesh, beasts taken in the hunt, fowl, fish 'and all that comes to us as food and drink', and a charter of Fergus son of Gille Brigte similarly includes in its reference to cain a wide variety of products.[44] Far from being restricted to specific foodstuffs, as it certainly was elsewhere in Scotland north of Forth,[45] cain in Strathearn may therefore have been levied on virtually all the produce of the earls' lands, woods, waters and even air. The evidence here is ambiguous, however, for a royal confirmation of Gille Brigte's gifts to Inchaffray, dated 1220, makes a careful distinction between cain and other customary renders,[46] and it may be that the Austin canons who acted as Gille Brigte's scribes mistakenly lumped together under an unfamiliar term two sets of distinct obligations. The grain produced in the arable portions of the earldom included not merely wheat, bere, and barley, but also oats, found in a charter of Fergus son of Gille Brigte in the mid 1240s, and perhaps rye, believed to have been grown on a small scale in the central belt of the kingdom.[47] The presence of numerous mills within the lordship and grants of multure further attest the cultivation of corn.

Of another traditional form of tribute, long owed in Scotland north of Forth, that is the obligatory hospitality known as conveth, Strathearn charters have rather less to say. The toun of Exmagirdle was rendering conveth in the early years of the thirteenth century, when it was commuted to a money payment.[48] At the end of the same century the earl was accustomed to receive from the tenants of Dunning a *frithelagium*, which by then had also been converted into a money payment, this one of four merks annually.[49] This reference suggests that within the lordship the unit of assessment for conveth was the shire or thanage, as it was in regions elsewhere in the kingdom where it was customary.[50] If so, the earl's representative in another comital thanage, that of Strowan, must also have been responsible for collecting such dues, first in kind, then later in money, but although the thane of Strowan appears as a witness in Strathearn charters, there are no other specific references in surviving documents to *coinmheadh*, *frithelagium*, or the Scots English equivalent, wayting. But echoes of the obligation there may well have been in the seven women who accompanied

---

43 *Inchaff. Chrs.*, no. 5. **44** Ibid., no. 16; *Lind. Cart.*, no. 24. **45** Duncan, *Making,* 153–4. **46** *Inchaff. Chrs.*, no. 40. **47** *Inchaff. Liber*, no. 10; Duncan, *Making,* 323. **48** *Lind. Cart.*, no. 42 **49** *Inchaff. Chrs.*, no. 113; *Inchaff. Liber,* no. 14. Frithelagium was 'the equivalent of conveth'; see Barrow, *Kingdom*, 39. **50** Ibid., 36.

Edward I with song and dance through the lands of Strathearn in 1296.[51] Customary rituals such as feasting and guesting were part and parcel of the general burden of hospitality that tenants owed their overlords from ancient times, and were especially deeply ingrained in native Gaelic society.[52] Edward I's summoning of the women of Strathearn shows that he understood only too well the symbolic value of using local custom to serve his interests. In the tense summer months of 1296 his appropriation of the ceremonies that had attended King Alexander III can hardly have gone unnoticed.

By the late thirteenth century the goods and services payable as conveth had become commuted to money payments in most parts of the realm, and the spread of such commutation to Strathearn probably accounts for the paucity of clear references to the obligation in surviving charter materials. Rather more surprising is the lack of specific reference to *can* and *coinmheadh* in written deeds from Lennox. A distaste for terms that were strongly Gaelic in flavour on the part of Latin-trained scribes may be wholly to blame here, for there is evidence that the native lords were as dependent on such renders as were their fellows elsewhere in Scotland. References to a tenth of 'corn, hay, multures, wool, cloth, cheese, butter, victuals, lambs, pigs, foals, and roe-bucks', such as that found in a grant of Earl Maoldomhnaich to the bishop of Glasgow, look very much like those of Earl Gille Brigte of Strathearn to his monastic foundation at Inchaffray, and may indeed replicate the blurring found in the latter of the distinction between traditional renders of cain and tithable goods generally.[53] The same charter, moreover, refers to the obligation of Lennox tenants to offer lodging and food to the *ketheres* of the earl, officials charged with travelling around the lands of the earldom on their lord's judicial business.[54] Not surprisingly, given the limited extent of arable liable for payment of cain and conveth, thirteenth-century Lennox charters include occasional mention of a limited variety of grains and their by-products, notably corn, flour, and malt.[55] Instead, renders were levied predominantly on the produce of the rich pastoral lands of the earldom. They must have included, above all, cheese, which is more certainly named as cain in other parts of Scotland north of Forth.[56] It was produced in such quantities in Lennox that it constituted the region's chief contribution to the king's common army,[57] and in the late thirteenth century Malcolm I could demand of a single tenant an annual rent of no less than twenty stones of cheese.[58]

Cain in Lennox may also have been assessed on another of its most abundant commodities, fish. The evidence here is problematic, but if cain is indeed to be understood as a render 'paid in the produce of the area',[59] then the abundant supply of fish from the numerous streams, rivers and lochs of the lordship

[51] *CDS*, iv, 475. [52] K. Simms, 'Guesting and feasting in Gaelic Ireland' (1978–9). [53] *Glasgow Reg.*, i, no. 141. [54] G.W.S. Barrow, 'Northern English society in the twelfth and thirteenth centuries' (1969), 22–3. [55] *Lennox Cart.*, 81; NLS Adv. MS. 35.2.4, ii, 402–6; *Paisley Reg.*, 158–9; *Glasgow Reg.*, i, no. 141. [56] Duncan, *Making*, 153. [57] Fraser, *Lennox*, ii, nos. 204, 207; *Lennox Cart.*, 19–20; RMS, i, no. 371; ii, no. 187; Royal Faculty of Procurators, Glasgow, Macfarlane Muniments ii, no. 73. [58] *Lennox Cart.*, 45–6. [59] Duncan, *Making*, 154.

may have been liable to this obligation. Animals such as pigs, lambs, cows, oxen and foals, all mentioned frequently in the charters, may similarly have been the stuff of lordly cain. More certainly, such commodities were considered tithable.

The image of the rural economy that emerges from Strathearn and Lennox charters is one of a predominantly pastoral society, regulated in its daily life and over its calendar year by the need to care for the oxen and cows, the sheep, the pigs, and the horses that were its most precious commodities. In the former, a zone stretching from the foothills of the Ochill range northwards to the braes of Fowlis Wester, and from there east to the Firth of Tay and the boundaries of the earldom of Fife afforded comital tenants, especially those newly introduced into the earldom, the opportunity to establish small nucleated settlements with infields and outfields of the type found in the borders and central and eastern lowlands. With much of its territory lying well above the twenty-five metre line, the topography of Lennox was considerably harsher. But in the southern and eastern reaches of the lordship, in the valleys of the Leven, the Blane, the Endrick and the Clyde Rivers, small nucleated settlements exploited to the full the limited extent of arable. In both lordships moors and pasture land alternated with dense regions of woodland, very little of it subject to the disafforestation that had already by the late thirteenth century altered irrevocably the landscape of Scotland south of Forth.[60]

As was the case all over western Europe, the expanding economy of the century or so after 1200 created new opportunities for lords in Scotland to establish lucrative monopolies in their lands and to exploit hitherto untapped sources of revenue. The native earls of Strathearn and Lennox were quick to adapt traditional notions of lordship to changing market conditions and, in some cases, were prepared to invest capital in the development or creation of promising new resources. Such, for example, were the establishment of stone quarries, the erection of mills and breweries, and the laying of turbaries that the lords of both regions undertook. The first, in particular, was an industry that required considerable financial outlay for labourers, both skilled and unskilled, but the judicious use of navigable rivers and other bodies of water greatly facilitated the transportation of stone and helped to offset costs. Earl Malise II of Strathearn established a quarry at Nethergask out of which he made gifts of building materials to Inchaffray abbey, but he jealously guarded its revenues from other tenants.[61] The construction of mills on the Pow Burn, at Gorthy, and at Dunfallin in Strathearn, and at Balloch, Croy and 'Aschend' in Lennox, similarly required considerable capital outlay. In the early years of the thirteenth century the brethren of Inchaffray were keen to secure similar revenues, and in 1200 they sought from Earl Gille Brigte leave to build an abbey mill. The earl agreed, but carefully reserved to himself the multures of his own tenants. The wording of a second grant concerning the abbey's mill, made some twenty years later, was considerably more terse and abrupt than the first had been, suggesting that com-

60 R.A. Dodgshon, 'Medieval rural Scotland' (1983), 52. 61 *Inchaff. Chrs.*, no. 95.

petition between the earl and the canons for limited resources from the structures had increased considerably.[62] The early earls of Lennox also carefully regulated access to the profits of their mills. They surrendered shares in multures as occasional gifts to Glasgow cathedral and, as the thirteenth century wore on and the value of these resources accrued, as the stuff of grants to especially favoured tenants.[63] The native earls were equally ready to turn the sale of peat, malt and ale into lucrative ventures,[64] and, in later thirteenth-century Lennox at least, to use shares in such revenues to supplement and complement small grants of land in order to attract new tenants to their territory. Still other, more modest, sources of ready money were the roads that ran through Strathearn and Lennox, the *viae* and *semitae* listed so conscientiously by the clerks who drafted later medieval charters. Malise II's grant to the canons of Inchaffray of free passage on the roads leading into Nethergask suggests that other travellers paid tolls for the privilege of using them.[65]

By the opening years of the fourteenth century the rents and revenues that flowed into comital coffers were rich and varied. The clauses listing the pertinents attached to lands, once believed by scholars to be meaningless jingles, are now much better understood as important indicators of the extent to which some lords exploited the resources at their disposal. By the time of Earls Malise IV and V in Strathearn and Earl Donald in Lennox the clauses were rich in detail and demonstrate clearly that these lords understood full well the substantial range of economic interests that comprised landed estates. The expansion of a 'monetized society' and a steady rise in prices for virtually all commodities enabled Scottish landlords of all ranks to turn the resources of their lands into new sources of wealth. The Gaelic lords of Srathearn and Lennox proved as adept at taking advantage of changing economic circumstances as did the English and continental newcomers. In some respects, in fact, the strength of traditional claims to the products of their lands and waters may better have positioned them to venture into the new economy, and to establish secure title over a still expanding range of lordly perquisites.

Lordly authority brought with it not merely valuable monopolies over such things as mills and breweries, but a host of lucrative rights over the labour and the persons of tenants and farmers, free and unfree. The shifting economic and cultural climates of the period between 1170 and 1365 exerted a powerful influence on the ways in which the native lords of Scotland gave expression to their authority over men, especially those of low status. The fines traditionally associated with legal servitude in Scotland, merchet, heriot and forfeiture, appear in the earliest Strathearn and Lennox charters, usually as appurtenances associated with estates of land.[66] Such, for example, were the *omnia forisfacta* that Gille Brigte granted to the prior and canons of Inchaffray when he gave them leave

---

62 *Inchaff. Liber*, no. 27; *Inchaff. Chrs.*, no. 39. **63** *Glasgow Reg.*, i, no. 141; *Lennox Cart.*, 40–1, 43–4, 46–8, 69–70. **64** *Inchaff. Chrs.*, nos. 76, 113; *Lennox Cart.*, 42, 46–8. **65** *Inchaff. Chrs.*, no. 95; see also *Lennox Cart.*, 40–1. **66** *Inchaff. Chrs.*, no. 43.

to hold courts of their own, and the *prisonibus et eschaetis et forisfactis et merchetis* that constituted part of Earl Maoldomhnaich of Lennox's grant of the lands of Luss to his kinsman Gille Moire son of Maoldomhnaich.[67] There was a marked tendency among the scribes employed in both lordships to use more sophisticated terminology as the thirteenth century wore on, and for the ambiguous 'forfeitures' and 'amercements' of early written deeds to become more clearly distinguished, after 1250, as merchets, heriots, escheats, and forfeitures. Later still, the scribes began to differentiate the fines levied for minor offences from those imposed on more serious infractions. Thus, the term 'bloodwite', signifying fines levied on assaults that involved the drawing of blood, does not appear in Strathearn until 1260, and only later still, around 1290, in Lennox.[68] Just what kinds of income these levies represented is almost impossible to determine. In the Gaelic regions of Scotland, as elsewhere, they may have amounted to little more than the 'trivial' sums that the earls of Fife are known to have collected.[69] But in Strathearn and Lennox, again as elsewhere, the symbolic importance of such fines was of far greater moment that their monetary value, particularly in the thirteenth century, when the changing culture and the quickening economy of the kingdom were profoundly affecting the relationship between lords and their peasants. In the early years of the century, Gille Brigte of Strathearn steadily augmented his gifts of a teind of the profits of his court to the canons of Inchaffray by including in his grants the monetary fines levied there, as well as the chattels of convicted offenders. Eventually, he even allowed the abbey to convene courts of its own. But outside the circle of his immediate family members, no other lay tenant enjoyed such comprehensive privileges.[70] Similarly, although Maoldomhnaich of Lennox occasionally included among his grants of land leave to hold courts and to collect the fines arising from cases heard in them,[71] it was not until after his death and the accession of his grandson and heir that the earls extended such prerogatives on a regular basis to their greater tenants, Gaelic or foreign. Magnates of all sorts constantly sought ways in which they might demonstrate their authority over men, and legal rights over the persons and the movements of their peasants still counted for a great deal in the later thirteenth century. Thus, Earl Malise II's grant of two serfs to Inchaffray abbey[72] served not only to build much needed capital for his afterlife, but also as a reminder to the unfree population of his lands that lordship might be exercised in all powerful ways.

Lordship over the lairdly and noble tenants of Strathearn and Lennox certainly weighed less onerously than it did over peasants, but the earls prized its prerogatives, real and symbolic, no less. The haphazard survival of written deeds

---

67 *Lennox Cart.*, 19–20. **68** NAS, GD 220/1/A1/3/3, 4; *Lennox Cart.*, 43–4. See also below, p. 126. **69** Duncan, *Making*, 338. **70** *Inchaff. Chrs.*, nos 25, 39, 43. Fergus son of Gille Brigte presided over a court, a prerogative which he inherited, together with his lands, from his uncle Maol Iosa. *Coupar Angus Chrs.*, i, no. 35. **71** Fraser, *Lennox*, ii, no. 7. **72** *Inchaff. Chrs.*, no. 87; *Inchaff. Liber* no, 58.

prior to the late twelfth century makes it difficult to define precisely both the nature of lordly authority and its relative value to the native earls. The richly varied entries in the Book of Deer leave little doubt that the mormaers of the early twelfth century enjoyed extensive rights even over lands that they alienated. From those directly under their control they derived a variety of 'taxes and services',[73] and such dues were rendered in kind, either in animals, grains, or other foodstuffs. Some of the cheese that Lennox farmers produced in such large quantities, for example, must have found its way into the earls' households in partial payment of his *cuit*, or 'cut'.[74] In addition, the juxtaposition of their roles as great territorial magnates and heads of extensive kin networks gave the mormaers of old an important say in the succession of estates form one generation to the next, and the passing of lands from father to son must also have offered lords the opportunity to demand and to receive tangible symbols of their rank and lordship. The thirteenth-century earl, Niall of Carrick, it has been shown, attached considerable significance to the economic benefits that accrued to him as ' kenkynnol', or head of his kindred.[75] Although the term *cenn cenéoil* does not appear in Strathearn or Lennox charters, the officials associated with the collection of tribute money on behalf of an early thirteenth-century earl of Lennox, the *ketheres*, certainly do,[76] and, as in Carrick, claims to *calp* and other forms of tribute were already old here in the thirteenth century.[77] The financial burdens of lordship were sometimes very onerous, and the exemptions from a long list of traditional exactions as well as from the obligation to house and feed his large entourage that Maoldomhnaich regularly granted to the monks of Paisley abbey clearly represented generous concessions.

The ambiguous rights and privileges characteristic of Gaelic lordship were ill suited to the precise terminology that, beginning in the twelfth century, scribes all over Scotland began to employ in royal and baronial charters. Yet, it took a remarkably long time for much of the vocabulary of English lordship to permeate written deeds in both Strathearn and Lennox. The one exception was the term 'aids' which, when it first appeared in a Strathearn charter dated 1211 x 1214, and in a Lennox deed about a decade later, had already become something of a catch-all word to designate a wide variety of renders arising out of the general obligation to perform military service.[78] The terms traditionally associated with classical 'feudalism', however, notably wardship, relief, and marriage, penetrated into Strathearn only in the early years of the fourteenth century.[79] Wards, reliefs, and the profits associated with the marriage of heiresses made their appearance earlier in Lennox, around 1240, but significantly these occur in a grant of land and privilege made in favour of a newcomer to the earldom, Sir David de Graham.[80] Tenants of native descent had to wait until after

---

73 K. Jackson, *The Gaelic notes in the Book of Deer* (1972), 19–24. **74** Ibid., 109, 119; Duncan, *Making*, 389. **75** H.L. MacQueen, 'The laws of Galloway: a preliminary survey' (1991), 131–8; idem, 'Survival and success: the Kennedys of Dunure' (2003), 76. **76** *Glasgow Reg.*, i, no. 141. **77** MacQueen, 'Laws of Galloway', 133. **78** *Lind. Cart.*, no. 42; Fraser, *Lennox*, ii, no. 204; Duncan, *Making*, 389. **79** *Inchaff. Liber*, App., no. 24. **80** Fraser, *Lennox*, ii, no. 2.

1300, and the rule of Maoldomhnaich's great-grandson, Malcolm II, to claim a share of the potentially lucrative revenues arising from such incidents, and it is perhaps no mere coincidence that when Malcolm II did agree to share his authority to demand wardship and relief and to control the marriage of heiresses, it was to a representative of one of the lordship's most ancient and prestigious families, Malcolm of Luss.[81]

The relative scarcity of terms normally associated with feudal incidents in Strathearn and Lennox may represent little more than a consequence of the uneven survival there of charters in favour of lay beneficiaries. But the preponderance of other evidence relating to the social, political and economic structure of these lordships suggests that other factors were at work. In recent years scholars have much debated military service and land tenure in later medieval Scotland, as well as the nature of the link between them. One school argues that the tenure of land was only one of an array of bonds that tied knights to barons, that it was merely 'coincidental', rather than integral to the lord-man relationship.[82] In such a view, lordly rights of wardship, relief, and marriage had little meaning other than as sources of revenue that might be commuted into annual cash payments and granted away at the lord's whim. Such 'fiscal tenure' was the feu ferm tenure so beloved of later medieval charter scribes, and reflected an 'essentially commercial attitude adopted towards feudal casualties' characteristic of Scotland by the early years of the thirteenth century. In this interpretation, moreover, tenure by blench ferme that is, by the periodic render of some symbolic object (gloves, spurs, sparrowhawks) served little purpose but to remind men that a conveyance of land had taken place; similarly, homage and fealty were merely 'reminders of obligations wider than an annual feu duty'. Critics of this fiscal interpretation of lord-man ties argue that, on the contrary, bonds between knights and barons were based ultimately on the tenure of land and the obligation to perform military service for it, however variably that obligation might be expressed. Thus, Alexander Grant has suggested that tenure by blench ferm relieved a tenant only of specific 'feudal' obligations (wardship, relief, and marriage), but not 'of the more general service that any lord would expect from his man',[83] and that the link between the 'more general' services and an estate of land remained the predominant model of lord-man relationships well into the early modern period.

The debate about lord-man ties and the tenure of land is of especial pertinence to a discussion of native lordship in the period 1170–1365, though the nature of surviving charter materials precludes a firm resolution of the historiographical debate. It is clear that the native earls exercised a wide ranging control over the lands of their tenants. The displacement of a handful of Gaelic tenants in favour of newcomers to their territories, the creation of what amounted to new tenancies out of lands long held by kin groups, and the records of

---

[81] *Lennox Cart.*, 23–4. [82] Duncan, *Making*, 391–409. [83] A. Grant, 'Service and tenure in late medieval Scotland, 1314–1475' (2000), 160.

inquests, such as the one held in 1263 to determine the age of the heir of a Lennox tenant, leave little doubt that those rights were extensive.[84] Yet the charter materials offer mixed evidence about the value that the native earls placed on such prerogatives. Around 1240, for example, Maoldomhnaich of Lennox was willing to surrender all his claims to wardships, reliefs, marriages, and other rights in Strathblane to Sir David de Graham for a mere three merks per annum, and he soon remitted the sum entirely.[85] In 1255, on the other hand, Malise II of Strathearn paid a fine of £100 in gold to the king of England for the custody, warship and marriage of his two daughters by Marjory de Muschamp, and subsequently spent considerable sums of money defending their title to their grandfather's estates in Northumberland.[86] But those lands were vast, and the expenses that Malise invested in the litigation must have been considered well worth the potential returns. Similarly, in 1310 Malise III fought hard to maintain control over the wardship of the young Strathearn nobleman, Malise de Logie, taking on that 'shifty opportunist', Gilbert de Malherbe of Stirlingshire.[87] By contrast, in the 1320s, when Malise IV ceded to John de Moravia of Drumsagard 'all wardships, reliefs, marriage fines and other customs and exactions which may in future be demanded' from the lands of Abercairney, he did so in blench ferme.[88]

If the monetary value of such casualties was negligible, their symbolic worth – like the earls' jurisdictional powers – was high, and for this reason alone worth preserving. Maoldomhnaich's son, Mael Coluim, objected strenuously to the arrangement his father made with Sir David de Graham in respect of the annual render from Strathblane.[89] His discontent can hardly have been caused by the loss of an income of three merks per annum. More intriguingly, it may have reflected Mael Coluim's uneasiness with the surrender of lordly prerogative that the grant represented. In similar fashion, the English phrase 'homage and service' meant something more than a mere abstraction to the native lords of Strathearn and Lennox, for it began to appear in their charters soon after 1200, much earlier than did other terms associated with 'feudal' tenure. Precisely what these terms represented is rather less certain, but a deed of Malcolm I of Lennox, dated c.1280, is instructive.[90] In it, the earl recalled his grandfather's grant in perpetuity of the lands of Luss to Gille Moire son of Maoldomhnaich, and noted that 'the said charter did not specify any form of homage due for the said lands'. The earl went on to confirm title to the estate to Malcolm and his heirs, required that 'as a sole mark of homage' Malcolm render two cheeses every year to the common army of the king, and specifically exempted the family from the obligation to pay 'wardships, reliefs, marriages, suits of court and all other services'. The unusual wording of this charter surely speaks to Earl Malcolm's attempt to emphasize and to publicise, in the language of his day, the especially close and loving relationship that existed between his own family and that of Luss. No

---

[84] See chapter 2.   [85] Fraser, *Lennox*, ii nos. 6, 7.   [86] Neville, 'Earls of Strathearn', i, 109–12.
[87] CDS, iii, no. 410; Barrow, *Robert Bruce*, 310.   [88] *Inchaff. Liber*, App., no. 24.   [89] Fraser, *Lennox*, ii, no. 8.   [90] *Lennox Cart.*, 23–4.

other tenant was so favoured: in Lennox, as in Strathearn, most men held their lands by knight service, in feu and heritage, or by blench ferme, and all owed homage as well as service of one kind or another to their overlords. It may well be that of all the new terms imported into Strathearn and Lennox in the wake of European settlement, the phrase 'homage and service', with its ambiguous connotation of loyalty, fidelity, and service accomplished most smoothly the transition from the cultural world of England and the continent to that of the Gaels, and why the terms appeared so much earlier in Strathearn and Lennox charters than did others. All lay tenants, great and small, native and newcomer, had traditionally been required to show the earls respect, and to render them the services associated with magnate status. What changed in the early thirteenth century was not the obligation to demonstrate such respect by performing 'homage' and rendering 'service', but the practice of articulating such duties in the formal language now current in land holding circles.

That the symbols of lordship weighed more heavily in the minds of the native earls of Strathearn and Lennox than did specific services is also revealed, if indirectly, in the frequency with which their charters required of lay beneficiaries only token renders for the lands and privileges they received. The significance of the objects that were the stuff of blench ferme renders has not attracted much attention from historians. Yet, the society in which such exchanges occurred was only just becoming familiar with the written deed as a normal feature of conveyance, and one still closely attuned to the symbolic meaning of objects as varied as gospel books, rods, jewels, and, above all, relics. The transition from the highly ritualized ceremonies in which land had been conveyed in pre-'feudal' Scotland into a setting in which title to estate was increasingly linked to possession of a written deed was a gradual process, perhaps nowhere more so than in the great native lordships that lay north of Forth, beyond the zone of intensive English and continental settlement. The slow pace in which change permeated the lands of Strathearn and Lennox, evident in so many aspects of its cultural, political and economic history, is apparent, finally, in the fact that until well into the thirteenth century annual blench ferme renders demanded of tenants of native descent continued to be offered in objects rather than coin: golden spurs and white gloves in Strathearn, golden spurs, roebucks and does in Lennox. By contrast, renders in coin, chiefly silver pennies, were demanded almost exclusively of tenants of English or continental background newly settled in the earls' territories. Only after 1260 did coin renders became the norm in either of the earldoms. In such small but significant ways did the native lords demonstrate their interest in preserving the cultural legacy of Gaeldom in the face of change.

The increasing monetization of thirteenth-century Scottish society effected profound changes in the ways that the great native lords ruled their territories and interacted with their tenants, but innovations in estate management and in the conveyance of land were nevertheless shaped by older notions of lordship and lordly authority. The enduring influence of the past was felt especially keenly in the development of the nascent common law of Scotland. It is now well understood that the legal system of the thirteenth century was very much a hybrid, in which customary practices were 'modified, re-named and adapted without doing too much violence to the native tradition'.[91] The blend of old and new is apparent in an examination of the ways in which the earls of Strathearn and Lennox governed their native tenants in the decades between 1200 and 1365, and in the changing nature of lord-man relationships.

In the late twelfth century all magnates, Gaelic-, French- and English-speaking, enjoyed a wide ranging authority to settle disputes that arose among their tenants, kinsmen, and followers. As heads of extensive kin groups, the native earls played especially important roles as arbitrators and mediators in settings other than formal tribunals. Such extra curial activity has left little trace in written record, but settlements achieved in this fashion may well lie concealed behind charters that describe the subdivision of large estates into smaller units, the carving out of new boundaries from previously unmarched lands, or the sale or exchange of tenancies, all of which are well attested in surviving documents. References to the *breitheamh (judex)* in Strathearn and Lennox deeds, however, suggest that justice was regularly meted out in courts attended by the free tenants of the province. When, as his father's heir, for example, Robert of Strathearn undertook to safeguard the interests of Inchaffray abbey, he did so in a formal gathering of Strathearn tenants.[92] The healing of the rift that developed between Maoldomhnaich of Lennox's son, Mael Coluim, and Sir David de Graham, marked by the issue of a charter, was also accomplished before an assembly of Lennox land holders.[93] In both territories, however, the formal language of Anglo-Norman style lordship and of English influenced law permeated the earls' written *acta* only gradually. Those hallmarks of English 'feudal' obligations, suit of court and head courts, do not make an appearance until after 1250, and when they do, these references are confined almost exclusively to charters issued in favour of non-native beneficiaries. Thus, the first mention of a tenant's duty to perform 'suit of the earl of Strathearn's court' comes in a deed of Earl Malise III, dated 1282 x 1289, when Malise de Logie, an up and coming young nobleman, was excused from the obligation.[94] The earl's capital courts are not noted until the 1320s.[95] In Lennox, suit of the earl's court occurs considerably earlier but, tellingly, only in deeds granted to French- and English-speaking tenants newly established in the earldom,[96] and not until the time of Malcolm I, towards the end of the thirteenth century, was the term used with any regularity in Lennox deeds.

The late date of these references suggests that for much of the thirteenth century the courts of the earls of Strathearn and Lennox retained much of their character as provincial assemblies, of the kind attested in Fife a hundred years earlier, as well as elsewhere north of Forth.[97] Although trained in the Latin char-

---

91 Sellar, 'Celtic law and Scots law', 6.   **92** *Inchaff. Liber*, no. 16.   **93** Fraser, *Lennox*, ii, no. 8   **94** Fraser, *Grandtully*, i, App., no. 69.   **95** *Inchaff. Liber*, App., no. 24; *RRS*, vi, no. 482.   **96** Fraser, *Lennox*, ii, nos. 7, 10, 11.   **97** Duncan, *Making*, 167–8; A. Grant, *Independence and nationhood:*

ter tradition, the clerics who wrote their deeds demonstrated a remarkable sensitivity to the ways in which the native earls conceived of, and in turn gave expression to, their lordship. They understood intuitively that these lords still held in great esteem the prerogatives that their predecessors had enjoyed. In this Gaelic world view, pre-eminence in a court of free tenants, a controlling interest in the disposition of lands, and the settling of quarrels among their followers all counted for at least as much as did cash revenues that might accrue to comital coffers from the sale, lease, or grant of the incidents of lordship, if not more. For much of the thirteenth century, moreover, the earls' native tenants thought likewise. The absence from the written deeds of both Strathearn and Lennox of the vocabulary found in the charters of English and continental magnates attests a strong preference on the part of native land holders for ambiguity in the language used to describe their lords' courts. Only towards the end of the thirteenth century, when the distinction between tenants of native Gaelic descent and those of English or continental provenance began to blur, did such conservatism begin to disappear. By the year 1300, the impulse to harken back to the cultural distinctions of an earlier age had waned among Scottish noblemen, great and small. Gaelic custom had merged with continental practice to create a uniquely Scottish nobility and new concepts of lordship. Equally important, the growing complexity of the rules governing land tenure had done much to stimulate the development of a common law of property in Scotland. The consequence of all these changes was a 'new endeavour to define rights and privileges' in written *acta*,[98] and an increasing emphasis on the privileges that distinguished the higher from the lesser nobility.[99] In jostling for a place among the privileged few entitled to describe themselves as barons, the earls of Strathearn and Lennox, like the lords of Galloway, Mar, Fife, and the other ancient provinces north of Forth consciously adopted the 'manners and modes' of Scottish courtly society, from which earlier distinctions of race and, to an increasing extent, language, were fast disappearing.[1] Their scribes likewise consciously adopted the language of Scottish courtly society to describe the business that was conducted in their courts. The assembly before which, in 1272, the heirs of Dùghall son of Ailin solemnly renounced their wives' titles to lands in Kilpatrick, over which Earl Malcolm I of Lennox presided, looked very much like those that would have been convened in the neighbouring Stewart lands.[2] Its suitors, Gaelic- and Scots-speaking, regarded attendance there no longer as a burden incumbent on them as tenants of these great lords, but as formal 'recognition of [their] social distinction'.[3] In the new cultural milieu of the early fourteenth century, moreover, status and prestige were enhanced by close association with the king's inner circle. Malcolm II's appointment in 1309 as sheriff of

Scotland 1306–1469 (1984), 136. **98** W.C. Dickinson, 'The administration of justice in medieval Scotland' (1952), 341. **99** Grant, *Independence*, 121–7. **1** K.J. Stringer, 'Acts of lordship: the records of the lords of Galloway to 1234' (2000), 210. **2** *Paisley Reg.*, 192–5, 197–203. **3** Duncan, *Making*, 407.

Clackmannan, then as sheriff of Dumbarton in 1321, must have done much to amplify his authority at home in Lennox, as did the king's grant of the right to conduct wappinshaws within his territories.[4]

If there is plentiful evidence of the native earls' capacity to summon the free tenantry of Strathearn and Lennox and to preside over them in the company of *breitheamhnan*, the extent of their jurisdiction over criminal offences is rather less certain. Understanding the nature of lordly justice in the period before 1200 has proved a vexatious exercise to even the most seasoned scholars,[5] and while it is now well known that the reigns of William I and Alexander II were crucial in the development of royal justice in much of the southern reaches of the kingdom, the pace and the nature of change in the great lordships north of Forth has been less well explored. Often cited in discussions of criminal justice is a royal assize of 1197, in which William threatened to suspend the franchisal courts of magnates who failed to punish violent offenders in their midst;[6] a decade earlier, in fact, the king had taken into his own hands the punishment of such malefactors in Galloway.[7] Such legislation suggests that jurisdiction over criminals was, and probably long had been, the responsibility of the mormaers, acting simultaneously as provincial governors and heads of extensive kin networks. Punishments varied according to the severity of the offence, but the system of kin based justice laid equal emphasis on the status of the victim, with compensation or restitution for acts of violence expressed in a series of tariffs resembling the 'Laws of the Bretts and Scots' that Edward I later condemned as antiquated and barbaric.[8]

In the closing years of the twelfth century change was very much in the air, and William's reign in particular saw the rapid development of the office of justiciar, the deployment of sheriffs across a considerable portion of the realm, and the steady reservation of the four pleas of the crown (murder, rape, arson, and violent affray) to the king's agents. Earl Gille Brigte of Strathearn's appointment as justiciar of Scotia neatly merged the extensive authority he exercised as mormaer with that of the crown, [9] and his intermittent tenure of that office in the later twelfth century must have elided the distinction between baronial and royal jurisdiction in that part of the realm. The crown had to wait a little longer to make a clear statement of its authority over legal affairs in Lennox, but in 1233 Alexander II successfully transferred the dispute over the lands of Kilpatrick to the court of his justiciar, ironically the earl's own father-in-law.[10] It was perhaps in assertion or defence of his customary prerogatives that, just three years later, when he accepted a royal charter for the earldom, Maoldomhnaich insisted that the deed include a clause reserving to him *sacca et socca cum furca cum tholo*

---

4 *RRS*, v, nos. 11, 194; NLS Adv. MS 34.3.25, fos. 80–81. As late as the 1350s, Donald earl of Lennox was still reserving to himself the summoning of wappinshaws; *RMS*, i, no. 371; *RRS*, v, no. 478. **5** See, for example, *RRS*, ii, 48–51. **6** Duncan, *Making*, 202–3. **7** Ibid., 185–6. **8** *APS*, i, 663–5; Grant, *Independence,* 158. **9** *RRS*, i, no. 337; Barrow, *Kingdom,* 66, 110. **10** *Paisley Reg.*, 170–1.

et theame et infangendthef; that is, the jurisdiction over life and limb that great native magnates had always enjoyed.[11]

Royal challenges to the exercise of baronial justice did not, however, provoke open resistance in Strathearn or Lennox. In part, this was because the new sheriffdoms created in the course of the later twelfth and the early thirteenth centuries lay beyond the lands controlled by the great native earls. In effect, the latter supplemented, rather than competed with, the work of the former,[12] and within their own territories Gille Brigte, Maoldomhnaich, and their successors remained largely undisturbed in the business of dealing with violent troublemakers. Equally important in this context was the nature of Scottish criminal justice itself. As has been aptly noted, its administration belonged above all to local communities, with suitors to the earls' courts responsible for detecting, apprehending, and prosecuting offences, and the *breitheamhnan* charged with passing sentence.[13] At once secure and competent in their role as conveners of the courts, the earls posed no threat to the Scottish crown's avowed aim of maintaining law and order in the localities. Together, these factors also explain why the native lords of Strathearn and Lennox found little need to seek the royal seal of approval that, increasingly after 1300, sent many important landowners to the royal court in search of grants *in liberam baroniam* or *in regalitatem*. The native earls of Lennox never sought from the crown the comprehensive authority inherent in such grants, although the powers they exercised were certainly commensurate with those of lords of regality elsewhere in the kingdom. Similarly, the lands of Strathearn were not erected into a regality until after the death of the last earl of the Gaelic line.[14] It is tempting, in fact, to see in the charter issued in favour of David Stewart earl of Strathearn a deliberate effort on the part of the crown to replicate there by royal fiat the kind of overweening authority over kinsmen and other lay tenants that a long line of native earls had previously enjoyed by right of custom and tradition.

The thirteenth-century earls of Strathearn and Lennox must have regarded the power of life and death inherent in the concept of high justice that English and continental settlers brought to Scotland with profound awe and respect, for the punishments for serious offences invoked in the kin based law with which they were familiar were above all those of compensation, reparation and restitution. They were certainly quick to grasp its potential for enhancing the already comprehensive judicial authority they enjoyed as provincial rulers. Accordingly, they shared it only rarely and selectively. Gille Brigte's generous grants to Inchaffray included permission for the brethren to convene a court of their own for tenants on priory lands, but he specifically reserved to his own officials the right to hang convicted felons.[15] Maol Iosa son of Fearchar acquired powers of high justice as a special gift from his brother Gille Brigte, and together with his estates passed these on to his nephew and heir Fergus. The latter proved equally

---

11 *Lennox Cart.*, 1–2.   12 Duncan, *Making*, 207.   13 Grant, *Independence*, 157–8.   14 *RMS*, i, nos. 404, 526, 538.   15 *Inchaff.Chrs.*, nos. 25, 43.

sensitive to the dignity that such privilege represented, and in a charter to the religious of Coupar Angus carefully stated that 'all sentences of judgment of water or iron, of loss of limb or beheading passed against the abbey's tenants shall be carried out by Fergus or his men' on his own gallows.[16] In Lennox, Maoldomhnaich was even more circumspect. He withheld the right to erect pit and gallows or to hold judicial duels even from Mael Coluim of Fife, for example, and from other great tenants.[17] Despite pressure from men who considered the privilege of high justice a hallmark of baronial status, in the fourteenth century his successors Malcolm I and Malcolm II were still reserving such rights to themselves; so, too, did Earl Donald and Walter de Faslane lord of Lennox as late as 1360.

The definition and expression of lordly authority were transformed in the course of the thirteenth century. So, too, were notions of lordly power. 'Power itself', it has been remarked, 'is not a resource ... but is exercised through material culture'.[18] In medieval Scotland, castles were the most ubiquitous sites of power, but so also were places identified closely with the exercise of lordly authority, popular courts and legal centres. The earls of Strathearn and Lennox used all of these in highly effective fashion as symbols and bulwarks of lordship, adapting their practices as the thirteenth century wore on to suit the changing nature of lordship itself.

Recent studies of castle architecture in the period between 1100 and 1300 in Scotland have revealed patterns of construction and fortification wholly distinct from those of neighbouring England. In areas of intensive English and continental settlement, chiefly (but not exclusively) the region south of Forth, the creation of new lordships was sometimes accompanied by the erection of the motte and bailey style structures typical of the 'feudal' nobility of post-Conquest England. But on many sites landowners appear to have been satisfied only with mottes, suggesting a lack of interest in establishing permanent garrisons designed to dominate the local countryside.[19] More intriguing still are the comparatively few sites on which early timber fortifications were replaced with more expensive, and more impressive, stone structures. 'Certain members of the Scottish nobility', it has been remarked, 'did build castles which were intended to signify wealth and status, but most were also content with the knowledge of who they were, and did not disguise themselves behind the grandeur of their curtain walls'.[20] A distinct lack of interest in building on a grand scale is readily apparent in many of the native lordships of Scotland. Richard Oram found plentiful evidence, documentary and archaeological, to support his contention that the Gaelic nobility of thirteenth-century Galloway had neither the need to build defensive fortifications in stone nor the inclination to make 'public statements

---

[16] *RRS*, ii, no. 136; *Coupar Angus Chrs.*, i, no. 35. [17] Fraser, *Lennox*, ii, nos. 11, 202. [18] S.M. Foster, 'Before Alba: Pictish and Dál Riata power centres from the fifth to the late ninth centuries AD' (1998), 2. [19] G.G. Simpson and B. Webster, 'Charter evidence and the distribution of mottes in Scotland' (1985), 2–11; Oram, *Lordship of Galloway*, 218–31. [20] F. Watson, 'The expression of power in a medieval kingdom: thirteenth-century Scottish castles' (1998), 76.

of their political status and economic power'.[21] The evidence concerning power centres in Strathearn and Lennox in the period between 1170 and 1365, although scattered and uneven, strongly supports the argument that these native lords, too, avoided equating impressive stone castles with social status, and lordly authority with the construction of stone castles. That they maintained permanent residences in which to live, and from which to administer their widespread territories, can hardly be doubted; that these halls and tower houses must have been sufficiently commodious to house a host of administrative officials, family members, and hangers-on is equally evident. A handful of charters that include place date clauses confirms the existence of such sites, for example at or near Crieff, Kenmore, Fowlis Wester and Innerpeffray in Strathearn, and Inchmurrin, Balloch, Fintry and Catter in Lennox. Early fieldwork undertaken by the Archaeological Field Survey of the Society of Antiquaries of Scotland, and more recently by the National Monuments Record of Scotland, have done much to unearth the physical remains of field systems, earthworks and planned fortifications. If a daunting amount of archaeological research remains yet to be completed in both regions, it is none the less possible to sketch more than a merely tentative map of lordly power centres in medieval Strathearn and Lennox.

The compact nature of the native lordships did not preclude the establishment of more than a single *caput* or power centre; in fact, varying levels of commitment to the Scottish royal court and different patterns of economic exploitation within their vast territories meant that the earls of Strathearn and Lennox must have lived a relatively peripatetic existence based on several residences. Mottes are distributed only thinly in Strathearn, suggesting a distinct lack of interest on the part of the earliest earls in imitating the new building styles of their foreign contemporaries. A charter of Earl Robert and two of Earl Malise II were dated at Crieff.[22] Preliminary surveys confirm nineteenth-century accounts of a motte or artificial mound on the nearby lands of Broich (NN82 SE14), some twelve yards in diameter, surrounded on all sides by a wall of earth and stone. Tradition asserts that it was on this 'stayt' of Crieff that the court of the earls of Strathearn was held from early times down to the late seventeenth century, when a tollbooth was erected in the town.[23] Charter reference, tradition, and local legend apart, there are other reasons for proposing Crieff as an important Strathearn power centre. The toun is located within the ancient comital thanage of Strowan, and in the heart of the arable portion of the earldom. Situated on the eastern edge of the earls' demesne lands it was from an early period also an important cattle market, and thus served as a convenient collection point for food and other renders. Crieff was also located in an area where the spiritual life of Strathearn was

---

21 Oram, *Lordship of Galloway*, 231.   **22** *Inchaff. Chrs.*, nos. 86, 95; *Inchaff. Liber*, no. 35.   **23** M. Headrick, 'The "stayt" of Crieff – a Bronze-age burial site' (1913–14), 366–8; R.S. Fittis, *Sketches of the olden times in Perthshire* (1878), 223–4; J. Shearer, *Antiquities of Strathearn* (4th edn., 1891), 82. See also below, p. 125.

concentrated. The parsons of the parish church there in the thirteenth and fourteenth centuries were almost invariably relations or close acquaintances of the earls, an indication of the status of the church in the locality. That there was probably some kind of residence in the area around Crieff is further attested in the record of an inquest held to examine the loyalty of Earl Malise III to Robert Bruce's cause, convened in Glasgow in 1307. Here, it is stated that the earl met with King Robert *a boys de Creff ou sa gents furent assemblees*.[24] Although no fortification is mentioned, the king spent the night in the area.

At Strowan there are still visible the remains of a motte of some size, possibly the site of a baronial residence, but perhaps equally likely that of the earls' man, the thane of Strowan.[25] A better documented site is Kenmore, on a small promontory situated where the River Earn meets the Loch, opposite present day St Fillans, and not far from the very ancient fortress at Dundurn. Two charters, dated 1258 and 1287, were issued form there;[26] in addition, the Glasgow inquest of 1307 heard that Earl Malise III was prevented form entering his stronghold on *leyle de Kenmer*, when Sir Neil Campbell and Sir Walter de Logie destroyed his path of retreat.[27] The site is palisaded and ditched, and in 1306 was sufficiently fortified to permit the earl to withstand the king's assault.[28] All traces of a residence or fortalice on the site have now disappeared; however, the reference to the 'island' of Kenmore is interesting. It suggests that, like nearby Neish Island (NN62 SE2), the dwelling was built on an artificial base, possible a crannog.[29] If this was the case, then the construction of a fortified residence at Kenmore attests the earls' deliberate choice of an ancient power site and, as late as the opening decades of the fourteenth century, a conscious effort on the part of the earls of Strathearn to associate their authority with the distant past. Such links stood in sharp contrast with the adoption of more recent architectural statements adopted by incomers from England and the continent, but they were no less impressive than mottes as visible manifestations of lordship. It is significant in this context that the native thane of Dunning, a representative of the earls' authority, also chose as a site for his chief residence a place close to an ancient hillfort.[30]

One of Malise II's charters was issued at Fowlis Wester,[31] and here again, the inquest of 1307 offers useful evidence in favour of regarding the site as the location of a comital residence. When King Robert first learned of Earl Malise III's refusal to perform homage, he gathered together his forces and marched on Fowlis, expecting to find the earl there.[32] Just over two kilometres east of the village, on a farm known for centuries as Castleton, there is visible a grassy

---

24 F. Palgrave (ed.), *Documents and records illustrating the history of Scotland* (1837), 320. **25** Simpson and Webster, 'Charter evidence', 20. **26** *Inchaff. Chrs.*, nos. 87, 118. **27** Palgrave (ed.), *Documents*, 320. **28** Duncan, *Making*, 441. **29** J. Stuart, 'Notices of a group of artificial islands in the Loch of Dowalton, Wigtownshire, and of other artifical islands or "crannogs" throughout Scotland' (1865), 175; with additional information from the RCAHMS CANMORE database. **30** S.T. Driscoll, 'Formalizing the mechanisms of state power: early Scottish lordship from the ninth to the thirteenth centuries' (1998), 41. **31** *Inchaff. Chrs.*, App., no. 5. **32** Palgrave (ed.), *Documents*, 319.

mound upon which lie the remains of a stone structure (NN92 SW9). Although the castle, if indeed that is what is was, is now long gone, there are good reasons for suggesting Fowlis Wester as a chief administrative and strategic centre of the earldom. The existence of the ancient shire of Fowlis, although long vanished already by the thirteenth century, has already been noted.[33] The name of Castleton is an old one, appearing in some of the earliest retours for the area.[34] Strategically, the site is not altogether sound, exposed as it is on the east and north sides, but it sits on a ridge commanding a clear view of the surrounding approaches. The village of Fowlis Wester is situated close by a road which, in the Middle Ages, ran north towards Buchanty, less than five kilometres from Inchaffray abbey, and in the centre of the arable region of the earldom. Many of the French and English speaking newcomers to Strathearn were settled within this area, and it was important for the earls to project a clear presence within their midst. Economic evidence further supports the argument for Fowlis among the chief residences of the earls. Their mills were located not far away at Dunfallin, itself the site of a meeting of the baronial court in 1284.[35] From 1200, if not earlier, there was a fishery in the Pow Burn, which would easily have supplied a comital establishment of some size, and in the later thirteenth century, there was a stone quarry not far away at Nethergask.

Several other sites appear to have fulfilled functions as comital residences. They include Innerpeffray, upstream from Dunfallin, which was certainly a fermtoun of some substance in the later Middle Ages, and probably the location of a contemporary fortification,[36] but also one or two places located in the western, highland reaches of the earldom. For most of the latter there remain but the barest of physical traces: a length of stone wall or earthen rampart datable to the later medieval period here, a suggestive placename there, a hill that might be of articificial construction, the possibility – increasingly likely as further excavations are completed – that a post-medieval building was erected on the foundations of an earlier fortification. Some two kilometres west of Crieff, on a bend of the River Earn, is a hill known as Tom-na-Chaisteal, 'hill of the castle' (NN82 SW3). Traces of fortification are now just discernible on the summit, but the foundations of a structure of some size are said to have been visible as late as 1832.[37] The top of the hill was once encircled by a double wall and, like Dunknock near Dunning, may have been the site of an early historic fort occupied well into the later medieval period. On the west side of the hill there was a series of ramparts. Tom-na-Chaisteal, if indeed it was a fortified site, would have served as an ideal nexus between lowland and highland portions of the earldom. Still another possible site of an early Strathearn hall or tower house lies in the vicinity of Dunning, itself the centre of a thanage, a stronghold of

[33] See above, p. 95. [34] T. Thomson (ed.), *Inquisitionum ad capellam Regis retornatarum abbreviatio* (Scotland) (3 vols, 1811–16), iii, nos. 66, 424, 672. [35] *Reg. Morav.*, App., nos, 13, 14. [36] Neville, 'Earls of Strathearn', i, 22; *Inchaff. Liber*, no., 30. [37] *The new statistical account of Scotland* (1845), x, 734.

considerable antiquity already in the thirteenth century, and a place long associated with the venerable St Serf. The site in question consists of the remains of an early earthworks, on which a castle was erected in the late Middle Ages (NN01 SW8).[38] Among the muniments of the Rollo family is a charter of David Stewart earl of Strathearn and Caithness, dated 1380, concerning estates nearby. These were the subject of a grant in which the earl reserved to himself the *cathedra comitis* and the site of the *domus capitalis* in the lands of Findony, *ex parte orientali cathedre supradicte*.[39] The term *cathair* may once have had some qualifying noun attached to it, now lost, but whatever its meaning in this context – seat, chair, dwelling or fortress – the reference suggests that the medieval earls used the site as a centre of local power.

The region west of Kenmore is poorly represented in surviving Strathearn charter materials, but the native earls drew substantial rents in kind from this area, and the parsons of the parish church of Balquhidder were frequent witnesses to the written deeds of Earl Malise III and his greater tenants.[40] The most likely site for a comital residence in this region lies at the far end of Loch Earn, on what appears to have been an artificial island, opposite Edinample, probably a crannog (NN52 SE3). As at Kenmore, the ready availability of foodstuffs for supplying the household together with the symbolic importance of an ancient site were a powerful combination in the choice of a residence.

Like the earls of Strathearn, the native lords of Lennox consciously avoided building residences in the continental style, and mottes are as thin on the ground here as they are in Strathearn. The parallels between the sites they chose and those preferred by the earls of Strathearn are, in fact, striking. Most obviously, Lennox boasted no single *caput*. For much of the period between 1170 and 1365 the earls moved from one hall or tower house to another, and were content with locations that were only lightly fortified, if at all. The one exception to this general rule was the massive fortress at Dumbarton, already in 1200 a venerable centre of law, administration and lordly power. In fact, the castle represented such an asset that in 1238 Alexander II assigned its care to a royal official, while his successor, Alexander III, used the newly created sheriffdom of Dumbarton as a means of checking the power of the native rulers of Lennox.[41] Dumbarton Rock was not, however, the only site in the lordship with ties to the historic past, and in the years after 1238 Maoldomhnaich and his kinsmen occupied residences in several other locations. Chief among these was the island of Inchmurrin, at the southern end of Loch Lomond. A stone castle was erected there in the fourteenth century, and after 1350 comital charters were dated here with come regularity.[42] Although the later medieval earls favoured the island as

---

38 Information from the RCAHMS CANMORE database. **39** *Historical manuscripts commission*, 3rd report (London, 1902), App., 406. **40** *Inchaff. Chrs.*, nos. 95, 103; *Inchaff. Liber*, nos. 32, 35, 44, 63, 66; *Morton Reg.*, ii, no. 6. **41** *Lennox Cart.*, 1–2; Duncan, *Making*, 389. **42** SAS, Archaeological Field Survey, *The archaeological sites and monuments of Dumbarton District, Clydebank District, Bearsden and Milngavie District, Strathclyde Region* (1978), 16; RCAHMS, *The historic landscape of Loch Lomond*, 15; *Lennox Cart.*, 45, 59, 60.

a rich hunting ground and kept much of it under forest, fieldwork and aerial photography have revealed traces of cultivation considerably earlier than the fourteenth century.[43] The island was also a hallowed place, the site of a chapel dedicated to St Mirren.[44] Inchmurrin afforded the earls of Lennox and their entourages plentiful and varied foodstuffs, a commanding presence on the largest of the islands of Loch Lomond, and a tangible link with the Gaelic past.

In the thirteenth century the native family already had a long association with Balloch: the bard Muireadhach Albanach referred to Ailin II as *mac righ bealagh*, 'son of the king of Balloch'.[45] Here, Maoldomhnaich erected a new residence on a low lying natural mound, and from there he and his successor issued a number of charters.[46] Balloch offered the earls, members of their large households, and their stewards and bailies ready access to the hunting grounds of the islands of Loch Lomond and areas further north, to the arable regions of southern and eastern Lennox, and to the resources of the River Leven. At Ballagan (NS48 NE3), Maoldomhnaich once again made use of naturally rising ground upon which to build a fortified hall, traces of which were removed in the eighteenth century.[47] The residence that he and his successors maintained here owed its importance to its proximity to the legal centre of the earldom at Catter,[48] but like Balloch it was also well situated for use as a collection point for foodstuffs and renders of various kinds.

A charter issued at Catter in 1217 shows that this portion of Strathblane parish, too, was already in use before Earl Maoldomhnaich abandoned Dumbarton.[49] It may have been chosen for its strong association with early Christian settlement in the region and more specifically with St Mirren.[50] Still another site of a comital residence was Fintry (NS68 NW6). Here, Maoldomhnaich constructed a motte on the crest of a ridge commanding a good view of the surrounding land.[51]

A noteworthy feature of this brief list of Lennox residences is their concentration in the lowland reaches of the earldom, south of Loch Lomond, in the valleys of the Leven, Endrick and Blane Rivers. Surviving charter evidence confirms that Maoldomhnaich and his successors were careful to establish a commanding presence in the richest arable and fishing parts of their lands. It argues, moreover, for the early conversion of these parts to the cash economy typical of the lowland regions of the kingdom, for the maintenance of several residences would have required, beyond significant quantities of foodstuffs, expenditures on the luxury items – clothing, spices, tapestries – that were such important aspects of the lordly culture of the day. As is the case with contemporary

---

43 NMRS, MS 993/1, fos. 9, 33. See Map 2.   **44** *Origines*, i, 35.   **45** L. McKenna (ed.), *Aithdioghluim Dána* (2 vols, 1939–40), i, 173.   **46** *Archaeological sites ... Dumbarton District*, 16; *Historic landscape*, 15; *Lennox Cart.*, 86; *Paisley Reg.*, 160–1, 171–2; W. Fraser, *The Stirlings of Keir and their family papers* (1858), 204–5; *Glasgow Reg.*, i, no. 284; Fraser, *Lennox*, ii, nos. 22, 30, 213; NAS, GD 430/76.   **47** *Archaeological sites ... Dumbarton District*, 15; RCAHMS, *Stirlingshire*, i. 269; SAS, Archaeological Field Survey, *The archaeological sites and monuments of Stirling District, Central Region* (1979), 38.   **48** See below, p. 125.   **49** Fraser, *Lennox*, ii, no. 202   **50** *Origines*, i, 34–5.   **51** RCAHMS, *Stirlingshire*, i, 175. For charters dated at Fintry, see *Lennox Cart.*, 25–6, 30–1.

Strathearn, however, the preponderance of written evidence from one part of the earldom should not obscure other indications that the native earls also devoted considerable time and energy to the upland portions of their territories. The heavy renders of cheese so typical of later medieval Lennox that were collected from the highland parishes of Luss, Arrochar and Drymen were the fruits of a vigorous pastoral economy, one that, together with the game taken from the extensive forests of northern Loch Lomondside, was more than sufficient to supply several comital households.

The efforts of late twentieth-century archaeologists to map the distribution of settlement in Argyll and Stirlingshire have brought to light the existence of several fortifications, many of them erected on sites occupied since prehistoric times, any number of which might have served the earls as residences. Likely sites include Elan Rossdhu (NS38 NE3), in the parish of Luss which, however, passed out of the direct control of Earl Maoldomhnaich in the early years of the thirteenth century. In addition to Inchmurrin, the family may also have built timber halls or houses on one or more of the numerous islands of Loch Lomond. Several of these are mentioned in contemporary deeds, and on most, prehistoric crannog sites provided the foundations upon which the earls (or their tenants) erected buildings of wood or stone.[52] Grants of estates in and around the toun of Edintaggart and along the Douglas Water in the hills above western Loch Lomond, as well as in Buchanan and Sallochy on the eastern side of the loch, reveal that the earls exploited these lands as intensively as they did their lowland possessions, if by different means. Archaeologists have associated moated homesteads like those that have been excavated at Garchell, Gartfarren and Gargunnock with the lairdly ranks of thirteenth-century Scottish society,[53] but the hall and manor houses of the earls were distinguishable from such structures perhaps only in being built on a grander scale. At Strathcashell (NS39 SE11), a crannog of a size large enough to accommodate a residence may have been regarded by the earls as a useful site from which to travel north or south along Loch Lomond, or eastward into the hills of Buchanan parish, perhaps especially given its proximity to the forested lands of Sallochy, Arrochymore and Balmaha, as well as to an ancient religious site.[54]

Noteworthy also is the readiness of the earls of Lennox and their greater tenants to adapt a variety of site types to their needs. The mottes and moated sites so often associated with the influence of Anglo-Norman and continental settlers eventually appeared in the region, but as was the case in Strathearn and other Gaelic lordships such as Galloway, the native earls by no means abandoned old fashioned building sites to reflect more up-to-date styles. Nor did they convert their timbered halls into the more lavish and expensive dwellings

---

[52] NMRS, MS 993/1, o. 43; F.O. Blundell, 'Further notices on the artificial islands in the Highland area' (1912–13), 265–6; Stuart, 'Artificial islands', 175; RCAHMS, *Stirlingshire*, i, 93. [53] RCAHMS, *Stirlingshire*, i, 178, 179; Duncan, *Making*, 441–2. [54] RCAHMS, *Stirlingshire*, i, 93, 167–8.
[55] Driscoll, 'Formalizing the mechanisms of power', 46.

once believed to have been the hallmarks of Anglo-Norman and continental lordship. With few exceptions, the thirteenth-century earls chose sites that projected a strong visual presence over waters, rivers, valleys, or roads. Many had long been occupied already by 1200, suggesting that associations with the remote past were of more than passing concern in a period when the cultural milieu of the lordship was undergoing considerable change. But few bristled with the defensive features of such famous castles as Edinburgh, Stirling, or Dumbarton. On the contrary, excavations have revealed scores of examples of medieval bank and ditch earthworks that afforded only minimal defence. Even that most ostentatious of parvenus, Sir David de Graham, appears to have been content with a modest hall of timber. Like his foreign fellows elsewhere in the kingdom, when he ordered the erection of a motte on which to build his tower house at Mugdock, he may have intended to make manifest his control over nature as well as men,[55] but in both Lennox and Strathearn Graham's visual expressions of power were the exception rather than the norm. The thirteenth-century earls of Lennox, like their counterparts in Strathearn, had little need to 'impress or overawe' with ostentatious displays of military architecture the inhabitants of lordships which, as descendants of ancient Gaelic families, they governed with uncontested authority.[56] Of greater interest are the uses that both families made of sites that had long fulfilled functions as power centres: ancient hill forts, prehistoric crannogs, places of early Christian worship. The rulers of Galloway, too, erected a handful of mottes in their lands, but in similar fashion built tower houses and halls in locations that had long been occupied.[57]

Such deliberate planning suggests more than a conservative reaction against new or 'foreign' building styles on the part of native lords, and more than just an aversion to financing expensive stone dwellings. The sophisticated central administration typical of so many of the Anglo-Norman and continental lordships of early thirteenth-century England, designed to facilitate the collection of rents in cash and kind, and dominated by the luxurious stone dwelling of a noble family and its retinue, accorded ill with the social and tenurial landscape of contemporary Scotland. Native lords in particular favoured many residences over a single *caput*. Their preferences were partly the consequences, of course, of an economy that, in Strathearn and Lennox, and indeed in much of the region north of Forth, was overwhelmingly pastoral, and that by its nature dictated a peripatetic existence for noble households based on the seasons. But something more appears to have been at work here. The strategic deployment of close family members meant that the earls' closest kindred were well represented in all corners of the lordships. Gille Brigte of Strathearn's placement of his brother Maol Iosa, then his nephew Fergus, in Strathtay, for example, ensured that in this distant part of the earldom there was a power centre associated with his household. In Lennox, similarly, Maoldomhnaich may not have

---

56 Watson, 'Expressions of power', 64; Duncan, *Making*, 441.   57 Oram, *Lordship of Galloway*, 219–31.

maintained a formal residence west of the Fruin Water along the mainland shores of the Gare Loch, or on the Rosneath peninsula, but he did establish a strong family presence at Faslane in the person of his brother Amhlaibh. In the fourteenth century, when the latter's descendant Walter succeeded to the title of earl in right of his wife, Faslane fell under the direct control of the comital family and became one of its principal seats.

After 1300 changes are apparent throughout Scotland in architectural styles, military requirements, and lordly consumption, each reflecting new and different attitudes toward domestic comfort and convenience. Such changes were apparent at all social levels in Strathearn and Lennox. Greater movable wealth was in some places translated into more ostentatious living arrangements. On the island of Inchmurrin, for example, the remains of a courtyard surrounded by the foundations of several stone buildings bear witness to an ambitious building programme on the part of Earl Malcolm II of Lennox.[58] More impressive still were the efforts of the Grahams, now long established in the earldom, to transform their seat at Mugdock castle into a residence befitting a family whose members had long since shed the stigma of upstarts. Here, Sir David (d. 1376) began construction on a whole new keep boasting massive walls and towers, together with a series of outlying buildings.[59] The castle conveyed an image of great strength and importance that, in conjunction with ongoing efforts to drain marshlands and develop hunting grounds, made Mugdock the equal of any baronial residence anywhere in the kingdom. The evidence for an increase in stone castle building in Strathearn has been much less intensively studied, but here, too, the earls and their greater tenants made efforts to improve the comfort and appearance of their dwellings. The fortification at Kenmore, possibly of stone, was tested against a royal assault in 1306.[60] A decade earlier, in the course of his progress through the earldom, Edward I broke his journey at Ogilvie Castle, perhaps then still in Malise III's hands, and presumably sumptuous and large enough to accommodate the king and his immediate entourage.

If the timbered halls and, later, the stone towers of the earls of Strathearn and Lennox fulfilled important functions as visible power centres, so must also have sites associated with the exercise of the earls' legal authority, albeit in different ways. The intrusion of agents of royal justice into the traditionally independent lordships in the course of the thirteenth century was perhaps most apparent in the expansion of the office of sheriff into the distant reaches of the realm. In some places, the sheriff simply replaced the thane, but in others, notably Fife, the duties of hosting and of dispensing royal justice were merged almost seamlessly with the powers already exercised by native earls.[61] In still others, royal sheriffs and comi-

[58] NMRS, MS 993/2; *Archaeological sites … Dumbarton District*, 17; with additional information from the RCAHMS CANMORE database. [59] RCHAMS, *Stirlingshire*, i, 249–53. [60] See above, p. 118. [61] N.H. Reid and G.W.S. Barrow (eds), *The sheriffs of Scotland: an interim list to 1360* (2002), xiv; Duncan, *Making*, 160–3, 168–70, 204–5; W.C. Dickinson (ed.), *The sheriff court book of Fife, 1515–1522* (1928), 369–88.

tal thanes shared some of these responsibilities until well after 1200. Justice in Strathearn, for example, was the responsibility both of the sheriff of Auchterarder and the native earls, and in 1290, significantly, it was Earl Malise III who accounted to the king's Exchequer for the ferme of the sheriffdom.[62] References to suit of the earls' courts, and in particular to tenants' obligation to attend the head or capital courts of the lordship do not begin to appear until the time of Malise III, though the frequency with which native men identified as *judices* witnessed Strathearn charters makes it clear that the comital courts were active throughout the thirteenth century. At least one of these was convened at Dunfallin in 1284, when the widow and son of the earl's steward resigned some of their lands to Sir William de Moravia of Tullibardine,[63] and others were held at or near the location of comital residences as required, such as Crieff.[64] The authority to dispense capital justice, on the other hand, was a much coveted prerogative, and the exercise of lordly power unfolded in highly ritualized ceremonies staged in public places long associated with such solemnity. In some regions of Scotland, Geoffrey Barrow has argued for a close link between place names containing the Gaelic element *comhdhail* ('assembly' or 'meeting') and the popular courts of the 'pre-feudal' age.[65] There is only one such site in Strathearn (Culthill, in the parish of Caputh), but a fourteenth-century deed of Robert Stewart earl of Strathearn, dated *in curia nostra tenta apud Creffe* is suggestive.[66] Eighteenth-century antiquarians made much of the local association of the so-called 'stayt' of Crieff with the medieval earls' courts, and more particularly the exercise of high justice. Whether or not the site fulfilled such a function, it was already in 1358 a place that had been in use for many centuries.[67]

The evidence, onomastic, archaeological, and written, for centres of legal power in thirteenth- and fourteenth-century Lennox is not much more plentiful. Royal centres of justice do not appear in record until 1234, when King Alexander II 'bought out' the native thane of Callendar, himself the descendant of a family that had long represented the crown on the eastern edges of the lordship.[68] A year before Alexander secured control of Dumbarton castle, he had already appointed a sheriff there,[69] but as the royal charter of 1238 to Maoldomhnaich made clear, over the lands of the earldom proper the king ceded full rights of justice. *Comhdhail* place names are as rare in Lennox as they are in Strathearn, but reference to *furcas nostras del Cathyre* in a written deed of Earl Donald reveals with some precision the location of at least one comital gallows. The existence of a motte at the site now known as Gallowshill or the Moathill is strongly suggestive of a place of some antiquity already when the charter was issued between 1333 and 1360.[70] The place name Catter, moreover, like the *cathair* of the Strathearn document of 1380, suggests a power centre of

---

62 *ER*, i, 51. **63** Fraser, *Grandtully*, i, App., no. 69; *Inchaff. Liber*, App., nos. 24; *RRS*, vi, no. 482. **64** *Reg. Morav.*, App., nos. 13, 14. **65** G.W.S. Barrow, 'Popular courts in early medieval Scotland: some suggested place-name evidence', in idem, *Scotland and its neighbours in the Middle Ages* (1992). **66** *Inchaff. Chrs.*, no.133. **67** Headrick, 'The "stayt" of Crieff', 366–8. **68** *RRS*, i, 46; Duncan, *Making*, 161. **69** *Paisley Reg.*, 218. **70** *RMS*, i, no. 371; Fraser, *Lennox*, i, 158–60.

some age, perhaps so widely known within the community it serviced that it required no qualifying noun to identify it clearly with the earl.

The native earls of Strathearn and Lennox maintained only one set of gallows within their respective lands. An exclusive setting accords well with the solemnity associated with such sites of lordly power, which offered a striking contrast with the more benevolent exercise of authority represented by tower houses and halls. For much of the thirteenth century the earls also jealously guarded their exclusive jurisdiction over criminals, sharing it only with a select few. When Maol Iosa son of Fearchar became a tenant of his brother Gille Brigte of Strathearn in the last decade of the twelfth century, he secured within his territories the privileges of sake, soke, toll, team and infangthief, together with the right to erect a pit and gallows. His nephew and heir Fergus enjoyed similar powers,[71] but it was not until 1260 that Malise II surrendered a measure of his extensive jurisdiction to one of his tenants, and even here, he allowed the latter only control over minor infractions causing bloodshed.[72] The earls of Lennox, too, long regarded power over life and limb and the gallows that symbolized it as exclusive privileges. Earl Maoldomhnaich granted Arthur Galbraith, a member of a very old Lennox family, the right to search within his own lands for stolen good, *quod anglice dicitur rancellis*,[73] but it was only in the last decade of the thirteenth century that Malcolm I allowed several of his more important tenants the right to take fines levied in cases of affray and assault (*abstractiones sanguinis quod dicitur bludwytys*). [74] Well after 1300 his successors were still requiring that tenants use the earls' gallows to carry out sentences of death, although several of them were by now licensed to hold superior courts of their own and to exercise jurisdiction over life and limb.[75] In the generations between 1170 and 1365 the prerogatives and perquisites of lordship in Scotland underwent a profound transformation, but in Strathearn and Lennox the authority to maintain pit and gallows remained a rare mark of privilege and a well nigh unchallenged symbol of magnatial power.

Although their lands yielded sufficient revenues to allow them to move in the highest social circles of their day, the earls of Strathearn and Lennox were nevertheless poorer in many respects than some of their contemporaries. In 1294–95 a report to the Exchequer estimated the annual income of the earls of Fife at £500, five-sixths of which they derived from rents.[76] The Scottish estates of Roger de Quincy (d. 1264) were worth £400 per annum.[77] Niall earl Carrick (d. 1256) and Gilbert of earl of Angus (assessed in 1263) enjoyed more modest incomes of £166 and roughly £85 respectively.[78] Such figures make it difficult

---

71 RRS, ii, no. 136; *Coupar Angus Chrs.*, i, no. 35.   **72** NAS, GD 220/1/A1/3/3, 4.   **73** *Lennox Cart.*, 28.   **74** Ibid., 43; see also reference to the bailies of Sir John de Luss, and the privileges understood in Malcolm II's grant to the same, RRS, v, no. 2.   **75** *Lennox Cart.*, 56–8, 81–2; *Paisley Reg.*, 205–6; NAS, GD 220/1/D5/1/4.   **76** Duncan, *Making*, 426–7, 585.   **77** G.G. Simpson, 'An Anglo-Scottish baron of the thirteenth century: the acts of Roger de Quincy, earl of Winchester and constable of Scotland' (1965), 79–81.   **78** Duncan, *Making*, 399, 427.

to counter the traditional argument that the thirteenth-century Scottish nobility lived in economic circumstances considerably more straitened than did their English counterparts, but it would be erroneous to assume that in the social and cultural contexts of the native lordships ranks, status, power and privilege depended exclusively, or even primarily, on annual income.

Early Exchequer records relating to Strathearn are disappointingly few, and the loss of a roll detailing the revenues of Earl Malise III in 1296, included among the records submitted to Edward I's agent, Hugh de Cressingham, is particularly regrettable.[79] An account of 1360 sheds little light on the (Stewart) earl's annual income, even in an age that devoted considerable attention to the details of rents and other revenues. A partial record of the contributions demanded of all lay and ecclesiastical lords for the ransom of King David II, it notes merely that the sums received from the lordship 'out of all goods, grain, chattels, ferms and returns, and [the work of] craftsmen' consisted of £67 9s. 8d. Similar evidence is available from the year 1366, when the earl paid £72 to the chancellor as part of his contribution to the ransom.[80] Both figures undoubtedly reflect the severe decline in rents and the 'general deflation' characteristic of the later fourteenth century which, it has been claimed, affected the value of money more than it did the production of 'real' wealth in the form of goods and services.[81] Neither does much to clarify questions concerning the rents in cash or kind to which the earls had access in the generations before 1360.

The earliest detailed description of the value of Strathearn estates is an account rendered in 1380 by Christian, mair of Dunning. He estimated annual revenues from ferms and other returns for a period of two Exchequer terms at over £300: £55 13s. 4d. from the 'shire' or thanage of Dunning, £89 8d. from Crieff and Fowlis Wester, £30 13s. 4d. from the lands of Trinity Gask and its surrounding area, and a lucrative £117 15s. from the vast estates lying westward from Crieff to Loch Earnhead and beyond.[82] These figures show that by the late fourteenth century the earldom's territories were yielding a favourable income, and certainly they suggest an intensified pattern of arable exploitation under the Stewart earls, especially in the region west of the arable heartland of the lordship. The difficulty here lies in identifying whether the increase in annual renders was the achievement of the later native earls, Malise IV and Malise V, or the consequences of more careful estate management by the Stewart newcomers. On balance, the evidence weighs slightly in favour of the latter. In the first years of the fourteenth century Malise III spent a great deal of time in captivity in England as a hostage of the English crown.[83] His grandson's flight to northern Scotland soon after assuming the title, and the unsettled fate of the earldom between 1333 and 1357,[84] did not favour either the implementation or

79 *APS*, i, 12. 80 *ER*, i, 51; ii, 43. The first assessment may have represented between 3d. and 6d. in the £, but the statutes that determined the precise amount of the contribution have not survived. See M.A. Penman, *David II, 1329–71* (2004), 219. 81 Nicholson, *Later Middle Ages*, 175; Penman, *David II*, 350. 82 *ER*, iii, 33–8. 83 C.J. Neville, 'The political allegiance of the earls of Strathearn during the War of Independence' (1986). 84 *SP*, viii, 254–9.

the supervision of a programme of land exploitation. The succession of the Stewarts to the lordship brought much needed stability in comital leadership and, it would appear, a thorough assessment of the economic challenges that the new lords encountered. In 1380, for example, the lands of Auchermuthill, on the edge of the vast Muir of Orchill, were recorded as almost totally waste: according to Christian the mair, 'no one has rendered [anything] to the earl for many years'.[85]

A hundred years earlier, yields from lands successfully set to the plough were insufficient to meet some of the native earls' financial obligations, and it is evident that they suffered from something of a chronic shortage of ready cash. Thus, in the early 1250s Malise II withheld payment of the relief owed from his English wife's Muschamp inheritance for a period of several years, perhaps because he experienced difficulty in raising the money; in 1259 needed to borrow the sum of thirty and one half merks from three merchants of Cahors to meet his debts.[86] In 1268 he was in arrears with the abbey of Inchaffray in respect of twenty-four merks, representing the sum of four years' annual rent from lands in Belnello.[87] His son, too, experienced problems mobilizing cash, and in 1293 it was in order to offset these difficulties that the earl reserved to himself for some five years the income from English lands settled on his daughter when she married the English lord, Sir Robert de Thony.[88] There are, then, few indicators in Strathearn of the kind of moneyed wealth that, in the thirteenth and fourteenth centuries, many of the earls' social equals enjoyed.

The same is true of Lennox. The earls were rich in title to a lordship covering a vast amount of territory, but there survives little evidence that they collected enough money rents to enable them to indulge in the kind of ostentatious display that some of the king's courtiers deployed so lavishly. The document known as Bagimond's Roll, drawn up around 1287, recorded that over a six-year period the teinds assessed on the parishes of the diocese of Glasgow were collectively worth the impressive sum of almost £5000.[89] In a single year those of the deanery of Lennox, within which a good portion of the medieval earls' lands lay, accounted for just over £50.[90] Such figures are not inconsiderable, though they can hardly be interpreted as reliable indicators of the revenues of lay land holders within the same region. There are no comparable numbers for the deanery of Luss, which also included a significant bloc of the western territories of the earldom of Lennox, but the much larger parishes characteristic of this region and the poor quality of its limited arable soil together suggest that annual cash revenues, ecclesiastical and lay, amounted to significantly less than those of the deanery of Lennox.

Records of the English Exchequer are of limited assistance in assessing the earls' wealth. Shortly before 1305 Malcolm II paid 100 merks to the English crown in relief to succeed to his inheritance.[91] The proportion of his landed

---

85 *ER*, iii, 33. **86** *CDS*, i, nos. 1792, 2160. **87** *Inchaff. Liber*, no. 35. **88** NRO, E 159/66 mm. 24, 45. **89** A.I. Dunlop (ed.), 'Bagimond's roll' (1939), 25. **90** *Glasgow Reg.*, i, lxvii. **91** NRO

revenues that this sum represented is open to question, but it looks like small beer indeed when set beside the 1097 merks paid over a decade earlier by the heir to the earldom of Buchan.[92] It is likely, moreover, that Edward I negotiated a much reduced fine with Malcolm in the hope that he might win the lord of Lennox to the English cause, but such a conclusion only further obfuscates an assessment of the annual revenues that the new earl expected to collect from his lands. Scattered references, however, suggest that Malcolm II and his successors reaped the rewards of the previous generations' efforts to exploit to the fullest the varied terrain of Lennox. In 1330 the sheriff of Dumbarton noted that the earl had been forgiven his contribution to a recently agreed tenth on movables, assessed at £14; in the same year another account revealed that the islands of Inchcailloch and Inchfad, formerly in the possession of Sir David de Graham, were yielding healthy rents of 60s. and 30s. annually.[93] Most of the other islands of Loch Lomond remained under the control of the earls of Lennox, and although some were set aside as hunting reserves, others, notably the large island of Inchmurrin, were probably also under the plough. It was not until 1434, however, some years after the forfeiture and death of the last native earl, that the crown undertook a thorough assessment of the lordship. Rents alone then totalled in excess of the princely sum of £700; and it is small wonder that in the mid-fourteenth century Walter of Faslane should have pursued the hand of the sole heiress of Earl Donald as vigorously as he did.[94]

Useful as such figures are for the late medieval period, they are not very helpful in providing reliable estimates for periods as far in the past as the time of Earl Maoldomhnaich. Well into the later fourteenth century military obligations discharged not in mounted service, but rather in cheeses, suggest that the lords of Lennox experienced only limited success in transforming the bulk of their annual rents into hard cash.[95] The survival there of the old fiscal 'houses' as units of assessment alongside measures such as the arable carucates more typical of the region north of Forth provides further evidence that agricultural improvement, and the cash rents that it generated, touched only some portions of the earls' lands. Like livestock, grain, and other foodstuffs, of course, cheeses were readily commutable into cash, and the growth of a money economy and the proximity of markets in Perth, Stirling and Glasgow cannot have failed to effect changes even in the most remote corners of either Starthearn or Lennox. In the waning years of the thirteenth century, moreover, the native earls conceived of their wealth in terms much broader than mere money rents, and their status as something much more complex than coined money alone might purchase. Awareness of a lack of ready money did not go unnoticed by these magnates. Earl Gille Brigte's generosity to the church was extensive, even by the standards of the day. Malise II and his successors, however, dramatically reduced the financial commitment of the Strathearn

---

SC 9/12 m 13d. **92** J. Stevenson (ed.), *Documents illustrative of the history of Scotland, 1286–1306* (1870), i, 418. **93** *ER*, i, 257–8, 268. **94** Ibid., iv, 589–90; *SP*, v, 337–8. **95** The obligation is mentioned as late as the time of Earl Donald, who died between 1361 and 1364.

family to the canons. In the middle years of the thirteenth century conditions no longer favoured such extravagance.

Both the earls of Strathearn and Lennox, moreover, actively sought to augment their revenues by exploiting their value as marriage partners. Malise II enjoyed rents from his Northumberland wife's estates for several years after her death; he parted with them reluctantly, and only after his two daughters by Marjory Muschamp had found husbands.[96] Two of his other three wives were noblewomen of the highest rank, and his marriages into the families of Caithness and Orkney, then into that of the king of Man, brought valuable new resources into his hands, albeit temporarily.[97] Similarly, the expenses that Malise III incurred in providing a tocher worth 1200 merks for his daughter Maud was nicely offset by the healthy annual returns he secured from his son-in-law's English estates, which by agreement he enjoyed for a period of five years.[98] Maoldomhnaich's marriage to the daughter of Walter II son of Alan brought much needed cash into the household from the rich arable lands of the Stewart lordship, possibly the estate of Polmadie known to have been in the earls' possession later in the thirteenth century. Malcolm II's friendship with King Robert likewise proved rewarding, securing for him the ferm, successively, of the sheriffdoms of Clackmannan and Dumbarton. For much of the medieval period the prestige associated with the ancient office of mormaer and headship of an extended kindred went a long way towards offsetting poor cash flow. Shrewd exploitation of social and political ties complemented the process.

[96] Neville, 'Earls of Strathearn', i, 239–40. [97] *SP*, viii, 246–7. [98] PRO, E 159/61, mm. 24, 45.

CHAPTER 4

Relations with the church

A great deal of land in Strathearn and Lennox was held of the earls not for knight service, or for customary renders or money rents, but for prayers and masses. The early earls and their kinsmen were generous patrons of several abbeys, including Inchaffray, Lindores and Paisley; in addition, the religious houses at Arbroath, Coupar Angus and Scone benefited from the munificence of the native families, if on a more modest scale. Contacts between the earls of Srathearn and the bishops of Dunblane were close, and their communication with the papacy more extensive than was usual between a distant Scottish lord and the holy see during the thirteenth century. Earl Maoldomhnaich, too, shared a host of interests (though these were not always harmonious) with the bishop of Glasgow.

The endowment patterns of Earls Gille Brigte and Maoldomhnaich in many respects reflect those found elsewhere north of Forth among native lords. Some years ago, Andrew McDonald noted that despite the emphasis that historians have laid on the role of the Scottish royal family in the establishment of new religious houses in twelfth-century Scotland, Gaelic princes and noblemen also 'embraced the Gregorian reforms ... and took an active role in shaping the monastic landscape of their territories'.[1] McDonald offers reliable evidence, for example, for regarding the monastic patronage of the lords of Galloway as on par with that of the house of Canmore, and further documents the active participation of Raonall son of Somhairle in the support of monastic religious houses in the western periphery of Scotland. His claims for the active involvement of native ruling houses in the monastic revival of the high Middle Ages in Scotland are echoed in other recent works,[2] and are amply illustrated in the lordships of Strathearn and Lennox.

On the surface, relations between the native lords and the church were cordial and fruitful for both parties. Discord between the abbey of Inchaffray and the see of Dunblane, on the other hand, began almost from the time of the foundation of the house in 1200, when both entered into competition for the

---

[1] A. McDonald, 'Scoto-Norse kings and the reformed religious orders: patterns of monastic patronage in twelfth-Century Galloway and Argyll' (1995), 189. See also *MRHS*, 7. [2] See, for example, B.T. Hudson, 'Gaelic princes and Gregorian reform' (1991), 61–2; K.J. Stringer, 'Reform monasticism and Celtic Scotland: Galloway, *c*.1140–*c*.1240' (2000), 127–65; and D. Brooke, *Wild men and holy places: St Ninian, Whithorn and the medieval realm of Galloway* (1998), passim.

special patronage of the Strathearn family. Moreover, a careful reading of surviving charters suggests that well into the thirteenth century Earls Gille Brigte, Robert and Malise II, as well as their immediate kinsmen, underestimated the gravity of these problems, and in failing to adjust to the complex changes that transformed the Scottish church in the wake of the European reform movement inadvertently exacerbated them. In similar fashion, problems relating to ecclesiastical jurisdiction over grants of land and privileges troubled the efforts of Maoldomhnaich of Lennox and his immediate family members to endow Paisley abbey. The circumstances under which the gifts of both families became the focus of sometimes bitter litigation reveal a great deal about the tensions between Gaelic custom and the tenets of the reforming church. They also shed valuable light on native beliefs about the ownership, transmission and bequest of land in a period that witnessed considerable change in the nature of lordship and land holding among both ecclesiastical and lay persons.

MONASTERIES AND PARISHES

From very early times there had been a community of brethren on a site known as Innis Aifreann, the Isle of masses (Inchaffray). Here, secular priests leading an eremitical existence enjoyed the patronage of Fearchar earl of Strathearn and his countess in the mid-twelfth century, when they assigned to the community the church of St Chattan of Aberuthven, deep in the heart of the lordship, and a small parcel of land pertaining to it.[3] The brethren of Inchaffray, led by the hermit Maol Iosa, lived a peaceful co-existence with another ancient establishment of religious men at nearby Muthill, this one consisting of Céli Dé priests who, in the years before the continental reform movement was fully established in Scotland, were an important presence within the kingdom.[4] Around 1194 Earl Gille Brigte made to the religious men of Inchaffray a modest grant of three acres of land 'next to the pond that lies beside the island at Fowlis'.[5] A few years later he added to the community's possessions the church of Madderty and a teind of his cain in wheat, meal, malt, cheese and fish.[6] The see of Dunblane approved these early gifts; indeed, in 1190 Bishop Simon had actively encouraged the formal endowment of the little house by granting it rights generally associated with a monastic church, including the privilege of sepulture 'to all who wish it'.[7] His successor, Bishop Jonathan, further granted the church possession of all episcopal rights in the abthane lands of the church of Madderty, a gift that gave to the brethren firm control over all the revenues associated with that church.[8]

There can be little doubt, however, that by the last decade of the twelfth century the community on the Isle of Masses was on the verge of a profound

---

[3] Reference to the grant survives in a confirmation by Earl Gille Brigte, c.1198; *Inchaff. Chrs.*, no. 3.   [4] For the Céli Dé of Muthill see *MRHS*, 3, 51.   [5] *Inchaff. Liber*, no. 118.   [6] *Inchaff. Chrs.*, nos. 4, 5.   [7] Ibid., no. 1, and xxiv.   [8] Ibid., no. 7.

change in its organization. The early grants of Earls Fearchar and Gille Brigte were made to the hermit priests serving the church, and certainly old-style religious men were still in residence there a decade after Bishop Simon of Dunblane's charter. A bull of Pope Innocent III dated in the winter of 1200, for example, was granted on the petition of 'J. the hermit of Inchaffray and his brethren',[9] and Maol Iosa the hermit together with his counterpart 'Malgegill' of Muthill, witnessed a charter of the bishop of Dunblane to the abbot of Cambuskenneth around the same time.[10] Both men were designated 'priors' of their respective houses, but by this time it is clear that Earl Gille Brigte, probably at the urging of Bishop Jonathan of Dunblane, had taken steps to initiate a reform of the house.

The effects of the continental reform movement in the church were felt as early as the mid-twelfth century in Scotland. Before the end of the century, under royal patronage at first, then under the influence of Scottish noble houses, orders of Cistercian, Premonstratensian, Tironensian and Augustinian monks and canons were established in houses both north and south of Forth.[11] The period also saw attempts to develop a network of parish churches and the stabilization of episcopal boundaries throughout the realm.[12] Two important developments accompanied this ecclesiastical reorganization. One was the granting to monastic houses of a variety of churches both by lay lords and by the bishops of Scotland. This process sometimes degenerated into an undignified scramble for possession of churches, appurtenances and revenues, and in some places created enmity among land holders, lay and religious. The second was the process by which most communities of secular priests and Céli Dé appear to have been suppressed or refounded as houses of Augustinian canons. Both features of the reform movement are apparent in early thirteenth-century Strathearn as well as in Lennox. The consequences of change, moreover, were remarkably similar in both regions.[13]

Traditionally, historians have linked the displacement of the native church in Scotland to the domineering influence of the Anglo-Norman royal court. The unabashedly glowing portrayal of Queen Margaret of Scotland (d. 1093) by her biographer, Turgot, as single-handedly responsible for bringing the light of reform to a corrupt native church has been the subject of considerable debate in recent years,[14] but few scholars are prepared to dismiss outright the tremen-

---

9 Ibid., no. 8. **10** W. Fraser (ed.), *Registrum monasterii S. Marie de Cambuskenneth A.D. 1147–1535* (1872), no. 217. 'Malgegill' is presumably the 'Malgirk de Mothel' (Maol Girig, 'devotee of St Cyricus') who witnessed a grant of Bishop Simon of Dunblane c.1190; *Inchaff. Chrs.*, no. 1; see also nos. 3, 13, and C. Innes (ed.), *Carte monialium de Northberwic* (1847), nos. 5, 11; G.F. Black, *The surnames of Scotland* (1996), 577. **11** Barrow, *Kingdom*, 169–86; M. Dilworth, *Scottish monasteries in the late middle ages* (1995), 5–7. **12** Duncan, *Making*, 142–51; I.B. Cowan, 'The development of the parochial system in medieval Scotland' (1961); G. Donaldson, 'Scottish bishops' sees before the reign of David I' (1952–53). **13** The transformation of hermitages in Augustinian houses occurred also in England; see J. Herbert, 'The transformation of hermitages into Augustinian priories in twelfth-century England' (1983). **14** For a useful summary of this debate and its various participants, see D. Baker, '"A nursery of saints": St Margaret of Scotland reconsidered' (1978), 119–41.

dous influence that she and her royal sons effected on religious devotion. It was chiefly in the face of Anglo-Norman and European cultural pressures, for example, that by the early thirteenth century the Céli Dé of Loch Leven were forcefully suppressed as a distinct community.[15] The religious foundations at Abernethy, Monymusk, Monifieth, Brechin and St Andrews survived the tide of change a little longer, but by the third quarter of the century these, too, had been transformed into Augustinian priories.[16] In like fashion the French-speaking earl of Buchan, William Comyn, refounded a once thriving house of secular priests at Deer as a Cistercian abbey in 1219.[17]

Similar developments occurred in the lordship of Strathearn. In the year 1200, in commemoration of the death of their eldest son and heir, Gille Crìosd, Earl Gille Brigte and his countess formally established an Augustinian priory at Inchaffray.[18] The intention was that the new order be superimposed on the secular priests living the eremitical life there. But unlike the forceful suppression of Céli Dé at some other sites in Scotland there is evidence that the earl wished to make the transition from one form of religious observance to another as gradual as possible, and that he had no wish to expel the brethren from the house by forcible or other means. The charter of foundation provided specifically that governance of the house be left in the hands of the current head, 'Malise, priest and hermit, in whose discretion we trust', and directed merely that newcomers to the priory be instructed in the rule of St Augustine. Although the earl's charters began to refer to the brethren specifically as 'canons' almost immediately after the erection of the priory, there remained resident in the little house men whose names are clearly of Gaelic origin, and who may well have remained hermits in the old tradition.[19] The religious foundation at Inchaffray may not, in fact, have abandoned altogether its older trappings until the year 1221, when the priory was raised to the status of an abbey under the direction of a canon imported from the royal abbey of Scone. The chronicler Walter Bower claimed that the motive for the replacement of the current head lay in the latter's 'incompetence',[20] quite possibly a reference to his status as a priest of the old order.

The list of the Strathearn family's endowments to the religious of Inchaffray, hermits and canons alike, is impressive. Most generous of all was Earl Gille Brigte himself. In addition to confirming his earlier gifts and those of his father, Fearchar, Gille Brigte's foundation charter bestowed on the canons the churches of Strageath, Auchterarder and Kinkell. It confirmed teinds of cain which Gille Brigte had granted in the late 1190s and added to these a further teind of all the food brought to the comital kitchens, of the profits accrued in the earl's court, and of other obventions. The canons secured license to fish in the Pow Burn

---

15 *MRHS*, 50. **16** Ibid., 46–7, 50–1; Barrow, *Kingdom*, 187–202. For a review of the principal locations of Céli Dé communities in Scotland, see W. Reeves, *The culdees of the British Islands* (1864), 33–58, 105–43. Reeves' account is dated and incomplete, but still useful. **17** Ibid., 74; A. Young, 'The earls and the earldom of Buchan in the thirteenth century' (1993), 185; K. Jackson, *The Gaelic notes in the book of Deer* (1972), 1–7. **18** *Inchaff. Chrs.*, no. 9. **19** Ibid., nos. 12–14, 19, 28, 33, 34, 37, 43, 44. **20** *Scotichronicon*, v, 112.

and to take kindling and timber from nearby woodlands. Soon after the foundation charter had been granted two deeds of *renovatio* confirmed the pre-1200 gifts of the churches of Aberuthven and Madderty,[21] an act intended to symbol the fresh start that the brethren had recently made. Around the same time the earl granted them additional lands, all lying close to the priory buildings and thus easily accessible to its inhabitants.[22] A series of subsequent charters made more detailed provision for shares of the grain, cheese, meat, fish and fowl consumed in his kitchens. The earl gave the brethren liberties to use his woodlands as a source of building materials and eventually awarded them freedom to fish in any of the waters of his territories.[23]

In the decade after 1200 the earl further set aside for the priory a site on the Pow Burn where the canons might construct a mill.[24] He assigned to them the chattels of convicted felons and the fines imposed on other transgressors charged with committing offences on the priory's lands.[25] During his lifetime the earl granted four more churches to the religious of Inchaffray: Dunning and Monzievaird before 1203–4, Fowlis around 1210, and Gask between 1220 and 1223.[26] The priory also secured control of the tenement of Bellyclone, a small portion of land situated next to the site that a few years earlier the earl had allocated for the erection of the priory's mill.[27] These early gifts suggest that Gille Brigte sought to establish at Inchaffray a self sufficient and economically independent community of holy men on the continental model. They are noteworthy not only for their generosity, but more generally because they bear witness to the success of the reformed church in conveying its materialistic ambitions to the great provincial aristocracy of Gaelic Scotland.

When the canons requested a second mill Gille Brigte granted them license to build and a parcel of land beside his own mill at Dunfallin. This time, however, the charter stipulated that the priory's servants must dig a pond to service both structures, and that all multures from comital demesne lands be reserved to the earl.[28] Gille Brigte appears to have decided that the religious house that he had founded and endowed had now been adequately provided for. Religious devotion, however strong, had its limits, and he was concerned that his generosity not diminish comital revenues further than it had already. Later gifts to the canons of Inchaffray confirm this change in attitude. In 1218, for example, the marshy land lying immediately adjacent to the Isle of Masses, hitherto waste, was turned over to the priory,[29] a none-too-subtle hint, perhaps, that the priory's ambitions to increase the value of its possessions should be channelled away from the earl's purse toward the more intensive exploitation of hitherto undeveloped lands.

One of Earl Gille Brigte's late grants to Inchaffray was license to hold its own courts for offenders dwelling on monastic lands. This charter also gave the

---

21 *Inchaff. Chrs.*, no. 13; *Inchaff. Liber*, no. 69. **22** *Inchaff. Chrs.* Nos. 11, 12. A charter of King William I, dated c.1205, confirmed these gifts as well as the two estates of Ardbennie and Balfour, for which no original deeds survive. *RRS*, ii, no. 464. **23** *Inchaff. Chrs.*, no. 16; *Inchaff. Liber*, no. 5. **24** *Inchaff. Liber*, no. 27. **25** *Inchaff. Chrs.*, no. 25. **26** Ibid., nos. 28, 45. **27** *Inchaff. Liber*, no. 34. **28** *Inchaff. Chrs.*, no. 34. **29** Ibid., no. 37

canons authority to take poinds from his tenants should they renege on their obligation to render teinds.[30] The concession of this important claim to judicial authority was the result of a series of arrangements and experiments designed to provide the canons with a regular income. The earlier grant of the right to collect fines and chattels from condemned priory tenants had apparently been the subject of complaint, perhaps owing to the irregularity or paucity of these revenues, and the earl exchanged these in 1219 for the income derived from the annual rent of the lands of Rahallo.[31] This settlement, too, proved, unsatisfactory, and Gille Brigte finally agreed that the least troublesome arrangement would be to grant the canons license to hold a court of their own.

The grant of jurisdictional privilege was sufficiently important to raise the profile of the priory of Inchaffray to abbatial status. In 1221 the native prior, Alpin, was removed from office and in his place Innocent, a canon of Scone, assumed the leadership of the newly instituted abbey.[32] Gille Brigte's first and perhaps only gift to the newly erected abbey was the grant of a local church and its revenues,[33] but his second wife, Iseulte of Kinbuck, assigned to the abbot and canons five acres of land from her own estate of Abercairney.[34]

Gille Brigte's gifts to the canons of Inchaffray were remarkably generous; in the century that followed they became the foundation of considerable wealth. In 1274–5, when Pope Gregory X imposed a kingdom wide tax on the Scottish clergy, his collector assessed the abbey's contribution of a teind of its revenues at £24 13s. 3d.,[35] placing Inchaffray's annual income well ahead of those of several other – and many larger – Augustinian houses.[36] By contrast, Gille Brigte's successors were notably less demonstrative of their piety. Indeed, after 1223 the canons increased their landed possessions at the hands of the Strathearn family very little, adding only a small plot of land near the mill at Dunfallin in the early 1220s,[37] and in 1266 two acres at Nethergask.[38] Gille Brigte's successors also assigned few wholly new sources of revenue to the abbey. Those they did relinquish were of a modest nature, including six marks annually from the lands of Belnello and a death bed grant from Malise II of four marks from Monkcroft for the support of an almshouse chaplain with the promise of monies to fund the purchase of chalice and ornaments there.[39] The canons also acquired from Malise the persons and labour of two serfs and their families,[40] but from Malise III only the advowson of a new parish church established at Strowan.[41]

Despite the uneven nature of surviving charter materials, the pattern of the earls' patronage of Inchaffray after the death of Gille Brigte in 1223 is clear. The deeds of Earls Robert, Malise II and Malise III offer good examples of the vari-

---

[30] Ibid., nos. 43, 44. [31] Included in a general confirmation of the earl's grants to Inchaffray abbey, ibid., no. 39. [32] No canon by the name of Innocent has been traced to Scone abbey, but Bower noted that Alpin's replacement came from there. *Scotichronicon*, v, 112. [33] *Inchaff. Chrs.*, no. 45. [34] Ibid., no. 46. [35] A.I. Dunlop (ed.), 'Bagimund's roll: statement of the tenth of the kingdom of Scotland' (1939), 53, 71. [36] G. Ewart, 'Inchaffray abbey, Perth & Kinross: excavations and research 1987' (1996), 47, table 1. [37] *Inchaff. Chrs.*, no. 52. [38] Ibid., no 95. [39] *Inchaff. Liber*, nos. 38, 52. [40] *Inchaff. Chrs.*, no. 87; *Inchaff. Liber*, no. 58. [41] *Inchaff. Chrs.*, no. 112.

ety of ways in which a powerful native family might balance pious obligations and more pragmatic considerations. Strathearn gifts to the abbey are also indicative of the changing economy of thirteenth-century Scotland and the concomitant pressure on landed resources about which historians are in general agreement.[42] The days of relinquishing title to entire estates, parish revenues and annual rents to the abbey were already waning before 1223; they had ceased almost altogether by the later years of the century. From the time of Earl Robert gifts to Inchaffray abbey were designed, rather, to provide the canons with the means to exploit the territories around them to maximum economic advantage. The change was subtle but unmistakable. Thus, one of Malise II's grants assigned to them twenty-four marks annually in place of teinds, which the earl felt he could use more fruitfully to his own advantage.[43] Malise III likewise converted the second tends promised by his predecessors into a fixed annual payment of twenty marks of silver,[44] leaving him free to reap the rewards of what had become, by the second half of the thirteenth century, a 'guilt-edged investment'.[45] Both charters were granted only grudgingly and in consequence of disputes with the religious concerning the regular payment of the promised teinds. Another gift included the advowson of Cortachy, a convenient grant in that the church, acquired by Malise II at the time of his marriage to Maud daughter of Gille Brigte earl of Caithness and Orkney, lay in distant Brechin.[46] By the closing years of the thirteenth century the abbey of Inchaffray boasted interests, directly or indirectly, in a wide variety of church lands and revenues, in multures and mills, in fishing and forest rights, in timber and quarrying privileges, in human labour and in structures such as mills and bridges. But it had not substantially increased its demesne at the expense of the earls of Strathearn since the time of Earl Gille Brigte.

In this later period, moreover, concessions from the comital family were sometimes hard won. In a lengthy deed granted to Inchaffray abbey before his father Gille Brigte's death, Robert, as heir, undertook to support and promote the interests of the religious house, confirming in a formal charter the numerous gifts that his father had made.[47] The document is overtly conciliatory in tone, and while there is no evidence that Robert sought to reverse his father's acts, the abbey's residents were sufficiently mistrustful to require a second solemn promise from him never to harass the abbot unjustly or to neglect to prosecute the legal concerns and interests of the house.[48] Malise II's grant of an annual money payment in place of teinds from rents and cain was made only after the religious of Inchaffray complained that they had not received these goods in full 'through the fault of his bailies'.[49] Further trouble was in evidence in 1268, when Malise II made provision for the repayment of several debts he had incurred with

---

[42] Duncan, *Making*, 425–7; I.D. Whyte, *Scotland before the industrial revolution* (1995), 46–50. [43] *Inchaff. Chrs.*, no. 76. [44] Ibid., no. 113. [45] Duncan, *Making*, 300. [46] *Inchaff. Chrs.*, no. 86. See also B. Crawford, 'The earls of Orkney-Caithness and their relations with Norway and Scotland: 1158–1470' (1971), 14, n. 1. [47] *Inchaff. Chrs.*, no. 41. [48] *Inchaff. Liber*, no. 16. [49] *Inchaff. Chrs.*, no. 76.

the abbey, some arising from the grant of a rent from Belnello near Fowlis that the earl had in fact assigned to his brother some time before.[50] Similarly, Malise III's gift of a fixed payment was the consequence of a dispute with Abbot Hugh of Inchaffray over the earl's attempts to circumvent the generosity of his predecessors.[51] Another struggle between earl and abbey, this one involving the patronage of the church of Strageath, resulted in the issue of a formal decreet in 1287.[52] By this time the abbey had clearly learned to be wary of its patron's intentions and in the same year it extracted from Earl Malise a written undertaking that monastic privileges would not in future be prejudiced by the canons' willingness on a recent occasion to supply him with military aid from their lands.[53]

The native family of Lennox, like that of Strathearn, established ties with a nearby religious house. The Cluniac monastery at Paisley was the chief beneficiary of its generosity, though like their counterparts in Strathearn, who also gave modest gifts to the Tironensian monks at Lindores and Arbroath and the Cistercians at Coupar Angus for a generation after Earl Gille Brigte's death,[54] members of the Lennox family granted charters of land and privilege to the religious of Arbroath and its mother house at Kelso. The pattern of monastic patronage in Lennox in the thirteenth century nevertheless differed substantially from that of Strathearn. The more marked insularity of Lennox, evident in so many aspects of the lordship until the late thirteenth century, is in evidence particularly in relations between the earls and their local bishop, as well as in the chronology and extent of ecclesiastical endowment. In the mid-1170s, during his brief tenure as earl, David of Huntingdon assigned to the abbey of Kelso the little churches of Campsie and Antermony. These were the only grant he appears to have made from the lordship, an indication, perhaps, of his unwillingness to plunder the territories during his temporary rule.[55] Some years later Earl Ailin II of Lennox, in a reassertion of his native independence, granted Campsie to the episcopal see of Glasgow, noting in his charter that he himself had founded the church and had gifted to it the surrounding lands at its dedication ceremony.[56] Ailin's son Maoldomhnaich, as heir to the earldom, confirmed the gift.[57] Soon after his accession, however, Maoldomhnaich renewed Earl David's grant of the church to Kelso,[58] thereby initiating litigation between the two

50 *Inchaff. Liber*, no. 35.   51 *Inchaff. Chrs.*, no. 113.   52 Ibid., no. 118.   53 Ibid., no. 117.   54 Earl Gille Brigte's brother Maol Iosa granted estates in Strathearn to the abbey of Lindores, founded by his father-in-law Earl David of Huntingdon, and to Arbroath abbey, a royal foundation colonized, like Lindores, from Kelso. *Lind. Cart.*, nos. 127 (1195 x 1198), 29 (1195 x 1214); C. Innes and P. Chalmers (eds), *Liber S. Thome de Aberbrothoc* (2 vols, 1848–56), i, no. 86 (probably late 1190s). Maol Iosa's heir, his nephew Fergus son of Gille Brigte, confirmed his uncle's grants to Lindores and gave the abbey small estates in Strathearn at Bennie and Cathermothel, *Lind. Cart.* nos. 32 (1214 x 1220), 26 (1233-4), 24 (1226 x 1234). Fergus likewise confirmed Maol Iosa's gifts to Arbroath; *Arbroath Liber*, i, no. 87 (1225–26). Earl Robert assigned a small portion of land in Strathtay to Coupar Angus abbey, a grant that was confirmed by his brother Fergus. Reference to the earl's gift survives only in Fergus's charter of confirmation; D.E. Easson (ed.), *Charters of the abbey of Coupar Angus* (1947), i. no. 35.   55 Printed in K.J. Stringer, *Earl David of Huntingdon* (1985), 238–9; see also 14, 93.   56 *Glasgow Reg.*, i. no. 101.   57 Ibid., i. no. 110.   58 C. Innes (ed.), *Liber*

establishments for control of Campsie, a contest out of which the bishop of Glasgow eventually emerged victorious.[59]

Earl Maoldomhnaich's tangles with Bishop Walter of Glasgow both before and after the débâcle over Campsie led him to direct his pious intentions elsewhere. Before 1228 the earl had made arrangements for his burial (together with his wife) and commemoration in Paisley abbey,[60] but the dispute over Campsie and the eruption of an even more bitter wrangle over the lands of Kilpatrick soured his relations with the see and with the abbey. By 1231 he had made alternate arrangements to join the fraternity of the Tironsensians of Arbroath, in whose martyrology he directed that his name, together with that of his brother Amhlaibh, be inscribed.[61] But this new link with the royal monastery was a fragile one, and neither Maoldomhnaich nor his brother appears to have had much further contact with Arbroath. The earl's grandson and successor, Malcolm I, formally conceded as much in 1273, when he noted that the family had long been in arrears in its payment of a gift of oxen and, under royal pressure, agreed to pay the monks of Arbroath an annual render of two shillings in their stead.[62]

The failure of Earl Maoldomhnaich to establish and endow a religious house within his own territories stands in marked contrast with the examples of other native lordships north of Forth, notably Strathearn, but also Galloway, Kintyre, Carrick, Fife, Mar and Angus, where Gaelic lords initiated or maintained close ties with religious orders. Moreover, the absence in the province of Lennox of pre-twelfth century houses of Céli Dé or hermit priests is notable, and several factors suggest that support for the church remained highly localized and that the region resisted the influence of reform much longer than was the case elsewhere. Surviving evidence in support of this hypothesis is fragmentary at best, but none the less intriguing. Lennox was a land in which small churches, shrines and wells dedicated to local holy men and women proliferated. The antiquary A.D. Lacaille noted over forty sites in the Loch Lomond area alone, and other early historians likewise remarked on the significant numbers of small holy places scattered throughout the lordship.[63] Place name evidence suggests that many of these sites were ancient already in the late twelfth century,[64] and that the clerics who lived there were under the protection and influence of lay lords. Well into the twelfth century the pious gifts of Lennox benefactors, modest and wealthy, were expended on the endowment of such sites. Maoldomhnaich's

S. Marie de Calchou (1846), i, no. 222. **59** Ibid., i, nos. 230, 279. **60** Paisley Reg., 159. **61** Arbroath Liber, i, no. 133. The earl's gift of four oxen annually and 20 more on the occasion of his death was confirmed by King Alexander II in January 1230–1; ibid., no. 134. **62** Arbroath Liber, i, no. 342. **63** A.D. Lacaille, 'The Capelrig Cross, Mearns, Renfrewshire ...' (1927), 138; idem, 'Ecclesiastical remains in the neighbourhood of Luss ...' (1928); idem, 'Loch Lomondside fonts and effigy' (1933–4); see especially the map facing p. 108; J.G. Smith, Strathendrick and its inhabitants from early times (1896), 125, 278; J.M. Mackinlay, Ancient church dedications in Scotland: non-scriptural dedications (1914), 26, 101–2, 136–7, 148, 152, 197–8, 209. **64** W.F.H. Nicolaisen, Scottish place-names: their study and significance (1979), 129–30, 172; idem, 'Gaelic place-names in Southern Scotland' (1970), 23–35; Barrow, Kingdom, 50–2; J.M. Rogers, 'The formation of the parish unit and community in Perthshire' (1992), 76.

father, Ailin II, for example, endowed the church of Campsie with nearby lands, and numerous churches in Lennox dedicated to Celtic saints were under the direct control and patronage of the earl and his immediate family.[65] Rulers of a region steeped in the Celtic religious tradition, the pre-thirteenth century lords of Lennox enjoyed the spiritual and religious services of a variety of ecclesiastical clients and tenants, and had little need to effect dramatic changes either to the spiritual life within their territories or to patterns of patronage. By the 1220s, however, the cultural pressure exerted by a European church intent on vigorous reform prevailed. Maoldomhnaich and his family settled on Paisley abbey as the focus of their support for the reform movement, but significantly they did so only after the earl's marriage to a daughter of one of the kingdom's most important new families, the Stewarts, had brought them into direct contact with the royal court.

Maoldomhnaich and his close kinsmen were never as generous to Paisley abbey as was the family of Strathearn to Inchaffray. The founder of the Cluniac monastery, Walter I son of Alan, had made plentiful provision for the house, and his descendants were still making grants of land and privilege two generations after his death. Lennox gifts in the time of Earl Maoldomhnaich and his successor, Malcolm I, were altogether less magnificent, and are notable chiefly for the information they reveal about the firm hold the native family maintained over ecclesiastical tenants in the lordship. In the early part of his rule Maoldomhnaich granted to the monks of Paisley only a single church with its lands (Kilpatrick, a gift that was fraught with difficulties), and also the advowson of a second.[66] Other donations resembled more closely the type of endowment that the successors of Gille Brigte earl of Strathearn assigned to Inchaffray. Like the Strathearn grants, these were designed to demonstrate generosity to the monks without seriously depleting the resources that members of the comital family exploited directly for their own benefit. One of Maoldomhnaich's grants, for example, assigned to Paisley abbey several small estates that had been let by courtesy to a native tenant, Feargus son of Cunningham.[67] Another early grant, dated 1227 x 1232, assigned to the monks lands around Duntocher and Duntiglennan in the parish of Kilpatrick, but required that income from them be assigned directly to the support of the chaplain who was then drawing revenues from the lands.[68] Still other early charters issued under the earl's name in the mid-1220s granted valuable fishing privileges in the River Leven.[69] When the abbey extended these fishing grounds thanks to a gift of one of the earl's tenants, Maoldomhnaich added to the grant access to nearby pasture and woodlands and to the entire water of Leven.[70] His last donation to the monks of Paisley was of another small estate in the parish of Kilpatrick, assigned as part of a confirmation of the several charters by which the monks held lands within the earldom.[71]

---

65 See, for example, *Paisley Reg.*, 158–9, 160 and the grant of the church of Kilpatrick to the abbey which initiated the bitter litigation discussed below, ibid., 157, 158. **66** Ibid., 158, 160. **67** Ibid., 159–60, 173. **68** Ibid., 158–9. **69** Ibid., 216–17. The grant was confirmed by King Alexander II in 1228, ibid., 214–15. **70** Ibid., 212–13. **71** Ibid., 174.

Like his brother, Maoldomhnaich, Amhlaibh son of Ailin II was restrained in his patronage of Paisley abbey, gifting to its brethren only a part of the salt works he had erected at Rosneath on the Gare Loch with access to his woodlands there and the right to present to the church of Rosneath.[72] The earl's grandson and successor, Malcolm I, was even less willing to part with the estates, revenues and privileges that made up the wealth of his lordship. Soon after the beginning of his personal rule he confirmed the abbey's possessions in Lennox in an elaborately worded charter.[73] But although it gave the monks access to woodlands in Bonhill, this grant provided no new landed endowments.

The restrained generosity of the Lennox family was both a reflection and a cause of the tension that characterized relations between the native lords and the reformed orders. The grasping manoeuvres typical of thirteenth-century monastic administrators were unfamiliar to members of the Gaelic aristocracy; they must also have represented a challenge to the earls' hitherto firm control over the priests and other religious men who dwelt within their territories. The early years of the thirteenth century saw Paisley abbey involved in a struggle to establish its authority as an autonomous house and to extricate itself from the influence of distant Cluny.[74] The efforts of the abbot and monks to assert independence made them particularly mistrustful of the competing ambitions of the see of Glasgow for control of the revenues of local churches, gifts which the native earls in turn used as rewards for the clerics in their entourages. In the midst of such tension it is hardly surprising that ties between the Gaelic magnates of the region and the powerful interests of the Cluniacs at Paisley should have been less than intimate. Both parties were certainly aware of the contentious issue of clerical endowments, and the numerous charters of confirmation that the earls and their kinsmen were asked to make over the course of the thirteenth century attest the abbots' determination to remind each generation of donors of its financial and tenurial obligations.

Adjustments in the monastic landscape of the twelfth and early thirteenth centuries were neither simple nor wholly satisfactory for the Gaelic families of Strathearn and Lennox. Scholars have long recognized that the reform of the Scottish church was very much a piecemeal affair, with some regions experiencing rapid change in the wake of Anglo-Norman and continental penetration and others – chiefly the native lordships – undergoing transformation much more slowly.[75] Resistance among native magnates to ecclesiastical encroachments on the exercise of lordly authority over local churches is apparent in the earldoms of Strathearn and Lennox well into the thirteenth century, and documents recording the struggles that ensued between lay and ecclesiastical powers in the changing milieu of the Scottish church are abundant. Surviving mate-

---

[72] Ibid., 210, 211. [73] Ibid., 215–16. [74] M. Dilworth, 'Cluniac Paisley: its constitutional status and prestige' (2000), 25–6; J. Durkin, 'Paisley abbey: attempt to make it Cistercian', (1956). [75] See, for example, M. Morgan, 'The organization of the Scottish church in the twelfth century' (1947); J. Dowden, *The medieval church in Scotland* (1910), 7–11.

rials suggest that despite pressure from the bishops of Dunblane (on Earls Gille Brigte and Robert of Strathearn) and Glasgow (on Maoldomhnaich of Lennox), the native lords nevertheless succeeded in maintaining a firm measure of control over ecclesiastical affairs within their territories. The later twelfth and the thirteenth centuries witnessed the creation of a distinctive Scottish church, a process that scholars have described as both promising and problematic. In the hundred years or so after the accession of King David I, the establishment of a new network of dioceses and parish churches covering most of the kingdom brought a new sense of organization, but it also generated difficult and sometimes contentious questions about control over the new churches. The accelerated pace of parish formation has been linked directly to the arrival in Scotland of Anglo-Norman and continental land holders; indeed, it has been claimed that the creation of estates for the newcomers, especially south of Forth, 'completely transformed' the Scottish church.[76] Sound arguments have been made in support of this statement,[77] but scholars also acknowledge that the laying out of new parishes did not destroy the pre-twelfth century network of small local churches designed to serve the surrounding countryside. Many of these small establishments were under the control of the lay patrons who had erected them within their territories and who retained strong proprietary interests in them. Thus, one of Maoldomhnaich of Lennox's grants to the bishop of Glasgow of the right of presentation 'to the next vacant church in Lennox' nevertheless reserved to the earl the right to make appointments in future.[78] In other charters to Lennox tenants the earl openly gave away not merely church buildings and the lands upon which they stood, but also his rights of presentation.[79] The earls of Strathearn, perhaps more sensitive to the views (or the pressure) of the newly reformed see of Dunblane, appear to have been more willing to relinquish control over the churches within their lands to the bishop, but as late as 1282–3 Earl Malise III still felt confident enough of his proprietary rights to found and endow a parish church at Strowan, the advowson of which he assigned as he saw fit.[80]

While ecclesiastical authorities enjoyed only varied measures of success in asserting their authority over the appointment of clerics to parish churches in thirteenth-century Strathearn and Lennox, they were less able to stem the steady process of appropriation. This was the practice by which a donor granted the revenues derived from the teinds and lands of churches to a third party, often a monastic corporation. Appropriation was by no means a phenomenon unique to Scotland,[81] but it was especially problematic here, because in the twelfth century episcopal sees were simultaneously consolidating their own boundaries and attempting to establish control over their provinces after a long period of desue-

---

76 Morgan, 'Organization of the Scottish church', 135. **77** I.B. Cowan, 'The appropriation of parish churches' (1995), 14–15, and idem, 'The development of the parochial system', 44–5. **78** *Paisley Reg.*, 160. **79** *Lennox Cart.*, 19–20, 30–1; NAS, GD 220/A1/2/2, GD 220/2/11. **80** *Inchaff. Chrs.*, no. 112. **81** Cowan, 'The appropriation of parish churches', 14 and the authorities cited there.

tude and decay.[82] In Scotland, moreover, the appropriation of churches coincided with the fixing of parish boundaries to such an extent that in some places one development was indistinguishable from the other.[83]

Proprietary interests of lay land holders in the churches scattered around their sees were the focus of ecclesiastical concern and legislation for more than a century after 1150,[84] but in Scotland as elsewhere in Britain and western Europe generally, lay appointments to clerical positions were a deeply entrenched practice. Within the native earldoms, moreover, kinship ties often reinforced relations between lords and clerics, further strengthening the family's interests in the appurtenances attached to ecclesiastical estates. One of Earl Gille Brigte of Strathearn's sons, for example, was parson of the parish church of Gask, and this Malise's son in turn parson, then rector, of the church of Crieff.[85] Members of the Lennox family also staffed the churches of their earldom: Maoldomhnaich's brother Dùghall, for example, became infamous in his own locality as rector of Kilpatrick.[86] Strathearn links with the ancient church of Muthill, and Dùghall of Lennox's reluctance to relinquish control over the historic site dedicated to St Patrick in turn led to bitter disputes with the religious houses of Lindores and Paisley, into which the bishops of Dunblane, Dunkeld and Glasgow quickly intruded their own concerns. Although the squabbles that erupted in respect of Muthill and Kilpatrick differed in their substance, both serve as illuminating examples of the challenge that native proprietary interests represented to the reform minded church as late as the third quarter of the thirteenth century. Both also serve as warnings against the tendency on the part of some scholars to treat the triumph of ecclesiastical reformers over a backward looking *ecclesia Scoticana* as an inevitable process.

The lands of Muthill, located deep within Strathearn and hard by the administrative centre of the lordship, had a long history already when troubles over the allocation of its church erupted around 1210. Originally an episcopal residence and perhaps the earliest seat of the bishops of Dunblane,[87] Muthill was also home to a community of Céli Dé whose members were still active well into the thirteenth century.[88] In the later twelfth century the church and the several estates attached to it were in the possession of Fearchar earl of Strathearn. When he died, they passed to his son and heir, Earl Gille Brigte, who in 1172 or 1173 granted them as part of a knight's feu to his brother, Maol Iosa.[89] In the

---

82 Ibid., 47–51; Duncan, *Making*, 281–302; I.B. Cowan, 'Vicarages and the cure of souls', in idem, *Medieval church*, 46–61: 46–9.   83 Morgan, 'Organization of the Scottish church', 143.   84 See, for example, *Glasgow Reg.*, i, no. 60; *Kelso Liber*, no. 427; D. Patrick (ed.), *Statutes of the Scottish church* (SHS, 1907), 11–14, 15, 43, 45, 49, 52, 53, 64, 66–7.   85 Neville, 'Earls of Strathearn', ii, nos. 49, 53, 54, 59, 61, 72, 73; App. B., nos. 12, 22–4, 27, 28, 31, 32, 49, 54.   86 *Paisley Reg.*, 163. See also below, pp 145–6.   87 *MRHS*, 204; A. MacQuarrie, 'Early Christian religious houses in Scotland: foundation and function' (1992), 17, 128–9.   88 Prior Mael Pol of Muthill and two of his brethren, Sitech and Mael Coluim, witnessed a charter dated 1178 x 1195; Innes (ed.), *Carte monialum de Northberwic*, 7; *Inchaff. Chrs.*, nos. 3, 13. This Sithech was probably the same 'Sythakh kelede' who witnessed Bishop Simon of Dunblane's confirmation of the church of St John the Evangelist to the Céli Dé of Inchaffray c.1190; *Inchaff. Chrs.*, no. 1.   89 *RRS*, ii, no. 136.

later 1190s, probably around the time of his marriage, Maol Iosa in turn made a gift of the church in free alms to the abbey of Lindores, founded by his father-in-law, Earl David of Huntingdon.[90] Maol Iosa's grant included 'all the lands attached to the church, with the teinds, oblations and everything else justly pertaining to it', an indication that by this time Muthill had acquired the status of a parish church.[91] In most respects the charter was typical of hundreds of others that assigned gifts in free alms to ecclesiastical corporations elsewhere in the kingdom. But Maol Iosa failed to take into account the determination of contemporary reform ideology to challenge the intrusion of lay patrons into local churches, and he underestimated the complex jurisdictional claims that were part and parcel of title to Muthill. Certainly, Bishop Abraham of Dunblane (ironically, a former chaplain of Earl Gille Brigte),[92] took a dim view of the native magnate's actions in disposing of ecclesiastical property. Like other bishops of his time he was struggling to assert control over the churches in his see in accordance with reform principles, and anxious to stem the tide of lay appropriations of these churches to monastic corporations. Abraham maintained that Muthill was a mensal church, that is, that its revenues had traditionally been rendered to episcopal coffers, a claim that appears to have been based in some fact.[93] The questions at issue were politically sensitive, given the close relationship between the see of Dunblane and the native lords of Strathearn, and were resolved only in stages, first during the time of Bishop Abraham between 1211 and 1214, then again in 1234–5, after a fresh attempt by Bishop Clement to achieve a settlement more satisfactory to episcopal interests. In the end the efforts and energy of each of the litigants were only partially rewarded, for the settlements gave title to the bishop but also imposed on him the obligation of rendering an annual rent to Lindores for the rights in several estates which the abbey had been compelled to cede with the church of Muthill.[94]

Around the same time as the litigation over Muthill was coming to a head Maol Iosa's heir, Fergus son of Gille Brigte, also became embroiled in another dispute with Lindores abbey, this time over an attempt to compensate the monks for the lordly rights he intended to exercise over newly developed lands in south western Strathearn. In one charter he granted them the lands of Bennie and Concraig, and in a second those of Fedale, in exchange for the second teinds of cain and rent that the abbey had been accustomed to receive since the time of Maol Iosa son of Fearchar.[95] The gifts, however, troubled Bishop Clement of Dunblane, a Scottish born Dominican noted for his efforts to effect a vigorous reorganization of episcopal revenues and ultimately to restore his ancient

---

90 *Lind. Cart.*, no. 127. **91** Cowan, 'Parochial System', 51; Morgan, 'Organization of the Scottish church', 136; Duncan, *Making*, 98–9. **92** J.H. Cockburn, *The medieval bishops of Dunblane and their church* (1959), 36–7. **93** I.B. Cowan, 'The post-Columban church' (1974), 249, 253–5, 258–9. **94** The lengthy dispute over Muthill and its pertinents is reviewed in detail in C.J. Neville, 'Native lords and the church in thirteenth-century Strathearn, Scotland' (2002), 454–67. For Muthill, see also Lord Cooper (ed.), *Select cases of the thirteenth century* (1944), 13–15. **95** *Lind. Cart.*, nos. 24, 26.

see to a strong and effective seat of episcopal authority.[96] This contest between Dunblane and Lindores over Fergus's gift resembled in many respect the argument over the church of Muthill and, as had occurred in the course of the earlier disagreement, the earl of Strathearn and members of his immediate family were inextricably caught up in the wrangling between see and abbey. Like Abraham before him, Clement took his grievance to the Roman curia, although this time with rather more success than his predecessor had enjoyed twenty years before. Papal judges delegate awarded the bishop a generous annual rent in lieu of revenues from the estates, and the monks of Lindores were permitted to retain only a portion of the teinds they had formerly enjoyed. They were also made to renounce afresh all claims to the church of Muthill.[97]

Tensions between native magnates and the changing thirteenth-century church were not confined to the lordship of Strathearn. The pious donations of Earl Maoldomhnaich of Lennox and his kin exhibit a strikingly lack of appreciation on the part of lay land holders for the determination of Scottish ecclesiastical authorities to secure widespread acknowledgment of episcopal rights and privileges. But they also demonstrate the defiance with which lay lords sometimes reacted against those ambitions. The clash of interests is nowhere more amply demonstrated than in the discord that arose over the church of Kilpatrick. As the birthplace of St Patrick and a pilgrimage site, Kilpatrick had an even more venerable history than did Muthill.[98] In the closing years of the twelfth century the church itself and its extensive lands were in the hands of Earl Ailin II of Lennox; attached to these was an equally ancient obligation to provide food and shelter for passing pilgrims and travellers.[99] Ailin was not ignorant of the ambitions of his contemporary, Bishop Jocelin of Glasgow, to assert control over ecclesiastical churches and lands in his see,[1] but neither was he prepared readily to cede his own authority over Kilpatrick and its estates. In a formal charter issued before the episcopal court he confirmed to Paisley abbey the church and several estates associated with it, and added a further gift of land, taking care to note that the grant bestowed on the monks 'all the liberties that I or any of my peers is capable of giving'.[2] Ailin's successor, Maoldomhnaich, confirmed the church to Paisley abbey soon after his succession in 1217. But here again, the terminology of his charter suggests that the earl was not prepared to surrender wholly his interest in Kilpatrick. Although the grant included the church itself 'with all its just pertinents', it was to be held 'as free, quit and honourably as any church in the realm of Scotland holds and possesses any other church *by gift of a [lay] patron*'.[3] The fact that Maoldomhnaich's brother, Dùghall, was installed as rector of Kilpatrick soon after the issue of this charter indicates

---

96 Duncan, *Making*, 143; *Lind. Cart.*, 258–62; Cockburn, *Medieval bishops of Dunblane*, 47–53. **97** *Lind. Cart.*, nos. 50–4. **98** Mackinlay, *Ancient church dedications non-scriptural*, 101–2; *Origines*, i, 20. **99** *Paisley Reg.*, 166. **1** Morgan, 'Organization of the Scottish church', 138–9; Cowan, 'Appropriation of parish churches', 16–20; Dowden, *Medieval church*, 115–16. **2** *Paisley Reg.*, 157; see also 321. **3** Ibid., 158, dated 1226 x 1228. Emphasis mine.

that the earl did indeed manage to retain considerable influence in the disposition of the church.

The reluctance of the Lennox family to abandon its longstanding control over Kilpatrick was a direct cause of the lengthy, bitter and expensive litigation that ensued, but also a symptom of the Scottish church's inability to disengage itself from the enduring grip of the native nobility. According to testimony presented to judges delegate in the mid-1230s, soon after his brother's charter concerning Kilpatrick had been issued to Paisley abbey, Dùghall commissioned a forged charter by which his brother the earl had allegedly detached several estates from the church and bestowed these as an hereditary feu on Dùghall himself. On the basis of this document Dùghall in turn granted the estates to several lay tenants, Gille Brigte son of Samuel de Renfrew, Dùghall son of Cristin the *judex* of Earl Maoldomhnaich, Feargus son of Cunningham and Robert de Reddehow. Dùghall claimed that his brother, Earl Maoldomhnaich, had confirmed these grants, but these charters, too, if they ever existed, were undoubtedly spurious. Abbot William of Paisley, however, wasted little time in asserting the rights of his house over the dubious claims of Dùghall and his men. His suit bears the hallmarks of a claim pursued efficiently, expeditiously, and with full expectation of a successful outcome. In June 1232, in response to a direct appeal from William, Pope Gregory IX issued a bull authorizing an inquest into lands 'unlawfully alienated and laid waste'.[4] Appointed to disentangle the whole matter were Lawrence, dean of Carrick, Richard, dean of Cunningham, and Alan 'master of the scholars of Ayr';[5] soon, Bishop William de Bondington of Glasgow and King Alexander II were also drawn into the litigation.[6] The documents produced in the several stages of the proceedings that followed Pope Gregory's mandate were extensive. Collectively, they provide rare and valuable information about the sophistication with which reform minded clerics pursued their aims and challenged their opponents in region like the lordship of Lennox.

The judges delegate, clearly predisposed to favour the claims of the Cluniac house of Paisley against those of the native family, set about resolving the dispute in a series of actions.[7] First to fall under their scrutiny in the autumn of 1233 was Gille Brigte son of Samuel, who had obtained from the cleric Dùghall a small plot of land on the Clyde known as Monackenneran (now lost). Gille Brigte himself never appeared before the judges, perhaps because like them he knew of the spurious nature of the charters he held, and his contumacy earned him sound condemnation. In his absence counsel for Paisley abbey produced in the first instance three, then at a second session of the court, twelve recognitors whose depositions a notary recorded virtually verbatim.[8] These testimonials reconstructed the recent history of the lands of Monachkenneran in vivid detail.

---

[4] Ibid., 164, 174. The dating of the several documents generated by the litigation concerning the lands of Kilpatrick is, with a few exceptions, that found in W.W. Scott, *Syllabus of Scottish cartularies: Paisley* (1996), 15–17.   [5] Ibid., 168.   [6] Ibid., 168–70.   [7] For a summary of these proceedings, see Cooper (ed.), *Select cases*, 32–40; see also *APS*, i, 95–7 (red pagination); *Origines*, i, 20–22.
[8] *Paisley Reg.*, 165–7.

One witness recalled how he himself as a child, some sixty years and more beforehand, had been entertained there by an old man named 'Bede Ferdan' (Gaelic Bredei Ferdomnach?), who lived in a house made of timber, and whose only obligation was to provide food and lodging 'for persons who passed by'. Another, younger, witness deponed that twenty years later he 'had seen' Cristin son of Bede in possession of the same land, and that the estates pertaining to the church of Kilpatrick consisted not merely of Monachkenneran but also of four other tenements, all currently in the possession of Dùghall son of Ailin. A second panel of witnesses summoned two months later, this one afforced by members from Earl Maoldomhnaich's own household, repeated similar testimony, though the tales they told reveal that Bede had been compelled to defend very strenuously his claims to the land of St Patrick. Thus, one of Maoldomhnaich's closest *familiares*, Mael Coluim Beg, revealed that Kilpatrick and its lands had always been under the jurisdiction of the church; another informed the court that as far back as the time of Earl David of Huntingdon the old man had successfully resisted attempts to raise a military aid; a third recalled that in fact Bede 'was killed in defence of the rights and liberties of the church'. In the face of such overwhelmingly damning testimony Dùghall had little choice but to capitulate. He tried, though, to implicate senior members of his family in the seizure of Kilpatrick lands, stating that he had agreed to their unlawful alienation 'because he did not wish to offend his father or his brother or his relations'.[9]

The judges delegate very quickly brought the matter to a close. They reported the findings of the inquests of September and November 1233 to the bishop of Glasgow, noting Dùghall's continued defiance even after his admission of fault,[10] awarded possession of Monachkenneran to Paisley abbey, dismissed Dùghall from the office of rector, and passed a sentence of excommunication against him. His tenant, Gille Brigte son of Samuel, meanwhile, was proving as unwilling as Dùghall to suffer the church's plundering of his landed possessions. In 1235 he brought suit against Earl Maoldomhnaich before the justiciar of Scotia in what appears to have been an action of warrandice, seeking compensation for the lands of Monachkenneran. In accordance with the findings of the inquest that had been held the previous year he agreed in the end to surrender the 'charter and confirmation' that he said he had received from the earl and his brother, and to abandon all claims to the estate. In return, Maoldomhnaich offered him payment of sixty marks, to be rendered in three instalments.[11]

The church's firm treatment of Gille Brigte's pretensions is equally evident in the series of actions pursued in respect of other lands belonging to Kilpatrick. Dùghall's alienation of no fewer than ten estates associated with the church was also the subject of Pope Gregory IX's bull of 1232, and an inquest convened in April 1234 found his tenants, Dùghall son of Cristin and Robert de Reddehow, guilty of attempting to wrest control of the lands by means of 'adulterine and illicit charters', as well as by resort to 'extortion'.[12] After avoiding the court for

9 Ibid., 167.   10 Ibid., 168.   11 Ibid., 170–1.   12 Ibid., 164–5, 173–4.

as long as he could, Dùghall finally appeared before the judges and personally admitted his wrongdoing. Earl Maoldomhnaich himself was also present at this session and, aware that his family could no longer defy the church, formally resigned all the lands of Kilpatrick to Paisley abbey.[13] Soon thereafter, in a flurry of written deeds, Dùghall son of Ailin and the men to whom he had in turn granted rights in the estates surrendered their claims (and their forged charters) into the hands of the earl, who in turn renewed his gift of the church in its entirety to Abbot William.[14]

If the litigation of 1233–5 represented a significant victory of the church over the power of native magnates, it did not see the wholesale triumph of reform principles over lordly prerogatives. Despite the sentence of excommunication with which the papal judges delegate responded to his contumacy, Dùghall son of Ailin won the right to retain his position of rector of Kilpatrick, together with a life rent from one of the estates that had been so bitterly contested.[15] Earl Maoldomhnaich's influence here is evident. Moreover, a final settlement of the dispute was by no means achieved in 1235. In the early 1270s Dùghall's heirs, three great-nieces, together with their husbands, initiated new suits in respect of Kilpatrick estates both against the earl and Paisley abbey. Their claims had some merit, for the plaintiffs received a measure of support from the king himself.[16] The resolution of these actions was as lengthy and complex (as well as expensive), as had been those of 1233–5, and this time the abbey won recognition of its title to the lands only after resorting to a substantial pay off of 140 marks and more to the complainants.[17] Even then, the issue was not allowed to rest: Earl Malcolm I of Lennox himself suffered excommunication in 1294 for attempting yet again to intrude into the lands of Kilpatrick.[18]

The examples of Muthill and Kilpatrick illustrate the difficulties that beset the reformed church in its endeavours to assert unchallenged authority over ecclesiastical properties held by native magnates. Similar struggles occurred in other parts of Gaelic Scotland and, as in Strathearn and Lennox, the settlement of these disputes was more often than not a matter of compromise rather than categorical victories for the church.[19] Drawing as they did on two centuries of reform inspired legislation, Scottish ecclesiastical tribunals of the thirteenth century were well equipped to undertake litigation on a broad front, but as late as 1250 the principle had yet to be accepted that ecclesiastical jurisdiction extended over all matters relating to church property.[20] Moreover, the relatively tardy reorganization of Scottish episcopal sees, which occurred simultaneously with the creation of new parishes and the introduction of reformed monastic orders from the continent, meant that bishops confronted at one and the same time the entrenched problem of the lay proprietary system and the quickening pace

---

13 Ibid., 165–6. **14** Ibid., 159–63, 173, 175–6, 178–80. **15** Ibid., 166. **16** Ibid., 180–204, 201*. **17** Ibid., 189–91. **18** Ibid., 201*–4*. **19** See, for example, Cooper (ed.), *Select cases*, 9, 12, 40–1, 51–2, 91–2; Stringer, 'Reform monasticism' 156, 159–60; P.C. Ferguson, *Medieval papal representatives in Scotland: legates, nuncios, and judges-delegate, 1125–1286* (1997), 136–54; R. Oram, *The lordship of Galloway*, 186. **20** Duncan, *Making*, 284–90; Ferguson, *Medieval papal representatives*, 187–90.

of lay appropriation. In such circumstances the ecclesiastical front could hardly be united in its aims. The vested interests of monastic bodies in securing wealthy endowments often clashed with those of bishops intent on imposing episcopal authority over their sees and creating cathedral prebends out of the same properties. Such was the case in both Strathearn and Lennox, where disputes between the religious houses of Inchaffray, Lindores and Paisley on the one hand and the sees of Dunblane and Glasgow on the other generated considerable tension. The intimate affiliations that Scottish monks and canons carefully cultivated with their lay founders and patrons were in some places paralleled in good relations between bishops and Scottish magnates. But in others, episcopal ambitions ran afoul of lordly intentions and relations were of a more antagonistic sort. The earldoms of Strathearn and Lennox offer pertinent examples of the latter and provide valuable case studies of the effects of reform on the structure of the Scottish medieval church.

EPISCOPAL AUTHORITY

Some two hundred years after the death of Gille Brigte of Strathearn, the chronicler Walter Bower noted that the earl 'divided his kingdom into three equal portions. One he gave to the church and bishop of Dunblane, the second to St John the Evangelist and the canons of Inchaffray, the third he kept for himself and his own needs, and for his heirs'.[21] Bower's praise was more fulsome than factual, but it offers strong evidence that in the eyes of later medieval churchmen Gille Brigte of Strathearn played a significant part in the restoration to preeminence of the see of Dunblane. More tellingly, it suggests the creation of an enduring memory, rather at odds with surviving evidence, of a close bond between bishopric and lordship. In the minds of the earl's own contemporaries, too, the ties between bishop and magnate were so intimate that the two were often blurred altogether.

The origins of the see of Dunblane are shrouded in mystery. Some type of episcopal organization had been established there before the time of David I, probably of the nature that Professor Donaldson described as 'monastic'; consisting, that is, of a series of local churches served by priests and headed by a monk-bishop.[22] The first mention of a reconstituted see dates from the year 1155, and a Bishop Lawrence was witnessing charters issued in the period of Earl Fearchar (d. 1171).[23] It was only in Gille Brigte's time, however, that efforts to reorganize the see gained momentum and that the centre of episcopal administration became firmly established at Dunblane.[24] The special patronage of the

---

21 *Scotichronicon*, iv, 458–9. **22** Donaldson, 'Scottish bishops' sees', 106–15: 115; see also *MRHS*, 204; Cockburn, *Medieval bishops of Dunblane*, 2–3, 6–7. See also Dowden, *Medieval church*, 10. **23** D.E.R. Watt, *Fasti ecclesiae Scoticanae medii aevi ad annum 1638* (2nd edn, 1969), 75; *RRS*, i, no. 182; *Cambuskenneth Reg.*, nos. 218, 219. **24** *MRHS*, 204.

earls of Strathearn is especially evident in the extant sources from the 1170s on; equally visible is the extraordinarily close relationship that Gille Brigte cultivated with the see. From the late twelfth century the bishops appear on record under the protection of the earls and, with the exception of a few detached parishes, the boundaries of the diocese and the bishops' area of influence were roughly coterminous with those of the lordship.[25] Indeed, for much of the thirteenth century the bishop and several dignitaries of the cathedral church were referred to by the name of Strathearn rather than that of Dunblane.[26] More noteworthy still was the role that the comital family played in staffing the chapter of Dunblane from the time of Gille Brigte down to the late fourteenth century, for the earls enjoyed the highly unusual privilege of appointing new bishops, and exercised their patronage whenever the opportunity presented itself. Candidates for the episcopal see were sometimes drawn from the earls' own *familiae*: Bishop Abraham, for example, served in the comital household as a chaplain for several years before his advancement to the see,[27] and was able to ride out the scandal over his marital status that followed his election because he had the backing of his patron, Gille Brigte.[28] The earls' overweening influence on episcopal elections was challenged soon after Gille Brigte's death, when Bishop Clement noted that elections rightly pertained to 'the whole clergy of Dunblane', but he himself openly acknowledged his need of Robert's support.[29] The papal curia addressed letters confirming new episcopal appointments to the earls as patrons of the see as late as 1361, illustrating the enduring association of the earldom with the bishopric, not merely in Scotland, but as far away as Rome.[30]

The close links between Strathearn and Dunblane had no parallel elsewhere in the kingdom. Richard Oram has noted the part played by Feargus of Galloway in the appointment of at least one bishop of Whithorn, but demonstrates that the events that led up to Gille-Aldan's election around 1128 were highly irregular. Thereafter, 'there is no evidence for their [the lords of Galloway] exercising control of the patronage of Whithorn in the fashion of the earls of Strathearn at Dunblane'.[31] Strathearn influence over the cathedral church was, moreover, deeply entrenched in areas other than episcopal elections. Throughout the thirteenth and fourteenth centuries the comital house-

25 Watt, *Fasti*, 78–9. 26 See, for example, *Inchaff. Chrs.*, nos. 3, 13; *Lind. Cart.*, no. 31; D.E. Easson (ed.), 'Miscellaneous monastic charters' (1951), 6–7. See also Dowden, *Medieval church*, 10. 27 *Inchaff. Chrs.*, nos. 3–5, 11–15, 25, 27, 28. In the last of these, dated *c.*1210, Abraham appears as bishop-elect. 28 Abraham's appointment was the subject of an angry letter from Pope Honorius III to Bishop William Malvoisin of St Andrews condemning the election of a cleric who, although unmarried, had a son. Abraham himself was the son of a priest. A. Theiner (ed.), *Vetera monumenta Hibernorum et Scotorum illustrantia* (1864), no. 6. For a reference to Arthur the son of Abraham, see *Inchaff. Chrs.*, no. 26. 29 Ibid., no. 60. 30 Theiner (ed.), *Monumenta*, nos. 284, 343, 355, 386, 442, 576, 644; *Lind. Cart.*, no. 31; W.H. Bliss et al. (eds), *Calendar of entries in the papal registers relating to Great Britain and Ireland (Regesta Romanorum pontificum). Papal letters* (14 vols, 1893–1960), i, 472–3, 567. 31 Oram, *Lordship of Galloway*, 182; see also 171–4. For a different view, see G. Donaldson, 'The bishops and priors of Whithorn' (1948–9).

hold supplied the see not merely with candidates for the bishop's throne but with a succession of deans, archdeacons, and other cathedral clergy.[32] From 1240 the abbots of Inchaffray, over whom the earls in turn exercised considerable authority, held the important office of precentor in the cathedral church.[33]

Walter Bower's comments notwithstanding, there is very little evidence in support of the contention that the thirteenth-century earls of Strathearn were actively involved in the establishment of a strong cathedral chapter at Dunblane. There survives little source material attesting the existence of anything resembling a chapter before c.1200, and there is no clear reference to a fully organized chapter until the time of Clement (1233–58). For a good part of the century after 1155 the bishops depended for counsel and advice upon a 'motley' group of clerics consisting of archdeacons, the occasional dean, the heads of nearby Inchaffray and Cambuskenneth abbeys, clerks, and a constantly changing selection of local clerics, including members of the Céli Dé community at Muthill.[34] Episcopal revenues were equally confused. The bishops claimed mensal incomes from the lands of Muthill, Aberuthven and Tullieden,[35] but the appropriation of these churches to Inchaffray priory under Earls Fearchar and Gille Brigte diverted those sources of income elsewhere. In addition, a series of valuable estates attached to the church of Madderty belonged to Dunkeld.[36] It was perhaps in response to the reallocation of such considerable resources to the canons that at the end of the twelfth century Bishop Simon invited clerics from Muthill to afforce his meagre chapter.[37]

Despite the growth of the episcopal entourage under Bishops Jonathan (c.1198–1210) and Abraham (1210–c.1225) and the involvement of the see in litigation over the teinds of local churches,[38] Dunblane experienced some very difficult years in the early thirteenth century. When the Dominican friar, Clement, became bishop in 1233 he found the cathedral church itself in a poor state of repair and, apparently, served only by a rural chaplain. It was not until 1240 that the chapter first issued a deed under a corporate seal of its own, and another generation had passed before a fully constituted chapter had been established.[39] The successful reform of the see was, in fact, accomplished almost exclusively as a consequence of the efforts of Clement and his successors, and in the face of considerable indifference on the part of the earls of Strathearn.

Clement was not long in office before he began to assert his episcopal authority and to attempt to reclaim for his church revenues and emoluments that he argued had been usurped. Prominent among his targets were the several churches that had been assigned by the earls of Strathearn to the canons of Inchaffray and the monks of Lindores, a process begun by Fearchar and his countess some sev-

[32] Watt, Fasti, 75–7, 78–81, 83, 86, 88–9, 91–2. [33] Ibid., 83; Inchaff. Chrs., xxxviii. [34] Duncan, Making, 281; Cockburn, Medieval bishops of Dunblane, 10–11, 237–40 [35] Inchaff. Chrs., nos. 60–2. [36] Ibid., no. vii, and 318. Earl Gille Brigte granted the church to the canons of Inchaffray in 1200. [37] Cockburn, Medieval bishops of Dunblane, 10–11. [38] Most notably, see the bitter dispute with Lindores abbey concerning the teinds of the church of Muthill. [39] Inchaff. Chrs., no. 67; Watt, Fasti, 79.

enty years before with the grant of the church of St Chattan of Aberuthven to the priests of the Isle of Masses.[40] Gille Brigte had assigned the church to his newly established priory and secured episcopal confirmations of his grant by two of his bishops.[41] The abbey later erected a vicarage with the teinds of the parish, reserving the right of presentation. In the litigation that he initiated in 1234, Clement asserted that both the vicarage and the second teinds from St Chattan and several other Strathearn churches belonged to him, and that the parish of Aberuthven in particular had been erected for the support of his table. The matter was put to arbitration before papal judges delegate and a compromise reached: Clement agreed to renounce his title to the church and its revenues in return for a hefty annual payment of £16 per annum payable by the abbot. The arrangement, which Clement might well have considered satisfactory, was rendered less attractive when Abbot Innocent admitted that the revenues at his disposal from St Chattan totalled barely £10 per annum. Clement had little choice but to remit the remaining £6 'out of compassion for the poverty of the house', but he made his agreement conditional on the abbey securing possession of the teinds of several other local churches then in the hands of the earl of Strathearn.[42]

This settlement, and others concerning parish teinds, rankled in the mind of the reform minded Bishop Clement. The arrangements made twenty years earlier for the collection of revenues from the parish church of Muthill had proved only partially successful and had been reached only after considerable time and expense to episcopal coffers.[43] Moreover, the award of fixed annual rents in lieu of teinds threatened further financial difficulties in future, for rents lost their value over time while tithal revenues increased. Less tangible, but perhaps of some concern as well, was the potential harm to relations with the earls of Strathearn that litigation in respect of parish churches might cause. Like his predecessors, Earl Robert was ambivalent in his support of episcopal ambitions against those of the family foundation at Inchaffray. Gille Brigte in particular had been sensitive to the reformed church's insistence that acts of appropriation be subject to episcopal approval,[44] and had sought confirmation of several of his gifts by the bishops of Dunblane, either by means of separate charters or by including their names in the witness lists of his deeds. His successors, Robert and Malise II, demonstrated a similar courtesy, but all three boasted poor records of real and tangible patronage to the episcopal see itself. The failure of the native family to endow the struggling cathedral church bore witness to a lack of concern with its prosperity, and probably also to recognition that the bishops' ambitions represented a challenge to their proprietary interests. Clement realized that the fortunes of Dunblane depended ultimately on a drastic reorganization of the diocesan administration and financial structures. In 1237, therefore, he went directly to the pope.

40 *Inchaff. Chrs.*, nos. 3, 13. **41** Ibid., nos. 10, 30. **42** Ibid., nos. 60–1. These churches were in the bishop's hands by 1239; ibid., no. 67. See also Cooper (ed.), *Select cases*, 41–2. **43** See above, p. 144, and *Lind. Cart.*, nos. 42, 50. **44** For the importance of episcopal approval in the early development of the Scottish parochial system, see Morgan. 'Organization of the Scottish church', 137; Cowan, 'Appropriation of parish churches', 15–16; and Duncan, *Making*, 299.

The complaint that Clement put before Gregory IX reads as an indignant indictment of the abuse of episcopal rights and privileges at the hands of both lay and religious authorities.[45] Clement began by stating that at the time of his succession in 1233 the see of Dunblane had been vacant for 'a hundred years or more', and that although bishops had been appointed, they had allowed the possessions of their office to be seized and plundered beyond possibility of recovery. When he came to Dunblane the church was in such an advanced state of decay that there was no longer any college of clergy, and the divine office was celebrated by a rural chaplain in a building that was roofless and near ruin. Episcopal revenues had been stolen by lay persons and alienated to such an extent that they scarcely sufficed to sustain him for even six months; in addition, there no longer existed a residence in which he might lay his head.

Clement's libel is a good example of reform rhetoric, and like most texts of this kind it includes as much invention as it does fact. There is little doubt that Dunblane was indeed languishing as a seat of episcopal authority in the time of Earls Fearchar and Gille Brigte, or that Clement's predecessors had been unable, despite the reforming climate of the late twelfth and earlier thirteenth centuries, to free themselves from the control of the native magnates. The diocese of Dunblane certainly suffered also from problems that plagued the heads of other sees during the thirteenth century, including the loss of parochial revenues to grasping monastic corporations and a poor state of physical repair.[46]

Clement's account of the state of his church nevertheless contained much that was true. When the early earls of Stathearn and their family members began to give tangible expression to their pious intentions it was chiefly to the religious men of Inchaffray and Lindores rather than to the cathedral church that they and their families directed gifts of lands and churches. Dunblane, moreover, lagged behind several other episcopal sees in the implementation of measures intended to reconstitute cathedral chapters, most apparent at Glasgow and St Andrews, but already in place in several other dioceses as well.[47] Fearchar and his successors were not so removed from events in the kingdom as to be wholly ignorant of the implications of ecclesiastical reform, and the close control that they strove to maintain over the episcopal office of Dunblane undoubtedly went some way towards ensuring the slow pace of change there.

---

45 Theiner (ed.), *Monumenta*, no. 91. The text of Clement's complaint has not survived, but its main points are preserved in the commission by which Pope Gregory initiated an inquiry into the matter on 30 April 1237. **46** Scholars, in fact, have linked the wave of new building at episcopal sites as far apart as Whithorn and Aberdeen to the implementation of reform measures designed as much to remedy the physical defects of the Scottish church as its spiritual malaise. D. MacGibbon and T. Ross, *The ecclesiastical architecture of Scotland* (3 vols, 1896–7), i, 46, 48–9; J.G. Dunbar, *The historic architecture of Scotland* (1966), 146; S. Cruden, *Scottish medieval churches* (1986), 92–3, 155–60, 181–3; Duncan, *Making*, 282–3; R. Cant, 'The building of St Andrews cathedral' (1974), 77–8. **47** N.F. Shead, 'The administration of the diocese of Glasgow in the twelfth and thirteenth centuries' (1976); I.B. Cowan, 'The organization of secular cathedral chapters' (1995); G.W.S. Barrow, *Kingship and unity*, 70–1; idem, *Kingdom*, 187–202; Duncan, *Making*, 281–2.

Pope Gregory's solution to the problems of Dunblane was to propose two plans for the thorough reform and reorganization of parish teinds in the diocese. He suggested that one quarter of the teinds of all parish churches in the see be assigned to the bishop for the erection of an episcopal residence and the support of a dean and a properly constituted chapter. Alternatively, the same portion of teinds from the several churches still in the hands of lay patrons was to be transferred, with the episcopal seat itself, to the canons of Inchaffray, who would henceforth become the clergy and chapter of a wholly new diocese and in whose hands would rest future episcopal elections. Not surprisingly, Clement opted for the first proposal. The second was unacceptable because, given the close relations between the Strathearn family and the abbey, it would seriously have compromised the independence of episcopal administration in the region. He therefore spent most of his remaining years in office negotiating with a wide variety of religious houses and lay patrons for the quarter teinds that would finance his reformed cathedral chapter. The disputes were complex and expensive, in part because the pope's mandate required that revenues be pursued 'only if it can be done without scandal' and because, by 1237, so many church lands had been assigned by appropriation to religious houses not only in Strathearn, but further afield in Menteith, Mar and Fife, too. Scandal was indeed avoided, though in the process of securing episcopal rights Clement clashed at virtually every remove.[48] In the end, moreover, his successes proved to be limited. Long after his death the chapter of Dunblane exercised direct control over a mere dozen of the twenty-six parish churches in the diocese,[49] with revenues from most of these consisting of fixed annual payments rather than more lucrative teinds. The number of prebends at the disposal of the bishop remained insufficient, and the grant of four canonries *ex officio*, while they added to the prestige of the chapter's membership, required stipends that proved difficult to fund adequately.[50] Clement's episcopate, moreover, did not see an end to stiff competition with Inchaffray abbey for scarce sources of revenue, and it was not until the early 1270s that the composition of the chapter of Dunblane was ultimately stabilized. The erection of a complete chapter was even longer in coming, not reaching its full complement until after 1500.

The thirteenth-century earls of Strathearn played only a muted role in the efforts of Clement and his successors to reform the see of Dunblane. When they did become involved it is difficult to discern the interests that motivated their actions. In the initial settlement of 1214 regarding the church of Muthill, for example, Earl Gille Brigte undertook the onus of rendering military service for one of the disputed estates,[51] but whether he did so in acknowledgment of his

---

48 For a summary of Clements' several suits, see Cockburn, *Medieval bishops of Dunblane*, 50–6 and the sources cited there. **49** Ibid., 14. **50** The abbots of Lindores, Cambuskenneth, Arbroath and Inchaffray were all granted prebends during Clement's episcopate. Theiner (ed.), *Monumenta*, no. 386; *Cambuskenneth Reg.*, nos. 125, 126; *Arbroath Liber*, i, nos. 1, 33, 34; *Inchaff. Chrs.*, no. 67; Cowan, 'Organization of secular cathedral chapters', 91. For the assessed value of the diocesan revenues of Dunblane in 1274–5, see Dunlop (ed.), 'Bagimond's roll', 26, 53–4. **51** *Lind. Cart.*,

responsibility as overlord for the unforeseen consequences of his brother Maol Iosa's grant or under pressure from Bishop Abraham is not clear. Robert remained distinctly aloof from Clement's pursuit of second teinds in 1234 and in 1259, when Bishop Robert de Prebenda sought assistance to pay the large debts of the see, it was from Pope Alexander IV that he sought assistance rather than his patron Malise II.[52] The earls of Strathearn, closely tied both to the religious house at Inchaffray and to the see of Dunblane, were in an invidious position in the scramble for revenues, rents and teinds that characterized most of the thirteenth century. Surviving evidence suggests that members of the comital family gave their allegiance primarily to the religious house on the Isle of Masses that Earl Gille Brigte had founded and endowed. They appear also to have been deeply suspicious of the efforts of Clement and his successors to reorganize the cathedral church. In the end, their choice of a favoured ecclesiastical client was a consequence of the competition generated by the conflicting aims of the reform movement.

Relations between the native earls of Lennox and the see of Glasgow were of a different nature, but here, too, episcopal authority and lay proprietary interests were a source of tension. By the later years of the twelfth century the bishops of Glasgow had embarked on an ambitious programme, the aim of which was the creation of a strong cathedral chapter that would reflect the status of the see as one of the most ancient and powerful in the realm.[53] Earlier incumbents, moreover, had begun the process of recovering churches, teinds and lands alienated to, or seized by, monastic and lay competitors. A study of churches newly dedicated in this period has found that significant numbers of these were returned to episcopal hands,[54] and that by the year 1200 the bishop 'was drawing on the incomes of about 35 churches'.[55] Pious grants offset many of the losses, and it was in support of Bishop Walter's efforts to reinvigorate his see that in the early thirteenth century Earl Ailin II of Lennox granted to Glasgow the church of St Machan of Campsie together with its adjacent chapels and all its revenues.[56]

Glasgow's insistence that authority to dispose of ecclesiastical property within the see belonged properly to the episcopal office alone was the cause of some disagreement between Ailin's successor, Maoldomhnaich, and Bishop Walter over the church of Campsie. [57] It is unclear whether the earl simply misunderstood the basis of the episcopal claim to preeminence, or if he interpreted Walter's designs to reclaim the church as a challenge to his lordly authority and decided openly to oppose it. Maoldomhnaich ultimately failed in his attempt to grant the church to Kelso abbey when Walter successfully pursued the abbot

nos. 43, 44. **52** W.H. Bliss et al. (eds), *Calendar of papal letters,* i, 367. **53** Shead, 'Diocese of Glasgow', 127–50. Cowan, 'Organization of secular cathedral chapters', 83–6. **54** N.F. Shead, 'Benefactions to the medieval cathedral and see of Glasgow' (1970), 3–4; *Glasgow Reg.*, i, no. 111. **55** Whyte, *Scotland before the industrial revolution*, 33. **56** *Glasgow Reg.*, i, no. 101. The grant was confirmed by the earl's eldest son and heir, Maoldomhnaich; ibid., i, no. 102. **57** Discussed above, p. 138.

and recovered title to it.[58] On this occasion at least, native pretensions were no match for ecclesiastical determination. The earl's next encounter with the bishop precipitated another episode in the conflict between episcopal intransigence and native resistance to reform measures, and proved equally troublesome. Early in 1226 Bishop Walter summoned Maoldomhnaich before a meeting of the cathedral chapter. There, the earl was compelled to acknowledge formally a series of episcopal privileges over which he had ridden roughshod to date, notably the obligation to render a teind of 'all the goods that by Christian law are owed to the church'. He agreed in future that he would from levying 'taxes and other exactions' from clerics in his lordship, that he would no longer require clerics to observe the onerous custom of providing hospitality to his serjeants, and that the clergy of Lennox should have unrestricted access to pasturage throughout his lands 'according to the traditions of the fathers and the statutes of the church'. Finally, he admitted that it was his duty as a lay magnate to enforce all sanctions levied against contumacious persons throughout his lands.[59]

The severity of the censure that Walter levied against the earl is itself extraordinary, but is rendered doubly so in that it echoed almost exactly a similar condemnation of the behaviour of Earl Gille Brigte of Carrick less than a year earlier.[60] The records of both incidents provide strong evidence that reform principles and all that these implied were not always received enthusiastically in the Gaelic regions of the kingdom. In 1225 Gille Brigte of Carrick, perhaps under episcopal duresse, made amends for the injuries that he and members of his family had inflicted on the see of Glasgow with a grant of a local church and its lands.[61] It is in this light that Maoldomhnaich's gift to the bishop of the church of Cardross *in usus mense episcopalis* should be interpreted.[62] There is little to suggest, however, that the litigation was successful in winning the earl over to the bishop's way of thinking, for Maoldomhnaich reserved to his mettlesome brother, the cleric Dùghall, all rights in the lands associated with the church. Moreover, several charters datable to the period after 1226 show clearly that Maoldomhnaich continued to include church buildings and properties, together with rights of presentation, in his grants to lay tenants.[63]

If relations between the bishops of Glasgow and the native earls of Lennox were not wholly amicable, each of the parties nevertheless managed to establish a *modus vivendi* with the other. Robert de Hertford, a prebendary of the cathedral church, was a tenant of Maoldomhnaich in the early 1220s, when he was in possession of a portion of the earl's fishery in the River Leven, and of Dùghall son of Ailin in the lands of Dalmanno.[64] The vicars of several of the churches belonging to the see were frequent witnesses to Lennox charters, revealing that bishop and magnate kept channels of communication open with

---

58 *Kelso Liber*, i, nos. 222, 230.   **59** *Glasgow Reg.*, i, no. 141. For a discussion of serjeanty service in Lennox, see p. 108, above   **60** *Glasgow Reg.*, i, no. 139.   **61** Ibid., i, no. 187; see also xxvii.   **62** Ibid., i, no. 108.   **63** See, for example, *Lennox Cart.*, 30–1, grant to William son of Arthur son of Galbraith, 1238, and NAS GD 220/2/11, a charter in favour of Stephen of Blantyre, *c.*1248.   **64** *Paisley Reg.*, 212–14, 217.

each other's household. Mistrust of episcopal ambitions that Bishop Walter had instilled in the family, however, endured for the rest of the thirteenth century. Although Earls Maoldomhnaich and Malcolm I were occasional witnesses to Glasgow deeds, and each confirmed to the see gifts that their tenants made to the bishop,[65] the latter made no further grants to the see, and indeed maintained a considerable distance from the cathedral church and its affairs. In Strathearn, accommodation to the new tenets of episcopal authority saw the earls consolidate their hold on the office of bishop. In Lennox, the native family adopted different strategies for protecting their proprietary interests in ecclesiastical matters. One of these, begun after the unsettling confrontation with Bishop Walter of Glasgow over Campsie and Antermony, was to resist openly further episcopal encroachments on lordly authority to make appointments to local churches. Throughout the thirteenth century the earls of Lennox kept in their hands the patronage of no fewer than seven parishes in the lordship, and in particular of those located deep within their own demesne lands.[66] The second was to secure firm control over the deanery of Luss, one of five included within the archdeaconry of Glasgow. From the late twelfth century on, the jurisdictional area of the deanery coincided with the boundaries of the lordship, and the region was in fact referred to by the name of Lennox, rather than Luss, throughout the medieval period. Scholars are unanimous in characterizing the influence of the earls over the incumbents to this office as highly unusual.[67] Maoldomhnaich dean of Lennox first appears in a charter of Ailin II dated 1182 x 1199,[68] and served as a frequent witness to the earl's deeds until he had reached a very advanced age.[69] More striking still was the fact that he had a son, named Gille Moire.[70] Both were tenants of the earl in a rich estate centred on the toun of Luss, itself a very ancient site associated with St Kessog.[71] The impious lifestyle of the dean was clearly a matter of concern to the bishop of Glasgow, and in the late 1220s the office was in the hands of an unrelated cleric. But the earl managed on this occasion, too, to secure the appointment of a favoured tenant, Michael de Fintry, who in turn passed the office on to his son, Luke, also one of the earl's clerks.[72] The control that Earl Maoldomhnaich enjoyed over the wealthy deanery of Lennox as temporal lord and ecclesiastical patron was thus all but absolute, and must have gone some way towards offsetting concerns about the pervasiveness of episcopal influence in the lordship. In this contest

---

65 See, for example, *Glasgow Reg.*, i, no. 178, datable to 1250 x 1270 by the presence in the witness list of Walter de Mortimer dean of Glasgow, and Luke dean of Lennox and, in Farbhlaidh daughter of Kerald's original grant, of Robert treasurer of Glasgow; Watt, *Fasti*, 153, 164, 179. **66** Baldernock, Balfron, Bonhill, Buchanan, Drymen, Fintry, Killearn, Kilmarnock, Kilsyth, Luss, Strathblane. *Origines*, i, 20–48; Morgan, 'Organization of the Scottish church', 143. **67** Morgan, 'Organization of the Scottish church', 143; Shead, 'Diocese of Glasgow', 145. **68** *Paisley Reg.*, 157. **69** Watt, *Fasti*, 179. **70** *Glasgow Reg.*, i, no. 102. **71** Fraser, *Lennox*, ii, nos. 204, 207, and facsimiles nos. 36, 37; *Origines*, i, 30. Maoldomhnaich's tenure of Luss dates to the time of Earl Ailin II of Lennox. See also below, p. 172. **72** *Lennox Cart.*, 34–5, with an eighteenth-century copy of the (now lost) original in NAS, GD 22/3/531; Watt, *Fasti*, 179.

the bishop of Glasgow was undoubtedly the loser, and it was presumably mistrust of the loyalty and objectivity of Michael de Fintry that in the early 1230s led him to entrust the settlement of the dispute concerning the estates of the church of Kilpatrick to the deans of Carrick and Cunningham.

CHANGES IN RELIGIOUS PATRONAGE IN THE LATER THIRTEENTH CENTURY AND BEYOND

By the later thirteenth century the contours of the ecclesiastical landscape in Scotland had been firmly drawn. As one scholar has noted, 'almost all its monasteries were established, organized and endowed with the bulk of their possessions';[73] the chief centres of episcopal administration had been settled, and well over a thousand parishes had been erected.[74] The great age of reform inspired pious giving was fast drawing to a close, and the fourteenth century was almost everywhere for monastic and episcopal lords a period of retrenchment and intensified exploitation of existing resources, rather than an era of new endowment. The causes of this momentous shift were numerous and complex. They arose out of the consequences of ongoing war and a rapidly changing (and generally worsening) economy. Both factors made it increasingly difficult for pious noblemen to balance religious devotion with the concerns for the integrity of family estates.[75]

Changes in the pattern of religious patronage are discernible in the comital families of Strathearn and Lennox as early as the second half of the thirteenth century, and accelerated in its third quarter. There is evidence, too, of reluctance on the part of the earls to take sides in disputes when the affairs of the bishops of Dunblane and Glasgow came into conflict with those of neighbouring religious houses; a sign, perhaps, of these magnates' by now wholly remote interests in the fortunes of the sees. In both lordships, moreover, the fourteenth century witnessed a move away on the part of the native earls from the purely localized environments of their territories to the broader context of Scottish politics and society. The reorientation of their energies and ambitions had marked consequences for the monks and canons who lived in their midst.

A shift in the material expression of religious devotion is most obviously revealed in Strathearn in the nature of extant charter materials relating to the lordship. Twenty-six of the thirty full texts of Earl Gille Brigte's charters and one of his lost acts are to ecclesiastical houses; the figure for Robert is ten full texts and two *notitiae* out of a total of fourteen. The number of ecclesiastical to lay beneficiaries begins to alter in the time of Earl Malise II, and is more than

---

[73] A. Grant, *Independence and nationhood: Scotland 1306–1469* (1984), 94. [74] Dowden, *Medieval church*, 2; I.B. Cowan, *The parishes of medieval Scotland* (1967), v; idem, 'Development of the parochial system', 43–55. [75] *MRHS*, 11; Whyte, *Scotland before the industrial revolution*, 84–8; Grant, *Independence and nationhood*, 93–119; T.C. Smout, *A history of the Scottish people, 1560–1830* (1969), 45.

reversed by the period of Malise V's rule between c.1329 and 1350. Seven of the sixteen acts of Malise II extant in full texts are deeds to lay individuals or corporations, with a single *notitia* bringing the total to eight, or half of his known grants. From the time of Malise III there survive only thirteen full charter texts and three lost acts, of which seven are in favour of religious recipients, but Malise IV and Malise V appear to have made no grants whatsoever to religious beneficiaries.[76] The distribution of surviving ecclesiastical and lay charters in Lennox between the periods of Earls Ailin II and Donald, that is, c.1185 to 1365, shows a strikingly different pattern, with almost three quarters of surviving full texts issued in favour of secular beneficiaries, and only thirty-five odds deeds granted to clerics of religious houses. The Gaelic lords of Lennox and their kindred were clearly not keen patrons of the reformed church. The preponderance of charters to lay persons, however, does not obscure a relative decline in grants to religious beneficiaries from the mid thirteenth century through the mid fourteenth, similar to that which occurred in Strathearn and indeed throughout the realm.[77]

Malise II was the last of the native earls of Strathearn to concern himself with the affairs of Inchaffray abbey, and the few grants that he made to the canons were modest.[78] Lack of interest in the welfare of the house also manifested itself in his unwillingness to take an active part in ongoing disputes concerning the appropriation of parish revenues that preoccupied the canons throughout the middle decades of the thirteenth century. The earl's indifference did not go unnoticed, and it is no coincidence that around this time the abbey intensified its programme of petitioning the pope for assistance in repossessing lands over which it had lost control, and initiated a series of suits designed to accomplish similar purposes.[79] The bishops of Dunblane, meanwhile, continued to struggle along on the improved but still inadequate finances secured by Clement during his epsicopate. In 1233 Robert de Prebenda received papal permission to claim the first year's revenues from all vacant benefices in the diocese, a gift intended to enable him to meet the debts of the see.[80] Neither Malise III nor his successors went out of his way to live up to his reputation as special patron of the see, and the later thirteenth-century bishops were compelled increasingly to fall back on the vicarage revenues of churches already annexed in order to endow their prebends.[81] Relations further deteriorated in 1291, when Bishop William appealed to the pope for permission to bequeath his movable possessions by testament, and sought an end to the practice by which the earls of Strathearn, 'by means of a wicked custom' had in the past confiscated these goods as their own.[82] Unwilling to surrender their historic if highly unusual

---

[76] Neville, 'Earls of Strathearn', ii, 302–5. [77] G.G. Simpson, 'An Anglo-Scottish baron of the thirteenth century: the acts of Roger de Quincy, earl of Winchester and constable of Scotland' (1965), 155–6; Stringer, *Earl David of Huntingdon*, 56, 91; idem, 'Acts of lordship: the records of the lords of Galloway to 1234' (2000), 203–34: 203, 206; Young, 'Earls and earldom of Buchan', 185–7. [78] See above, p. 137. [79] *Inchaff. Chrs.*, nos. 104, 107, 110, 111, 113–15, 117, 118, 120, 122; see also xxxi. [80] Bliss et al. (eds), *Calendar of papal letters*, i, 367. [81] Cowan, 'Organization of Scottish secular cathedral chapters', 34. [82] Theiner (ed.), *Monumenta*, no. 343.

control over the office of bishop, the later earls nevertheless expended little energy in ensuring the material prosperity of Dunblane. Walter Bower's comments notwithstanding, the see of Dunblane enjoyed its pre-eminence in despite of, rather than thanks to, the efforts of the native earls of Strathearn.

In the late thirteenth and early fourteenth centuries the earls of Lennox demonstrated a similar reluctance to give up valuable lands and lordly prerogatives on behalf of the church of their day. Despite the royal favour that greatly increased his wealth and standing in the kingdom, Malcolm II was remarkably parsimonious towards the monks of Paisley, perhaps a legacy of the enduring arguments about the lands of Kilpatrick which in 1294 had seen his father condemned as an excommunicate and the laying of an interdict over his territories.[83] In an elaborately worded document issued at Dumbarton in 1330 that belied a great deal of tension, Malcolm confirmed his acceptance of the monks' title to Kilpatrick and further granted them the privilege of holding courts of their own for the trial and punishment of all felons taken on their Lennox lands.[84] The gift of jurisdictional rights may have reflected a sincere wish to assist the abbey's efforts to augment its revenues, but because the concession was linked to a solemn promise to end the practice of levying fines and other unlawful dues from the abbey's tenants, it is more likely that it was a concession made under duresse. Malcolm II's only other benefaction was a grant of 1333 to the inmates of the hospital at Polmadie of an exemption for twenty years from customary dues.[85] But despite a later claim that members of the Lennox family had been founders and patrons of the hospital, Malcolm and his successors failed miserably in their roles as donors to the house. In 1394 the bishop of Glasgow sought to appropriate the hospital 'in which for a long time little or nothing has been done for the poor',[86] and soon thereafter earl and bishop were in conflict over presentation rights to Polmadie.[87] The records of Earl Donald and his successor as lord of the territories of Lennox, his son-in-law Walter of Faslane, as patrons of the church are equally unimpressive. In 1364 Arbroath abbey was still attempting to collect a monetary gift once granted by Earl Maoldomhnaich, a promise long since forgotten by Malcolm I, Malcolm II and Donald.[88] Like their fellow magnates in Strathearn, the native earls of Lennox appear to have found the demands of ecclesiastical administration and monastic exploitation alike less than attractive. Their retreat from the practice of regular patronage affected the material prosperity of the church in their regions as profoundly as did similar actions by other lay lords elsewhere in the realm.

---

83 *Paisley Reg.*, 201*–4*. **84** Ibid., 205–6. **85** *Glasgow Reg.*, i, no. 284. **86** W.H. Bliss (ed.), *Calendar of entries in the papal registers relating to Great Britain and Ireland* (1896), 614. The hospital was still derelict seventy years later, when Isabella countess of Lennox transferred its revenues to a new collegiate church; Bliss et al. (eds), *Calendar of papal letters*, x, 623–4. **87** *MRHS*, 188; *Glasgow Reg.*, i, nos. 317–18. In the fifteenth century Duncan earl of Lennox was still arguing with the bishop of Glasgow about the right of presentation to the hospital at Polmadie. Ibid., ii. no. 344. **88** *Arbroath Liber*, i, no. 342; ii, nos. 29–30.

THE NATIVE CHURCH AND EUROPEAN INFLUENCES

The history of what might be termed 'church-state relations' in medieval Strathearn and Lennox reveals that the introduction of continental reform ideas was no simple process. The teachings of reform minded clerics certainly did not fall on deaf ears. The earls of Strathearn and Lennox fostered and maintained firm links with the canons and monks who shared their territories. In this sense, both comital families participated actively in an ethos shared not only by the great majority of the Gaelic magnates of their age, but also by European newcomers to Scotland. The motives that led noble men (and women) to follow the example of the royal house in endowing new religious houses were many and varied. They included genuine piety and simple acceptance of the church's teachings about heaven and hell and, more particularly, of the efficacy of charitable acts in the afterlife. In their foundation charter to Inchaffray, for example Gille Brigte and Maud of Strathearn expressed at once sincere grief at the death of their son, and realistic hope of eternity, and it was belief in the church's teachings about the fate of their souls that prompted Earl Maoldomhnaich of Lennox and his brother, Amhlaibh, to make arrangements for memorial masses in the church of St Thomas the martyr of Arbroath. In like fashion the establishment and support of no fewer than nine religious houses by the native lords of Galloway reflected the family's status as a 'major ally of the reformed orders' and as profoundly devout believers in the teachings of the contemporary church.[89] The dedication of still other houses by the lords of the western isles, as well as by the Gaelic earls of Carrick, Fife, Menteith and Mar, demonstrates that in the later twelfth and the thirteenth centuries the church's teachings were disseminated as thoroughly among native magnates as they were among their French- and English-speaking fellows, and indeed that the latter by no means held a monopoly over concrete expressions of religious devotion.

Gaelic lords were equally active to grasp the political, economic and social benefits of participating actively in the implementation of reform principles. Studies of Galloway have demonstrated the strong link between the religious patronage of Feargus and the rehabilitation of his character in the minds of ecclesiastical commentators; at the same time, they underscore his untrammelled success in deploying political opportunism to brilliant effect in the aggrandizement of his own authority in south-western Scotland.[90] The sons of Somhairle were moved to support religious reform for reasons as much devotional as political,[91] and similar efforts by the earls of Fife and Dunbar and by other native patrons within their own territories were in equal parts pious and self-serving. The establishment of the new orders, moreover, brought wholly new sources of revenue to royal and baronial coffers, and lay magnates were quick to grasp the poten-

---

[89] Stringer, 'Reform monasticism and Celtic Scotland', 128. [90] Ibid., 127–65; Oram, *Lordship of Galloway*, 172–4; Hudson, 'Gaelic princes and Gregorian reform', 73. [91] McDonald, 'Scoto-Norse kings', 215–19.

tial of the religious economy. The 'major redistribution of economic resources' that has been traced in the lands of the Cistercian monks of Galloway is evident, too, in Scotland north of Forth.[92] In Strathearn, for example, the vigorous efforts of the canons of Inchaffray to exploit their natural resources opened up new lands for cultivation and helped to turn the waters of the Pow Burn and the River Earn into profitable sources of ready cash.[93] In the rapidly developing economy of post-reform Scotland no native lord, however devout, was foolish enough to reject the tremendous economic benefits that followed everywhere on the heels of monastic revival. It is equally evident that the struggles between bishops and Gaelic magnates for control of ecclesiastical appointments involved the pursuit of the profits arising from rights of presentation as much as they did the resolution of matters ecclesiological.

And yet, a proprietary interest in the churches of their lands was deeply engrained in notions of lordship among the native earls of Strathearn and Lennox, and ecclesiastical claims to a plenitude of power throughout the realm struck at the heart of these beliefs. Despite increasing pressure from their local bishops, the earls of Strathearn and Lennox refused wholly to relinquish traditional prerogatives in church lands. The consequences of the enduring strength of the earls' claims were several. One was the continuation in both lordships of much of the personnel, and some of the practices, of the older church, exemplified in the survival of communities of Céli Dé and the widespread popularity of ancient religious sites dedicated to the worship of local saints. A second was the tension generated by the conflicting aims of reform minded bishops and conservative Gaelic lords, manifested in bitter disputes such as those which erupted over the churches of Muthill in Strathearn and Kilpatrick in Lennox. For much of the late twelfth and the thirteenth centuries, then, the establishment of the reformed church within the Gaelic territories of the kingdom was by no means a foregone conclusion, but rather a matter of conflict, compromise, and accommodation.

POPULAR RELIGION

If the experiences of Strathearn and Lennox in the arena of church-state relations were roughly similar, there is also considerable evidence in the two regions of shared attitudes in lay people's sensibilities to the spiritual mission of the reformed church. Lay piety is a feature of the medieval cultural scene that has long interested historians of Scotland, but one that a dearth of surviving record materials has made very difficult to assess. The various enactments – and reenactments – of Scottish church councils speak volumes about the difficulties that beset ecclesiastical authorities in their efforts to convey messages about good

---

[92] Stringer, 'Reform monasticism and Celtic Scotland', 146. See also Oram, *Lordship of Galloway*, 250–3. [93] Neville, 'Earls of Strathearn', i, 7–9, 21–2. See also above, pp 82, 97–8.

Christian living. Long after the clerical author Turgot lamented the shortcomings of the lay people and clerics of St Margaret's day,[94] local and provincial councils continued to legislate against the casual ways in which common folk and their priests treated the sacraments, conducted themselves in church, and demonstrated inappropriate Christian behaviour.[95] A repeated emphasis of statutes well into the fourteenth century on the special status of church buildings, the provision of adequate teinds for clerics charged with the cure of souls, and the independence of priests and monks from lay control provide unmistakable indications that the separation of sacred and profane affairs, although clearly articulated in theory, was much more difficult to implement on the ground.[96] In particular, close relations between clerics and lay persons were aspects of pre-twelfth-century devotional life that no ecclesiastical administration, however determined, could easily dismantle. One scholar has suggested that in the lordship of Galloway 'it can hardly be imagined that the teachings of the post-Gregorian church penetrated deeply into everyday life',[97] and there is certainly evidence that elsewhere in the Gaelic-speaking parts of the kingdom pre-reform practices survived in only mildly attenuated form. Proponents of the reform programme who promulgated new measures modelled on the continental church faced in the native lordships an especially difficult challenge when they tried to effect change among a population unfamiliar with their tongue and accustomed to forms and expressions of devotional belief that owed little to English or European practice.

The strict and admonitory tone of ecclesiastical statutes might suggest that the encounter between the reformed church and its Scottish flock was above all an antagonistic one. But there is much evidence from the Gaelic regions of the realm to support the belief that the process of reforming popular belief was in many respects one of accommodation and acculturation by both Latins and Gaels. On the one hand, custom was adapted in favour of new standards of Christian conduct; on the other, the formal church was sufficiently flexible to permit the preservation of much that was traditional and familiar. The later twelfth and thirteenth centuries were, in short, a key period in the development of hybrid forms of popular piety. By the year 1300 there can be little doubt that religious practices in most of the regions north of Forth reflected the influence of the continental church. But the tenacity of local custom and the survival of devotional practices not found elsewhere in western Europe are equally visible. Scottish popular religion of the later medieval period owed as much to the Celtic past as it did exposure to more recent continental experience.

Scholars who have explored the first manifestations of the reform impulse in Scotland are virtually unanimous in identifying the reign of King David I as

94 W. Forbes-Leith (ed.), *Life of St Margaret, queen of Scotland, by Turgot, bishop of St Andrews* (1884), 42–52. **95** Patrick (ed.), *Statutes of the Scottish church*, 30–4, 40, 42, 48, 51–2, 57–8. **96** Ibid., 8–77. For a study of late medieval conditions in the diocese of Dunblane, see J.R. Todd, 'Pre-Reformation cure of souls in Dunblane diocese' (1975). **97** Stringer, 'Reform monasticism and Celtic Scotland', 137.

a turning point in the history of ecclesiastical government. If David is no longer credited with reviving a moribund church single-handedly, he was more certainly responsible for restoring a number of episcopal sees, facilitating the gradual establishment of a network of parishes throughout the kingdom, and generally promoting the efforts of reformers to give expression to their tenets.[98] The degree to which royal enthusiasm for ecclesiastical reorganization actually transformed spiritual practices is more difficult to trace. In the late eleventh century Queen Margaret is said to have taught her rough-edged husband, Mael Coluim III, how to pray and to express his devotion in acts of Christian piety, and to have instructed his magnates to conduct themselves as proper sons of the church.[99] The survival of the Céli Dé movement well into the thirteenth century and of such irregular practices as secular marriage, however, suggest that Margaret's efforts to abolish the 'barbarous rites' she found among the ignorant Scots proved only partially successful.

Evidence for the piety of lay Christians in medieval Scotland is at once widespread and ambiguous. The wave of monastic foundations stretching from the border region as far north as Buchan and west into the still largely independent region of the highlands and islands offers vivid testimony of the success with which European religious orders as varied as Cluniacs, Augustinians, Cistercians, Premonstratensians and Tironensians spread the message that generosity to the earthly church was directly linked to heavenly rewards. When native magnates like Mael Coluim earl of Fife, Raonall of the Isles, Feargus lord of Galloway and Gille Brigte earl of Strathearn founded new monasteries at Culross, Saddell, Glenluce, Soulseat and Inchaffray or, like Gille Criosd earl of Mar endowed ancient monastic settlements at places like Deer and Monymusk[1] they were responding not merely to the influence of the Scottish royal house, but were dutifully emulating the pious activities of the larger community of European magnates for whom religious patronage was both an act of generosity and a sound spiritual investment. St Margaret herself could hardly have asked for a stronger indication that the reform message was beginning to fall on receptive ears.

Genuine piety there undoubtedly was among a significant section of the Scots nobility in the twelfth and thirteenth centuries. The texts of the written deeds that members of the Strathearn and Lennox families granted to ecclesiastical beneficiaries offer valuable windows into the piety of Scottish lay men and women. They also serve as a useful foundation for an exploration of the ways in which the formal church both accommodated and helped to shape native spirituality in the age of reform. The 'credo of the native community at large' may well, as Keith Stringer has commented, be '[v]irtually beyond discovery',[2]

---

98 See, for example, Barrow, *Kingship and unity*, 67–74; Donaldson, 'Scottish bishops' sees', 106–7, 115–16. **99** Forbes-Leith (ed.), *Life of St Margaret*, 38–9, 40–4. **1** McDonald, 'Scoto-Norse kings', 187–219; Jackson, *Gaelic notes*, 117–24; W.D. Simpson, *The province of Mar* (1943), 109–11; T. Thomson (ed.), *Liber cartarum prioratus Sancti Andree in Scotia* (1841), 306, 372–5; M. Ash, 'The diocese of St Andrews under its 'Norman' bishops' (1976), 109. **2** Stringer, 'Reform monasticism and Celtic Scotland', 137.

but there is every reason to conclude that genuine piety played a significant role in directing the actions of the Gaelic magnates of Scotland. Reform minded clerics might well deplore the usage in the Scottish church of customs and observances they considered backward, even detrimental to Christian souls, but the religious impulses they sought to harness were familiar to native leaders. The act of endowing the church with gifts of land had a long history among the Gaelic peoples, one which churchmen of the reform period acknowledged and nurtured. Beyond the politically motivated fulminations of such harsh critics as the late thirteenth-century Archbishop John Pecham, who was still in this late period bemoaning the manifest inferiority of the Celtic church,[3] local clerics acknowledged the wisdom of permitting older practices to survive alongside newly introduced rules, regulations and notions. The result of this fruitful accommodation of old and new was the fashioning of a popular piety that was widely attractive to lay Scots people, noble and common alike.

It has been suggested that the teachings of reform minded clerics about penance, salvation and personal morality 'may well have had a real impact' on the devotional practices of the late twelfth- and early thirteenth-century lords of Galloway.[4] Feargus and his sons had an unusually poor record of depredation and impious behaviour for which to make amends, but there is plenty of evidence in support of this statement in the Gaelic regions of Strathearn and Lennox. The chronicler John of Fordun relates that Fearchar earl of Strathearn, leader of the quickly suppressed revolt of 1160, was returned to the king's peace through the mediation of the clergy.[5] It was perhaps as an act of penance that he offered the brethren on the Isle of Masses the church of St Chattan of Aberuthven and its attached lands, and that he formally assigned to it a teind of his goods. It was more certainly in acknowledgment of his own failings in respect of his Christian duties that soon after 1226 Earl Maoldomhnaich of Lennox gifted the church and teinds of Cardross to the episcopal see of Glasgow. A deeper spirituality still is visible in other comital deeds. Foundation charters of twelfth- and thirteenth-century religious houses constitute fine examples of the rhetorical style of the period. Replete with superfluous verbiage and exaggerated expressions of filial piety appropriate to such solemn documents, they are for the most part untrustworthy measures of devotional intensity. On occasion, however, it is possible to read into the language of these texts expressions of genuine sentiment. Such, for example, is the foundation charter of Inchaffray, granted in 1200 by the earl and countess of Strathearn soon after the death and burial in the chapel there of their eldest son, Gille Criosd.[6] The size, shape and handwriting style of this document, as well as the fine quality of the parchment upon which it was written, set it apart from all of the earl's other written deeds, and demonstrate the care with which Gille Brigte and Maud chose to record

---

[3] See, for example, H. Pryce, *Native law and the church in medieval Wales* (1993), 71–2. [4] Stringer, 'Reform monasticism and Celtic Scotland', 140–1; see also 142–4. [5] *Chron. Fordun* i, 251; ii, 256. [6] *Inchaff. Chrs.*, no. 9 (see also facsimile no. 4).

their actions and the depth of their grief. The beauty of the opening clauses has been described as 'a fine expression of the spirituality which could come forth from secular love under the stress of bereavement',[7] and in many respects the charter is as impressive as any royal deed of foundation. The generosity with which Earl Gille Brigte eventually endowed the new house may be viewed in similar terms, not merely as conventional declarations of piety, but as acts intended to establish spiritual links with his kinspeople, past and future. His gifts were many and varied, and the tradition of familial patronage that Gille Brigte initiated endured for several years after his death.[8] The desire for an enduring association between the Strathearn family and the religious house of Inchaffray carried over to Earl Gille Brigte's second marriage to the daughter of a Gaelic tenant, who made a gift of some of her tocher lands to the Isle of Masses.[9]

Evidence attesting the piety of the Gaelic earls of Lennox is equally plentiful. Relations with the ecclesiastical officials in the territories of the lordship were not particularly amicable, but neither Earl Ailin II nor his successor, Maoldomhnaich, was oblivious to the notion that acts of munificence were appropriate to men of their rank. Maoldomhnaich entrusted the care of his bodily remains and the welfare of his soul to the Cluniac house of Paisley patronized by his neighbour and father-in-law, Walter II son of Alan,[10] then, after the dispute over the church of Kilpatrick had soured relations with Paisley, to the royal monastery at Arbroath. The care with which the earl made arrangements for the inclusion of his name and that of his brother, Amhlaibh, in the abbey's martyrology and the request that a mass be celebrated annually for the care of their souls betray more than a conventional concern for the afterlife.[11] Despite the bitterness of the disagreement with Paisley, moreover, Maoldomhnaich, his brothers Amhlaibh and Dùghall, and his successor Malcolm I made other grants of land and privilege to the Cluniacs, the former of parish churches and their valuable pertinents, the latter of access to the rich fishing grounds of the River Leven and the Gare Loch.[12] The determination of the earls of Strathearn and Lennox to maintain close control over several of the parish churches in their lordships, moreover, may be interpreted as more than just self-serving. It bears witness also to the concern, appropriate to Gaelic magnates of their rank, for the provision of religious services to the Gaelic speaking population of their respective territories. The witness lists of charters granted by members of the families of Strathearn and Lennox abound in the names of clerics whose first language was almost certainly Gaelic, and whose duties must have included ministering to their flocks in their native tongue: Mael Giric the Céli Dé of Muthill, Mael Coluim the clerk, Brice the parson of Crieff, Maol Iosa the parson of Fowlis, Maol Iosa the rector of Kilbride and Gille Moire the dean;[13] Gille

---

7 Duncan, *Making*, 452.   **8** The religious endowments of Earl Gille Brigte's brothers, nephews and later descendants are reviewed in Neville, 'Earls of Strathearn', i, 55–7, 73–75, 84.   **9** *Inchaff. Chrs.*, no. 46.   **10** *Paisley Reg.*, 159. The earl's wife was included in these arrangements.   **11** *Arbroath Liber*, i, no. 133.   **12** *Paisley Reg.*, 209–10, 215–16.

M'Aodhán son of the parson of Rosneath (later parson himself), Thomas de Carrick the clerk, Maurice son of the dean of Luss and Somhairle the parson.[14] Although the fact that several of these religious officials were fathers of (illegitimate?) children must have been deeply offensive to the more conservative clerics of the day, episcopal and monastic officials could hardly deny the valuable services they performed among native communities in communicating the church's spiritual teachings. It was doubtless through the mediation of Gaelic-speaking representatives of the church as much as it was the fulminations of episcopal and monastic authorities that the Gaelic people of Scotland absorbed the message of reform.

In matters spiritual, as in so much else, the native lords of Strathearn and Lennox governed by example as well as by mandate. Their kinsmen and the few tenants of English or continental origin who inhabited their lands duly emulated them in providing endowments for the church. Patterns of religious benefaction were remarkably similar in both territories. In Strathearn, Earl Gille Brigte's brother, Maol Iosa, developed close links with the Scottish royal family and the rarified entourage of the royal court.[15] His chief beneficiaries were the monks of the Tironensian abbey of Lindores founded by his father-in-law (David earl of Huntingdon), who received the church of Muthill and the valuable estate of Redgorton in Strathtay, and the abbey of Arbroath, established by King William I, to which he gifted an annual income from his fishery of Meikleour in Strathearn.[16] Maol Iosa's heir, Fergus son of Gille Brigte, followed his uncle's example by directing his pious donations to Lindores and Arbroath,[17] but he, too, was a benefactor of the family's religious house at Inchaffray,[18] as was another of Gille Brigte's sons, Malise.[19] The proximity of the abbey to the administrative centre of the earldom, its importance to the comital family and, no doubt, genuine belief in the efficacy of the canons' prayers dictated that some Strathearn tenants should follow their lords' lead. Thus, as early as 1208, one of Earl Gille Brigte's few non-native tenants, Tristram of Gorthy, granted a croft near the mill he had built on a tributary of the Pow Burn,[20] and Tristram's descendants remained closely involved in the abbey's fortunes until well into the thirteenth century.[21] At least one member of another new family, the Methvens, was also a patron of Inchaffray,[22] as were some of Earl Robert's tenants, among them the

---

13 *Inchaff. Chrs.*, nos. 1, 3, 13, 15, 27, 28, 30, 31. **14** *Paisley Reg.*, 157, 211; *Lennox Cart.*, 31. **15** Neville, 'Native lords and the church', 459. **16** *Lind. Cart.*, nos., 29, 127 (late 1190s x 1214); *Arbroath Liber*, i, no. 96 (late 1190s). **17** *Lind. Cart.*, no. 26, grant of the lands of Bennie, located just south of the Muir of Orchill, with the lands pertaining to it at Concraig (1233–34); no. 24, grant of Fedale, also close to the Muir of Orchill, in exchange for teinds and revenues from his uncle's lands in Srathearn and Strathtay (1226 x 1234); *Arbroath Liber*, i, no. 87, confirmation of Maol Iosa's grant of an annual rent from Meikleour, exchanged as above (1225–26). **18** *Inchaff. Liber*, no. 10; *Inchaff. Chrs.*, no. 74, grant of a chalder of oatmeal from his lands of Auchtermachany (1245 x 1247). **19** *Inchaff Liber*, no. 63; *Inchaff. Chrs.*, no. 102, grant of lands in Maol Iosa's tenement of Rossie, *c.*1273. **20** *Inchaff. Chrs.*, no. 26 (see also facsimile no. 8). **21** *Inchaff. Liber*, nos. 47, 48, 59. **22** Ibid., no. 59.

Luvetots of Dalpatrick and Theobald son of William and his kinsmen.[23] It is, however, noteworthy that with the exception of Gille Brigte's second wife, Iseulte, native donors to the priory or abbey of Inchaffray were strikingly few. Extant charter materials suggest that the canons received little from the Gaelic-speaking inhabitants of Strathearn other than the renders in food and kind that the earls' deeds and current ecclesiastical law require them to give.

A similar situation obtained in thirteenth-century Lennox. Earl Maoldomhnaich's brothers, Amhlaibh and the infamous Dùghall, endowed the Cluniac house of Paisley. But as in Strathearn, the church's teachings about the importance of benefactions to the reformed monastic orders appears to have gone largely unheeded among the family's native tenantry, and in the thirteenth century Paisley based its prosperity above all on gifts from its founder's family, the Stewarts, and their French- and English-speaking followers. The grasping practices of the monks may well have been at fault here. When, towards the middle of the century, Dùghall son of Cristin the *judex* of Lennox and his wife resigned to the abbey the lands they held in Knock in exchange for a smaller estate in Walkinshaw, they did so not as an act of devotion but as a consequence of their poverty and indebtedness.[24] Dùghall had been one of the targets of the abbey's ruthless pursuit of the lands belonging to the church of Kilpatrick,[25] and his impoverishment can hardly have endeared the Cluniacs to him. Farbhlaidh, daughter of Kerald and wife of Norrinus de Monorgrund was the target of similar litigation. Her attempts to assert title to several estates attached to Kilpatrick similarly came under the attack of monastic lawyers in the early 1270s and, conscious of the bitterness that had characterized the earlier dispute, in later life it was rather to the fabric of the church of St Kentigern of Glasgow that she made a formal gift.[26] There is little reason to mistrust the pious motivations behind a grant of c.1277 by Malcolm lord of Luss in aid of the construction of the bell tower and treasury of Glasgow cathedral,[27] but the gift is all the more noteworthy for its rare representation of conventional piety among the native population of the lordship. The notion of gift giving to the church was hardly unknown in Strathearn and Lennox. Yet, beyond the ranks of the earls and their kinsmen, native tenants did not closely equate Christian piety with grants of land to the monastic orders. In both lordships, Gaelic people expressed their devotion in ways distinct from those of their English and continental fellows, and it is to other areas that historians must look in order to understand the nature of popular piety among the native population of the thirteenth and early fourteenth centuries.

In his biography of St Margaret, Turgot made brief mention of the queen's interest in the numerous hermits of her realm, who led 'lives of great strictness in the flesh, but not according to the flesh'.[28] The ascetic tradition was equally

---

[23] Ibid., nos. 32, 59, 66; *Inchaff. Chrs.*, nos. 56, 103.   [24] NAS, GD 90/1/17; *Paisley Reg.*, 178–80.
[25] *Paisley Reg.*, 173–6.   [26] *Glasgow Reg.*, i, no. 177, confirmed in no. 178 by Earl Maoldomhnaich.
[27] Ibid., i, no. 229.   [28] Forbes-Leith (ed.), *Life of St Margaret*, 58.

important in the devotional life of Margaret's subjects. The community of priests who lived on the Isle of Masses before Gille Brigte's erection of an Augustinian priory there was under the earl's protection, and it was probably at his behest that around 1190 Bishop Simon of Dunblane confirmed its members in the possession of the church of St John the Evangelist with its landed endowments.[29] Gille Brigte's early gifts to the brethren indicate that his support was more than merely nominal,[30] and it was perhaps owing to his direct influence that Bishop John of Dunkeld surrendered to them the lands of the abthane of Madderty, revenues from which had belonged to the see from a very early period.[31] Gille Brigte's appointment in 1200 of the hermit Maol Iosa as head of the newly reconstituted community further ensured that the holy men of Inchaffray would continue to play a vital role in the spiritual life of his tenants. The Céli Dé of Muthill also remained members of the religious community of Strathearn.

The tradition of hospitality to pilgrims and travellers is well attested in the church of Gaelic Ireland,[32] and is found also in late twelfth- and early thirteenth-century Lennox. Earl Maoldomhnaich and his tenants were patrons of a variety of small religious communities. Not all were recognized by the reform minded clerics of the day, but they played an important role in the devotional practices of the region. The hermit Bede Ferdan, for example, was responsible for the housing and feeding of pilgrims, and for a while at least enjoyed the protection of the comital family. His hermitage, a timber house, was located on lands attached to the church of Kilpatrick long known as Patrick's Seat,[33] and his obligation to provide hospitality resembled closely that of the ascetic who lived on the isle of Incholm, and who on one occasion entertained King Alexander I himself.[34] Recent archaeological work has uncovered evidence in the Lennox region of the remains of small medieval ecclesiastical sites at locations such as Inchmurrin and Inchcailloch in Loch Lomond, in the heart of the lordship, which may have served as hermitages.[35] Bede's responsibility for the care of pilgrims passed to his son and successor Cristin, and presumably also to Dùghall son of Earl Ailin II when he gained possession of the church of Kilpatrick, but among the charges levied against Dùghall in his conflict with Paisley abbey were the unlawful use of the lands associated with the church and improper Christian conduct, perhaps references to the activities of his predecessors. When Dùghall lost control of the lands the ancient eremitical tradition at Kilpatrick may well have come to an end.

29 *Inchaff. Chrs.*, no. 1. **30** *Inchaff. Liber*, no. 18; *Inchaff. Chrs.*, nos. 3–5. **31** *Inchaff. Chrs.*, no. 7. The abthane lands included an estate known in the fifteenth century as Bordlands, a name that recalls its ancient status as mensal. Ibid., 318. For the meaning of the term, see G.W.S. Barrow, 'The Lost Gàidhealtachd' (1992), 121–3; A.L. Winchester, 'The distribution and significance of "Bordland" in medieval Britain' (1986); and A. Macdonald, 'Major early monasteries: some procedural problems for field archaeologists', in D.J. Breeze (ed.), *Studies in Scottish antiquity presented to Stewart Cruden* (1984), 74–5. **32** K. Simms, 'Guesting and feasting in Gaelic Ireland' (1979), 67–79. **33** *Paisley Reg.*, 162, 166–8. **34** *Scotichronicon*, iii, 111. **35** Lacaille, 'Loch Lomondside fonts', 114–15; with additional information from RCAHMS CANMORE database.

It might be supposed that the reformed church of the thirteenth century was less than supportive of the ascetic tradition in Strathearn and Lennox, for references to hermits decline rapidly after 1200, and the Céli Dé brethren were soon replaced entirely with reformed canons. Yet the disappearance of hermits is probably more apparent than real. Notices of such men and their dwellings occur elsewhere in the kingdom well into the later medieval period: King Alexander II, for example, is known to have extended his protection to two hermits of Moray.[36] Of some pertinence here is an intriguing argument offered some years ago by David McRoberts, who linked the use of the terms 'chaplain' and 'chaplainries' in written *acta* to priest hermits and their houses, and who suggested that the ascetic tradition in Scotland, as elsewhere, long survived the efforts of thirteenth-century reformists to restrict it to monastic precincts.[37] In regions such as Strathearn and Lennox, moreover, chapels such as those of St Michael in Glen Luss, associated with a nearby hill named 'Edentaggart' ('priest's hillside'), in the parish of Luss, Aber in Kilmarnock parish, and St Blane's, Lochearnhead, Strathearn, to name only a few,[38] and the presence of tiny shrines now surviving only in place-names such as Tom-na-Clog ('hill of the bell' [of St Kessog]), Inchtavvanach ('island of the monk's house') in Lennox, and Struc a' Chabeil ('pinnacle of the chapel') in Killin, Perthshire,[39] suggest that devotion to the Celtic saints remained an important focus of religious life among common folk. As late as the first decade of the fourteenth century, a grant of Earl Malcolm II to Sir John de Luss made specific mention of St Kessog, and styled him 'our patron'.[40]

Although they were determined to channel the pious impulses of their flocks into conventional forms of expression, twelfth- and thirteenth-century ecclesiastical reformers were not wholly insensitive to the special requirements of common people who understood little of the Latin language or of the European context of reform. The bishops of Dunblane and Glasgow could not afford to turn a blind eye to overt resistance against reform among Gaelic magnates and major land holders: the responsibility to lead their tenants by example incumbent on men of such status mandated that conformity to reform principles must be enforced. But below the exalted ranks of the Gaelic nobility the bishops were prepared to demonstrate greater lenience and to be more accommodating of

---

36 G.W.S. Barrow, 'Badenoch and Strathspey, 1130–1312: 2. The church' (1989), 10. For evidence of early hermitages at Whithorn and in the parish of Logie, see C.A.R. Radford, 'Excavations at Whithorn (final report)' (1955–6), 152–3, and D.M. Anderson, 'Hermitages in Logie parish' (1967), 58–9. **37** D. McRoberts, 'Hermits in medieval Scotland', in *Innes Review* 16 (1965). Such attitudes certainly help to explain the decline of the Céli Dé movement in Scotland. **38** Lacaille, 'Ecclesiastical remains', 97–8; idem, 'Capelrig Cross', 132–8; idem, 'Loch Lomondside fonts', 114–15. The lands on which the chapel of St Michael was located passed into the hands of Walter lord of Buchanan in the mid-fourteenth century; NAS, GD 220/2/22. **39** A.D. Lacaille, 'Notes on a Loch Lomondside parish' (1965), 152; idem, 'Loch Lomondside fonts and effigies', 114; C.A.R. Radford, 'The early cross and shrine of St Mahew, Cardross, Dumbartonshire' (1966); J.R. Walker, '"Holy wells" in Scotland' (1892–3), 161–2, 187, 190, 194–5, 199–201. **40** Fraser, *Lennox*, ii, no, 211.

native practice. Very occasionally, conventional miracles of the European sort became the stuff of local talk,[41] but the popularity of Celtic saints remained strong in thirteenth-century Strathearn and Lennox, and the dedication of newly erected churches to worthies such as St Serf, St Bean and St Kessog proceeded unhindered well after 1250. A recent study of parish formation in medieval Perthshire, moreover, reveals that in the drawing of new boundaries the bishops of Dunblane allowed great latitude to the earls of Strathearn:

> It may also be the case that the formation of parishes utilized existing local churches because of an established relationship to and status within the territorial communities that became their parishes. The prominent role of native earls, who would have been well acquainted with the estate and community organization and with ecclesiastical provision in their earldom in parochial formation may have contributed greatly to the survival of existing churches in parochial guise.[42]

The native earls' familiarity with the religious and territorial communities of their lordship may, as this author has argued, have transformed them into 'royal agents ... in the implementation of royal policy for ecclesiastical reform'.[43] But circumstances are equally likely to have been the other way around: the bishops of Dunblane must have been under considerable pressure to accede to the earls' influence in the process of delineating new administrative boundaries.

Sensitivity to the local customs, beliefs and practices of the rural population of native Scotland is particularly apparent in the creation of archdeaconries and rural deaneries, whose officials were the chief agents of episcopal administration in the localities, and acted as vital links between the bishops and their flocks. In Dunblane, the late twelfth-century archdeaconry of Muthill (also known as Dunblane or Strathearn) was roughly coterminous with the two lordships of Strathearn and Menteith, but by the third decade of the thirteenth century it had been split into two smaller units.[44] It is tempting to attribute this division to the growing cultural differences that distinguished the former, under the rule of a Gaelic-speaking native magnate, from the latter, now governed by the family of the Comyns and their tenants. Clearer evidence of the deliberate recognition of the distinct needs of native communities comes from the see of Glasgow, where in the late twelfth century the archdeaconry of Glasgow was divided into five smaller units, one of whose boundaries coincided almost exactly with those of the Gaelic-speaking lordship of Lennox.

In the creation of the rural deanery of Lennox (or Luss, as it is identified in early record) the bishops found an unusual opportunity for the reformed church

---

[41] See, for example, the miracle performed by the monk Adam of Lennox, reported in A.O. Anderson and M.O. Andersdon (eds), *The Chronicle of Melrose from the Cottonian Manuscript, Faustina B. IX, in the British Museum* (1936), 121. [42] Rogers, 'Formation of the parish unit and community', 84. [43] Ibid., 57. [44] Watt, *Fasti*, 88, 91.

to respond in meaningful fashion to the devotional peculiarities of a native population. The church of Luss itself boasted a long and historic association with one of the most revered of Scottish saints, the sixth-century Irish martyr, Kessog,[45] and it was doubtless in recognition of its ancient status as a holy site that the church became the centre of a parish created in the late twelfth century. When the bishop of Glasgow then erected a deanery based in Luss he acknowledged simultaneously the importance of the local cult of St Kessog, the distinct nature of the Gaelic people who lived within the lordship of Lennox and, not least, the special status of the native family whose landed possessions were situated in the vicinity of the church. The lords of Luss had held the lands and the patronage of the church from the late twelfth century at least,[46] and their position as hereditary keepers of the relic known as the bachall or crozier of St Kessog meant that they enjoyed considerable status as local religious dignitaries. They were both appropriate and promising representatives of the formal church in the region,[47] and notwithstanding the existence of a son, Gille Moire, Maoldomhnaich of Luss was appointed to the office of dean of Lennox sometime between 1178 and 1199, a position he held until at least 1214.[48] Gille Moire did not follow him in office, but he did retain patronage rights in the church of Luss. Royal charters of the early fourteenth century attest the enduring importance of the site as a centre of native worship; thus, in 1315 King Robert I granted to the church of St Kessog the privilege of sanctuary 'for a space of three miles around, both on land and on water'.[49] Chartered sanctuaries ('girths') were rare in western Scotland, and the king's act bespoke 'recognition by the Crown of an ancient and well-established custom', and special honour for a particularly favoured saint.[50]

References to Luss and its unusual privileges in the records of medieval Lennox are numerous; they are also sufficiently intriguing to suggest that the church's hereditary patrons enjoyed unusual status within native society. Scholars have long appreciated the profound influence of Ireland on the ecclesiastical landscape of Scotland, particularly in the western reaches of the kingdom. Of particular relevance here is the office of coarb (Irish *comharba*), whose incumbent was both the spiritual heir of the saintly founder of a religious house and an hereditary guardian of lands that had belonged in ancient times to monastic establishments. The coarb of Ireland was appointed by a bishop as 'headman of the

---

45 A.D. Lacaille, 'Some ancient crosses in Dumbartonshire and adjoining counties' (1925), 144; idem, 'Notes on a Loch Lomondside parish', 148–51; Mackinlay, *Ancient church dedications non-scriptural*, 136; A. Macquarrie, *The saints of Scotland: essays in Scottish church history, AD 450–1093* (1997), 7. The medieval parish of Luss was extensive. Until the early seventeenth century it included the detached lands of Buchanan and portions of the modern parishes of Bonhill and Arrochar. **46** See above, pp 54–5. **47** G. Hay and D. McRoberts, 'Rossdhu church and its books of hours' (1965), 16. McRoberts cites here a charter of King Robert I in which Sir John of Luss appears as *bachelarius* of Earl Malcolm II of Lennox. *RRS*, v, no. 81. **48** *Paisley Reg.*, 157; *Glasgow Reg.*, i, no 101; *Lennox Cart.*, 12. **49** *RRS*, v, no. 55. **50** Dowden, *Medieval church*, 148. For other sanctuaries and a general discussion of girth in medieval Scotland, see H.L. MacQueen, 'Girth: society and the law of sanctuary in Scotland' (2001).

family or families of hereditary tenants occupying church lands within the parish'.[51] Scholars have not found hereditary coarbships in Gaelic Scotland, though they admit that the concentration of ecclesiastical office in a single family over more than a single generation was not unheard of. In Strathearn, for example, Nicholas succeeded his father Malise son of Earl Gille Brigte as a cleric, as did Luke son of Michael in the church of Fintry in Lennox.[52] The earliest written evidence relating to the church of Luss, however, offers tantalizing suggestions that a coarbship on the Irish model did in fact exist in Lennox, and that ecclesiastical reformers there enacted a series of measures to suppress it.

In Ireland coarbs were often charged with the specific task of safeguarding saintly relics; in County Louth, for example, members of the family of O'Mulholland were keepers of the St Patrick's Bell, just as the lords of Luss were guardians of St Kessog's crozier.[53] Reforming clerics were as determined there as they were in Scotland to secure universal acknowledgment of the church's jurisdiction over spiritual matters and an untrammelled hold on ecclesiastical property,[54] and one of the consequences of their efforts was the transformation of the once independent coarbs into rural deans directly answerable to episcopal authority.[55] A similar process appears to have taken place at Luss, and the earliest written deeds relating to the church suggest that it was well under way already in the early years of the thirteenth century. When he is first mentioned in written record, the native man Maoldomhnaich was simultaneously lord of the lands of Luss and and rural dean of Luss/Lennox. His son, Gille Moire, can hardly have expected to succeed him in ecclesiastical office under the watchful eyes of the reformist bishops of Glasgow, but he did manage to retain the right to present to the parish church, and he inherited from his father (and passed along to his successors) the obligation to safeguard the relic of St Kessog. In Ireland, the lands of the coarbs almost everywhere enjoyed special sanctuary rights over and above the normal privileges of protection that all churches afforded fugitives.[56] The claim of Luss to status as a sanctuary of especial importance was not formally recognized by the Scots crown until the early

---

51 K. Simms, 'Frontiers in the Irish church – regional and cultural' (1995), 177–200: 177. The literature on the coarbs and erenaghs of medieval Ireland is considerable. See S.J.D. Seymour, 'The coarb in the medieval Irish church (c.1200–1500)' (1933), and a series of articles by J. Barry in *Irish Ecclesiastical Record* published between 1957 and 1960 (5th ser., vols 88–94). 52 Neville, 'Earls of Strathearn', ii, nos. 49, 53, 54, 59, 61, 72, 73; App. B, nos. 12, 22–4, 27, 28, 31, 32, 49, 454; NAS, GD 22/3/531; *Lennox Cart.*, 34–5. For other examples, see Barrow, 'Lost Gàidhealtachd', 113–14, and D.S. Thomson, 'Gaelic learned orders and *literati* in medieval Scotland' (1968), 66–8. 53 Simms, 'Frontiers in the Irish church', 184 Similar examples in Scotland include the keepers of the pastoral staff of St Moluag at Lismore and of the *coigreach* of St Fillan; W.D.H. Sellar, 'Celtic law and Scots law: survival and integration' (1989), 8. 54 See, for example, K.W. Nicholls, 'Rectory, vicarage and parish in the western Irish dioceses' (1971); and J. Watt, *The church in medieval Ireland* (1972), 1–27. 55 J. Barry, 'The coarb and the twelfth-century reform' (1957), 21. 56 Seymour, 'The coarb in the medieval Irish church', 21; Hughes, 'Frontiers in the Irish church', 178. On the privilege of sanctuary in Scotland, see Patrick (ed.), *Statutes of the Scottish church*, 39–40; Dowden, *Medieval church*, 145–52; MacQueen., 'Girth', 333–52.

years of the fourteenth century, but there is reason to believe that Robert I's charter of 1315 merely acknowledged the long standing tradition enjoyed by the church.[57] The argument for the existence at Luss of a coarbship on the Irish model is admittedly speculative, but evidence of an early religious house there suggests that the site had a very ancient history, and surviving documents make it clear that twelfth-century reformers were hard pressed to ignore it.[58]

The mendicant orders of medieval Scotland were above all an urban phenomenon, and they were firmly established in Perth and Glasgow by the year 1250. But precisely because they preferred the towns, the friars did not have much of an impact on the native populations of the Gaelic countryside. Neither did the gift giving ethos of native culture find an outlet in provision for hospitals. The development of such institutions in Scotland is greatly complicated by the fact that a large variety of services fell under the general rubric of the term 'hospital', and very few of these had an unbroken record of continuous existence.[59] Ian Cowan interpreted the obligation of the keeper of Patrick's Seat in Lennox to provide food, drink and shelter to pilgrims and travellers as proof of the existence of a hospital at Kilpatrick,[60] but the witnesses who testified in 1233 about the lands belonging to it reported that these services were no longer offered.[61] The church and its lands maintained their prestige as an important cultic site well after they had passed under the control of Paisley abbey, but clear evidence of the existence of a hospital there is lacking. In the mid fifteenth century Countess Isabella of Lennox claimed that an almshouse for poor men and women had been founded at Polmadie by her ancestors, but if such a place did exist in the thirteenth, it failed to attract support from the earls' native tenants.[62] Similarly, a gift of Malise II of Strathearn provided funds for the purchase of a chalice and ornaments for an almshouse at Inchaffray abbey,[63] but archaeological excavation has uncovered no trace of a building specifically dedicated to the care of the ill and infirm, and the earl's endowment was not emulated by any of his tenants. Although it is unwise to draw firm conclusions from the very limited nature of the records surviving from medieval Strathearn and Lennox, it would seem that in contrast to the land holding ranks of native society, common folk absorbed only slowly, if at all, the reformed church's message about the efficacy of some acts of piety that, elsewhere in Europe, were regarded as conventional.

If the reformed church tolerated the cult of Celtic saints in Strathearn and Lennox and sometimes turned a blind eye to unusual religious practices among native lay people, it could not afford to ignore flagrant abuses of canon law, least of all by its own members. The complaints of Turgot bishop of St Andrews about the irregularities of marriage among the Scots of St Margaret's day was

---

57 *RRS*, v, no. 55.   **58** C.A.R. Radford, 'The early curch in Strathclyde and Galloway' (1967), 118. Macdonald, 'Major early monasteries', 81, notes that 'the presence at a site of a large body of sculptured stones ... may suggest that the site in question was formerly that of a monastery'. The environs of Luss boast many such stones.   **59** *MRHS*, 30; J. Durkan, 'Care of the poor: pre-reformation hospitals' (1959), 268.   **60** *MRHS*, 182–3.   **61** *Paisley Reg.*, 166–8.   **62** See above, p. 130.   **63** *Inchaff. Liber*, nos. 38, 52.

echoed a generation later by a monk of Rievaulx, who vilified the customs practised by the Galwegians.[64] The penetration of ecclesiastical legislation into the native regions of the realm was a process of several centuries' duration, and scholars have shown that secular marriage there survived until the end of the Middle Ages and beyond.[65] The extent to which the teachings of the church affected marriage customs in Strathearn and Lennox remains obscure. At the highest social levels the earls and their immediate families must have been under considerable pressure from vigilant episcopal authorities to conform to the laws of marriage as defined by the contemporary church, and there is little reason to doubt that union such as those between Earl Gille Brigte and his first wife, Maud, daughter of Sir William d'Aubigny, or Maoldomhnaich and his wife, Elizabeth Stewart, were anything but valid either in ecclesiastical eyes or from the perspective of foreign families who were most attuned to the tenets of the reformed church. Gille Brigte's second wife, however, was the daughter of a native tenant, and the tendency of most of his kinsmen (as well as those of the earls of Lennox) to look to native women as marriage partners reflects a preference for Gaelic cultural *mores*, perhaps including secular marriage and handfasting. Below the ranks of the land holding nobility, however, surviving records generate next to no tangible evidence concerning marriage customs.

Concubinage among the clergy was a more serious concern. The conduct of Scottish clerics, like that of their counterparts throughout western Europe, fell well below the rigorous standards set by the high and later medieval church. As elsewhere, however, ecclesiastical authorities legislated determinedly (if ultimately in vain) against the keeping of women and cohabitation with concubines.[66] In the twelfth and thirteenth centuries the problem was particularly acute in the native lordships, where tenacious religious conservatism and the fundamental challenges of language impeded the efforts of ecclesiastical authorities to effect a transformation of morals among its members. Many years ago Bishop Dowden argued that Gaelic lords deliberately sought to safeguard their proprietary interests in the parish churches of their territories by assigning responsibility for the cure of local souls to their own kinsmen. He was of the opinion that 'it would be hazardous to conclude' that such men 'were ecclesiastics in more than name', and he cited as a particular egregious example Malise son of Earl Gille Brigte of Strathearn, parson of Gask.[67] Dowden's criticism of the moral laxity of native clerics like Malise or his near contemporary, Maoldomhnaich dean of Luss, reflect accurately the concerns of the official church in Scotland as these were expressed in episcopal statutes. But such comments, like the ecclesiastical legislation that forms their basis, obscure the very

---

64 Forbes-Leith (ed.), *Life of St Margaret*, 51–2; F.M. Powicke (ed.), *The life of Ailred of Rievaulx by Walter Daniel* (1950), 45. **65** W.D.H. Sellar, 'Marriage, divorce and concubinage in Gaelic Scotland' (1978–80), 474–84; Barrow, 'Lost Gàidhealtachd', 115–16. **66** For discussions of the legislation on marriage in medieval Scotland, see Patrick (ed.), *Statutes of the Scottish church*, lxxxvii–lxxxviii and the statutes cited at 14–15, 28, 37, 44, 51, 55, 59–60, 68–9; also Dowden, *Medieval church*, 251–71. **67** Ibid., 128.

real dilemma that contemporary churchmen encountered in trying to provide meaningful spiritual services to the native communities of the kingdom who understood neither Latin nor French. Moreover, they credit the church with too little success in achieving its aims. A significant segment of the clerical population of Strathearn and Lennox may well have fallen short of the strict standards set out in local and provincial church councils of their day, and there can be little doubt that these conditions must deeply have troubled champions of the reform movement. Yet, toleration of irregularities among the clerics of the native lordships must only ever have been regarded as a stage in the eventual triumph of reform values. In the meantime, even the most determined episcopal officials in Dunblane and Glasgow must have welcomed the presence of Gaelic-speaking parsons, rectors, vicars and chaplains in the small parishes of Strathearn and Lennox as promising channels of communication with the native population. It was thus as the agent of a church prepared to bend its own rules, despite contemporary injunctions against the holding of courts in parish churches, that in the early 1220s the priest of Strageath summoned an assembly of lay and clerical tenants of the earl of Strathearn in a ceremony that was at once solemn and festive.[68] Appropriate or not, the parish church was the focal point of religious and secular life in the native lordships, just as it was elsewhere in the realm, and the numerous churches of Strathearn and Lennox were places where the formal ecclesiastical establishment of the day interacted most fruitfully with the common people of the region.[69]

Religious life in twelfth- and thirteenth-century Strathearn and Lennox was a rich blend of Celtic custom and more recent devotional rituals. Keith Stringer has argued for similarly 'harmonious cross-cultural encounters' in Galloway in this same period, and evidence of the accommodation and integration of native values and practices has been found in other regions of the kingdom, including the western highlands, the lordship of Buchan and, perhaps most successfully, in Fife.[70] By the fourteenth century the interaction of native and European cultures had created a church that was uniquely Scottish. Local saints shared feast days in monastic martyrologies and liturgical calendars with worthies familiar to the English and continental faithful.[71] In some areas ecclesiastical offices remained firmly in the hands of families that had long controlled them, while in others monastic and episcopal appointments went to clerics trained in the Latin tradition.[72] In the parishes of the Gàidhealtachd sermons were preached

---

68 *Inchaff. Liber*, no. 16. **69** On parish life generally in the Middle Ages, see G. Donaldson, *Scottish church history* (1985), 223–4. **70** Stringer, 'Reform monasticism and Celtic Scotland', 153; McDonald, 'Scoto-Norse kings', 201–2, 218; Young, 'Earls and earldom of Buchan', 185–6; M.O. Anderson, 'The Celtic church in Kinrimund', (1974); Barrow, *Kingdom*, 187–202. **71** A.I. Doyle, 'A Scottish Augustinian psalter' (1957), 75–9; F. Wormald, 'A fragment of a thirteenth-century calendar from Holyrood abbey' (1934–5), 474; J. Durkan, 'The place-name Balmaha' (1999), 88; A. Budgey, '*Commeationis et affinitatis gratia*: medieval musical relations between Scotland and Ireland', in R.A. McDonald (ed.), *History, literature, and music in Scotland, 700–1560* (Toronto, 2002), 221. **72** Thomson, 'Gaelic learned orders', 67–8.

in Gaelic, but elsewhere in the kingdom they might be delivered in Scots or French, or both.[73] The owner of a book of hours fashioned in distant Paris felt comfortable adding to the manuscript's Latin text some lines in Gaelic – including two charms.[74] The transformation of popular piety in Scotland was a lengthy and sometimes conflictual process, and one that was by some measures never fully accomplished in parts of the kingdom. But in the later fourteenth century the common people of Strathearn and Lennox participated in devotional rituals that drew as much on their native past as they did on the ideology of the post-Gregorian reform movement.[75]

THE EXPERIENCE OF STRATHEARN AND LENNOX IN THE LARGER CONTEXT OF THE SCOTTISH GÀIDHEALTACHD

The challenges and the promises that confronted the reformed church in Strathearn and Lennox were not, of course, peculiar to those lordships. One of the most pervasive themes in the history of Scotland in the twelfth, thirteenth and fourteenth centuries is the church's attempt to bring religious practice and belief throughout the realm into conformity with the ideology of the universal church in Rome. Progress towards this goal was by no means uniform or steady. Streathearn and Lennox were conservative native lordships, and the successes of the reform movement were measured only incrementally here over the *longue durée* between *c.*1150 and 1400. There were, moreover, significant differences between the regions. The unusually intimate relationship between the earls of Strathearn and the bishops of Dunblane, for example, went some way towards facilitating the establishment of episcopal authority in the lands of the earldom to a much greater degree than occurred in neighbouring Lennox, where the bishops of Glasgow frequently aroused the ire and the suspicion of the native magnates. In some areas of Scotland Gaelic conservatism and lordly ambitions hindered the efforts of reform minded clerics in only the mildest of ways. The native earls of Fife most notably and, after 1212, the lords of remote Buchan absorbed post-Gregorian tenets remarkably quickly, and proved valuable allies in the transmission of reform principles to their tenants. At the other extreme, in some provinces relations between secular and ecclesiastical dignitaries, far from being harmonious, were antagonistic and in some cases violent. Thus, the reform message did not take fast root in Caithness, where opposition to the establishment of an episcopal seat on the continental model witnessed a 'clash of cultures' in which

---

[73] I.B. Cowan, 'The medieval church in the highlands', in L. McLean (ed.), *The middle ages in the highlands* (Inverness, 1981), 91–100: 93, 99. [74] J. Higgitt, *The Murthly hours: devotion, literacy and luxury in Paris, England and the Gaelic west* (2000), 15. [75] For a general discussion of popular piety in Scotland in the Middle Ages, see D. Ditchburn, *Scotland and Europe: the medieval kingdom and its contacts with Christendom, 1214–1560* (2000). Although the thrust of Ditchburn's argument here is the Europeanization of belief, he provides numerous examples of 'the universal and the parochial' features of popular religious practices; ibid., 34.

two bishops fell victim to brutal assault.[76] In like fashion, royal efforts to initiate reform by introducing Scottish bishops to the western isles and to Galloway met with rebellion and armed opposition.[77] In areas like these, where the mere presence of new agents of episcopal authority generated profound tension, ecclesiastical reform could not progress steadily, if at all.

Reactions to the reformist ideology of Rome in the native lordships of Scotland were diverse, and to date scholars have avoided suggesting that there was anything 'typical' or 'normative' in the experience of one region or another. The analysis that follows offers some general observations concerning the consequences of reform in Strathearn and Lennox. It links developments here to patterns that scholars have identified in some of those other regions, and weighs the relative successes and failures of reformers to effect change. The strength of such a broad approach is that it serves to illuminate changes in the ecclesiastical and political history of Scotland that previous studies of individual lordships, although these are now abundant, have not always fully appreciated.

The success or failure of reform proponents to win acceptance for their plans to reinvigorate the Scottish church ultimately hinged on the support (or lack thereof) of the secular lords responsible for governing the affairs of their tenants, great and small. In Strathearn and Lennox this acquiescence was only partially achieved in the short term. As early as the time of Fearchar in the late twelfth century, the earl of Strathearn demonstrated a willingness to listen to the reformed church's teachings about the spiritual value of granting lands and other resources to the holy men who lived in their midst, and his successor, Gille Brigte, founder and patron of Inchaffray, proved himself a fine example of the kind of munificent lord that clerics hoped would assist their efforts in the Gaelic regions of the kingdom unfamiliar with the essence of reform ideology. The earls of Strathearn also accepted in cautious but encouraging fashion the church's teaching that strong episcopal authority was an essential component of ecclesiastical, political and social governance. Although they exercised unusual influence over the bishops of Dunblane, members of the comital family acknowledged the importance of the episcopal presence in their territories. They demonstrated this in their willingness to seek confirmation from Dunblane of their numerous grants to Inchaffray, and in their acceptance of the transformation of the priests resident there into Augustinian canons. Yet, the lords of Strathearn clung tenaciously, and for a long time successfully, to their traditional roles in the election of bishops and the appointment of priests to parish churches. The earls of Lennox proved rather more reluctant to promote actively the process of administrative reform within their lands. They founded no new religious houses, and only grudgingly made gifts of land and privilege to the church; moreover, they began

---

[76] B.E. Crawford, 'Norse earls and Scottish bishops: a clash of cultures' (1995), and idem, 'The earldom of Caithness and the kingdom of Scotland, 1150–1266' (1985), 27–30. [77] A. McDonald, 'Monk, bishop, impostor, pretender: the place of Wimund in twelfth-century Scotland' (1992–4); Oram, *Lordship of Galloway*, esp. 164–90; Duncan, *Making*,166.

to make donations to Paisley abbey only after Earl Maoldomhnaich's marriage into a prominent Anglo-Norman family made such acts of lordly munificence *de rigueur*. The grants of the earl and his kinsmen to the Cluniac house, however, were never more than modest. They submitted only reluctantly to the authority of the bishops of Glasgow, and only definitively after 1226, when Maoldomhnaich was taken to task for violating the privileges of the church.

In some respects the church's experience in Strathearn and Lennox resembled those of other native lordships. What counted most, irrespective of place, was the degree to which Gaelic lords were prepared to accept and implement meaningfully the imperatives of the reform agenda. In the eyes of earnest clerics the earls of Fife were shining exemplars, to be emulated by all native lords. Patrons of a variety of new monastic communities and important allies of a vigorous episcopal seat based in St Andrews, Donnchad III and Donnchad IV, Mael Coluim I and Mael Coluim II were crucial agents in the dissemination of the church's ideology. Professor Barrow's comment that the native family of Fife 'could adapt itself successfully not only to the customs and institutions of feudalism, but also, on the social level, to the dominant French aristocracy of the Angevin period' might just as well be extended to the arena of ecclesiastical policy.[78] At the other end of the spectrum stood the largely independent rulers of the western and northern reaches of the kingdom. Houses of reformed monks and canons were thin on the ground here for much of the thirteenth century,[79] and the sees of Argyll, Moray and Caithness were not firmly established until the late twelfth and the early thirteenth centuries respecitvely. In these regions the intrusion of bishops into the authority that lords exercised over their tenants were deeply resented and actively opposed. The proximity of the lands of Lennox to Argyll and the isles, and the western focus of the earls towards the heart of the Scottish Gàidhealtachd and Ireland for much of Maoldomhnaich's lengthy tenure of the comital title account in large part for the conservatism apparent in all aspects of his lordship. It was not until the time of his grandson and great-grandson, Malcolm I and Malcolm II, at the end of the thirteenth century, that the earls of Lennox became fully integrated into the political nexus of central and eastern Scotland. Until then, their support for ecclesiastical reform was lukewarm at best. The lords of Strathearn, by contrast, were linked more closely by social and familial ties to the French- and English-speaking magnates who surrounded the king, and as a consequence were more widely exposed to the profound changes that were occurring in the church. Although they experienced a period of adjustment to the assertion of episcopal authority in the first part of the thirteenth century, by the time of earl Robert's succession in 1245 the tenets of reform had begun to take root there.

The importance of the foreign nobility in promoting the implementation of the reform programme in Scotland was another key factor in winning over

---

78 G.W.S. Barrow, *The Anglo-Norman era in Scottish history* (1980), 89–90.   **79** Those that were established, moreover, were almost all creations of the rulers of Argyll.

the native magnates. The generous gifts of the lords of Galloway to new monastic orders in their lands have been described as proof that they were 'very much in tune with the cosmopolitan religious sentiment of the age'.[80] A wish to emulate the largesse of their English and continental fellows was also a factor in the establishment of new religious houses at Saddell and Iona (Raonall son of Somhairle), Ardchattan (Donnchad MacDùghalll), Culross (Mael Coluim earl of Fife), Fearn (Fearchar earl of Ross), Blantyre (Patrick earl of Dunbar) and Inchaffray (Gille Brigte earl of Strathearn),[81] as well as in the ongoing endowment of the reformed orders by native lords such as Morgrund and Gille Crìosd earls of Mar (Arbroath, Moray, St Andrews), Maol Coluim earl of Atholl (Arbroath, Coupar Angus, Dunfermline, Lindores, St Andrews) and Maoldomhnaich earl of Lennox (Arbroath, Paisley).[82]Although lords of English and European descent were as likely to clash with episcopal dignitaries and to challenge the right of bishops to intrude into the affairs of their territories as were native magnates, when the former first settled in Scotland, by and large they brought with them acceptance of the notion that the governance of their lands must properly be shared with diocesan authorities. There can be little doubt, moreover, that the inculcation of reform ideas and influences occurred most rapidly in regions that passed by reason of inheritance or royal intervention into the hands of newcomers. The earldoms of Buchan and Menteith and the lordship of Badenoch are particularly pertinent examples. Buchan remained in native hands until the early thirteenth century, when King William I granted the last earl's heiress in marriage to William Comyn and elevated the latter to the status of earl. Almost immediately William introduced the Cistercian order to north-east Scotland when he founded a new house at the ancient site of Deer in 1219, and he proved a generous patron of other churches within his lands and beyond.[83] Significantly, the development of a cathedral chapter at Aberdeen and the decline of old monastic communities at Deer, Turriff, Monymusk and Clova coincided with his rule and that of his immediate successor.[84] In Moray, the creation of the office of warden, then the erection of the lordship of Badenoch, the first entrusted to William Comyn, the second to his son, Walter, similarly accelerated the pace of ecclesiastical change there.[85]Although the reformed religious orders found little support in Badenoch, the establishment of a permanent cathedral at Elgin in 1224 saw the creation of a chapter proceed apace.[86] Continental influence first began to touch the earldom of Menteith in 1233 or 1234, when Walter Comyn lord of Badenoch married the daughter of

---

[80] McDonald, 'Scoto-Norse kings', 217. [81] *MRHS*, 59, 74, 77, 83, 89, 91, 101. [82] *Arbroath Liber*, i, nos. 1, 33, 100, 206; C. Rogers (ed.), *Rental book of the Cistercian abbey of Cupar-Angus* (2 vols, 1879-80), i, 33; C. Innes (ed.), *Registrum de Dunfermelyn* (1842), nos. 58, 147, 148; *St Andrews Liber*, 59, 232–6, 245–7, 363; *APS*, i, 405; NLS, Adv. MS. 15.1.18, no. 66. [83] A. Young, *Robert Bruce's rivals: the Comyns, 1212–1314* (1997), 26, 50; idem, 'Earls and earldom of Buchan', 185–6. [84] *MRHS*, 47, 51, 7, 202–3; W.D. Simpson, 'The Augustinian priory and parish church of Monymusk, Aberdeenshire', (1925), 42–4. [85] Young, 'Earls and earldom of Buchan', 177–8. [86] *MRHS*, 206; Barrow, 'Badenoch and Strathspey: 2. the church', 1–16.

the last native earl. Here, too, the pace of ecclesiastical change noticeably quickened thereafter. Bishop Clement of Dunblane considered it advisable, for example, to carve out of his episcopal lands a new rural deanery based on the boundaries of Comyn's lordship,[87] and the latter's acts of munificence in founding and endowing an Augustinian house at Inchmahome[88] brought the influence of the new monasticism and the tenets of the reform programme directly into the heart of this region. To varying degrees, then, the accommodation of secular and ecclesiastical interests that was so vital a feature of the lands that came under the control of foreign magnates helped to pave the way for the spread of the reform agenda to the native regions of the kingdom, and to bring the conservative world of the Gaelic lordships into the orbit of the post-Gregorian church.

The process of ecclesiastical transformation was most successfully accomplished in areas where lordly authority was supportive of change. New principles were also most likely to flourish when reforming clerics demonstrated respect for, and sensitivity to, native custom and tradition, and remained cautious in introducing new forms of authority. Even the most determined of reformers were aware that they did not have at their disposal a blank slate upon which they might impose change and effect improvement. The early bishops of St Andrews, Brechin and Dunkeld, for example, struggled with a sometimes bewildering variety of claims to the patronage of parish churches and other lands lying that lay beyond their diocesan boundaries.[89] In the more compact territorial bishoprics of Dunblane and Glasgow, by contrast, the extent of episcopal authority approximated in the ecclesiastical sphere the control that the earls already exercised in the secular. In both regions, the division of authority between bishop and earl was accomplished with relatively little dislocation of existing conditions.

The importance of toleration for the exercise of traditional lordly influence was perhaps of greatest consequence in the process of parish formation that began in earnest under King David I and picked up pace after the promulgation of the decrees of the Fourth Lateran Council.[90] The most beloved of Scottish bishops were those who carved new parishes our of lands associated since ancient times with holy sites, as well as out of lands linked to specific kin groups. The practice of respecting long recognized territorial division, for example, served the thirteenth-century bishops of Moray well in the regions of Badenoch and Strathspey,[91] and similar policies were followed in regions as far apart as Mar, Fife, Angus, Argyll, Galloway and Caithness, where ancient shires and thanages were given new life as parish units.[92] In Strathearn, likewise, the

---

[87] Watt, *Fasti*, 91. [88] *MRHS*, 91–2. [89] Ash, 'Diocese of St Andrews', 105–26; idem, 'Celtic church in Kinrimund', 67–76; Barrow, *Kingdom*, 187–202; M. Anderson, 'St Andrews before Alexander I' (1974); M. Dilworth, 'The dependent priories of St Andrews (1976), 157, 162–3 [90] Barrow, *Kingship and unity*, 72–3. [91] Barrow, 'Badenoch and Strathspey: 2. the church', 1–16. For the example of Duffus, see *Moray Reg.*, no. 81. [92] Barrow, *Kingdom*, 50–4, 233–49; Ash, 'Diocese of St Andrews', 112–13, 117; Simpson, *Province of Mar*, 89 and table at 151–3; idem, 'Augustinian priory and parish church of Monymusk', 34–5; I.B. Cowan, 'The church in Argyll and the Isles',

boundaries of the newly created parish of Muthill represented the area once served by a community of Céli Dé priests. In Lennox, the parish of Luss was built around a church staffed by the hereditary keepers of an ancient shrine dedicated to St Kessog, as was that of Kilpatrick, further south.

The realignment of old territories in many of the native lordships stands in some contrast to the creation of new parishes in the parts of Scotland settled by English and continental newcomers. Here, new parishes were often coterminous with recently delineated lay feus. This was the pattern in the Stewart lands of upper Clydesdale, for example, a region that boasted 'as perfect a group of manorial churches as we are likely to find',[93] and in Lothian, where the parish of Legerwood was constituted in part from an estate granted by King Malcolm IV to Walter son of Alan.[94] The preservation of old divisions in the network of new parishes begun in the twelfth century, as well as in new administrative units such as archdeaconries and rural deaneries, went some way towards providing useful channels of communication for ecclesiastical reformers, not only with the native lords of Scotland, but with their Gaelic-speaking parishioners.

The accommodation of traditional devotional practices served the church well not only in Strathearn and Lennox, but throughout the realm. It can hardly be doubted that in regions newly settled by French- and English-speaking lords some changes must have troubled the native population. Throughout Scotland, Roman reformers subjected the conventions that governed Christian marriage to the rigorous scrutiny of canon lawyers, theologians and episcopal leaders. The voluminous legislation that they generated was known in remote Scotland as early as the reign of St Margaret, and the magnates who arrived in the twelfth century brought with them familiarity not only with the new teachings on marriage, but with the closely related business of inheritance. Scottish bishops were likewise determined to reform the objectionable marriage practices among the ranks of the highest nobility, and their efforts were felt especially keenly by members of the native aristocracy. The twelfth-century chronicler, Walter Daniel, lamented the resort to secular marriage among the Galwegians,[95] but less than a century later, the Gaelic lord Muireadhach of Menteith had to resign his title to the earldom when questions were raised about the legitimacy of his parents' union.[96] The church's stance on this occasion can hardly have failed to impress upon Strathearn and Lennox magnates the importance of conformity to clerical teachings about marriage.

While ecclesiastical reformers were concerned to ensure the observance of appropriate Christian behaviour among the native nobility of Scotland, they were

---

139; Brooke, *Wild Men*, 69; Crawford, 'Norse earls', 133; R.G. Cant, 'The medieval kirk of Crail' (1983), 368. More generally, see T.O. Clancy, 'Annat in Scotland and the origins of the Parish' (1995), a useful corrective to A. MacDonald, '"Annat" in Scotland: a provisional review' (1973); and Morgan, 'Organization of the Scottish church', 143–4. **93** Ibid., 142; for examples in parts of the country settled by men of Flemish descent, see L. Toorians, 'Twelfth-century Flemish settlements in Scotland' (1996), 8, 12. **94** Barrow, *Kingdom*, 325. **95** Cited in Brooke, *Wild Men*, 98; see also Oram, *Lordship of Galloway*, 57. **96** Fraser, *Red book of Menteith*, ii, 214–15; *SP*, vi, 125.

nevertheless prepared to allow less rigorous standards to obtain among people of lesser rank. The accommodation of old customs and practices evident in thirteenth-and fourteenth-century Strathearn and Lennox was a feature of religious life in other lordships as well, both native and newly settled. Earl Malise II of Strathearn's grant of two serfs to Inchaffray abbey[97] is but one example of the ways in which reform era clerics weighed the complex matter of personal freedom among Christian peoples against the dangers of intruding too heavily into the social fabric of the kingdom, and the exchange of *nativi* and their families was a vigorous feature of the human economy throughout rural Scotland in Mar, Garioch and elsewhere.[98] Just as they encouraged the revitalization of shrines to Celtic saints in Strathearn and Lennox, so too did churchmen find room in the new network of parishes for venerable sites from Banchory-Ternan in Mar and Cromdale in Strathspey, to Iona in the western isles and Kirkmabrech in Galloway.[99] The bishops of Moray and St Andrews welcomed Gaelic-speaking priests in Badenoch and Fife as much as did those of Dunblane and Glasgow in Strathearn and Lennox,[1] not merely because there was a lack of candidates to fill parish offices. While they can hardly have been naïve enough to expect that the message of reform would alter popular belief and devotional custom in the short term, no change whatsoever would be forthcoming if priests, parsons and vicars could not communicate at the most fundamental levels with their flocks.

Historians interested in measuring the relative successes and failures of the reform movement in the native lordships of twelfth-, thirteenth- and fourteenth-century Scotland would probably place Strathearn and Lennox somewhere in the middle reaches of a notional spectrum, with the former more quickly and more comprehensively adopting change than the latter. By the middle years of the thirteenth century, and especially from the time of Earl Malise II on (1245–*c.*1271), change is apparent in the religious landscape of Strathearn, for example in the proliferation in witness lists of lay and ecclesiastical charters of men whose personal and family names link them closely to the land holding nobility of English and continental descent. The comital family demonstrated considerable respect for, and conformity with, the rules governing the conveyance of church lands and the appointment of clerics to parish livings, even if they abandoned the pattern of generous giving that had characterized the rule of their predecessor, Gille Brigte.

In Lennox, the grip of custom in matters relating to the church and its property was still strong enough to provide the great-nieces of a disgraced cleric with a reasonable expectation of success in a fresh claim to lands associated with the church of Kilpatrick, even when these had long ago been assigned to the see of

---

97 *Inchaff. Chrs.*, no. 87; *Inchaff. Liber*, no. 58. **98** *Aberdeen-Banff illustrations*, ii, 18–19, iv, 693–4; Duncan, *Making*, 331–4. **99** Simpson, *Province of Mar*, 86–7; Barrow, 'Badenoch and Strathspey: 2. the church', 1–2; Cowan, *Parishes of medieval Scotland*, 90; Brooke, *Wild Men*, 75–6. For a wide variety of other sites, see A.D.S. Macdonald and L.R. Laing, 'Early ecclesiastical sites in Scotland: a field survey, part I' and 'part II', (1967–8), and 102 (1969–70). **1** G.W.S. Barrow, 'Badenoch and Strathspey, 1130–1312: 1. secular and political', (1988), 10; *Inchcolm Chrs.*, no. 1.

Glasgow. In the second half of the thirteenth century the native earls still had few direct links with the cosmopolitan world of the universal church represented by church councils and luminaries such as David Bernham (who spent part of his career as precentor of Glasgow cathedral),[2] or William Wishart, renowned not only within Scotland but in England and the continent.[3] These magnates preferred to focus their energies inward on the several parish churches over which they maintained personal control. Relations with the Cluniac monks of Paisley were cool. It was not until the very end of the century that profound cultural change began to transform the political, economic and social complexion of Lennox. That the region should have remained equally conservative in its popular religious beliefs and practices is hardly surprising.

2 M. Ash, 'David Bernham, bishop of St Andrews, 1239–1253' (1976), 34.   3 Barrow, *Kingdom*, 193, 219.

CHAPTER 5

Gaelic lordship in 'Anglo-Norman era' Scotland

In 1216, as the young King Alexander II was preparing to lead the army of Scotland into the northern English border lands, another war was touching the earldom of Lennox. Internecine conflict in northwestern Ireland had long troubled the lives of local residents, but it also offered exciting opportunities to adventurous men, and in a rare coincidence both aspects of Irish warfare influenced the Scottish lordship directly. In Donegal, Muireadhach the son of Earl Ailin II of Lennox was busy winning fame in battle against Trad h-ua Mailfhabhaill, the leader of Cenél Fergusa, killing the latter together with several of his kinsmen.[1] Around the same time, an Irish bard, also named Muireadhach, one of seven sons of Aenghus Fionnabhrach, and distinguished already as an *ollamh*, set out for Lennox. It was not his first visit. A decade and a half earlier he had fled Sligo and eventually Ireland itself after falling afoul of a powerful man, and had found refuge with Ailin's father; in return for the protection he was given there he had composed a praise poem in honour of the earl. His second journey saw him settle permanently in Lennox, and write a second song, this one addressed to another of Ailin II's sons, Amhlaibh.[2]

The two Muireadhaìch were part of a steady movement of men and women back and forth across the Irish Sea, a body of water that was more a bridge than it was an obstacle. Ireland was a rich recruiting ground for Scottish lords seeking mercenary troops, and the challenges to the authority of the Canmore kings that magnates such as the lords of the Isles, the Mac Uilleim kindred, and the rulers of Galloway were able to mount owed as much to Irish as they did Scottish resources.[3] Close communications between the realms favoured an equally free flow of ideas and cultural practices. The earldoms of Strathearn and Lennox were thus part of the Gàidhealtachd, 'a great crescent of cultural homogeneity' spanning the entire Irish Sea region.[4] Well into the late medieval period

---

[1] W.M. Hennessy and B. McCarthy (eds), *Annala Uladh: the annals of Ulster* (4 vols, 1887–1901), ii, 261. [2] D.S. Thomson, 'The Mac Mhuirich bardic family' (1960–3), 278–9; L. McKenna (ed.), *Aithdioghluim Dána* (3 vols, 1939–40), i, xxxii–xxxiii. The song addressed to Ailin II *c*.1200 is discussed in B. Ó Cuív, 'Eachtra Mhuireadhaigh Í Dhálaigh' (1921), and T.O. Clancy (ed.), *The triumph tree*, 258. [3] S. Duffy, 'The Bruce brothers and the Irish Sea world, 1306–29' (1991), 59–83; R.A. McDonald, *Outlaws of medieval Scotland* (2003), 71, 106; D. Brooke, *Wild men and holy places: St Ninian, Whithorn and the medieval realm of Galloway* (1994), 130–4; Duncan, *Making*, 530–1. [4] C. McNamee, *The wars of the Bruces: Scotland, England and Ireland, 1306–1328* (1997), ii; see also W. McLeod, *Divided Gaels: cultural identities in Scotland and Ireland c.1200–c.1650* (2004), 3–13.

Gaelic remained in both lordships the everyday language of the majority of the landed ranks (and of their peasants), but increasingly in the century and a half after 1170, exposure to European influences altered the profile not merely of the native language, but of the contexts in which it was employed.

The genesis of a distinctively Scottish culture in Strathearn and Lennox during this crucial period is evident in a host of aspects, some easily discernible, others more subtle and, for the historian, frustratingly difficult to grasp. Some changes were momentous. Such, for example, was the introduction of written charters and other deeds related to the tenure of land, which hastened the intrusion of Latin, French, and English into the business of conveyance and, ultimately, the relationship between native lords and the people who held estates of them. Other changes were mundane, but none the less significant. Thus, the choices that the earls of Strathearn and Lennox and their countesses made when they named their children reveal much about their understanding of their families' past, but also about aspirations for their future. Still other changes, although they may on the surface appear to have been simple, were symptomatic of a much deeper shift in modes of thought, expression, and conduct. When, for example, Earl Ailin II of Lennox welcomed the gift of song that his Irish refugee Muireadhach Ó Dálaigh offered him, he simultaneously affirmed a specifically Gaelic and Irish origin for his lineage and imitated the latest European fashion of patronizing a wandering minstrel. Which of these cultural mores was the more dominant? Likewise, when they considered suitable marriage partners, the earls of Strathearn and Lennox must have borne in mind a variety of criteria: the rank and status of candidates, certainly; the size and location of the tocher lands that the women would bring to the marriage, equally certainly. But to what extent did they ponder the future countess's ability to communicate clearly with household servants, local tenants and, most obviously, their own children?

This chapter examines these and other aspects of native lordship in Strathearn and Lennox between the late twelfth and the mid fourteenth centuries. One of its themes repeats the arguments made elsewhere in this work in showing that, until about 1250, the earls consciously strove to preserve, and in some cases openly to champion, Gaelic customs and practices in the face of powerful European influences. Resistance to the wholesale abandonment of traditional practices under the pressure of new ideas is apparent in the way the earls organized their households, in the relationships that they maintained with their tenants, and in their acceptance of the mandates of a reforming church. It is manifest also in the strategies that Gille Brigte and Robert of Strathearn, and Ailin II and Maoldomhnaich of Lennox adopted to maintain their status as Gaelic provincial rulers. They were by no means impervious or overtly hostile to foreign ideas about lordship and its trappings, and indeed found in some English and continental practices new ways of expressing their lordship over their free tenants and peasants. At the same time, however, and in myriad ways, they successfully cultivated a distinct identity within the community of the Scottish aristocracy and, for much of this period, continued to wield their authority much as had the mormaers of old.

The overwhelmingly Gaelic flavour of Gille Brigte of Strathearn's lordship began to wane perceptibly under the rule of his son Robert; by the time the latter's son in turn succeeded to the title of earl it had well nigh disappeared. Malise II's involvement in the disruptive events of Alexander III's minority kept him close to the court for much of the decade after 1249; thereafter, service to the crown meant that he had to divide his time equally between the national political scene and his landed estates. Frequent and ongoing contact with the political, economic, and cultural world of the larger Scottish realm brought an end to the relative isolation and conservatism that had characterized Strathearn society since 1200. In Lennox, the loosening of the earls' commitment to cultural and political isolationism did not take place for another generation at least, and when in 1248 Earl Maoldomhnaich's son Mael Coluim quarrelled with Sir David de Graham, the assembly before which the parties convened must have included not merely Gaelic- and French- or English-speaking arbitrators, but clerks and scribes capable of understanding all these languages.[5] Malcolm I's assumption of the title in the early 1270s saw the pace of change in Lennox quicken, then accelerate further in the years immediately after the death of Alexander III, when the family sided with the cause of Robert Bruce.

In both Strathearn and Lennox the changing nature of lordship was the consequence of more than merely the earls' choice of friends, tenants, and courtly contacts. Alexander III's achievements in establishing firm control over the furthest reaches of a united kingdom also had important effects on the forging of a distinctly Scottish nobility. As the inhabitants of the western isles found after 1263, sustained political independence was no longer possible in the later thirteenth century. The economic boom of this period, moreover, encouraged the movement of people and ideas across the Forth-Clyde line, and helped to dissolve some of the linguistic, cultural and social barriers between the regions that had marked the later twelfth century. The burghs of Perth and Glasgow offered not only promising markets for the traditional products of agrarian and pastoral farmers, but exciting new venues within which to enact the rituals associated with Gaelic lordship. Thus, in 1274 a charter of Malcolm I required of the beneficiary 'as much food for the army of the lord king as pertains to a quarter of land in Lennox', but specified also an annual rent of ten shillings, 'to be rendered to us each year at the fair of Glasgow'.[6] In this fashion, Malcolm brought the small, local community of his lordship into the larger world.

The 'relative prosperity' of Alexander III's reign provided a backdrop for the gradual integration of the foreign cultural practices that the newcomers had brought to Strathearn and Lennox into the customs of native society.[7] The process by which this was accomplished in the context of several key features of lordship is the focus of this chapter. The pace of transculturation discernible in both regions in the late twelfth century might well have occurred only slowly

5 Fraser, *Lennox*, ii, no. 8. 6 *Lenn. Cart.*, 85–6. 7 N. Reid, 'Alexander III: the historiography of a myth' (1990), 181–208: 207.

and haltingly but for the events of the 1290s, when Scottish landowners, great and small, were caught up in another crisis, this one more serious and more disruptive than anything the political community had experienced since the days of Mael Coluim III. The struggle for independence and nationhood that began at Norham in 1291 profoundly altered the personal histories of most of the kingdom's great families. Malise of Strathearn lost his freedom and his earldom to the fortunes of war; his contemporary, Malcolm II of Lennox, forfeited his title to a wrathful Edward I. As Geoffrey Barrow's comprehensive study of Robert Bruce's career has made clear, Scottish noblemen were by no means united in their opposition to the English king's designs. But all shared the uncertainty and dislocation of open war. The events of the precarious political world of the post-1296 period overtook them all, and compelled them to fight conquest and assimilation on much more than merely the cultural front. The first phases of the wars of independence thus affected not only the personal careers of individual noblemen, but the structure of the Scottish aristocracy as a body. The earls of Strathearn and Lennox who were alive in the middle years of the fourteenth century ruled their territories with a comprehensive authority that would have been immediately recognisable to their early thirteenth-century predecessors. But the ways in which they now manifested that lordship had changed beyond all recognition.

CHARTERS AND CHARTER WRITING IN STRATHEARN AND LENNOX

One of the most profound consequences of the encounter between Gaels and Europeans in Scotland was the gradual but steady spread of written documents beyond the royal chancery into the world of ecclesiastical and noble land holding. Written records were by no means unknown before the later twelfth century, as the collections of royal and noble charters edited by Archibald Lawrie and, more recently, Professors Barrow and Duncan have shown.[8] By mid-century, the brethren of the distant monastery of Deer in Aberdeenshire thought it wise to begin recording their property rights in the margins of an old gospel book. Unusually, these notations were in Gaelic; so, too, apparently, were the lists of lands and privileges kept in 'an old volume written in the ancient Scottish tongue', subsequently lost, by the Céli Dé of Loch Leven.[9] The practice of writing, in short, was fast becoming an important aspect of lordly governance in Scotland well before 1150. Thereafter, a number of factors came together to establish the Latin language deed as a permanent feature of the cultural landscape. One of these was the general process that scholars refer to as the 'Europeanization' of the king-

---

[8] A.C. Lawrie (ed.), *Early Scottish charters prior to A.D. 1153* (1905); G.W.S. Barrow (ed.), *The charters of King David I* (1999); A.A.M. Duncan, 'The earliest Scottish charters' (1958); idem, 'Yes, the earliest Scottish charters' (1999). [9] T. Thomson (ed.), *Liber cartarum prioratus Sancti Andree in Scotia* (1841), 113.

dom, which saw the 'fuller and deeper incorporation' of the realm 'into the Latin and Frankish world'.[10] In this sense, the adoption of written documents initially by the Scottish royal house, then by its ecclesiastical tenants and, eventually, by lay magnates was but one manifestation of a Europeanization process also evident in a host of other secular and ecclesiastical contexts, among them the development of the office of king, the standardization of coinage, the growth of burghs, and the creation of a network of parishes in the kingdom.

There can be little doubt, however, that the establishment of the reformed religious orders in Scotland during the reigns of David I and his immediate successors provided added impetus to the spread of charter writing from the royal chancery into significant portions of the kingdom. Like their counterparts in England, Wales, and Ireland, monkish landlords in Scotland quickly came to associate the writ charter, authenticated with the donor's seal, with title to the vast estates with which they were endowed, and it was chiefly owing to their evidentiary value that in the course of the later decades of the twelfth century written records found their way into charter chests, cartularies and, beyond these, royal, ecclesiastical, and baronial courts.[11]

The native earls of Scotland were not ignorant of the new weight that their king and their ecclesiastical tenants accorded to written charters. The survival of early deeds from Strathearn and Lennox, as well as from Mar, Buchan, and other lordships in old Scotia attests the growing awareness of the importance of parchment documents. From Strathearn, there survive 40 extant texts of charters from the time of Earls Fearchar, Gille Brigte and Robert,[12] together with fragments or notitiae of 8 others; similarly, there remain 44 full texts from the Lennox of Earls Ailin II and Maoldomhnaich (including several issued by the latter's son, Mael Coluim), and 10 other notitiae. The overwhelming majority of Strathearn charters (41 full and partial texts) relates to grants to ecclesiastical beneficiaries, especially Inchaffray abbey. The Latin trained canons who came from Scone to join the newly established house on the Isle of Masses clearly had a shrewd appreciation of the value of written instruments. They found within Strathearn, moreover, much to concern them in the closely intertwined claims of the native rulers and the nearby bishops of Dunblane and Dunkeld to the estates and churches that constituted the priory's early endowments. The canons' insistence on keeping sealed charters that would protect their titles accounts in turn for the splendid collection of deeds relating to this otherwise modest house, and for the close relationship between the scriptorium at Inchaffray and the earls' household.[13]

---

10 R. Bartlett, *The making of Europe* (1993), 286. See also D. Ditchburn and A.J. Macdonald, 'Medieval Scotland, 1100–1560' (2001), 176; D. Ditchburn, *Scotland and Europe: the medieval kingdom and its contacts with Christendom, 1214–1560* (2000), passim; and M.-T. Flanagan, 'The context and uses of the Latin charter in twelfth-century Ireland' (1996), 120.   **11** Barrow (ed.), *Charters of King David I*, 4–55; *RRS*, i, 57–8; *RRS*, ii, 69–70; T.M. Cooper (ed.), *Select cases of the thirteenth century* (1944).   **12** These numbers refer to texts that survive either as single sheet originals or cartulary copies.   **13** Neville, 'Earls of Strathearn', i, 338–9.

The monkish tenants of the Gaelic lords of Lennox were no less vigilant, and about half of the deeds issued by the earls that survive from the period c.1185–1250 (twenty-five) were granted in favour of ecclesiastical beneficiaries, chiefly Paisley abbey, but also the cathedral church of Glasgow and Kelso abbey. The more even distribution of documents between secular and ecclesiastical beneficiaries reveals, however, that the native rulers of Lennox and at least some of their lay tenants were as likely as were their religious fellows to regard sealed charters as valuable commodities. A brief study of these documents yields some interesting observations about the use of writing among lay persons in the lordship. Both Gaelic and foreign tenants, for example, employed sealed charters to plan, then to promote, strategies of family inheritance. The native earls, for their part, came to see in them a way of consolidating their authority, not only in relation to the crown but, equally important, within the changing tenurial world of their own territories. Lay persons in Lennox – donors, beneficiaries, lords, and tenants – found tangible benefits in the practice of charter writing. The authority accorded to parchment documents in turn initiated profound transformations of a system of land holding that to date had rested on predominantly oral tradition.

Although few in number, newcomers to Lennox such as Simon Croc, Simon son of Bertolf, and David de Graham brought with them a keen appreciation of the significance of charters of infeftment. As did settlers everywhere, they no doubt sought to receive from their new lord 'as much as they could get ... on the most favourable terms';[14] accordingly, they requested, and received, formally executed charters, drafted in the latest diplomatic style, and authenticated with Maoldomhnaich's newly fashioned seal.[15] In one instance at least, David de Graham replaced a sitting (native) tenant, a situation that must have lent greater urgency still to the formal recording of the earl's will.[16] In the middle decades of the twelfth century, all over Scotland, such deeds, written on small pieces of parchment or vellum, became increasingly commonplace wherever English or continental newcomers settled. As Professor Barrow has aptly noted, by the reign of Malcolm IV 'the practice of issuing written documents for laymen was in no way uncommon';[17] that they survive in relatively small numbers reflects nothing more than the poor survival rate of fragile, single sheet originals of any kind. Lay tenants were much less likely than the large monastic establishments to copy their charters into cartularies; indeed, the fact that a late medieval earl of Lennox actually thought to do so explains the unusual richness of the family's muniments.[18]

In Lennox at least, and almost certainly in other Gaelic provinces, native tenants came to appreciate fully and quickly the value of sealed charters. They may simply have done so, of course, in imitation of the sophisticated newcomers

---

[14] S. Reynolds, 'Fiefs and vassals in Scotland: a view from outside' (2003), 182.   [15] Fraser, *Lennox*, ii, nos. 3, 6, 7, 9, 11; Blair Castle, Muiments of the Duke of Atholl, volume of inlaid charters, no. 4.   [16] Fraser, *Lennox*, ii, no. 7.   [17] *RRS*, i, 57.   [18] *Lennox Cart.*, xvi–xviii.

then settling in their midst, and thus merely to have been swept up, willy-nilly, into the 'age of charters' that historians once attributed to the coming of the foreigners.[19] Some Gaels, moreover, may have sought to have their titles to land fortified by written documents because they themselves were newcomers to the lordship and, like English and continental settlers, saw in such records a form of insurance against future challenges to their titles. To still other native tenants, the sealed deed may have represented no more than one among an array of artefacts associated with, but incidental to, the business of conveyance. Like gospel books, knives, rings, staffs, and clods of turf, documents were powerful symbolic tools that might be produced for use in court should the need to display them arise. In the Gaelic world of the twelfth and early thirteenth centuries, however, the drafting of written instruments had not yet superseded the staging and performance of public rituals associated with the conveyance of land.[20] The oral testimony of old and wise men likewise remained a widely used method of proof, as the proceedings relating to the church of Kilpatrick in Lennox reveal.

Some native tenants must have regarded possession of sealed charters as a mark of their lord's preferment, a means not only of establishing a unique and special relationship with their earl, but of positioning themselves at the top of the landed hierarchy in relation to other tenants within Lennox. Such, for example, were the rulers of Luss, whose status as guardians of an ancient local shrine already set them apart from their fellows. The series of charters they secured from Maoldomhnaich may in fact have marked the family's rise from a purely honorial status into the ranks of the earl's wealthiest and most prestigious tenants. Another such family was that of Galbraith. Although originally of British origin, its members had become thoroughly Gaelicized by the later twelfth century,[21] and already in Maoldomhnaich's time they counted among the earl's most trusted advisors.[22] They would have regarded written deeds as a singular mark of distinction. More important still, in this context, was the series of charters issued in favour of the earl's several brothers, who became the chief beneficiaries of Maoldomhnaich's well executed strategy to consolidate the hold of his kindred, current and future, over the earldom lands.[23] For all these reasons, possession of sealed charters by native tenants had significance beyond the mere imitation of the new fangled practices of a foreign aristocracy. The charter itself was still at this time a flexible instrument, its clauses adaptable to a variety of circumstances,[24] and, above all, capable of responding to the legal and tenurial concerns of native and newcomer alike.

19 R.L.G. Ritchie, *The Normans in Scotland* (Edinburgh, 1954), 185. **20** M. Clanchy, *From memory to written record: England 1066–1307* (2nd edn., 1993), 254–5; G.W.S. Barrow, 'The Scots charter' (1992), 94. See also the discussion of a dispute between the bishop of Dunblane and the abbot of Inchaffray which was resolved without recourse to written deeds, in C.J. Neville, 'Charter writing in thirteenth century Celtic Scotland' (2001), 75. **21** See below, p. 211. **22** See, for example, *Lennox Cart.*, 26–7, 30–1. **23** See above, p. 56; also M. Brown, 'Earldom and kindred: the Lennox and its earls, 120–1458' (2003), 207–8. **24** Barrow, 'The Scots charter', 99.

It was not long before Gaelic tenants in Lennox began to deploy written instruments in the setting of lordly and royal courts, but early examples of such activities reveal both the unfamiliarity of native land holders with the customs that continental culture associated with charters, and the ambivalence of the foreigners, especially the church, concerning the validity of documents that originated among native men. In 1233–4, Gille Brigte son of Samuel based his claim to the lands of Monachkenneran on possession of a charter granted him by Dùghall son of Ailin II and a written confirmation of this deed by Earl Maoldomhnaich himself. Both were subsequently ruled 'adulterine' and 'illicit', and Paisley abbey regained possession of the estate.[25] The abbot compelled the earl to issue a new charter recording the restoration of the lands to the monks, and to acknowledge that any future attempts on the part of his kinsmen to produce written documents intended to challenge the abbey 'will not be considered binding'.[26] A second tenant caught up in the dispute also had to surrender his records,[27] and thereafter, resignations of estates into the earls' hands were sometimes marked not merely *per fustum et baculum*, but with the handing over of all sealed instruments relating to the property. In similar fashion, native tenants also came to grasp quickly the evidentiary weight that Anglo-Norman and continental legal customs associated with waxen seals. Despite the existence of two early written instruments, William son of Arthur Galbraith did not consider his family's title to the lands in Lennox secure until he had received from the earl a third deed, this one authenticated with his lord's seal.[28]

Documents also served the myriad interests of native rulers; in some respects, indeed, more than they did those of tenants. To the Gaelic lord who issued them, written *acta* had a multiplicity of meanings. Over the long period of their respective rules, both Gille Brigte of Strathearn and Maoldomhnaich of Lennox came to grasp fully the authority inherent in their seals, and to turn to their advantage the new practice of issuing charters. The grant of written charters to families newly established in their territories, such as the Luvetots in Strathearn and the Crocs in Lennox, was an act of lordship that had resonance among Gaelic and incoming magnates alike, one that was coming to have almost as much significance as the act itself of granting the land. Even the rapacious David de Graham cannot have failed to appreciate that the deeds he secured from Maoldomhnaich placed him in a position of subservience, however honourable, to the earl of Lennox. Charters granted in favour of native thanes, both in Strathearn and Lennox, served the Gaelic rulers' ambitions in equally meaningful fashion. They established a firm hierarchy of status and power between the magnates and these traditionally powerful officials; in addition, they placed the thanes of Strowan, Dunning and, in part at least, of Callander on an equal footing with royal thanes. Above all, the lords of Strathearn and Lennox found in the new practice of charter writing an important means of reshaping the ancient bonds that linked them to their native tenants. In the early thirteenth century traditional Gaelic notions

---

25 *Paisley Reg.*, 164–70.   **26** Ibid., 170–1.   **27** Ibid., 173.   **28** *Lennox Cart.*, 26–7, 30–1.

about land ownership were still a living part of native custom and law, and claims to land were still closely associated with membership in a kin group.[29] Heads of kindred therefore played especially crucial roles in controlling the distribution of estates among their followers. The written charters to lay persons that survive from Lennox offer glimpses of this role in practice; they suggest also that the earls saw in their *acta* an opportunity to exercise their lordly prerogatives in new and powerful ways. Of especial relevance in this context are clauses of perambulation, which appear frequently in Maoldomhnaich's deeds. When the earl summoned tenants from one or another area within Lennox and directed them to march the bounds of a patch of land, he accorded the recognitors a say in the creation of new estates out of lands that had once been held in common. But he also, simultaneously and implicitly, gave expression to a kind of authority that only a great lord and a head of kin might licitly exercise. In the early years of the thirteenth century, for example, Maoldomhnaich assigned lands in the parishes of Luss and Arrochar to a family of native tenants, but he carefully excepted from his grant the estates with which he intended to endow his brother Gille Criosd, later known as MacGilchrist's Land.[30] Similarly, when he displaced the native tenant Farquhar MacGille Mhartainn in order to settle David de Graham in Strathblane and assigned the former new estates elsewhere in the earldom, Maoldomhnaich exercised a prerogative shared only by a handful of social and political equals. Preserving written records of such lordly acts amounted to a public declaration of the earls' authority.[31]

The adoption of written deeds had implications, finally, for the establishment of the native magnates' kinsmen within the community of their own lordships. Both in Strathearn and Lennox, the names of the earls' close male relations, most often brothers and sons, but sometimes also nephews, were almost always included among the witness lists of comital *acta*, attesting their presence at the highly ritualized ceremonies that accompanied the conveyance of land. The inclusion of these names served several purposes. Recording the presence of male members of the family permitted Gaelic lords to identify publicly the men whose advice, counsel, and friendship they valued most. Witness lists had a commemorative function as well, according specific members of the earls' family a permanent place in the collective memory of the wider kin long after the donor and his relatives had 'gone the way of all flesh', as a contemporary phrase piously put it. The attestation of brothers and sons also signalled to all and sundry the assent of the grantor's siblings and heirs to the alienation, in some cases in perpetuity, of family property. There are echoes here not merely of the Gaelic custom that accorded important kinsmen a say in the distribution of land

---

29 R.A. Dodgshon, *Land and society in early Scotland* (1981), 110–11. **30** *Lennox Cart.*, 19–20; Fraser, *Lennox*, ii, no. 204; Royal Faculty of Procurators, Glasgow, Hill Collection of MSS, Macfarlane Muniments, ii, no. 73; *RMS*, ii, no. 187; *Origines*, i, 31–2. More generally, see Neville, 'Charter writing', 81–4. **31** Anglo-Saxon lords had exercised similar prerogatives in the making and shaping of their landscapes. See M. Reed, 'Anglo-Saxon charter boundaries' (1984).

once held collectively, but also, if distantly, of the continental practice known as the *laudatio parentum*, by which noblemen made gifts of land 'with the approval of relatives, rather than acting unilaterally'.[32] In their double roles as witnesses and co-alienors, moreover, brothers and sons undertook on behalf of themselves and their heirs to protect the future title of the beneficiaries' descendants to an estate; in effect, to offer an early form of warrandice.[33]

In imitating the practice of the newcomers and choosing to commit their actions to parchment, the early earls of Strathearn and Lennox initiated complex and profoundly important changes to the dynamics of land ownership within their respective territories. Charters empowered. In a period during which the tenurial world was in a state of flux written deeds possessed for some beneficiaries a *gravitas* that outweighed the spoken word or the symbolic artefact. To others they were indispensable adjuncts to land ownership, weapons to be carefully stored against the day when they might be needed in defence of rival titles and claims. To still others they were tangible symbols of status, authority, and place within a shifting social and political hierarchy. From both lordships there is some evidence that charter writing by native donors did not remain the exclusive preserve of the earls. Members of the Strathearn *familiae*, for example, began to imitate their lord and to issue written deeds under their own seals as early as the 1190s. Thus, Maol Iosa son of Fearchar, Iseulte the countess, Fergus and Gille Brigte sons of Gille Brigte, and Joachim of Kinbuck all recorded grants in writing.[34] In Lennox, similarly, the earliest charters of Amhlaibh son of Ailin II are contemporary with those of his brother Maoldomhnaich.[35] It is none the less noteworthy that each of these grants was made to an ecclesiastical beneficiary, and that from both regions the earliest surviving deeds by Gaelic-speaking laymen to other lay persons date only from the very late thirteenth century.[36] Such patterns serve as cautionary reminders, if indeed any more are needed, that foreign customs penetrated the Gaelic lordships in piecemeal fashion and only under specific circumstances.

Among a large segment of the native tenantry written instruments remained rare. It is something of a commonplace among Scottish charter scholars to lament the loss of deeds issued in favour of lay persons in comparison with grants to ecclesiastical beneficiaries.[37] The predictability with which historians wrestle with problems associated with medieval sources in no way diminishes the unfortunate fact that 'the chances of survival have worked against the layman's document and (relatively) in favour of the ecclesiastical'.[38] The records of Strathearn

---

32 S.D. White, *Custom, kinship, and gifts to saints: the laudatio parentum in western France, 1050–1150* (1988), 1. **33** C.J. Neville, 'Women, charters, and land ownership in Scotland, 1150–1350'. **34** *Lind. Cart.*, nos. 24, 26, 28, 29, 32, 112, 127; *Inchaff. Chrs.*, no. 46; *Inchaff. Liber*, no. 10; C. Innes and P. Chalmers (eds), *Liber S. Thome de Aberbrothoc* (2 vols, 1848–56), i, nos. 86, 87; D.E. Easson (ed.), *Charters of the abbey of Coupar Angus* (2 vols, 1947), i. no. 35; *Moray Reg.*, no. 80. **35** *Paisley Reg.*, 209–11. **36** *Moray Reg.*, App., nos. 13, 14; *Lennox Cart.*, 79–80, 83–5; NAS, GD 220/1/A1/4/4. **37** *RRS*, i 57–9; B. Webster, *Scotland from the eleventh century to 1603* (1975), 80–2; K.J. Stringer, *Earl David of Huntingdon*, 153–4. **38** *RRS*, i, 57–8.

and Lennox are no different. It is undoubtedly true, as Keith Stringer has opined, that in some parts of the kingdom (especially those settled by newcomers to the realm) lay persons had as much use for written titles as did their clerical fellows.[39] But scholars should not apply such generalizations indiscriminately to the regions of Scotland that lay under the control of Gaelic magnates. Here, the reason why so few charters to lay beneficiaries survive may well be that they were never written. Nor were they needed. Well into the thirteenth century few native people would have thought to question the traditional authority of an Earl Gille Brigte or an Earl Maoldomhnaich to make grants from lands that belonged to the extended kin group. Moreover, given the importance that Gaelic society attached to gift giving, fewer still may have thought it seemly to demand written proof of their lords' largesse. Among the majority of people in Strathearn and Lennox, possession of a charter might be viewed as enhancing title to an estate, access to the rivers, lochs, forests and other natural resources, or a claim to a share in a rent of grain or other foodstuffs. But for much of the later medieval period parchment proofs did not displace a lord's spoken word or diminish the probative value of symbolic objects that represented that lord's promise.

The written deeds that have survived from the first half of the thirteenth century bear eloquent witness to the complicated process of transculturation, accommodation, and change that characterized the social and tenurial environments of Strathearn and Lennox. The 'coming of the Normans' with charters clutched in their hands did not signal the wholesale imposition of alien customs and practices over those of the Gaels nor, in either lordship, did it spell the demise of orality. Influence the native culture the newcomers certainly did, and some land holders enthusiastically adopted the charter. However, contact with the Gaelic culture of Scotland had an equally profound effect on the ways in which the foreigners lived, held their land, and negotiated lord-man relations. Charters had important consequences for all who came into contact with them. Not least among these were concepts of 'good' lordship. The following section examines this topic in the context of a type of clause often found in Strathearn and Lennox charters, that of warrandice.

FINDING CULTURAL HYBRIDITY IN SURVIVING SOURCES:
'GOOD' LORDSHIP IN GAELIC SCOTLAND

In an article written almost sixty years ago, the legal historian Stanley Bailey argued that '[i]n its ordinary form, the warranty of land was an obligation, owed to the tenant of certain land, to defend him in his possession of that land against all men'. Clauses of express warranty, he observed, became customary in English charters in the early years of the thirteenth century, and 'almost universal' by the 1290s.[40] Bailey's article was based on a careful study of several hundred writ-

---

[39] Stringer, *Earl David*, 153. [40] S.J. Bailey, 'Warranties of land in the thirteenth century'

ten deeds, and although a handful of scholars have elaborated on his findings since he wrote, his conclusions have remained essentially unchallenged. Thus, Paul Hyams showed that clauses of warranty should be more correctly dated to the twelfth century in England. He elaborated Bailey's argument, moreover, by suggesting that the act of warranty implied both the 'positive promise' of a lord to support his vassal's claim to an estate against any challenges, and the 'negative promise' of the lord to renounce forever his title to such lands.[41] Like Bailey, he demonstrated that the concept of warranty was closely identified with the 'age-old duty of "good lordship"', and that in England, at least, it developed as a consequence of specific political, social, and legal circumstances. More recently still, John Hudson has examined the language of charters written in the century or so after the Norman Conquest of England. His conclusions generally support Hyams' suggestion that warranty was an Anglo-Norman, rather than an Angevin, innovation, and that it reflected legal notions current in Normandy in the period just before 1066. Hudson is not convinced, however, that the negative and positive aspects of warranty were as distinguishable as Hyams argued.[42]

The notion of a lord's obligation to protect his tenants' rights in land eventually came to Scotland, too, part and parcel of the cultural, social, and legal baggage that, beginning in earnest in the reign of David I, accompanied the process that historians have variously dubbed the 'feudalization', the 'Normanization', or the 'Europeanization' of the northern kingdom, and the adoption of the written charter as a record of conveyance. The discussions of warranty first articulated by the English legist known as *Glanvill* were eventually copied into one of the earliest and most influential compilations of Scottish law, *Regiam Majestatem*. Although dating from the early fourteenth century, the treatise none the less shows that the concept was 'well established' there much earlier.[43] Indeed, *Regiam Majestatem* borrowed so heavily from the English model that its author eschewed altogether an attempt to offer a fundamental definition of warranty at Scots law, and proceeded instead to review the circumstances under which, at English law, litigants might vouch their warrantors in court.[44] Familiarity with the notion of warrandice (as it was known in Scots legal parlance) there may well have been: one of King David's charters, for example, included a clause of explicit warrandice that read as follows: 'And if I or my heirs are not able to warrant this land to Walter [of Ryedale] or his heirs against the just claims of another, I and my heirs will grant him and his an exchange of equal value, to their reasonable satisfaction'.[45] Yet, such clauses remained rare for many years yet in royal deeds,[46] as well as in the charters of English and continental lords who controlled property both in Scotland and

---

(1944), 274, 275–6. **41** P. Hyams, 'Warranty and good lordship in twelfth century England' (1987), 440. **42** J. Hudson, *Land, law, and lordship in Anglo-Norman England* (1994), 55 and, more generally, 51–8. **43** H.L. MacQueen, *Common law and feudal society in medieval Scotland* (1993), 46. **44** T.M. Cooper (ed.), *Regiam majestatem and Quoniam attachiamenta* (1947), 80–3, 84–6, 88–93. **45** Barrow (ed.), *Charters of David I*, 141, probably dated 1150 x 1153. **46** *RRS*, ii, 73.

England, and who were therefore in close touch with legal and jurisprudential developments south of the border.[47] Thus, of the fifty-five full charter texts that survive from Earl David's tenure of the honour of Huntingdon between 1185 and 1219, only four include such a clause.[48] Extant deeds from the lordships of Strathearn and Lennox, however, reveal that although the newcomers to Scotland transplanted the notion of warranty to the lands they settled in Scotland and, in the course of the century or so after their arrival, secured its place in early Scottish common law procedure, the notion of warrandice did not penetrate the Gaelic regions of the kingdom until relatively late in the thirteenth century. More important still, it developed in the native earldoms along distinctly different lines than it did elsewhere in the realm, even in lordships that, like Buchan and Menteith, passed into the hands of newcomers at an early date. In the Gaelic regions of Scotland, moreover, the English concept of warranty was not a uniquely foreign import; it owed a great deal, too, to indigenous influence.

The comparative paucity of clauses of express warrandice in Scottish charters until the middle years of the thirteenth century has not gone entirely unnoticed by scholars. Keith Stringer has sought to explain their omission from written deeds by suggesting that 'the continued strength of lord-man ties played a part in ensuring that for Scottish freeholders implied warrandice often sufficed in itself'.[49] In the absence of centralized control over a standardized legal system, he argues, the independence and autonomy of great lords allowed them to preempt challenges to their grants of sasine by all but the most determined of litigants. Following up on this observation, Hector MacQueen has noted that the increasing use of express clauses of warrandice in the course of the thirteenth century 'suggests that conditions were changing, perhaps as a result of a more active land market and the development of more regular royal justice, both of which may have tended to reduce the certainty flowing from a lord's grant of land'.[50] Both arguments have much merit. Implicit in them, however, is the assumption that both the onus for requesting, and the concern for including, clear statements of the lord's obligation lay squarely on the shoulders of the tenant — each, in short, stresses what Paul Hyams would describe as the 'negative promise' associated with warranty in English *acta*. The charters of the thirteenth-century earls of Strathearn and Lennox, however, suggest some very different ideas about the purpose of clauses of warrandice than those advanced by scholars like Stringer and MacQueen. First, the clauses, when they do appear, may have been included in written *acta* as frequently in the interests of lords as they were at the behest of the latters' tenants. Second, and more important, the obligation to safeguard a tenant's title to land was as much testimony to the strength

---

[47] See also the comparison of warranty clauses in documents of English and Scottish provenance in K. Stringer, 'The charters of David, earl of Huntingdon and lord of Garioch: a study in Anglo-Scottish diplomatic' (1985), 91. [48] Stringer, *Earl David*, 223, 226, 253, 262. [49] Stringer, 'Charters of David earl of Huntingdon', 90–1. [50] MacQueen, *Common law*, 47.

and resilience of native Gaelic custom as it was a reflection of more recent Anglo-Norman legal and cultural influences.

In both England and Scotland, the elucidation of a clause that would simply and, above all, effectively, guarantee a tenant his rights in lands and privileges was the result of a lengthy process. This development is nicely illustrated in Strathearn and Lennox deeds. Notable, when the clause does begin to appear, is the considerable variety of phrases used to pledge the grantor's promise. A charter of Fergus son of Gille Brigte earl of Strathearn to Lindores abbey, dated 1233 or 1234, includes the phrase '[a]nd I and my heirs warrant [the brethren] the said lands against all men, and acquit them of all wordly services'.[51] Not much later the abbey sought confirmation of this gift from Fergus's brother, Earl Robert, and it was perhaps at the instigation of these particularly shrewd monks that the latter's scribe included in the text of his general confirmation specific mention of Fergus's original warrandice.[52] Earl Gille Brigte's written deeds also demonstrate the fluidity of phraseology that scribes might employ in the early thirteenth century: a grant to Lindores abbey stated that 'I and my heirs acquit the monks from all services and secular exactions that the lord king and his heirs and all men generally might [demand] of the land';[53] still another included the equally elaborate, if inelegant, '[a]nd know that, in order to prevent anyone attempting any injury whatsoever in respect of the land or anyone dwelling on it in the way of exaction, I and my heirs acquit the said estate'.[54] Such clauses echo those found in charters issued by the newcomers to Scotland, but they are also strikingly reminiscent of the 'quenching' of obligations that characterized the grants of some twelfth-century Gaelic lords to the abbey of Deer.[55] In the Lennox of Earl Maoldomhnaich, likewise, comital scribes included a clause of warrandice only occasionally in their written instruments, opting when they did for simple phrases, such as 'I and my heirs warrant and acquit [the said lands] against all men and women', or 'against all men'.[56] Variety of usage in all these deeds attests not only the fact that in neither region was there as yet anything approaching standard charter formulae but, more obviously still, the unfamiliarity of Lennox scribes with English conventions concerning the language appropriate to express warrandice.

The late twelfth century English legist generally referred to as 'Bracton' wrote that a clause of warranty should always include the verbs *warantizare*, *adquietare*, and *defendere*. The first understood the obligation on the part of the lord to defend his tenant's claims to a specific estate of land; the second embodied his undertaking to declare his tenant quit of all services, military or financial, save those stipulated in the terms of the grant. The verb *defendere* signified the magnate's willingness to appear in court on behalf of a tenant if called upon to defend the latter's title.[57] These careful distinctions are

---

[51] *Lind. Cart.*, no. 26. [52] Ibid., no. 27. [53] Ibid., no. 31. [54] Ibid., no. 44. [55] K. Jackson, *Gaelic notes in the book of Deer* (1972), 120–4. [56] *Lennox Cart.*, 19–20; Fraser, *Lennox*, ii, nos. 6, 10, 11. [57] G.E. Woodhouse (ed.), *Bracton De legibus et consuetudinibus Angliae* (4 vols, 1968–77),

absent from the thirteenth-century *acta* of the native earls of Strathearn and Lennox. It is not, in fact, until the end of Malise II's time in late 1260s and early 1270s that all three verbs begin to appear in clauses of warrandice in Strathearn. The same can be said of Lennox charters and, incidentally, of written deeds from the Gaelic regions of Menteith, western Moray, and Galloway as well.[58]

Debate in the English context about the *raison d'être* behind clauses of warranty is as yet ongoing, with one school of legal historians arguing that the promise to protect rights in land was the consequence of tenants' determination to win recognition of heritable rights in property;[59] another suggesting that the impetus came, rather, from lords concerned to protect their vassals from future depredations by the lord's own heirs;[60] and still another, which proposes that the influences at work here were exogenous rather than endogenous, a consequence of the late twelfth-century crown's attempts to move questions regarding seisin (and disseisin) into royal courts.[61] Focused above all on finding links between concepts of warranty as they developed in England and warrandice in a rapidly 'feudalising' Scotland, Scottish legal scholars have as yet speculated little on other cultural influences that were at work in the elucidation of the concepts of feu and heritage that became fundamental aspects of tenure at Scottish common law. Underlying the few discussions that have arisen, moreover,[62] are the twin assumptions that clauses of warrandice were a foreign import to Scotland, that they had no native history there; and that overwhelmingly, it was ecclesiastical tenants, notably monastic houses and episcopal beneficiaries, who agitated for the inclusion of the clauses in the charters they received. Put another way, these scholars tie the appearance of the clauses in Scottish records uniquely to the reception of Anglo-Norman law in the kingdom; a process, moreover, that they regard as somehow inevitable. Ultimately, then, they see in the clauses evidence to support the argument that Gaelic lords readily shed their own notions about lord-tenant relationships immediately upon coming into contact with English land law, and that they showed themselves equally willing to adopt wholesale the trappings of a more highly sophisticated legal culture. A study of the corpus of charters issued in the great Gaelic lordships of ancient Scotia is therefore especially relevant to this debate. In some cases, Gaelic magnates did include clauses of warrandice in their written deeds. But when they did so, it was not merely in slavish imitation of the latest legal trend. Rather, they recognized in the clauses unique opportunities to give new and meaningful expression to the trappings of native lordly authority and power.

---

ii, 117–19; Bailey, 'Warranties of land', 274, 276.   **58** W. Fraser, (ed.), *The red book of Menteith* (2 vols, 1880), ii, nos. 2, 6, 13, 17; W. Fraser, *The chiefs of Grant* (1883), iii, nos. 6, 10, 11; and some of the charters edited in K. Stringer, 'Acts of lordship: the records of the lords of Galloway to 1224' (2000), 212–34.   **59** See, for example, S.F.C. Milsom, *The legal framework of English feudalism* (1976).   **60** See, for example, Hyams, 'Warranty and good lordship'.   **61** This theme runs through J. Hudson, *Land, law, and lordship;* see also idem, *The formation of the English common law* (1996), esp. 112–17.   **62** See, for example, MacQueen, *Common law*, 47; Duncan, *Making*, 407–8.

Clauses of express warrandice begin to appear in charters issued under the seals of the earls of Strathearn only in the latter half of the thirteenth century. They are found almost exclusively in deeds granted to religious houses – the Augustinians at Inchaffray priory, and later, abbey, and the Tironensians of Lindores abbey – or to tenants who had come to the lordship as colonizers, either from Anglo-Norman England or from regions south of Forth originally settled by English and continental lords, men like David de Graham, Gilbert de la Hay, John of Johnstone, and Walter Stewart.[63] Scottish clerics, like their counterparts elsewhere in Britain and Europe, were particularly anxious to ensure that gifts in alms would endure well beyond the lifetime of the grantor, for such men conceived of themselves as trustees of the corporate religious bodies of which they were members, and ultimately of a universal church that welcomed offerings of all sorts from pious persons. Lay tenants newly settled from England, well versed in the customs and practices that governed lord-vassal relationships there, were similarly bound to want to ensure for themselves in Scotland the same kind of proprietary rights and, in the case of problematic title, the same kind of access to mechanisms of dispute resolution that they enjoyed south of the border. In this sense, their insistence on clauses of express warrandice that would protect not only their own tenure, but that of their future heirs, should not merely be expected, but is perhaps even predictable in the charters they secured.

The absence of clauses of express warrandice in Strathearn charters before 1257 is therefore noteworthy, and particularly so in the written instruments that commemorated gifts of land and privilege to the brethren of Inchaffray. Earl Gille Brigte's first recorded grants to the religious on the Isle of Masses were generous and varied, and included not only estates of land, but also parish kirks and their appurtenances, and tiends of all the foodstuffs, grain, animals, and drink that came into his kitchens in the form of annual renders known collectively as cain.[64] We would not expect in this period to find clauses of warrandice in written deeds that recorded gifts of animals or cain, but none of the charters in which Gille Brigte granted land included the clauses, express or implicit; neither did those of his son and successor, Earl Robert. The canons of Inchaffray probably supplied the early thirteenth-century earls with a secretarial pool of sorts, for there cannot have been many men permanently in their entourages well enough versed in the intricacies of charter writing to assume this responsibility.[65] It is well known, moreover, that when the priests who lived on the Isle of Masses were disbanded in 1198 and formally reestablished as Austin canons, the transition was effected smoothly. One of the resident native holy men assumed the new position of prior,[66] and several other Gaelic-speaking brethren choose to remain among the newly reconstituted group on the Isle of Masses. In the early

---

[63] See, for example, *Inchaff. Liber*, App., nos. 12 (Hay) and 14 (Johnstone), the latter a marriage portion to Annabella, daughter of Earl Robert; NAS, GD 220/1/A1/3/3, 4 (David de Graham); *Morton Reg.*, ii, no. 6 (marriage portion to Cecilia daughter of Earl Gille Brigte on the occasion of her marriage to Walter II son of Alan).   [64] *Inchaff. Liber*, no. 18; *Inchaff. Chrs.*, nos. 3–5.   [65] Neville, 'Earls of Strathearn', i, 339.   [66] *Inchaff. Chrs.*, no. 9.

years of the thirteenth century these men retained a good deal of influence within the priory, and it is not unlikely that they were instrumental in perpetuating there Gaelic customs and traditional values in the matter of gift giving. All would have considered it a grave breach of etiquette to demand of a great magnate such as Gille Brigte of Strathearn some sort of written guarantee that his word was good and his gifts secure. It is interesting to note, in this regard, that the Tyronensian monks of Lindores abbey, generously patronized by Earl Robert and several of his Strathearn kinsmen, did not share the implicit trust of the holy men of Inchaffray in the family's intentions. Several deeds to Lindores issued under the seals of Maol Iosa son of Fearchar, Fergus son of Gille Brigte, and Earl Robert himself include clauses of express warrandice.[67] But Lindores was not a Strathearn foundation, and despite the generosity of the family, it never enjoyed the intimate links that characterized relations between Inchaffray and these native lords.

If the large number of extant charters to Inchaffray priory (and, after 1221, abbey) make it possible to posit there the resilience of native beliefs and customs, there is much less evidence in the documents for a comparable survival of Gaelic practices in grants of land to lay persons. There survive only one complete text to lay beneficiaries from Gille Brigte's time (a grant of tocher on the occasion of his daughter's marriage to Mael Coluim of Fife, 1194 x 1198), and only one from the period of Earl Robert's rule (another grant of tocher, this one to his sister Cecilia and her husband, Walter II son of Alan, 1223 x 1229).[68] Both deeds include clauses of express warrandice. Yet, the effect of these gifts was to alienate valuable estates from patrimonial lands to the newlyweds, in all likelihood in perpetuity. These were precisely the sorts of grant that might be expected to generate opposition in future from the earls' heirs, and so precisely the kind of gift that shrewd beneficiaries would seek to protect with the provision of formal warrandice.

Lennox charters to lay persons survive in significant numbers from the thirteenth century, and an examination of these texts lends considerable weight to the suggestion that native lords included clauses of express warrandice only in specific circumstances. Immediately apparent from a perusal of the Lennox charters is the chronology of the clauses: from Earl Maoldomhnaich's time there are only a handful, and it is not until the period of his grandson and successor, Malcolm I, that they begin to appear with any regularity. Equally notable is the frequency with which the clauses were included in the texts of charters in favour of French- and English-speaking newcomers to the earls' territories. Throughout the thirteenth century foreign influence within Lennox remained limited and subject to the earls' firm control. The most privileged of the incomers was Sir David de Graham, already in the 1240s a speculator in lands throughout central and southern Scotland (and, incidentally, soon to become a tenant also of Earl

---

[67] *Lind. Cart.*, nos. 24, 26–9. [68] Edinburgh University Library, photographic negative of Scottish charters belonging to John Maitland Thomson, no. 26; NAS, RH 6/19, GD 90/1/15.

Malise II of Strathearn). Graham first gained a foothold in Lennox by displacing two native tenants, securing in the parish of Strathblane estates that had belonged to Farquhar Mac Gille Mhartainn and a man by the name of Luke. Thereafter, he also won exemption from a traditional money render that the former had owed the earl.[69] Each of the written *acta* recording these grants included a clause of express warrandice, but the specific circumstances under which Maoldomhnaich replaced one tenant with another created conditions that might in future have imperiled Graham's claim to the lands. In this case, then, the earl and his new tenant each had an interest in exacting, and offering, the clause. Maoldomhnaich's establishment of a well connected and highly influential Anglo-Norman lord within his territories bore witness, among his Gaelic tenants and kinsmen, to his authority as a great lord, and more specifically to his actions in disposing of earldom lands in the manner of a Gaelic head of kindred.

Such statements were not merely symbolic. In the complex cultural world that Lennox was becoming in the course of Maoldomhnaich's long rule, there was a very real need to assert the traditional prerogatives that attended Gaelic notions of lordship. Just as important was the earl's concern to make a statement to the king, for in this same period the precise tenurial relationship between the crown and the rulers of the ancient provinces north of Forth remained ambiguous. Graham's reasons for wanting his charters to include clauses of warrandice were equally pressing, though different. Well versed in the English laws and customs governing heritability and warranty, he, like any number of other foreign lords of his time, sought to establish clear title to his new Scottish possessions. This was all the more immediate a concern given the circumstances under which he had acquired the properties. Nor was Sir David's vigilance misplaced. Maoldomhnaich's son, displeased with his father's attempts to alienate the lands in perpetuity, attempted to prevent Graham from entering the estates, and eventually agreed to the latter's settlement within Lennox only after submitting to formal arbitration.[70]

Lennox charters, in fact, reveal quite clearly that for much of the thirteenth century clauses of express warrandice were included in written instruments issued in favour of lay persons only when the circumstances of a grant were potentially problematic. Early in the century one of Maoldomhnaich's native tenants experienced difficulty in securing firm title to promised estates, largely owing to defective charters and to his lord's unintended violation of the conventions governing gifts of land then current in England, which the latter understood only poorly. A first charter to Maurice son of Gilleasbuig Galbraith and his son Arthur granted them lands that the earl had acquired as a marriage portion in the Stewart lordship of Renfrew, in exchange for others 'which', the earl noted, 'I could not warrant them'. There were problems with the new grant, however, and it was cancelled *pro defectu sigillj*.[71] A second gift of still another estate, although it included warrandice 'against all men, forever', was similarly deemed defective for want of

[69] Fraser, *Lennox*, ii, nos. 6, 7, 10.   [70] Ibid., no. 9.   [71] *Lennox Cart.*, 27.

a seal,[72] and eventually in 1238 Arthur's son William secured a third charter, which included a witness list made up not only of a group of local Gaelic tenants, but also of an impressive array of foreign worthies, among them Alexander Comyn of Buchan, William Douglas, David de Graham and the justiciar of Lothian, David de Lindsay. The document itself included a clear, unambiguous (and quite Bractonian) statement on the part of the earl that 'I and my heirs warrant, acquit, and defend all the said lands in all their particulars ... to William and his heirs forever against all men and women'.[73] A native family established already for many generations around the little toun of Luss on Loch Lomond, similarly compelled to press its claims in the wake of the earl's attempts to introduce newcomers, also sought charters with clauses of express warrandice from him.[74]

Examples of this kind might be multiplied, drawn not only from written instruments issued in the name of Earl Maoldomhnaich, but from those of other local donors as well. During the period of Maoldomhnaich's rule, at least, in the majority of these cases the appearance of clauses of warrandice may be linked either directly or by inference to estates from which sitting Gaelic tenants were being removed to make way for newcomers, or were being planted afresh in parts of the earl's territories where they had not previously held land. By the time his grandson Malcolm I succeeded him around 1270, native and incomers alike had become familiar with the implications of warrandice. Few were as prescient as the abbot of Paisley, who in 1273 had his scribe write into a charter concerning a valuable fishery the following words: 'And I and my heirs will support the said religious in their possession of the fishery and its fruits and in all that they might wish to do in the way of improvements to it, until such time as we can formally warrant and defend them'.[75] In 1273, however, the abbey had good reason to be wary. Its abbot was still deeply entangled in bitter litigation concerning lands in the parish of Kilpatrick (a dispute that was not finally resolved until the 1290s), which an earlier generation of Lennox lords had tried to wrest from church control.[76] But other tenants, most notably Malcolm's foreign settlers, were eager to secure the legal protection that warrandice offered, and almost always had the clause inserted into their charters of infeftment.

The cases discussed to date fall squarely within Paul Hyams's category of 'negative' promise as described above. In other words, they would seem to lend weight to the school of thought that places the concept of warrandice firmly (and, for some historians, solely) in the context of the struggle by land holders for security of tenure against voracious, unscrupulous lords. They also support, albeit by implication rather than explicitly, the view that warrandice of land was primarily an import from England rather than a manifestation of indigenous custom. But warrandice, especially in the Gaelic culture north of Forth, offered compelling opportunities for native magnates anxious to give real and meaningful expression to their 'good lordship', and its attraction to men such as

---

[72] Ibid., 26–7. [73] Ibid., 30–1. [74] Fraser, *Lennox*, ii, no. 207. [75] *Paisley Reg.*, 215–16. [76] For a summary of this litigation, see Cooper (ed.), *Select Scottish cases*, 32–40.

Malise II of Strathearn and Maoldomhnaich of Lennox lay as much in its appeal to Gaelic notions of lordship as it did to English influence. The cultures of the nearby Gaelic realms of Wales and Ireland boasted customs and practices designed, like warrandice, to emphasize the authority of great lords over their lands and tenants. Here, concepts of honour and its antithesis, shame, were indelibly linked; indeed, in pre-state forms of society such as early medieval Wales and Ireland, they were 'twin foundation stones'.[77] Closely tied to the notion of honour, moreover, was the concept of status. Scholars have written at some length about legally defined honour in both realms, and about the role that honour played in determining how individuals conceived of their 'rightful place in a social group'.[78] Much of what they argue may fruitfully be applied to Gaelic Scotland in the early thirteenth century. In all three realms, challenges to lordly authority and affronts to honour were met with an array of sanctions of varying degrees of severity. Chief among these was the practice of malediction.

Echoes of pre-twelfth-century beliefs about honour, status, and the appropriate practice of malediction abound in the early charters of Scottish Gaelic lords. The purpose of warrandice, in Scotland as in England, was clear and quite simple. It was designed to protect the beneficiary's rights in a parcel of land should there arise a claim against these in future, and its inclusion in written deeds 'is probably best explained by the parties' awareness of other possible claims which might be made good in some forum, and against which precautions required to be taken'.[79] The Gaelic tradition of ritual cursing, practised widely among lay folk and clerics alike, had a similar purpose. Although its origins were traceable ultimately to the spread of Benedictine monasticism on the continent in the early medieval period, the Gaelic cultures of Britain absorbed, adapted, and revivified the tradition of malediction, then embedded it deeply into their own systems of custom and belief.[80] Like the clause of warrandice, ritual cursing was intended ultimately to ensure that the descendants of a donor did not tamper with gifts of land and privilege that their predecessors had made, and in respect of Ireland at least the cultural link between malediction and clauses of sanction in written deeds is well attested.[81] Cursing was likely to occur, moreover, when honour and status were denied or otherwise compromised.[82] By the thirteenth century the honour of the Gaelic earls of Strathearn and Lennox as landowners of the highest rank, as heads of extensive native kindred, and as ultimate guarantors of tenure within their territories, depended to a great extent on the protection they afforded their tenants, and the honour that these men in turn accorded them. Even in the comparatively insular environment of these

[77] T. Charles-Edwards, 'Honour and status in some Irish and Welsh prose tales' (1978), 137. [78] N. Patterson, 'Honour and shame in medieval Welsh society: a study of the role of burlesque in the Welsh laws' (1981, 1982), 87. See also W. Davies, 'Anger and the Celtic saint' (1998), 199. [79] MacQueen, *Common law*, 47. [80] L.K. Little, *Benedictine maledictions: liturgical cursing in Romanesque France* (1993), 192–202; L.M. Bitel, *Isle of the saints: monastic settlement and Christian community in early Ireland* (1990), 152–5; idem, 'Saints and angry neighbors: the politics of cursing in Irish hagiography' (2000), 127. [81] Ibid., 125. [82] Ibid., 202.

two intensely Gaelic regions, wide ranging changes in the social, legal and cultural environment characteristic of this period throughout Scotland raised new questions about, and posed new challenges to, traditional forms of lordship. Clauses of warrandice and the tradition of cursing that they echoed offered the native earls an opportunity to sound clear warnings to all, present and future, against an affront to their honour as lords. If, as has been suggested,[83] the native earls carved new estates for individual tenants out of lands once held collectively by kin groups, then clauses of warrandice may have promised a measure of security for tenants newly established on Strathearn and Lennox lands, and further served as a formal notice to future generations that the earls had the authority to effect changes to existing tenurial and territorial structures.

Clauses of warrandice had legal as well as social consequences. Here, too, charter texts suggest an unbroken process of acculturation, adaptation, and maturation through which native custom of an early period survived remarkably intact into the twelfth and early thirteenth centuries. On the few occasions when they included the clauses in their written deeds, the earls of Strathearn and Lennox demonstrated a concern for the integrity of their gifts that is strikingly reminiscent of the curses invoked by the 'angry saints' of a previous age. When, for example, Earl Gille Brigte of Strathearn and his countess arranged for the conversion of Céli Dé priests on the Isle of Masses to the rule of St Augustine, they marked the occasion with the issue of a beautifully executed charter of foundation, elaborately (if quaintly) scripted in a formal book hand, and drawn up in accordance with the new fangled diplomatic conventions then current among English and continental lords, complete with invocations to God and Jesus, a generous landed endowment, and provision for ample future income. There was in this document no formal clause of warrandice. Gille Brigte did, however, make a direct appeal to Gaelic tradition when he called down divine wrath on any and all who might cause 'trouble or injury to that place, or its ministers, or to anyone fleeing to it'.[84] In this statement, it is possible to grasp at first hand the beginning of a process by which English concepts of warrandice and native cultural practices and beliefs came together. Again, in 1220/1, when he granted to the canons of Inchaffray leave to hold a court for tenants from their lands, Gille Brigte strictly forbade any of his servants or their men to cause violence or disturbance within the priory lands or to exact anything from the religious against their will *super forisfactum meum*.[85] Similarly, in a charter to Paisley abbey Maoldomhnaich of Lennox prohibited his men from presuming to commit any injury to the monks 'on pain of full forfeiture'.[86] The monitory tone underlying these strictures, although updated to conform to thirteenth-century convention, was evocative of the maledictions that, it has been observed, 'characteristically terminate' charters from other Gaelic areas in the several preceding centuries. They convey the same message as the following phrases: 'he who

---

[83] Neville, 'Charter writing', 82–3. [84] *Inchaffray Chrs.*, no. 9. [85] Ibid., nos 43, 44; *Inchaffray Liber*, no. 4. [86] *Paisley Reg.*, 213.

violates this will be cursed', found in an early document from South Wales;[87] and 'if anyone shall presume by any violence or device, to take away this my grant ... may God Almighty take away from him the life of the kingdom of heaven and may he undergo everlasting punishment with the devil and his angels', and 'by St Columba whosoever of my heirs molests them [the monks of Paisley] shall have my eternal curse', both found in charters from twelfth-century Scotland.[88] In the great lordships of Strathearn and Lennox, as well as in others, including Fife, Galloway, and even the Buchan of the Comyns, Gaelic cultural beliefs and practices coexisted comfortably with newer European ideas well into the thirteenth century. In this sense, clauses of warning such as those that Earls Gille Brigte and Maoldomhnaich sometimes included in their charters should best be understood as marking a transitional or intermediate phase between the old practice of formal malediction and the newer English style of warrandice. In Ireland, the tradition of cursing began to decline in the aftermath of Norman colonization;[89] the evidence from Strathearn and Lennox suggests that a similar argument may be applied to Scotland.

The Scottish earls' frequent resort to clauses of warrandice, then, reveals the adaptability of the charter form to native custom and tradition and the equally receptive nature of the early Scottish common law. While warrandice had a manifestly different origin than the ritual curse, clauses of warrandice, like malediction, had an important role to play in the transmission and disposition of landed property. The consequences of the clauses, exactly like those of the ritual curse, extended well beyond the lifetimes of individuals whose intentions might be forgotten or ignored by future generations. It is small wonder that great lords should have had good reason to include them in their written instruments.

In the specifically Gaelic context, then, warrandice might be at once 'positive' and 'negative': the two were not mutually exclusive. As a legal device it may well have been introduced to Scotland by English and continental newcomers; so, too, of course, was the written charter itself. But exposure to the cultural and legal practices of the newcomers did not entail the wholesale abandonment or the suppression of the modes of thought and behaviour of an earlier age. The native lords of Lennox and Strathearn may well have adopted the written charter in response to pressure from their ecclesiastical tenants, the monastic houses at Paisley, Arbroath, and Inchaffray and the bishops of Glasgow, Dunkeld, and Dunblane. More definitely, they did so as members of a pan-European cultural movement that acknowledged the growing importance and authority of written deeds. But they found uses for the written word far beyond the conventional recording of acts of piety and charity. The flexibility of the basic charter form provided them with a medium through which to give concrete expression to

---

[87] This and other curses from Wales, Ireland, Scotland and Brittany are noted in Davies, 'Anger and the Celtic saint', 193.   [88] G. Donaldson, 'Aspects of early Scottish conveyancing' (1985), 161; *Paisley Reg.*, 125. For other Scottish curses see the charters collected and discussed in Lawrie (ed.), *Early Scottish charters*.   [89] Bitel, 'Saints and angry neighbors', 127.

indigenous concepts about lordship and property, and an instrument with which to consolidate their governance of large blocs of Scottish territory at a time when the tenurial landscape of Scotland was changing dramatically. They may, in fact, have seen in the English concept of warranty an opportunity to express their authority as lords more extensively than the old custom of malediction had allowed them. The sanctions consequent on a breach of the Gaelic practice of cursing were, above all, spiritual. Disgruntled saints sometimes manifested their wrath in a physical assault on the violator's person, and often by damning his soul in the afterlife.[90] The satisfaction a lord achieved from such a transgression was almost entirely vicarious, consisting of knowledge of the offender's eternal fate, but offering little guarantee that the donor's original intentions in making a gift or grant of land would ultimately be respected. The sanctions available to an aggrieved party as a consequence of an offer of warrandice were of a more earthly, pragmatic sort. In the event of a grantor's gift being challenged, thirteenth-century legal process promised the beneficiary the support of the king himself in recovering his property. In short, implicit in the lord's offer of warrandice was royal acknowledgment of his title to the estates that he chose to alienate, and of his right to do so. Lordly warrandice might thus be put to shrewd use in the reinforcement of property rights both by the donor and the beneficiary. In the shifting social, political, and legal milieus of thirteenth century Scotland, native lords must have found such expressions of lordly prerogatives immensely appealing.

Clauses of express warrandice provide a particularly apt example of the ways in which the thirteenth-century native lords of Scotland incorporated into, and encoded within, deeds written in the English style the practices and traditions peculiar to their own culture. So, too, do other features of the charter form, including lists of the appurtenances attached to lands, detailed descriptions of the boundaries of estates, and even witness lists, which performed the function of identifying formally and publicly the men (and, incidentally, the women) whom the earls of Lennox and Strathearn wished to include among their entourages. More generally, the act of making grants of land itself was tremendously appealing to the native earls, because it gave real and meaningful expression to the 'gift-exchange ethos of Gaeldom'.[91] Far from being wholly novel and a foreign import, then, the practice of warrantying land became a useful, and welcome, tool in the hands of native earls.

CULTURAL INTERGRATION IN OTHER CONTEXTS

The family

The adoption of the charter form and its consequences for the law of real property reveal the ease with which Gaelic and European ideas interacted in thir-

---

90 Little, *Benedictine maledictions*, 167–72; Davies, 'Anger', 191–3; Bitel, 'Saints and angry neighbors', 129.   91 K.J. Stringer, 'Reform monasticism and Celtic Scotland: Galloway, c.1140–c.1240' (2000), 140.

teenth century Strathearn and Lennox. The process of cultural integration and accommodation between the peoples occurred also in more subtle, if equally complex ways. Chief among these was marriage. Reed Davies has noted the leading role that matrimonial alliances played in the period of 'adjustment' that followed the settlement of Norman and French noblemen in Ireland, Wales, and Scotland. The home, he has shown, acted as a powerful locus for the interplay of native and foreign customs at the most personal and intimate levels.[92] But Davies also portrays the forging of marriages as 'a subtle instrument of domination' on the part of the newcomers, and as 'a strategy of subjection, however honourable',[93] and scholarly discussions about noble marriage in Scotland have tended to focus on the ways in which the crown used these unions to create ties of cultural and political dependence with a dominant and potentially dangerous native aristocracy.[94] The process of transculturation, however, was not unidirectional, with Gaelic customs associated with the family setting necessarily giving way to European mores. Strathearn and Lennox charters offer compelling evidence that the flow of ideas and influences was equally strong in the opposite direction.

At first glance, the marriage strategies of the native earls appear to have reflected their acceptance of the political aims of the crown, designed as these were to encourage close and friendly links with the newly established foreign nobility. For much the same reason as Earl Donnchad III of Fife and his son Donnchad IV chose wives from among the Warenne and Corbet families, and Earl Patrick of Dunbar sought the daughter of King William himself as his first wife, and Christina widow of William de Brus as his second,[95] Gille Brigte of Strathearn became associated with a family intimately connected with the royal family when he married Maud d'Aubigny. She was the daughter of Sir William d'Aubigny 'the Breton' and Maud de Senlis, the cousin of Kings Malcolm IV and William I.[96] Similarly, the earl's brother Maol Iosa and his sister Christian chose spouses from among the prestigious Anglo-Norman and continental families of their day: Earl David of Huntingdon, whose natural daughter Ada married the former, and Walter Oliphant, who became the husband of the latter.[97] All three alliances must have been approved, if they were not actually planned, by William I, with the dual purpose of strengthening royal connections with a leading native family, and introducing its members into the charmed circle of the king's foreign friends. Precisely the same kind of benefits accrued to another of the crown's most prestigious Gaelic subjects when Maoldomhnaich of Lennox

---

[92] R.R. Davies, *Domination and conquest: the experience of Ireland, Scotland and Wales 1100–1300* (1990), 52. [93] Ibid., 53. [94] See, for example, G.W.S. Barrow, *The Anglo-Norman era in Scottish history*, 89; idem, 'The earls of Fife in the 12th century' (1953); R. Oram, *The lordship of Galloway*, 194, 203–4; K. Stringer and A. Grant, 'Scottish foundations' (1995), 88; C.J. Neville, 'A Celtic enclave in Norman Scotland: earl Gilbert and the earldom of Strathearn, 1171–1223', 78. [95] Barrow, 'Earls of Fife', 53–4; idem, *Anglo-Norman era*, 87; *St Andrews Liber*, 278; *SP*, iv, 7; Anderson and Anderson (eds), *The chronicle of Melrose*, 92–3; *CDS*, iv, no. 700. [96] *SP*, viii, 242; Neville, 'Earls of Strathearn', i, 62–3. [97] Ibid., i, 55; idem, 'A Celtic enclave', 78.

chose as his countess Elizabeth Stewart, the daughter of Walter II son of Alan.[98] As Davies has aptly noted, these kinds of marriages were critical in helping natives and newcomers 'to adjust to each other ... and to begin the process of cultural integration'.[99]

Less often discussed, however, are the circumstances under which husbands and wives sought spouses not among the leading new families of the realm, but from the indigenous Gaelic nobility. Earl Fearchar of Strathearn married a woman whose antecedents are unknown, but whose personal name, Ethne, is clearly of Irish provenance.[1] After the death of Maud d'Aubigny their son Gille Brigte chose as his second wife a woman of considerably less exalted native status.[2] The name of Earl Robert's wife, the mother of Malise II, is unknown, perhaps because she was not a member of one of the leading new families of the realm. More noteworthy still is the silence of contemporary source materials with respect to Lennox wives. The spouse of Earl Ailin II went unrecorded altogether, as did the names of the women who married Maoldomhnaich's many brothers, his son Mael Coluim, Robert Bruce's friend Malcolm II, and even Earl Donald. Early modern genealogists noted these omissions only laconically,[3] but such lacunae are of great significance in a period in which chroniclers, courtiers, and clerks alike were closely attuned to the markers of rank and status. The anonymity of Strathearn and Lennox wives reflects more than just the chauvinism of medieval scribes; on a deeper level, it may speak to the prejudice of Latin trained authors against persons whose status they considered unworthy of notice, an observation that has been made in regard to other aspects of contemporary Scottish culture.[4]

Surviving charter materials offer other intriguing indications that, despite their close contact with the cultural influences of England and Europe, the Gaelic lords of Strathearn and Lennox did not consider marriage into the incoming aristocracy a *sine qua non* of position and rank. In fact, the evidence suggests otherwise, and in both lordships the earls used the intimate setting of the home as crucibles for the preservation and promotion of their indigenous culture. They manifested their intentions, for example, in the names that they chose for their children, in the life plans they made on behalf of their sons and daughters, and in the personal ties that they forged between their offspring and the wider network of the kindred.

Scholars have long appreciated the central importance of lineage in the social, political, and cultural organization of the Gaelic-speaking peoples of the British Isles.[5] The language of Scots law in the thirteenth and fourteenth centuries preserved a host of terms associated with kin based society, and the survival of these words and concepts well into the sixteenth century demonstrates the resilience

---

98 *SP*, v, 332. **99** Davies, *Domination and conquest*, 52. **1** *Inchaff. Chrs.*, nos. 3, 13. **2** See Table 1. **3** See, for example, *SP*, v, 332–6; viii, 244. **4** See above, pp 99, 104; Barrow, *Kingdom*, 240. **5** See, for example, R. Davies, 'Kinsmen, neighbours and communities in Wales and the western British Isles, *c*.1100–*c*.1400' (2001).

of native custom within the lordships that lay at the heart of the Scottish Gàidhealtachd.[6] Within this setting, it was as members of a kin group that 'the individual found his identity, both in terms of his descent from the lineage founder and laterally in terms of his *parentes* and *cognati*'.[7] The simplest and most effective strategy for ensuring that the link between revered ancestors and future generations remained living lay in parents' choice of personal names for their children. The earls and countesses of Strathearn and Lennox understood well the implications of commemorating their kindred and, more generally, of privileging the ethnic origins of the earls' lineage, and well into the fourteenth century both families favoured Gaelic names for their sons. Maol Iosa, Latinized as Malisius, recurred in all but one of the eight generations of the Strathearn family between the mid-twelfth century and *c*.1350; from the time of Malise II (d. 1271) it was always given to the oldest son and heir.[8] French names appear only rarely, the exceptions being several Roberts, the son of Gille Brigte and his wife Maud, Robert the second son of Malise II, and Robert the third son of Malise III. Far more often, the earls and their kinsmen insisted on Gaelic names for their sons, among which pride of choice was Gille Brigte, Latinized as Gilbertus. Strathearn women, destined both by tradition and, increasingly, by Scottish legal custom to leave the immediate surroundings of the agnatic kin group upon marriage, were by contrast endowed with Christian names popular throughout the European world of the day. Maria, perhaps commemorating the mother of Jesus, and Maud, the name of Gille Brigte's first wife, were frequent choices, though the name of Gille Brigte's youngest daughter, Ethne, recalled that of her grandmother, Fearchar's wife. The uncertain history of Ailin II's succession to the title of earl of Lennox after its tenure by the king's brother David may have cast a shadow over the naming of his descendants, for the name Ailin does not reappear in any of the five generations of Lennox men who succeeded him as earl.[9] But the native rulers of this province laid claim to a more venerable ancestor still in the Irish king Conall Corc, legendary founder of the kingship of Cashel. In the poem he addressed to Ailin around the year 1200, the bard Muireadhach Albanach Ó Dálaigh retold the story of Conall's journey to Scotland, where he married Leamhain, the daughter of Fearadhach Finn Feachtnach, the (equally legendary) king of the Picts. When she drowned, she gave her name to the river that flowed through the lands where she had lived. Muireadhach thus identified Ailin as 'descended from royal Irish stock, and also, in a sense, from the river which flows through his lands'.[10] By implication, each successive generation of his descendants bore an eponymous association with the territory of Lennox. Ailin nevertheless emphasized the link with his exalted royal ancestor when he named one of his sons Corc.[11] Male members of the Lennox lineage held a variety of names, but from Maoldomhnaich's generation onwards, almost

---

6 J. Bannerman, 'The Scots language and the kin-based society' (1988), 1–19. **7** Davies, 'Kinsmen', 176. **8** See Table 1. **9** See Table 2. The son of Maoldomhnaich's sister Eva, however, had that name. **10** Clancy (ed.), *Triumph tree*, 258. **11** Fraser, *Lennox*, ii, no. 207.

all were of Gaelic origin, including Mael Coluim, (Malcolmus), Amhlaigh (Amelec, Hauel, Hamelon), and Donnchad (Duncanus). Such choices constituted potent declarations of ethnic identity and allegiance in thirteenth- and fourteenth-century Scotland.

Quite apart from distinguishing native noblemen from members of the newly established aristocracy, the reuse of specific family names accomplished other important functions. From one generation to the next familiar Gaelic names constantly reiterated the earls' standing in relation to the lower ranking groups over which they ruled. Continuity of nomenclature among male members of the kindred thus kept alive the memory of the Gaelic past and the continuity of a family's rule. Far from rushing to adopt the Christian names that might have allowed their sons to be assimilated more quickly and more easily into the polyglot society of the royal court, as some scholars have claimed was the norm in thirteenth-century Scotland, Gaelic personal names signalled the determination of the native rulers to minimize both the intrusion of foreign influence into the physical setting of the home and, if less tangibly, the erosion of long cherished ideas about the central importance of the kindred.

It is no accident, in fact, that in the opening years of the thirteenth century the Lennox family should have found particularly attractive the opportunity to associate its members with a decidedly Irish Gaelic past. Genealogies like the one composed by the bard Muireadhach for Ailin II set the native lords apart from a vast majority of incoming tenants, many of whom were landless younger sons and who, in a very real sense, had no history of their own before coming to Scotland. The reign of Malcolm IV saw the intensification of settlement by the newcomers in the Clydesdale area lying just to the south of Lennox.[12] The earliest earls much have felt the presence of the settlers especially keenly, and never more than during the 1170s and '80s, when control of the province of Lennox was wrested forcefully from the native family and bestowed upon one of the newcomers.[13] Ailin II's negotiations for the marriage of his son and heir Maoldomhnaich to the daughter of Walter II son of Alan must likewise have served, if indirectly, to underline the potential threat to the native culture of the region represented by the new lordships south of the Clyde.

During Ailin's time, moreover, Lennox was a land with a varied history. Originally part of the Brittonic kingdom of Strathclyde, the region and its inhabitants had been influenced by Gaelic and Norse settlers, each of whom left their marks on the landscape in early fortifications, place names, and local customary practices. Some important Lennox families still celebrated their British past. Such, for example, were the men who called themselves Galbraith, already in this period among the wealthiest and most important of the earl's tenants. The representative of one generation invoked his distinctive past openly with the use of the personal name Arthur, another by referring to himself as Mac an Bhreatnaich, 'son of the Britons'.[14] The construction of family pasts may have

---

[12] Barrow, *Kingdom*, 257–9.   [13] Stringer, *Earl David*, 13–19.   [14] *Lennox Cart.*, 29–30; G.F. Black,

been entirely fanciful, for by the late twelfth century the Galbraiths, like other land holding families in Lennox, had been thoroughly Gaelicized. But the history of the lordship, recent and distant, was varied enough to warrant Ailin's warm support of a poet whose skills might usefully be employed in the shaping of a thoroughly orthodox past for the Lennox region. In the changing ethnic profile of late twelfth-century Scotland 'pedigree making' (and 'pedigree faking') were very much the order of the day.[15] The Scottish royal house itself set a powerful example here, for this was precisely the period during which members of the Gaelic learned orders were busy promoting the figures of Mael Coluim III and his saintly wife Margaret as progenitors of the Mac Donnchada dynasty.[16] The squaring off of the cultures of the European settlers against that of the old established Gaelic families proved a rich and lucrative field for imaginative *seanchaidhean*, and despite the poor survival rate of manuscript sources, there is no reason to doubt that other bards like Muireadhach Albanach Ó Dáiligh, trained in the tradition of pedigree making, found gainful employment throughout the lands north of Forth.[17] The Lennox family never lost its appreciation of the importance of the bardic tradition to their social and political status within the wider Scottish realm. Around 1400 Earl Duncan commissioned another genealogy to celebrate his family's ancient origins,[18] an undertaking perhaps all the more pressing as the earl's title had descended to him in the female line.

If the earls of Lennox worked hard to establish their Gaelic credentials by locating their past in Ireland, the earls of Strathearn and their kindred had no such pressing concerns. Their descent from the ancient Gaelic ruling orders of pre-twelfth century Scotland was impeccable and undisputed. There is considerable evidence to suggest that Strathearn was recognized as a distinct region as early as the ninth century, and almost certainly in the tenth, when the old provinces of Pictland were reorganized in preparation for defence against Viking attacks.[19] The late twelfth-century tract entitled *De situ Albanie* affirmed among contemporaries the antiquity of the earldom as a unit of lordship,[20] and Gille Brigte of Strathearn enjoyed so secure a place among the Gaelic elite of his day

---

The surnames of Scotland (1946), 306. **15** The terms are David Sellar's; see idem, 'Highland family origins – pedigree making and pedigree faking', in *The middle ages in the highlands* (1981), 103–16. **16** D. Broun, *The Irish identity of the kingdom of the Scots in the twelfth and thirteenth centuries* (1999), 195–6. **17** D.S. Thomson, 'Influences of medieval thinking on the Gaelic world in Scotland in the sixteenth century and later' (1997), 18–19; idem, 'Three seventeenth-century bardic poets: Niall Mór, Cathal and Niall MacMhuirich' (1977), 221. See also the list of bards working in medieval Scotland compiled in McLeod, *Divided Gaels*, 233–6, and the early poems collected in Clancy (ed.), *Triumph tree*. **18** K.A. Steer and J.W.M. Bannerman, *Late medieval monumental sculpture in the west highlands* (1977), 205; M. MacGregor, 'Genealogies of the clans: contributions to the study of MS 1467' (2000), 143–5. **19** M.O. Anderson, *Kings and kingship in early Scotland* (1973), 140; Duncan, *Making*, 110–11. The region of Fortriu is mentioned frequently in the Irish annals; see, for example, A.O. Anderson (ed.), *Early sources of Scottish history 500 to 1286* (2 vols, 1922), i, cxvii, 192–3, 220–2, 230, 233, 236, 253, 292, 367, 407, 474. **20** Anderson, *Kings and kingship*, 242.

that he may have considered the need to assert his family's pedigree superfluous. The antiquity of the family and of the territorial unity of the province it governed collectively represented an 'ultimate badge of Scottish identity',[21] and was patently evident to the foreign noblemen who surrounded the king. It is no accident, moreover, that in royal witness lists, clerks almost always accorded Gille Brigte's name precedence even over those of the most important new families.[22] In the complex and shifting social hierarchy of William I's reign the status of the native earls of Strathearn stood very high. It remained so well after Gille Brigte's death, and was dramatically reiterated at the inauguration of Alexander III in 1249. On this occasion Malise II of Strathearn was one of only two earls responsible for enkinging the young prince, and he was thus depicted in two early illustrations of the event, one a near contemporary seal, the other an illuminated miniature in a manuscript of Walter Bower's *Scotichronicon*.[23] In the latter, Malise of Strathearn stands directly in front of a small figure playing the *clàrsach*, who accompanies with music the *seanchaidh*'s recital of Alexander's antecedents. No one seeing the seal or, later, the manuscript would have failed to appreciate the importance of the earl of Strathearn as a link to Alexander's Gaelic antecedents.

While some of the customs that the native rulers of Strathearn and Lennox nurtured were intended to limit the influence of the foreigners, other traditions specific to the intimate setting of the home may have encouraged the freer interplay of the European and native cultures. Such, for example, were the practices associated with fosterage. Thirteenth-century European noblemen frequently sent their sons to the households of great lords, often magnates with whom they had personal or tenurial ties.[24] Noble youths used these years to develop skills in war and in the gentler arts of *courtoisie*, but also to forge social and political ties that would stand them in good stead in future. The Gaelic world also knew such a custom, the purpose of which was the education of youths in the Gaelic language and the establishment of contacts that would lead to fruitful military and political alliances in later life.[25] King David I himself spent several years at the court of Henry I of England 'among the household youngbloods';[26] two hundred years later, his descendant Robert Bruce also became a foster son.[27] Maoldomhnaich of Lennox entertained such youths in his home, among them,

---

[21] J. Bannerman, 'The king's poet and the inauguration of Alexander III' (1989), 149. [22] Neville, 'Earls of Strathearn', i, 257–8. [23] Bannerman, 'The king's poet', 124–5; A.A.M. Duncan, *The kingship of the Scots, 842–1292* (2002), 136–7; *Scotichronicon*, v, Plate 1, facing p. 288. [24] See, for example, the experience of the young William Marshal so elegantly described in D. Crouch, *William Marshal: court, career and chivalry in the Angevin empire 1147–1219* (1990), 19–52; also S. Shahar, *Childhood in the Middle Ages* (1990), 209–20; D. Alexandre-Bidon and D. Lett, *Children in the Middle Ages, fifth–fifteenth centuries* (1999), 43–5; G. Duby, *The chivalrous society* (1977), 111–22; R. le Jan-Hennebicque, 'Apprentissages militaires, rites de passage et remises d'armes au haut moyen âge' (1993), i, 211–32. [25] Bannerman, 'Influences', 18–20; McLeod, *Divided Gaels*, 42–3; G.W.S. Barrow, *Kingship and unity: Scotland, 1000–1306*, 107. [26] M. Chibnall (ed.), *The ecclesiastical history of Orderic Vitalis* (6 vols, 1969–80), iv, 274–5; Davies, *Domination and conquest*, 51. [27] R. Nicholson, *Scotland: the later Middle Ages* (London, 1974), 73.

perhaps, the son of the poet Muireadhach Albanach Ó Dáiligh.[28] Strathearn charters do not refer specifically to foster sons, but it is possible that some of the landless youths known to have been resident there, the *militi comitis* and *amici comitis* of Latin language *acta* were present in such a capacity.[29] The Gaelic custom of sending sons away from the household, then, was not so far removed from that practised by the newly settled foreign lords, and the shared experience of living outside the home in their youth may well have played an important role in promoting social relations between the sons of great lords, native and newcomer.

Although surviving Strathearn and Lennox charters have scarcely more to reveal about noble women's roles in the home than they do on the subject of fosterage, there are indications that within the setting of the Gaelic household wives and daughters were accorded greater opportunities to participate in the business of governing the kin group than contemporary European custom allowed. Unusual among the charters of Earl Gille Brigte of Strathearn, for example, is the frequency with which the countess appears as a witness to her husband's *acta*; on two occasions, their daughter, Maud's namesake, was also included among the list of attestors.[30] Maud d'Aubigny, moreover, secured pride of place with her husband as co-founder in the charter that transformed Inchaffray into an Augustinian priory,[31] and she is found among the witnesses to a deed of her neighbour and kinswoman by marriage, Ela of Fife.[32] Elizabeth Stewart, the wife of Maoldomhnaich of Lennox, granted no charters, but her husband gave careful consideration to her spiritual future when he made careful provision for the singing of annual masses for her soul in Paisley abbey.[33]

Women's occasional appearance in early charter materials is noteworthy, chiefly because the nascent common law of Scotland afforded them few opportunities to act independently, either as single women or within marriage. The weight of their testimony accordingly counted for little.[34] Gaelic custom, however, appears to have allowed women greater agency in the disposal of landed property. Thus, the early entries in the Book of Deer note joint grants of estates by husbands and wives of the ruling dynasty of Buchan.[35] In the middle years of the thirteenth century Elena de Croc, the wife of an Anglo-Norman tenant of Maoldomhnaich of Lennox, corroborated her husband's account of the sale of a carucate of family land to a local cleric before a royal inquest,[36] indicating that within this lordship, at least, women's testimony counted for something. The presence of women in the witness of lists of deeds dated later in the same century, and then more generally as donors and co-alienors in a growing number of *acta* from both north and south of Forth, may therefore attest the influence of Gaelic custom on the law of property in this period.[37] More certainly,

---

28 Bannerman, 'King's poet', 143; Thomson, 'Mac Mhuirich bardic family', 281. **29** See above, p. 70. **30** *Inchaff. Chrs.*, nos. 2–4, 11–14, 17, 25, 28; *Inchaff. Liber*, App., no. 2 **31** *Inchaff. Chrs.*, no. 9. **32** C. Innes (ed.), *Registrum de Dunfermelyn* (1842), no. 153. **33** *Paisley Reg.*, 158–9. **34** G.W.S. Barrow, 'Witnesses and the attestation of documents in Scotland, twelfth-thirteenth centuries' (1995), 8. **35** Jackson, *Gaelic notes*, 34–5, 58, 76, 118. **36** NAS, RH 5/21. **37** Neville,

the inclusion of women's names in written records relating to the conveyance of estates infers their presence at the public ceremonies that marked the occasion of lordly grants. Their disappearance from lists of attestors after c.1250 need not imply their banishment from the ritual performances of native lordship; it reflected more probably the chauvinism of the scribes, and marked the growing conformity of native charter writing practices with English and continental convention.

Language
One of the most challenging obstacles to the fruitful exchange and absorption of ideas, customs and practices between the Gaelic and European noble cultures of medieval Scotland was the very obvious matter of language. The retreat of Gaelic before 'Inglis' in the course of the century and a half after 1500 has been amply documented and sometimes lamented.[38] But in the generations that followed the settlement of the first foreigners the population of much of the highland zone of Scotland was a complex mosaic in which a notable majority of Gaelic-speakers, noble and common, rubbed shoulders with men and women whose first, and sometimes only, language was French, English, Breton, or Flemish. To that polyglot mixture must also be added persons who were considered the *literati* of contemporary society, that is, men skilled in writing Latin.

As the written charter became increasingly associated with the tenure and conveyance of land, the need for clerks able to speak, understand, and write in more than one language accelerated. Multilingual social interactions must have generated novel methods of social interaction between natives and newcomers all over the kingdom, but they must also have given rise to very real problems of communication in regions of intensive Gaelic settlement like Strathearn and Lennox. In England, the aftermath of the Norman conquest created a need for what Michael Clanchy has called 'pragmatic literacy', and brought to prominence a class of royal and baronial servants who had a sound working knowledge not merely of Latin, but of English and French as well.[39] A similar process operated a century later in Scotland, though its course followed a very distinctive path. Here, the onus of establishing and maintaining contact between native lords on the one hand and English- and French-speaking incomers on the other fell in large part to the *oes dána*, 'the learned orders of the kin based society' who were such crucial figures in the cultural landscape of the Gàidhealtachd.[40] Long before 1300 such men were providing a 'range of services' to native lords, chief among which was the preservation of family histories in genealogical poems and songs.[41] Command of spoken Gaelic and skills in written Latin gave such

'Women, charters land ownership'. **38** McNeill and MacQueen (eds), *Atlas of Scottish history to 1707*, 427; D. Murison, 'The historical background' (1979), 6, 8; idem, 'Linguistic relationships in medieval Scotland', in (1974); D. Thomson, 'Gaelic literature [Scotland]' (1993). **39** Clanchy, *From memory to written record*, 206, 211–12, 236. **40** Thomson, 'Scots language', 11. **41** Thomson, 'Influences', 18.

men added stature in the increasingly polyglot environments of the twelfth century, especially in regions like Strathearn and Lennox, which straddled the linguistic divide between the highlands and lowlands of the kingdom. In Scotland, as in Ireland, moreover, members of the learned orders performed equally vital functions in their lords' courts, where they acted as custodians of the native legal tradition. Indeed, scholars have linked the enduring influence of offices such as that of the *breitheamh* directly to the strength of kin based law in precisely such regions as Strathearn and Lennox.[42] After 1150 the learned men were active also as interpreters, for Gaelic tenants noble and common, of the Latin language deeds that more and more often recorded the earls' acts of lordship. As occurred in England, moreover, the increasing sophistication of baronial governance was in turn manifested in the spread of pragmatic literacy among a greater proportion of lordly servants. The 'attorneys', 'bailies' and stewards mentioned in the earls, written *acta* attest the ability of a growing number of household and estate officials able to function in bilingual, and probably trilingual, environments.[43]

From the late twelfth century the earls of Strathearn and Lennox themselves numbered among the bilingual elite of their territories. Gille Brigte of Strathearn's marriage to Maud d'Aubigny brought him into direct contact with the spoken English and French of the Anglo-Norman and continental aristocracy, and perhaps also, through members of her retinue, with the English of Yorkshire, where her father held several estates.[44] It was perhaps his familiarity with these languages that, quite apart from his status as a great provincial lord, made him such an attractive candidate to King William I for the position of justiciar of Scotia. Maoldomhnaich of Lennox's marriage to Elizabeth Stewart must likewise have provided the earl with a rough and ready ability to communicate in a language other than his native Gaelic, if only on a personal level. In both lordships the presence of monastic establishments offered still another important pool from which to draw linguistic expertise. The transformation of the priests resident on the Isle of Masses in Strathearn into a body of Augustinian canons, for example, did not see the expulsion of the Gaelic-speaking brethren; they were, in fact, encouraged to stay on, and their presence is well attested long after 1198.[45] Such men represented valuable resources to the earl and his kinsmen as translators, and even more as advisors on Gaelic custom to the Latin-trained scribes who began almost immediately to keep parchment records of grants of land and privilege to the house.

On occasion, it is even possible to glimpse, if only fleetingly, the role of native Gaelic speakers in their roles as translators and, through them, the changing nature of the linguistic landscape of Strathearn and Lennox. This is particularly the case in a study of the morphology of some of the Gaelic terms found

---

[42] Thomson, 'Scots language', 12–13; see also above, pp 61–3. [43] See, for example, *Inchaff Chrs.*, nos. 43, 76, 77, 115; *Lennox Cart.*, 45–6; Fraser, *Lennox*, ii, no. 211. [44] W. Farrar (ed.), *Early Yorkshire charters* (3 vols, 1914–16), i, 460–3; G.E. Cokayne, *The complete peerage* (new edn., 13 vols in 14, London, 1910–59), iv, 93–4. [45] *Scotichronicon*, v, 112; *MRHS*, 91.

in the written *acta* of the thirteenth-century earls. Among the Strathearn charters that survive as original parchment sheets, for example, the name Inchaffray underwent considerable change between roughly 1190 and 1250. In no fewer than sixteen of the documents issued by Gille Brigte the name appears in some variation of its Gaelic form of Innis Aifreann,[46] and only twice under the Latin guise of Insula Missarum.[47] The earl's foundation charter of the year 1200 refers to the site as *Inche Affren quod latine dicitur Insula Missarum*. These observations suggest that Strathearn scribes were familiar with both Gaelic and Latin, but that in Gille Brigte's lifetime, at least, the former remained the language of choice in references to the spiritual heart of the lordship, and perhaps also the name that his scribes heard when, in formal ceremonies of infeftment, the priory's name was recited aloud. A study of the seven scribes responsible for penning the earl's charters, almost all of them drawn from the ranks of Inchaffray residents, reveals that one of these, at least, was almost certainly a native Gaelic speaker. In his deeds the name Inchaffray appears in a form that most closely resembles its spelling in Gaelic, Inseaffrenn or Inseafren, and renditions of other native proper nouns, including Gillebertus, Ferthed, Gillenanemh, Anachol, Macbeth, Gillemichel, Stratherenn, Edardoennech, Melkinh, Kenbuc, Gaisk, all preserve clear elements of Gaelic phonetics or orthography.[48] So, incidentally, did the earl's seals. On the two styles that have survived, the obverse shows a figure dressed in the full equestrian gear typical of the European fashion of the day, but the legends preserve the Gaelic form of his name in reproducing its first syllable as 'Gille'.[49]

Only three of Earl Robert's charters to Inchaffray abbey survive as originals. In all three the priory's name appears in a Latinized version of its Gaelic designation.[50] But if the transcripts of the fifteenth-century cartulary which preserves three other deeds represent faithful copies of the original single parchment deeds, already in his time the earl's scribes were becoming accustomed to referring to the abbey by the fully translated name of Insula Missarum.[51] Such a pattern reflects the demographic profile of the residents of Inchaffray, for by Robert's time the former Céli Dé priests who had formed the core of the house when it was first transformed in 1200 would have died, and a newer group, followers of the canon imported from Scone in 1220 to head the newly erected abbey, were well established. The transition period had ended by Malise II's time (1245–71), when the Latin form of the name had become the norm. Four original charters addressed to the canons use the name Insula Missarum;[52] in a fifth document the name appears as Inchafran, but significantly this is a letter of notification addressed to the earl's Gaelic-speaking tenant, Brice thane of Dunning.[53]

The evidence of thirteenth-century Lennox charters is at once more jejune and difficult to assess. The proximity of Paisley abbey offered the earls ready

---

46 *Inchaff. Chrs.*, nos. 4, 6, 9, 11, 12, 13, 15, 16, 25, 27, 28, 34, 37, 39, 43, 44. **47** Ibid., nos. 3, 45. **48** Ibid., nos. 12, 27. **49** Neville, 'Earls of Strathearn', i, 341. **50** *Inchaff. Chrs.*, nos. 41, 51, 52. **51** *Inchaff. Liber*, nos. 12, 16, 59. **52** *Inchaff. Chrs.*, nos. 76, 86, 87, 95. **53** Ibid., no. 77.

access to men skilled in the minutiae of contemporary diplomatic, and it is likely that many of the written *acta* of the early lords of Lennox, including those issued in favour of lay beneficiaries, were produced in the scriptorium of the Cluniac house. Paisley was not, however a native foundation. It was the creation of Walter son of Alan, who staffed the monastery (located first at Renfrew) with men imported form Much Wenlock in Shropshire.[54] Few, if any, of its inmates were of native stock. An additional obstacle to understanding pragmatic bilingualism or trilingualism in Lennox is the relatively poor survival rate of charters as single parchment sheets among the Paisley muniments. Most of its grants are known only through the survival of a late medieval cartulary.

Despite these problems, an examination of the texts of extant deeds suggests that the scribes responsible for recording early Lennox charters had at least some access to native Gaelic speakers. The place name Lennox derives from the Gaelic Leamhain, and the early earls adapted the nominative form of the noun to Leamhainach. Unlike Inchaffray, the word could not easily be translated into Latin. Its pronunciation, however, was amenable to phonetic representation, and from the late twelfth century it was some form of the latter that became standardized in royal and baronial *acta*. Thus, in the earliest charters it appears as Leuenachs or Leuenax.[55] It retained this form until well into the fourteenth century, when the guttural consonant of the final syllable softened to a dental, producing Leuenas or Leuenaus, reflecting the influence of spoken Inglis. More striking examples of the struggles that attended the Latinizing of Gaelic occur in personal names, especially Maoldomhnaich, Amhlaibh, Gille- compound names, and proper nouns generally that contained gutturals, or that required lenition. Predictably, the *literati* of the Lennox region demonstrated no interest in learning even the most fundamental rules of Gaelic grammar. But intellectual snobbery did not prevent them from seeking out Gaelic speakers and from trying to devise phonetic renditions of personal and place names. From a very early period Ailin became Alwinus, and Maoldomhnaich, Maldoun' or Maldouen'.[56] By about 1240, the latter had become sufficiently standardized to acquire a proper Latin declension. Amhlaibh proved especially difficult. The best that scribes unfamiliar with Gaelic orthography could manage was Hamel' (transformed, later still, to Amelec), then, by the mid-thirteenth century, Aulech, a pronunciation that became fixed in the family name MacAulay.[57] Sensitivity to the subtleties of spoken Gaelic in the earliest Lennox documents is more apparent still in the spelling of proper nouns as varied as Muradach and Ferchar/Feruwar,[58] and of place names like Clarines and Letarchore.[59] The *literati* of Strathearn and Lennox almost certainly believed that Latin 'served but poorly to express … barbarous names',[60] and probably accorded native Gaelic speak-

---

54 *MRHS*, 64.   **55** *RRS*, ii, no. 367; NAS, GD 1/88/2, 3.   **56** W. Fraser (ed.), *Facsimiles of Scottish charters and letters* (1903), no. 37; NAS, GD 1/88/2, 3; GD 220/2/4; GD 220/1/A1/2/2.   **57** NAS, GD 1/88/2, 3; GD 220/2/10; Fraser, *Facsimiles*, no. 37.   **58** NAS, GD 1/88/2, 3; GD 220/1/A1/2/3.   **59** NAS, GD 220/2/4, 9.   **60** *Paisley Reg.*, xxiv.

ers only grudging respect. But they could not have played as important a role as they did in introducing the written charter to either lordship without the assistance of men capable of communicating with the indigenous population, form the earls themselves to their tenants, to the labourers bound to the soil.

Literature
The resilience of the Gaelic language in the written and oral cultures of medieval Strathearn and Lennox, even in the face of tremendous pressure to conform to the linguistic conventions of the new aristocracy (and of the crown itself), was impressive. Surviving charter materials offer compelling evidence against portraying cultural change within the old Gaelic provinces of the kingdom in the period following the accession of David I as anything but a foregone conclusion. Language, it has been aptly noted, was 'the expression of the soul or character of a people'; especially in the regions where distinct peoples met and interacted with each other, 'language sensitivities were most likely to be acute'.[61] If historians have not been able to reconstruct fully the 'lost' Gàidhealtachd of medieval Scotland,[62] they have made compelling arguments for reversing the still surprisingly dominant tendency to portray Scottish society as having inevitably surrendered indigenous mores and practices before an overwhelming wave of Europeanizing influence.[63] Occasionally, surviving records afford glimpses of an equally telling 'surrender' on the part of the incomers. The failure of romance literature to find fertile soil in late twelfth- and thirteenth-century Scotland offers one such example. Although native lords all over the kingdom (including the leading men of Strathearn and Lennox) proved receptive to the allures of the chivalric ethos, and quickly embraced some of its most ubiquitous trappings, among them honorific titles, armorial bearings, and equestrian seals, the literature that was so popular a feature of courtly society was not one of them. In England, within a generation of the conquest, the genre of prose and poetry known as *romans lignagères* became widely popular, taking the place of the family chronicle that had been a staple of aristocratic culture in France. The *romans* were designed specifically to suit the social and cultural aspirations of a conquering nobility whose members had no connection with English soil.[64] From Scotland, by contrast, there survives only a single example of the genre of ancestral romance, the *Roman de Fergus*. It was commissioned by Alan of Galloway, probably on the occasion of his marriage.[65] This work, however, cir-

---

[61] R.R. Davies, 'The peoples of Britain and Ireland, 1100–1400: IV. Language and historical mythology' (1997), 9, 12. [62] G.W.S. Barrow, 'The lost Gàidhealtachd' (1992); see also Sellar, 'Celtic law', 1–27, and the several works of Derick Thomson cited in this chapter. [63] For recent examples, see R.R. Davies, *The first English empire: power and identities in the British Isles, 1093–1343* (2000), 157; R.A. McDonald, 'Matrimonial politics and core-periphery interactions in twelfth- and early thirteenth-century Scotland' (1995). [64] D.M. Legge, *Anglo-Norman literature and its background* (1963), 138, 141; N. Thomas, 'The Old French *Roman de Fergus*: Scottish mise-en-scène and political implications' (1993), 94–5. [65] Duncan, *Making*, 530; D. Legge, 'Some notes on the *Roman de Fergus*' (1950), 163. But see also Oram, *Lordship of Galloway*, 54, and Brooke, *Wild men*, 118.

culated only poorly, and like others of its genre generated little interest among patrons in Scotland, Gaelic or European.

Few scholars have attempted to explore why family romances never took root in Scotland when other aspects of the chivalric ethos clearly did and, more specifically, given the Galwegian provenance of *Fergus*, why English and continental newcomers, parvenus all, did not consider it important to establish their credentials and to enhance their prestige as lordly rulers, as they manifestly did in England. Only one has ventured to opine that, written as it was in French, *Fergus* 'was based on a language that had no future in the poet's adopted country'.[66] Another, more complex reason, however, might explain why family romances were not successfully transplanted into the kingdom. Like William of Normandy himself, the European aristocrats who settled in England after 1066 set out simultaneously to celebrate and to legitimise their conquest in prose, poetry, and song. They found there few indigenous antecedents of the *romans lignagères* they had known in France. Early works, notably *Guillaume d'Angleterre* (c.1130), the *Estoire de Waldef* (1190s), and *Boeve de Haumbre* (late twelfth century) reveal how quickly and successfully the newcomers began to reproduce the genre in England; they attest, moreover, the relative ease with which poets and prose writers were able to appropriate the heroic figures, real and legendary, of the Anglo-Saxon past, to establish ownership of these figures, to recast them into new moulds, and to deploy them to suit the needs of a new and ethnically distinct aristocracy.

The English and European noblemen who migrated to Scotland in such significant numbers almost a century later found the field of family history writing much more hotly contested. Gaelic culture had a rich tradition of writing and celebrating family, tribal, and royal genealogies. The custodians of this heritage, moreover, members of the *oes dána,* were part of the very 'power structure' of the eleventh- and twelfth-century kingdom.[67] Long before the foreigners settled in Scotland these men had been jealous defenders of their near monopoly over the cultural past of the Gaelic people, a frame of mind that can only have intensified in response to the growing tide of foreign settlement after 1125. In the face of such deeply entrenched vested interest, French language family histories in the style of the *romans lignagères* were perhaps doomed to a fraught existence in all but the most thoroughly Frenchified regions of the kingdom.

CONCLUSION

In the century or so after 1150 the encounter between Gaelic and European customs and mores in Scotland generated cultural confrontations, some of which are now almost entirely lost to the gaze of the historian. Echoes of the tension

---

[66] D.R.R. Owen, *William the Lion, 1143–1214: kingship and culture* (1997), 152. [67] Thomson, 'Influences', 18; idem, 'Scots language', 10; see also Davies. 'Language', 18.

between natives and newcomers are sometimes heard in the comments of contemporary observers such as the Melrose chronicler who, describing the rising against King Malcolm IV in 1160, noted the anger of Fearchar of Strathearn and five other earls at the young king's subservience to Henry II of England,[68] and more clearly still in the derision (and wistfulness?) of the English monk who, towards the end of William I's reign, wrote that 'the more recent kings of Scots profess themselves to Frenchmen in race and manners, language and culture, and, after reducing the Scots to utter servitude, admit only Frenchmen to their friendship and service'.[69]

A great deal more evidence of the interactions between the cultures lies veiled behind the laconic wording of charters and other written deeds. But as this chapter, and this work more generally have demonstrated, the surviving Latin language records do not obscure altogether the vitality of Gaelic traditions in Strathearn and Lennox during the so-called 'Anglo-Norman era' of Scottish history. The heads of both families were fully committed to the survival of the kindred as the chief unit of social and tenurial organization within their lordships, to the perpetuation of kin based justice, to the sense of history of their families, to the preservation of their language, and to the inculcation of their children in the customs of the Gàidhealtachd. Their efforts to resist and ultimately to control the cultural imperialism of an aggressive European aristocracy in turn bore fruit in the creation of a distinctly Scottish style of lordship, a style not impervious to foreign influence, but one still rich in its indigenous elements.

---

[68] *Chron. Melrose*, 36. [69] W. Stubbs (ed.), *Memoriale fratris Walteri de Convetria* (2 vols, 1872–3), ii, 206.

Conclusion

From Castile northward to Sweden, and Portugal eastward to Hungary, later medieval noble authority rested ultimately on lordly power, however formally or informally this might be expressed.[1] Perhaps at no time was this simple dictum of greater significance in Scotland than in the years 1214 to 1286. This period, which spanned the reigns of Kings Alexander II and Alexander III, witnessed a concerted, and largely successful, effort by the crown to assert its firm control over the distant reaches of the realm and to forge a united kingdom. That the Alexanders came near to achieving their goal was partly the legacy of their military and political victories in regions as far apart as Moray, Argyll, and Galloway, and partly the result of the strong direction that they rulers provided in developing a unique and highly sophisticated system of common law. More important still in the making of the later medieval kingdom, however, was the crown's recognition of the strength of local particularism.

In the thirteenth century the earls of Scotland, still few in number, were very much 'links between the provinces and the kingdom ... middle men, so to speak, providing a national focus for local affairs',[2] and much of the stability that the realm enjoyed rested on the fact that the crown was prepared to allot a significant share in its governance to its greatest subjects. The ways in which the magnates in turn exercised that authority changed profoundly in the course of the years between 1140 and 1365, and especially in the first century of this period. Within the ancient earldoms north of Forth the transformation of lordly power that has been the focus of this work was the consequence of a carefully orchestrated accommodation between Gaelic and European ideas. Here, the native ruling families not only survived the shifting political and cultural environments of the Alexandrian age, but helped to direct it by marrying successfully the traditional rights of Gaelic lordship over men and property with the highly structured prerogatives of Anglo-Norman and continental magnates. The process had a difficult start, and until the second half of the thirteenth century the early earls resisted both passively and actively the intrusion of new men and ideas into their lands.

It is no small irony that the attempt to recover the experience of the native Gaelic lords of Strathearn and Lennox that has been the focus of this book has

---

1 For two important studies of medieval lordship, see R. Bartlett, *The making of Europe* and S. Reynolds, *Kingdoms and communities in Western Europe, 900–1300* (1984).   2 A. Grant, 'Aspects of national consciousness in medieval Scotland' (1994), 92.

rested almost exclusively on the interpretation of written records first introduced to their territories by a foreign culture. Among the many innovations that European newcomers brought with them to Scotland, none was to have greater significance than the sealed charter. Written documents, it has been remarked, created 'textual communities', and in turn generated 'new rituals of everyday life'.[3] The work of scholars interested in the subject of medieval literacy, however, has made it equally clear that societies which depended on the oral transmission of history and tradition 'worked perfectly well without written narrative',[4] and that orality, that is, the power of the spoken and remembered word, never lost its grip in medieval Europe. In Scotland, as elsewhere, the rituals associated with fundamental notions of land ownership changed profoundly over the course of the two centuries between 1140 and 1365. The language of landed society became the Latin of clerics and lawyers, and the record of the transactions of landed persons that of the formal charter. The native earls of Strathearn and Lennox consciously accepted and absorbed the literate mentality of the Europeans, and in doing so initiated a new phase in their expression of lordly power and authority. Although they never abandoned altogether the concept of mormaership that had defined lordly authority in the pre-twelfth century period, their use of charters added a new dimension to their place in society as heads of kindred, provincial rulers, and Gaelic magnates.

The thirteenth and fourteenth century earls of Strathearn and Lennox thus boasted a newly contextualized series of lordly powers, and they exercised these in myriad ways. They summoned, provisioned, and led provincial armies. They erected fortified residences. They exercised broad jurisdiction when, presiding in person or by proxy over their baronial courts, they set conditions on the tenure of land or imposed sentences of life and limb over malefactors. They constantly sought and found new methods of exploiting their territories in order to augment their fiscal, material, and human resources. They exerted firm control over the lives of their tenants, great and small, free and unfree, Gaelic-, English-, or French-speaking. Borrowers of concepts and modes of behaviour from the incoming aristocracy of England and the continent they certainly were; yet, well into the late medieval period the native rulers never abandoned their commitment to the strongly kin based nature of lordly authority that had defined aristocratic power in the period before the coming of the foreigners. The prerogatives that set fourteenth century magnates apart from the lesser nobility owed as much to the preservation of old native custom as it did to the acceptance and incorporation of Anglo-Norman and continental ideas first introduced in the reign of David I.

The 'good lordship' of the earls meant different things to different men. The rulers of Strathearn and Lennox understood well that their households exerted strong drawing power among noble tenants seeking the promise of support in

---

[3] B. Stock, 'Medieval literacy, linguistic theory, and social organization' (1984–5), 18.   [4] M. Innes, 'Keeping it in the family: women and aristocratic memory, 700–1200' (2001), 24.

the lawsuits that were the stuff of medieval litigation, opportunities for promotion into the ranks of the comital entourage, and the chance of a share of lucrative revenues, and throughout the years 1140–1365 these magnates successfully attracted into their political, cultural, and territorial orbits men of English, continental, and Gaelic background. It was thus in the expectation of advancing their own fortunes and those of their families that men like the Luvetots and Tristram (later known as de Gorthy) first came to the Strathearn of Earl Gille Brigte, and that Simon Croc and Simon son of Bertolf ventured beyond the confines of Renfrewshire into what must have looked like the wilds of Earl Maoldomhnaich's Lennox. Even men who already boasted status and wealth saw advantages in fostering strong tenurial ties with the native magnates, such as Sir David de Graham, who in the mid-thirteenth century successfully gained a foothold in both regions. The lands of the earls were more welcoming still of Gaelic-speaking families who sought to find a place, or to enhance their standing, in the changing cultural conditions of the period, among them men such as Anecol of Dunning in Strathearn, and Galbraiths and Colqhuouns in Lennox.

As the heads of extended kinship groups, the earls of Strathearn and Lennox were almost as powerful within their lordships as was the king himself, and they did not hesitate to express their traditional authority over local society in real and meaningful fashion. Surviving charter materials afford valuable glimpses of the ways in which they did so, for example in the notice that one deed includes of Maoldomhnaich of Lennox's decision to uphold the Gaelic custom that provided for the equal division of a native tenant's estates among his several sons,[5] or in the extant documents that record the native rulers' frequent confirmations of deeds issued under the seals of lesser lords.[6] The earls exercised broader authority still in carving out new estates for favoured tenants. Here, too, charter materials offer indications of the rituals by which they created new fermtouns and settled (or resettled) families, either directly, as in clauses of perambulation, or indirectly, in preserving onomastic evidence of the division of established estates into smaller units. The late medieval tenurial landscapes of Strathearn and Lennox reveal the successful amalgamation of the customs by which Gaelic lords had once controlled the distribution of land among members of an extended kin group with the newer practices of settlers familiar with the obligations and conditions that defined lord tenant relationships in England and the continent.

Men of lowly rank in medieval Strathearn and Lennox experienced lordly power and authority in more personal, and certainly more onerous, fashion. Both regions knew an order of unfree peasants, bound to the soil or to a specific owner, though the clerical scribes who drafted the documents in which they are noted

---

[5] Fraser, *Lennox*, ii, no. 207.   [6] For example, charters of Malcolm I of Lennox confirming grants to Sir Patrick de Graham and Mael Coluim son of Gille Mícheil, and a deed of Robert earl of Strathearn confirming a charter of his brother Fergus; ibid., ii, nos. 14, 15; *Lennox Cart.*, 85–6; *Lind. Cart.*, no. 27.

eschewed the native terms *cumelache, cumherba*, and *scoloc* found elsewhere in Gaelic Scotland.[7] Malise II of Strathearn transferred ownership of two such men, together with their families, to the canons of Inchaffray.[8] Although references to unfree persons are intriguingly absent from the early thirteenth-century records of Lennox, it is hardly to be expected that the earls exploited their landed resources as vigorously as they did without a servile labour force of considerable size. Charters from as early as Maoldomhnaich's time, moreover, make mention of the lordly perquisite of merchet and, by mid-century, heriot, both widely associated in English legal parlance with unfree status;[9] their use a reflection, probably, of the Latin trained scribes' preference for familiar terms.

Good lordship also had a spiritual context. Among the many currents of change sweeping through Scotland in the period between 1150 and 1300, few had a more lasting influence than the reformed church. Over the course of these years men and women living in Strathearn and Lennox found new ways to express their faith under the leadership of their secular lords: physically, in the many small churches that sprang up in both regions; spiritually, in the introduction of new saints and feast days to the liturgy; and theologically, in seeing and experiencing on a more regular basis the fruits of the work of sermonizing priests and praying monks. Here (sometimes despite the grumbling of reformers) opportunities abounded for the native earls to encourage and direct the harmonious blending of Gaelic custom and continental innovation.

In the late 1340s, when he made a last, and ultimately unsuccessful, attempt to regain possession of the earldom of Strathearn, Malise V might well have had cause to reflect on the nature of lordship. His swift departure for the security of northern Scotland after the battle of Halidon Hill abruptly severed his ties with the territory that his family had ruled for some two centuries, a breach that intensified with the passage of years and the earl's success in forging new social and familial alliances in Caithness, Orkney, and beyond.[10] News from the south would undoubtedly have kept him well informed of the several magnates whose claims to his lordship were upheld according to the waxing or waning fortunes of the Balliol or Bruce governments. Securing title to the earldom of Strathearn was a matter of concern to all these men for the same fundamental reasons. Amidst the clutter of increasingly small and fragmented honours, baronies, and lordships that comprised the tenurial structure of late medieval Scotland great territorial blocs like Strathearn were exceptional, both in their geographical extent and in the lucrative and wide ranging jurisdictional rights associated with them.[11] Holdovers from 'pre-feudal' Scotland,[12] lordships like Strathearn were

7 G.W.S. Barrow, *Kingship and unity: Scotland, 1000–1306* (1981), 17; Duncan, *Making*, 328–30. 8 *Inchaff. Chrs.*, nos. 57, 58. 9 See, for example, *Lennox Cart*, 19–20, 34–5, 42; Fraser, *Lennox*, ii, no. 207. 10 Neville, 'Earls of Strathearn', i, 154–5; B. Crawford, B., 'The earls of Orkney-Caithness and their relations with Norway and Scotland: 1158–1470' (1971), 30–6. 11 See here especially the work of Alexander Grant, 'The development of the Scottish peerage' (1978), 1–8; idem, 'Earls and earldoms in late medieval Scotland (*c*.1310–1460)' 24–40; and idem, 'The construction of the early Scottish state' (2000), 54–7. 12 McNeill and MacQueen (eds), *Atlas of Scottish*

the richest and rarest of prizes among ambitious aristocrats of the late medieval period. It is small wonder that, after the death of Malise V and the fall from favour of his rivals, Robert Stewart should have expended such energy and effort to win for himself the title of earl.[13] Lennox, similarly, was such a prize, and preserving the integrity of his ancient lordship much preoccupied the childless Earl Donald. As early as the 1340s he set about making arrangements for the transmission of the title to his daughter's (and only heir's) husband Walter of Faslane, and eventually to their son Duncan. His designs were accomplished only in the face of powerful efforts by the Stewart family to encroach upon his territories.[14] The stature that set the late medieval rulers of Strathearn and Lennox apart from their noble fellows was apparent in the solemn grandeur of the title of earl palatinate that David Stewart eventually acquired in 1371,[15] and in the alacrity with which James I seized the revenues and lands of Lennox following the condemnation to death of Earl Duncan in 1425.[16]

The covetous eyes that the Stewarts cast on both regions was a reflection only in part of the wealth in land and money that each represented. It spoke also to a shrewd appreciation on the part of fourteenth- and fifteenth-century men of the legacy of the mormaerships of old. If the close knit societies that Earls Fearchar of Strathearn and Ailin II of Lennox had fostered, held together by unwritten bonds of extended kinship, neighbourliness, Gaelic custom, and a distinct language are no longer as recognizable in the fourteenth century as they are in the late twelfth and the early thirteenth, neither had they vanished altogether. The success of the early earls in integrating the kin-based culture of the Gaels with the tenurial structures of the Europeans had made later medieval Strathearn and Lennox quintessential symbols of authority, independence, and power in a world in which status, rank, and privilege were the only measures of a nobleman's worth that really mattered.

---

history to 1707 (2000), 183. **13** M. Penman, *David II, 1329–1371* (2004), 145, 182, 200. **14** M. Brown, 'Earldom and kindred: the Lennox and its earls, 120–1458' (2003), 211–18. **15** *RMS*, i, nos. 404, 526, 538. **16** M. Brown, *James I* (1994), 73; R. Nicholson, *Scotland: the later middle ages* (1974), 286–7; R. Tanner, *The late medieval Scottish parliament: politics and the three estates, 1424–1488* (2001), 17–18.

Bibliography

MANUSCRIPT SOURCES

Blair Atholl, Pethshire, Muniments of the Duke of Atholl
Crimonmogate House, Aberdeenshire, Muniments of the Earl of Erroll
Darnaway Castle, Moray, Muniments of the Earl of Moray
Dollerie House, Perthshire, Muniments of Mr Anthony Murray
Durham, Muniments of the Dean and Chapter
Edinburgh
Edinburgh University Library
  Laing Charters
  Photograhic negatives of Scottish charters belonging to John Maitland Thomson
Messrs Macrae Flett and Rennie, Colquhoun of Luss Muniments
National Archives of Scotland
  AD 1   Crown Office Writs
  C 2/1, 3 Great Seal Register
  CS 6   Acta Dominorum Consilii et Sessionis
  GD 1/88 Stevenson Charters
  GD 1/91 Leckie Charters
  GD 16   Papers of the Earls of Airlie
  GD 22   Cunninghame Graham Muniments
  GD 24   Abercairney Muniments
  GD 25   Ailsa Muniments
  GD 38   Papers of the Blair Oliphant Family of Arblair and Gask
  GD 45   Papers of the Maule Family, Earls of Dalhousie
  GD 55   Charters of the Abbey of Melrose
  GD 86   Fraser Charters
  GD 90   Yule Collection
  GD 97   Duntreath Muniments
  GD 150 Papers of the Earls of Morton
  GD 160 Papers of the Drummond Family, Earls of Perth
  GD 124 Papers of the Erskine Family, Earls of Mar and Kellie
  GD 175 Papers of the Earls of Erroll
  GD 198 Haldane of Gleneagles Charters
  GD 212 Maitland Thomson Papers
  GD 220 Muniments of the Dukes of Montrose
  GD 248 Seafield Grant Charters
  GD 430 Napier Charters
  PA 1/4 Rolls of Parliament
  RH 1   Register House Transcripts
  RH 3   Microfilm of records held in the NAS
  RH 4/23 Ordnance Survey Original Name Book.
  RH   Documents transferred from the PRO, London

RH 6   Register House Charters
RH 9   Miscellaneous Papers
National Library of Scotland
   Acc. 10301   Adv. MS. 34.4.2   Adv. MS. 35.4.9
   Adv. MS. 15.1.18   Adv. MS. 34.4.3   Adv. MS. 43.2.35
   Adv. MS. 17.1.15   Adv. MS. 34.4.10   Adv. MS. Charters
   Adv. MS. 19.2.17   Adv. MS. 34.4.14   MS. 72
   Adv. MS. 34.1.2   Adv. MS. 34.5.1   Dep. 313
   Adv. MS. 34.3.25   Adv. MS. 35.2.4
National Monuments Record Scotland, MS 993/1
Glasgow
Glasgow University Library, MS Gen 198
Royal Faculty of Procurators, Hill Collection of Manuscripts, Macfarlane Muniments
London
British Library
   Add MSS. 11545   Lord F. Campbell Charters, xxx
   Add MSS. 19747   Stone MS., 351
   Add MSS. 33245   Cotton Charters, xviii
   Add MSS. 34794   MS. Harleian 83.C.24
National Archives
   C 47   Chancery, Miscellanea
   C 54   Chancery, Close Rolls
   C 60   Chancery, Fine Rolls
   C 66   Chancery, Patent Rolls
   C 145   Chancery, Inquisitions Miscellaneous
   E 30   Exchequer, Treasury of Receipt, Diplomatic Documents
   E 159   Exchequer, King's Remembrancer, Memoranda Rolls
   E 368   Exchequer, Lord Treasurer's Remembrancer, Memoranda Rolls
   SC 1   Special Collections, Ancient Correspondence
Perth, Messrs Condie, Mackenzie and Co., Kinnoull Trustees' Muniments

PRINTED SOURCES
Primary sources are indicated by an asterisk.

*Aithdioghluim Dána, ed. L. McKenna (2 vols, Irish Texts Soc., 1939–40).
Alexandre-Bidon, D., and Lett, D., *Children in the Middle Ages, fifth-fifteenth centuries* (Notre Dame, 1999).
Anderson, D.M., 'Hermitages in Logie parish', in *Innes Review* 18 (1967), 58–9.
Anderson, M., 'St Andrews before Alexander I', in G.W.S. Barrow (ed.), *The Scottish tradition: essays in honour of Ronald Gordon Cant* (Edinburgh, 1974), 1–13.
Anderson, M.L., *A history of Scottish forestry* (2 vols, London, 1967).
Anderson, M.O., 'The Celtic church in Kinrimund', in *Innes Review* 25 (1974), 67–76.
——, *Kings and kingship in early Scotland* (Edinburgh, 1973).
**Anglo-Scottish relations 1174–1328: some selected documents*, ed. E.L.G. Stones (Oxford, 1965).
**Annala Uladh: The annals of Ulster*, ed. W.M. Hennessy and B. McCarthy (4 vols, Dublin, 1887–1901).
**The annals of Roger de Hoveden*, ed. H.T. Riley (2 vols, London, 1853).
**Annals of the reigns of Malcolm and William, kings of Scotland*, ed. A.C. Lawrie (Glasgow, 1910).
Ash, M., 'David Bernham, bishop of St Andrews, 1239–1253', in D. McRoberts (ed.), *The medieval church of St Andrews* (Glasgow, 1976), 33–44.
——, 'The diocese of St Andrews under its "Norman" bishops', in *SHR* 55 (1976), 105–26.
*'Bagimond's roll: statement of the tenths of the kingdom of Scotland', in *Scottish History Society Miscellany VI*, ed. A.I. Dunlop (SHS, 1939), 3–77.

Bailey, S. J., 'Warranties of land in the thirteenth century', *Cambridge Law Journal* 8 (1944), 274–99.
Bain, E.C., *A short guide to deserted settlements in Glen Lednock* (Auchterarder, 1976).
Baker, D., '"A nursery of saints": St Margaret of Scotland reconsidered', in idem (ed.), *Medieval women* (Oxford, 1978), 119–41.
Bannerman, J., 'The king's poet and the inauguration of Alexander III', in *SHR* 68 (1989), 120–49.
——, 'MacDuff of Fife', in A. Grant and K.J. Stringer (eds), *Medieval Scotland: crown, lordship and community* (Edinburgh, 1993), 20–38.
——, 'The Scots language and the kin-based society', in D.S. Thomson (ed.), *Gaelic and Scots in harmony: proceedings of the second international conference on the languages of Scotland* (Glasgow, 1988), 1–19.
Barrell, A.D.M., *Medieval Scotland* (Cambridge, 2000).
Barrow, G.W.S., *The Anglo-Norman era in Scottish history* (Oxford, 1981).
——, 'The army of Alexander III's Scotland', in N.H. Reid (ed.), *Scotland in the reign of Alexander III* (Edinburgh, 1990), 132–47.
——, 'Badenoch and Strathspey, 1130–1312: 1. Secular and political', in *Northern Scotland* 8 (1988), 1–15.
——, 'Badenoch and Strathspey, 1130–1312: 2. The church', in *Northern Scotland* 9 (1989), 1–16.
——, *David I of Scotland (1124–1153): the balance of new and old* (Reading, 1985)
——, 'The earls of Fife in the 12th century', in *PSAS* 87 (1953), 51–62.
——, *Feudal Britain* (London, 1956).
——, 'King David I, earl Henry and Cumbria', in *Transactions of the Cumberland and Westmorland Antiquarian and Archaeological Soc.*, 99 (1999), 117–27.
——, *Kingship and unity: Scotland 1000–1306* (London, 1981).
——, 'The Lost Gàidhealtachd', in idem, *Scotland and its neighbours in the Middle Ages* (London, 1992), 105–26.
——, 'Northern English society in the twelfth and thirteenth centuries', in *Northern History* 4 (1969), 1–28.
——, 'Popular courts in early medieval Scotland: some suggested place-name evidence', in idem, *Scotland and its neighbours in the Middle Ages* (London, 1992), 217–45.
——, *Robert Bruce and the community of the realm of Scotland* (1st edn, Berkeley and Los Angeles, 1965, and 3rd edn, Edinburgh,1988).
——, 'The Scots charter', in idem, *Scotland and its neighbours in the Middle Ages* (London, 1992), 91–104.
——, 'Witnesses and the attestation of documents in Scotland, twelfth-thirteenth centuries', in *Journal of Legal History* 16 (1995), 1–20.
Barry, J., 'The appointment of coarb and erenagh', in *Irish Ecclesiastical Record*, 5th ser. 93 (1960), 361–5.
——, 'The coarb and the twelfth-century reform', in *Irish Ecclesiastical Record*, 5th ser. 88 (1957), 17–25.
——, 'The coarb in medieval times', in *Irish Ecclesiastical Record*, 5th ser. 89 (1958), 24–35.
——, 'The distinction between coarb and erenagh', in *Irish Ecclesiastical Record*, 5th ser. 94 (1960), 90–5).
——, 'The extent of coarb and erenagh in Gaelic Ulster', in *Irish Ecclesiastical Record*, 5th ser. 94 (1960), 12–16.
——, 'The lay coarb in medieval times', in *Irish Ecclesiastical Record*, 5th ser., 91 (1959), 27–39.
Bartlett, R., 'The Celtic lands of the British Isles', in D. Abulafia (ed.), *The new Cambridge medieval history, vol. V: c.1198–c.1300* (Cambridge, 1999), 809–27
——, *The making of Europe: conquest, colonization and cultural change, 950–1350* (Princeton, 1993).
Bedos-Rezak, B.M., 'Medieval identity: a sign and a concept', in *American Historical Review* 105 (2000), 148–1533.
Bil, A., 'Transhumance place-names in Perthshire', in *PSAS* 122 (1992), 383–402.
Bitel, L.M., *Isle of the saints: monastic settlement and Christian community in early Ireland* (Ithaca, 1990).
——, 'Saints and angry neighbors: the politics of cursing in Irish hagiography', in S. Farmer and B. Rosenwein (eds), *Monks and nuns, saints and outcasts: religion in medieval society* (Ithaca, 2000), 123–50.

Black, G.F., *The surnames of Scotland* (New York, 1946, repr. Edinburgh, 1996).
Bliese, J.R.E., 'Aelred of Rievaulx's rhetoric and morale at the battle of the Standard, 1138', in *Albion* 20 (1988), 543–56.
Blundell, F.O., 'Further notices on the artificial islands in the Highland area', in *PSAS* 47 (1912–13), 257–302.
Boardman, S., *The early Stewart kings: Robert II and Robert III, 1371–1406* (East Linton, 1996).
—— and Ross, A., 'Editors' introduction', in S. Boardman and A. Ross (eds), *The exercise of power in medieval Scotland, c.1200–1500* (Dublin, 2003), 15–22.
The Book of the Dean of Lismore, ed. T. Mc'Laughlin (Edinburgh, 1862).
Bracton De legibus et consuetudinibus Angliae, ed. G.E. Woodhouse (4 vols, Cambridge, MA, 1968–77).
Brooke, D., 'Fergus of Galloway: miscellaneous notes for a revised portrait', in *Trans. of the Dumfriesshire and Galloway Natural History and Archaeological Soc.*, 3rd ser. 66 (1991), 47–58.
——, *Wild men and holy places: St Ninian, Whithorn and the medieval realm of Galloway* (Edinburgh, 1998).
Broun, D., 'The birth of Scottish history', in *SHR* 76 (1997), 4–22.
——, *The charters of Gaelic Scotland and Ireland in the early and central Middle Ages* (Quiggan pamphlets on the sources of medieval Gaelic history, Cambridge, 1995).
——, 'Defining Scotland and the Scots before the wars of independence', in F. Broun and M. Lynch (eds), *Image and identity: the making and re-making of Scotland through the ages* (Edinburgh, 1988), 4–17.
——, *The Irish identity of the kingdom of the Scots in the twelfth and thirteenth centuries* (Woodbridge, 1999),
——, 'The seven kingdoms in *De situ Albanie*: a record of Pictish political geography or imaginary map of ancient *Alba*?', in E.J. Cowan and R.A. McDonald (eds), *Alba: Celtic Scotland in the medieval era* (East Linton, 2000), 24–42.
Brown, E.A.R., 'The tyranny of a construct: feudalism and the historians of medieval Europe', in *American Historical Review* 79 (1974), 1063–88.
Brown, M., 'Earldom and kindred: the Lennox and its earls, 120–1458', in S. Boardman and A. Ross (eds), *The exercise of power in medieval Scotland, c.1200–1500* (Dublin, 2003), 201–24.
——, *James I* (Edinburgh, 1994).
The Brut or The chronicles of England, ed. F.W.D. Brie (Early English Text Soc., 1906).
Buchanan, W., *A historical and genealogical essay upon the family and surname of Buchanan* (Glasgow, 1723).
——, *An enquiry into the genealogy and present state of ancient Scottish surnames* (Glasgow, 1820).
Budgey, A., '*Commeationis et affinitatis gratia*: medieval musical relations between Scotland and Ireland', in R.A. McDonald (ed.), *History, literature, and music in Scotland, 700–1560* (Toronto, 2002), 208–32.
Calendar of entries in the papal registers relating to Great Britain and Ireland (Regesta Romanorum pontificum): Papal letters, ed. W.H. Bliss et al. (14 vols, London, 1893–1960).
Calendar of entries in the papal registers relating to Great Britain and Ireland (Regesta Romanorum pontificum): Petitions to the pope, ed. W.H. Bliss (London, 1896).
Campbell, N.D., 'MacEwans and MacSweens', in *Celtic Review* 7 (1911–12), 272–84.
Cant, R., 'The building of St Andrews cathedral', in *Innes Review* 25 (1974), 77–94.
Cant, R.G., 'The medieval kirk of Crail', in A. O'Connor and D.V. Clarke (eds.), *From the stone age to the 'forty-five: studies presented to R.B K. Stevenson* (Edinburgh, 1983), 368–83.
Carpenter, D., *The struggle for mastery, Britain, 1066–1284* (London, 2003).
Carte monialium de Northberwic, ed. C. Innes (Bannatyne Club, 1847).
Charles-Edwards, T., 'Honour and status in some Irish and Welsh prose tales', *Ériu* 29 (1978), 123–41.
The charters of King David I: the written acts of David I king of Scots, 1125–53 and of his son Henry earl of Northumberland, 1139–52, ed. G.W.S. Barrow (Woodbridge, 1999).
Charters of the abbey of Coupar Angus, ed. D.E. Easson (2 vols, SHS, 1947).

The chronicle of Melrose from the Cottonian Manuscript, Faustina B. IX, in the British Museum, ed. A.O. Anderson and M.O. Andersdon (London, 1936).
The chronicle of Walter of Guisborough, ed. H. Rothwell (Camden Soc., 1957).
Chronicles of the reigns of Stephen, Henry II, and Richard I, ed. R. Howell (4 vols, London, 1884–89).
Chronicon Henrici Knighton, vel Cnithon, monachi Leycestrensis, ed. J.R. Lumby (2 vols, London, 1889–95).
Clanchy, M.T., *From memory to written record: England 1066–1307* (2nd edn, Oxford, 1993).
Clancy, T.O., 'Annat in Scotland and the origins of the Parish', in *Innes Review* 46 (1995), 91–115.
——, 'Scotland, the 'Nennian' rescension of the *Historia Brittonum*, and the *Lebor Bretnach*', in S. Taylor (ed.), *Kings, clerics and chronicles in Scotland, 500–1297* (Dublin, 2000), 87–107.
Cockburn, J.H., *The medieval bishops of Dunblane and their church* (Edinburgh, 1959).
Cokayne, G.E., *The complete peerage* (new edn, 13 vols in 14, London, 1910–59).
Collectanea de rebus Albanacis, ed. Iona Club (1947).
Cowan, E.J., 'The invention of Celtic Scotland', in E.J. Cowan and R.A. McDonald (eds), *Alba: Celtic Scotland in the medieval era* (East Linton, 2000), 1–23.
——, 'Norwegian sunset – Scottish dawn: Hakon IV and Alexander III', in N. Reid (ed.), *Scotland in the reign of Alexander III* (Edinburgh, 1990), 103–31.
Cowan, I.B., 'The appropriation of parish churches', in idem, *The medieval church in Scotland* (Edinburgh, 1995), 12–29.Cowan, I.B., 'The church in Argyll and the Isles', in idem, *The medieval church in Scotland* (Edinburgh, 1995), 129–43.
——, 'The development of the parochial system in medieval Scotland', in *SHR* 41 (1961), 43–55.
——, 'The medieval church in the highlands', in L. McLean (ed.), *The Middle Ages in the highlands* (Inverness, 1981), 91–100.
——, 'The organisation of secular cathedral chapters', in idem, *The medieval church in Scotland* (Edinburgh, 1995), 77–96.
——, *The parishes of medieval Scotland* (Scottish Record Soc., 1967).
——, 'The post-Columban church', in *Records of the Scottish Church History Soc.* 18 (1974), 245–60.
——, 'Vicarages and the cure of souls', in idem, *The medieval church in Scotland* (Edinburgh, 1995), 46–61.
Crawford, B., 'The earls of Orkney-Caithness and their relations with Norway and Scotland: 1158–1470' (PhD thesis, University of St Andrews, 1971).
Crawford, B.E., 'The earldom of Caithness and the kingdom of Scotland, 1150–1266', in K.J. Stringer (ed.), *Essays on the nobility of medieval Scotland* (Edinburgh, 1985), 25–43
——, 'Norse earls and Scottish bishops: a clash of cultures', in C.E. Batey, J. Jesch and C.D. Morris (eds), *The Viking age in Caithness, Orkney and the north Atlantic* (Edinburgh, 1995), 129–47.
Crawfurd, G., *The peerage of Scotland* (2 vols, Edinburgh, 1716).
Crouch, D., *William Marshal: court, career and chivalry in the Angevin empire 1147–1219* (London, 1990).
Cruden, S., *Scottish medieval churches* (Edinburgh, 1986).
Davies, R., *The age of conquest: Wales, 1063–1415* (Oxford, 1991).
——, *Domination and conquest: the experience of Ireland, Scotland and Wales, 1100–1300* (Oxford, 1990).
——, *The first English empire: power and identities in the British Isles 1093–1343* (Oxford, 2000).
——, 'Kinsmen, neighbours and communities in Wales and the western British Isles, c.1100–c.1400', in P. Stafford, J. Nelson and J. Martindale (eds), *Law, laity and solidarities: essays in honour of Susan Reynolds* (Manchester, 2001), 172–87.
——, *Lordship and society in the march of Wales, 1282–1400* (Oxford, 1978).
——, 'The peoples of Britain and Ireland, 1100–1400: IV. Language and historical mythology', in *TRHS*, 6th ser. 7 (1997), 1–24.
Davies, W., 'Anger and the Celtic saint', in B. Rosenwein (ed.), *Anger's past: the social uses of an emotion in the Middle Ages* (Ithaca, 1998), 191–202.
——, 'Charter-writing and its uses in early medieval Celtic societies', in H. Pryce (ed.), *Literacy in medieval Celtic societies* (Cambridge, 1996), 99–112.
——, 'The Latin charter-tradition in western Britain, Brittany and Ireland in the early medieval period', in D. Whitelock, R. McKitterick and D. Dumville (eds), *Ireland in early medieval Europe: studies in memory of Kathleen Hughes* (Cambridge, 1982), 258–80.

Davis, G.R.C., *Medieval cartularies of Great Britain* (London, 1958).
Denholm-Young, N., *Seignorial administration in England* (Oxford, 1937).
Dickinson, W.C., 'The administration of justice in medieval Scotland', in *Aberdeen University Review* 34 (1952), 338–51.
—, 'The *toschederach*', in *Juridical Review* 53 (1941), 85–111.
Dilworth, M., 'Cluniac Paisley: its constitutional status and prestige', in J. Malden (ed.), *The monastery & abbey of Paisley* (Renfrew, 2000), 23–36.
—, 'The dependent priories of St Andrews, in D. McRoberts (ed.), *The medieval church of St Andrews* (Glasgow, 1976), 157–66.
—, *Scottish monasteries in the late Middle Ages* (Edinburgh, 1995).
Ditchburn, D. and Macdonald, A.J., 'Medieval Scotland, 1100–1560', in R.A. Houston and W.W.J. Knox (eds), *The new Penguin history of Scotland: from the earliest times to the present day* (London, 2001), 96–181
Ditchburn, D., *Scotland and Europe: the medieval kingdom and its contacts with Christendom, 1214–1560* (East Linton, 2000).
Dixon, P.J., 'Settlement in the hunting forests of southern Scotland in the medieval and later periods', in G. de Boe and F. Verhaeghe (eds), *Rural settlements in medieval Europe: papers of the 'Medieval Europe Brugge 1997' conference, Vol. 6* (Zellik, 1997), 345–54.
*Documents and records illustrating the history of Scotland, ed. F. Palgrave (London, 1837).
*Documents illustrative of the history of Scotland 1286–1306, ed. J. Stevenson (2 vols, Edinburgh, 1870).
Dodgshon, R.A., 'Changes in Scottish township organization during the medieval and early modern periods', in *Geografiska Annaler* 59B (1977), 51–65.
—, *Land and society in early Scotland* (Oxford, 1981).
—, 'Medieval rural Scotland', in G. Whittington and I.D. Whyte (eds), *An historical geography of Scotland* (London, 1983), 47–71.
Donaldson, G., 'Aspects of early Scottish conveyancing', in P. Gouldesbrough (ed.), *Formulary of old Scots legal documents* (Stair Soc., 1985), 153–86.
—, 'The bishops and priors of Whithorn', in *Trans. of the Dumfriesshire and Galloway Natural History and Archaeological Soc.* 3rd ser. 37 (1948–9), 127–54.
—, 'Scottish bishops' sees before the reign of David I', in *PSAS* 87 (1952–53), 106–77.
—, *Scottish church history* (Edinburgh, 1985).
Donaldson, G. and Morpeth, R., *A dictionary of Scottish history* (Edinburgh, 1977).
Dowden, J., *The medieval church in Scotland: its constitution, organisation and law* (Glasgow, 1910).
Driscoll, S.T., 'The archaeology of state formation in Scotland', in W.S. Hanson and E.A. Slater (eds), *Scottish archaeology: new perceptions* (Aberdeen, 1991), 81–111.
—, 'Formalising the mechanisms of state power: early Scottish lordship from the ninth to the thirteenth centuries', in S.M. Foster, A. Macinnes and R. MacInnes (eds), *Scottish power centres from the early Middle Ages to the twentieth century* (Glasgow, 1998), 33–58.
Drummond, W., *The genealogy of the most noble and ancient house of Drummond* (Glasgow, 1889).
Duby, G., *The chivalrous society* (London, 1977).
Duffy, S., 'The Bruce brothers and the Irish Sea world, 1306–29', in *Cambridge Medieval Celtic Studies* 21 (1991), 55–86.
Dumville, D.N., 'The chronicle of the kings of Alba', in S. Taylor (ed.), *Kings, clerics and chronicles in Scotland 500–1297* (Dublin, 2000), 73–86.
Dunbar, J.G., *The historic architecture of Scotland* (London, 1966).
Duncan, A.A.M., 'The earliest Scottish charters', in *SHR* 37 (1958), 103–35.
—, *The kingship of the Scots, 842–1292* (Edinburgh, 2002).
—, *The nation of the Scots and the Declaration of Arbroath (1320)* (London, 1970).
—, 'Yes, the earliest Scottish charters', in *SHR* 78 (1999), 1–38.
Durkan, J., 'Care of the poor: pre-reformation hospitals', in *Innes Review* 10 (1959), 268–80.
—, 'Paisley abbey: attempt to make it Cistercian', in *Innes Review* 7 (1956), 60–2.
—, 'The place-name Balmaha', in *Innes Review* 50 (1999), 89–101.
*Early Scottish charters to A.D. 1153, ed. A.C. Lawrie (Glasgow, 1905).

Early sources of Scottish history, A.D. 500–1286, ed. A.O. Anderson (2 vols, Edinburgh, 1922, repr. Stamford, 1990).
Early Yorkshire charters, ed. W. Farrar (3 vols, Edinburgh, 1914–16).
The ecclesiastical history of Orderic Vitalis, ed. M. Chibnall (6 vols, Oxford, 1969–80).
Edward I and the throne of Scotland, 1290–1296, ed. E.L.G. Stones and G.G. Simpson (2 vols, Oxford, 1978).
Ewart, G., 'Inchaffray abbey, Perth & Kinross: excavation and research, 1987', in *PSAS* 126 (1996), 469–516.
Facsimiles of the national manuscripts of Scotland (3 vols, London, 1867–72).
'Families of the Lennox: a survey', in *Scottish Genealogist* 22 (1975), 29–46.
Ferguson, J., 'The seven earls of Scotland', in *Juridical Review* 25 (1913), 185–208.
Ferguson, P.C., *Medieval papal representatives in Scotland: legates, nuncios, and judges-delegate, 1125–1286* (Stair Soc., 1997).
Fittis, R.S., *Sketches of the olden times in Perthshire* (Perth, 1878).
Flanagan, M.-T., 'The context and uses of the Latin charter in twelfth-century Ireland', in H. Pryce (ed.), *Literacy in medieval Celtic societies* (Cambridge, 1996), 133–32.
——, 'Strategies of lordship in pre-Norman and post-Norman Leinster', in *Anglo-Norman Studies* 20 (1997), 107–26.
Foster, S.M., 'Before Alba: Pictish and Dál Riata power centres from the fifth to the late ninth centuries AD', in S.M. Foster, A. Macinnes and R. MacInnes (eds), *Scottish power centres from the early Middle Ages to the twentieth century* (Glasgow, 1998), 1–31.
Frame, R., 'Aristocracies and the political configuration of the British Isles', in R.R. Davies (ed.), *The British Isles 1100–1500: comparisons, contrasts and connections* (Edinburgh, 1988), 142–59.
——, *The political development of the British Isles, 1100–1400* (Oxford, 1990).
*Fraser, W., *The book of Caerlaverock* (2 vols, Edinburgh, 1873).
*——, *The chiefs of Grant* (Edinburgh, 1883).
*——, *Facsimiles of Scottish charters and letters* (Edinburgh, 1903).
*——, *Memoirs of the Maxwells of Pollock* (2 vols, Edinburgh, 1863).
*——, *The red book of Grandtully* (2 vols, Edinburgh, 1868).
*——, *The red book of Menteith* (2 vols, Edinburgh, 1880).
*——, *The Stirlings of Keir, and their family papers* (Edinburgh, 1858).
*——, *The Sutherland book* (3 vols, Edinburgh, 1892).
Gaffney, J., 'Summer shielings', in *SHR* 38 (1959), 20–35.
Gemmill, E. and Mayhew, N., *Changing values in medieval Scotland: a study of prices, money, and weights and measures* (Cambridge, 1995).
Genealogical collections concerning families in Scotland, made by Walter Macfarlane, 1750–1751, ed. J.T. Clark (2 vols, SHS, 1900).
Geographical collections relating to Scotland made by Walter Macfarlane, ed. A. Mitchell and J.T. Clark (3 vols, SHS, 1906–8).
Gesta Regis Henrici Secundi Benedicti abbatis, ed. W. Stubbs (2 vols, London, 1867).
Gilbert, J., *Hunting and hunting reserves in medieval Scotland* (Edinburgh, 1979).
Graeme, L., *Or and sable: a book of the Graemes and Grahams* (Edinburgh, 1903).
Graham, E.M., *The Oliphants of Gask* (London, 1910).
Grant, A., 'Aspects of national consciousness in medieval Scotland', in C. Björn (ed.), *Nations, nationalism and patriotism in the European past* (Copenhagen, 1994), 68–95.
——, 'The construction of the early Scottish state', in J.R. Maddicott and D.M. Palliser (eds), *The medieval state: essays presented to James Campbell* (London, 2000), 47–71.
——, 'The development of the Scottish peerage', in *SHR* 57 (1978), 1–27.
——, 'Earls and earldoms in late medieval Scotland (c.1310–1460)', in J. Bossy and P. Jupp (eds), *Essays presented to Michael Roberts* (Belfast, 1976), 24–40.
——, 'Fourteenth-century Scotland', in M. Jones (ed.), *The new Cambridge medieval history, vol. VI: c.1300–c.1415* (Cambridge, 2000), 345–74
——, *Independence and nationhood: Scotland 1306–1469* (London, 1984).

—, 'Scotland's "Celtic fringe" in the late middle ages: the Macdonald lords of the Isles and the kingdom of Scotland', in R.R. Davies (ed.), *The British Isles 1100–1500: comparisons, contrasts and connections* (Edinburgh, 1988), 118–41.

—, 'Service and tenure in late medieval Scotland, 1314–1475', in A. Curry and E. Matthews (eds), *Concepts and patterns of service in the later Middle Ages* (Woodbridge, 2000), 145–79.

—, 'Thanes and thanages, from the eleventh to the fourteenth centuries', in A. Grant and K.J. Stringer (eds), *Medieval Scotland: crown, lordship and community* (Edinburgh, 1993), 39–81.

Hall, D., 'The Middle Ages', in D. Omand (ed.), *The Perthshire book* (Edinburgh, 1999), 59–74.

Halliday, S.P., 'Marginal agriculture in Scotland', in T.C. Smout (ed.), *Scotland since prehistory* (Aberdeen, 1993), 64–78.

Hay, G. and McRoberts, D., 'Rossdhu church and its books of hours', in *Innes Review* 16 (1965), 13–17.

Headrick, M., 'The "stayt" of Crieff – a Bronze-age burial site', in *PSAS* 48 (1913–14), 365–9.

★*Hector Boece, The chronicles of Scotland*, ed. E.C. Batho and H.W. Husbands (2 vols, Scottish Text Soc, 1936–41).

Herbert, J., 'The transformation of hermitages into Augustinian priories in twelfth-century England', in W.J. Shiels (ed.), *Monks, hermits and the ascetic tradition* (Oxford, 1983), 131–45.

Herbert, M., 'Charter material from Kells', in F. O'Mahony (ed.), *The book of Kells: proceedings of a conference at Trinity College, Dublin, 6–9 September, 1992* (Aldershot, 1994), 60–77.

Higgitt, J., *The Murthly hours: devotion, literacy and luxury in Paris, England and the Gaelic west* (London, 2000).

★*Highland papers*, ed. J.R.N. MacPhail (4 vols, SHS, 1914–34).

Hopkins, P, 'The symbology of water in Irish pseudo-history', in B. Hillers and J. Hunter (eds), *Proceedings of the Harvard Celtic colloquium XII* (Cambridge, MA, 1992), 80–6.

Hudson, B.T., 'Gaelic princes and Gregorian reform', in B.T. Hudson and V. Ziegler (eds), *Crossed paths: methodological approaches to the Celtic aspect of the European Middle Ages* (New York, 1991), 61–82.

—, *Kings of Celtic Scotland* (Westport, 1994).

—, 'The Scottish chronicle', in *SHR* 77 (1998), 129–61.

Hudson, J., *The formation of the English common law: law and society in England from the Norman conquest to Magna Carta* (London, 1996).

—, *Land, law, and lordship in Anglo-Norman England* (Oxford, 1994).

Hyams, P., 'Warranty and good lordship in twelfth century England', *Law and History Review* 5 (1987), 437–503.

Innes, M., 'Keeping it in the family: women and aristocratic memory, 700–1200', in E. van Houts (ed.), *Medieval memories: men, women and the past, 700–1300* (Harlow, 2001), 17–35.

★*Inquisitiones ad capellam Regis retornatarum abbreviatio (Scotland)*, ed. T. Thomson (3 vols, London, 1811–16).

★*Instrumenta publica sive processus super fidelitatibus et homagiis Scotorum domino regi Angliae factis A.D. MCCXCI– MCCXCVI*, ed. T. Thomson (Bannatyne Club, 1834).

Irving, J., *History of Dumbartonshire* (rev. edn, 3 pts, Dumbarton, 1917–24).

—, *Place names in Dumbartonshire* (Dumbarton, 1928).

Jackson, K., *The Gaelic notes in the Book of Deer* (Cambridge, 1972).

Jan-Hennebicque, R. le, 'Apprentissages militaries, rites de passage et remises d'armes au haut moyen âge', in *Éducation, apprentissgae, initiation au moyen âge: actes du 1er colloque international de Montpellier* (Université Paul Valéry) de novembre, 1991 (2 vols., Montpellier, 1993), i, 211–32.

★*John Barbour, The Bruce*, ed. A.A.M. Duncan (Edinburgh 1997).

Johnstone, J.B., *Place-names in Scotland* (London, 1934).

—, *The place names of Stirlingshire* (Stirling, 1904).

Jones, G.R., 'Multiple estates and early settlement', in P. Sawyer (ed.), *Medieval settlements: continuity and change* (London, 1976), 16–40.

Lacaille, A.D., 'The Capelrig Cross, Mearns, Renfrewshire …', in *PSAS* 61 (1927), 122–42.

—, 'Ecclesiastical remains in the neighbourhood of Luss …', in *PSAS* 62 (1928), 85–106.

—, 'Loch Lomondside fonts and effigy', in *PSAS* 68 (1933–4), 100–16.

—, 'Notes on a Loch Lomondside parish', in *Innes Review* 16 (1965), 147–58.

——, 'Some ancient crosses in Dumbartonshire and adjoining counties', in *PSAS* 59 (1925), 143–53.
Lees, J.C., *The abbey of Paisley from its foundation till its dissolution* (Paisley, 1878).
Legge, D., 'Some notes on the Roman de Fergus', *Trans. of the Dumfriesshire and Galloway Natural History and Archaeological Soc.*, new ser. 27 (1950), 163–72.
Legge, D.M., *Anglo-Norman literature and its background* (Oxford, 1963).
Liber cartarum prioratus Sancti Andree in Scotia, ed. T. Thomson (Bannatyne Club, 1841).
Liber cartarum Sancte Crucis, ed. C. Innes (Bannatyne Club, 1840).
Liber s. Marie de Calchou, ed. C. Innes (2 vols, Bannatyne Club, 1846).
Liber sancte Marie de Balmorinach, ed. W.B.D.D. Turnbull (Abbotsford Club, 1841).
Liber sancte Marie de Melros, ed. C. Innes (2 vols, Bannatyne Club, 1837).
Liber s. Thome de Aberbrothoc, ed. C. Innes and P. Chalmers (2 vols, Bannatyne Club, 1848–56).
The life of Ailred of Rievaulx by Walter Daniel, ed. F.M. Powicke (London, 1950).
Life of St Margaret, Queen of Scotland, by Turgot, bishop of St Andrews, ed. W. Forbes-Leith (Edinburgh, 1884).
Lindsay, J., 'The heritable bailies of the Lennox', in *Publications of the Clan Lindsay Soc.* 1:3 (1904), 3–40.
Little, L.K., *Benedictine maledictions: liturgical cursing in Romanesque France* (Ithaca, NY, 1993), 192–202.
Low, M., *Celtic Christianity and nature: early Irish and Hebridean traditions* (Edinburgh, 1996), 57–78.
Loyd, L.C., *The origins of some Anglo-Norman families* (Harleian Soc., 1951).
MacDonald, A., '"Annat" in Scotland: a provisional review', *Scottish Studies* 17 (1973), 135–46.
——, 'Major early monasteries: some procedural problems for field archaeologists', in D.J. Breeze (ed.), *Studies in Scottish antiquity presented to Stewart Cruden* (Edinburgh, 1984), 69–86.
Macdonald, A.D.S. and Laing, L.R., 'Early ecclesiastical sites in Scotland: a field survey, part I' and 'part II', in *PSAS* 100 (1967–68), 123–34 and 102 (1969–70), 129–45.
Macdonald, W.R., *Scottish armorial seals* (Edinburgh, 1904).
MacGibbon, D. and Ross, T., *The ecclesiastical architecture of Scotland* (3 vols, Edinburgh, 1896–7).
MacGregor, M., 'The genealogical histories of Gaelic Scotland', in A. Fox and D. Woolf (eds), *The spoken word: oral culture in Britain 1500–1800* (Manchester, 2002), 196–239.
——, 'Genealogies of the clans: contributions to the study of MS 1467', in *Innes Review* 51 (2000), 131–46.
Mackinlay, J.M., *Ancient church dedications in Scotland: non-scriptural dedications* (Edinburgh, 1914).
——, *Ancient church dedications in Scotland: scriptural dedications* (Edinburgh, 1910).
MacQuarrie, A., 'Early Christian religious houses in Scotland: foundation and function', in J. Blair and R. Sharpe (eds), *Pastoral care before the parish* (Leicester, 1992), 110–33.
——, *The saints of Scotland: essays in Scottish church history AD 450–1093* (Edinburgh, 1997).
MacQueen, H.L., *Common law and feudal society in medieval Scotland* (Edinburgh, 1993).
——, 'Girth: society and the law of sanctuary in Scotland', in J.W. Cairns and O.F. Robinson (eds), *Critical studies in ancient law, comparative law and legal history* (Oxford, 2001), 333–52.
——, 'The kin of Kennedy, "kenkynnol" and the common law', in A. Grant and K.J. Stringer (eds), *Medieval Scotland: crown, lordship and community* (Edinburgh, 1993), 274–96.
——, 'The laws of Galloway: a preliminary survey', in R.D. Oram and G.P. Snell (eds), *Galloway: land and lordship* (Edinburgh, 1991), 131–43.
——, 'Survival and success: the Kennedys of Dunure', in S. Boardman and A. Ross (eds), *The exercise of power in medieval Scotland, c.1200–1500* (Dublin, 2003), 67–94.
Matthaei Parisiensis monachi Sancti Albani chronica majora, ed. H.R. Luard (7 vols, London, 1972–3).
McDonald, A., 'Monk, bishop, impostor, pretender: the place of Wimund in twelfth-century Scotland', in *Transactions of the Gaelic Soc. of Inverness* 58 (1992–4), 247–70.
——, 'Scoto-Norse kings and the reformed religious orders: patterns of monastic patronage in twelfth-century Galloway and Argyll', in *Albion* 27 (1995), 187–219.
McDonald, R.A., 'The foundation and patronage of nunneries by native elites in twelfth- and early thirteenth-century Scotland', in E. Ewan and M. Meikle (eds), *Women in Scotland c.1100–c.1750* (East Linton, 1999), 5–15.
——, *The kingdom of the isles: Scotland's western seaboard, c.1190–c.1336* (East Linton, 1997).

——, 'Matrimonial politics and core-periphery interactions in twelfth- and early thirteenth-century Scotland', in *Journal of Medieval History* 21 (1995), 227–41.
——, *Outlaws of medieval Scotland: challenges to the Canmore kings, 1058–1266* (East Linton, 2003).
——, 'Rebels without a cause? The relations of Fergus of Galloway and Somerled of Argyll with the Scottish kings, 1153–1164', in E.J. Cowan and R.A. McDonald (eds), *Alba: Celtic Scotland in the medieval era* (East Linton, 2000), 166–87.
McLeod, W., *Divided Gaels: cultural identities in Scotland and Ireland, c.1200–c.1650* (Oxford, 2004).
McNamee, C., *The wars of the Bruces: Scotland, England and Ireland, 1306–1328* (East Linton, 1997).
McNeill, P.G.B. and MacQueen, H.L. (eds), *Atlas of Scottish History to 1707* (Edinburgh, 2000).
McRoberts, D., 'Hermits in medieval Scotland', in *Innes Review* 16 (1965), 199–217.
——, 'Rossdhu church and its book of hours', in *Innes Review* 16 (1965), 3–17.
Meek, D.E., 'The Scots-Gaelic scribes of late medieval Perthshire: an overview of the orthography and contents of the book of the Dean of Lismore', in J.H. Williams (ed.), *Stewart Style 1513–1542: essays on the court of James V* (East Linton, 1996), 254–72.
*Memoriale fratris Walteri de Convetria, ed. W. Stubbs (2 vols, London, 1872–3).
Milsom, S.F.C., *The legal framework of English feudalism* (Cambridge, 1976).
*'Miscellaneous monastic charters', ed. D.E. Easson, in *Scottish History Society Miscellany VIII* (SHS, 1951), 3–16.
Morgan, M., 'The organisation of the Scottish church in the twelfth century', in *TRHS*, 4th ser. 29 (1947), 135–49.
Murison, D., 'The historical background', in A. J. Aitken and T. McArthur (eds), *Languages of Scotland* (Glasgow, 1979), 2–13.
——, 'Linguistic relationships in medieval Scotland', in G.W.S. Barrow (ed.), *The Scottish tradition: essays in honour of Ronald Gordon Cant* (Edinburgh, 1974), 71–83.
Murray, D.C., 'Notes on the parish of Duthill', in *Transactions of the Gaelic Soc. of Inverness* 43 (1960–3), 24–45.
Napier, M., *A history of the partition of the Lennox* (Edinburgh, 1835).
Neville, C.J., 'A Celtic enclave in Norman Scotland: earl Gilbert and the earldom of Strathearn, 1171–1223', in T. Brotherstone and D. Ditchburn (eds), *Freedom and authority: Scotland c.1050–c.1650* (East Linton, 2000), 75–92.
——, 'Charter writing in thirteenth century Celtic Scotland', in A. Musson (ed.), *Expectations of the law in the Middle Ages* (Woodbridge, 2001), 67–89.
——, 'Native lords and the church in thirteenth-century Strathearn, Scotland', in *Journal of Ecclesiastical History* 53 (2002), 454–75.
——, 'The political allegiance of the earls of Strathearn during the war of independence', in *SHR* 65 (1986), 133–53.
——, 'Women, charters, and land ownership in Scotland, 1150–1350', in *Journal of Legal History* 26 (2005), 1–29.
The new statistical account of Scotland (15 vols., Edinburgh, 1845).
Nicholls, K. W., 'Rectory, vicarage and parish in the western Irish dioceses', in *Journal of the Royal Soc. of Antiquaries of Ireland* 101 (1971), 53–84.
Nicholson, R., *Edward III and the Scots* (Oxford, 1965).
——, *Scotland: the later Middle Ages* (Edinburgh, 1974).
Nicolaisen, W.F.H., 'Gaelic Place-names in Southern Scotland', in *Studia Celtica* 5 (1970), 15–35.
——, *Scottish place-names: their study and significance* (London, 1979).
Nisbet, A., *A system of heraldry* (Edinburgh, 1722).
Ó Corraín, D. and Maguire, F., *Gaelic personal names* (Dublin, 1981).
Ó Cuív, B., 'Eachtra Mhuireadhaigh Í Dhálaigh', in *Studia Hibernica* 1 (1921), 56–69.
Oram, R., 'Continuity, adaptation and integration: the earls and earldom of Mar, c.1150–c.1300', in S. Boardman and A. Ross (eds), *The exercise of power in medieval Scotland, c.1200–1500* (Dublin, 2003), 46–66.
——, 'David I and the Scottish conquest and colonisation of Moray', in *Northern Scotland* 19 (1999), 1–20.

——, 'A family business?: colonization and settlement in twelfth- and thirteenth-century Galloway', in *SHR* 72 (1993), 111–45.
——, *The lordship of Galloway* (Edinburgh, 2000).
Owen, D.R.R., *William the Lion, 1143–1214: kingship and culture* (East Linton, 1997).
Parry, M.L., 'Upland settlement and climatic change: the medieval evidence', in D. Spratt and C. Burgess (eds), *Upland settlement in Britain: the second millennium B.C. and after* (Oxford, 1985), 35–49.
Patterson, N., 'Honour and shame in medieval Welsh society: a study of the role of burlesque in the Welsh laws', in *Studia Celtica* 16–17 (1981, 1982), 73–103.
Penman, M., *David II, 1329–71* (East Linton, 2004).
——, '*A fell coniuracioun again Robert the doughty king*: the Soules conspiracy of 1318–20', in *Innes Review* 50 (1999), 22–57.
Pollock, D., 'The Lunan Valley project: medieval rural settlement in Angus', in *PSAS* 115 (1985), 357–99.
Pryce, H., *Native law and the church in medieval Wales* (Oxford, 1993).
RCAHMS, *The historical landscape of Loch Lomond and the Trossachs* (Edinburgh, 2000).
RCAHMS, *Stirlingshire: an inventory of the ancient monuments* (2 vols, Edinburgh, 1963).
Radford, C.A.R., 'The early church in Strathclyde and Galloway', in *Medieval Archaeology* 11 (1967), 105–26.
——, 'The early cross and shrine of St Mahew, Cardross, Dumbartonshire', in *Innes Review* 17 (1966), 3–10.
——, 'Excavations at Whithorn (final report)', *Trans. of the Dumfriesshire and Galloway Natural History and Archaeological Soc.* 3rd ser. 34 (1955–6), 131–94.
Reed, M. 'Anglo-Saxon charter boundaries', in idem (ed.), *Discovering past landscapes* (London, 1984), 261–306.
Reeves, W., *The culdees of the British Islands* (Dublin, 1864).
*Regiam majestatem and Quoniam attachiamenta, T.M. Cooper (Stair Soc., 1947).
*Registrum de Dunfermelyn, ed. C. Innes (Bannatyne Club, 1842).
*Registrum episcopatus Aberdonensis, ed. C. Innes (Edinburgh, 1845).
*Registrum honoris de Morton, ed. T. Thomson, A. Macdonald and C. Innes (Bannatyne Club, 1853).
*Registrum monasterii s. Marie de Cambuskenneth, A.D. 1147–1535, ed. W. Fraser (Grampian Club, 1872).
Reid, N., 'Alexander III: the historiography of a myth', in idem (ed.), *Scotland in the reign of Alexander III* (Edinburgh, 1990), 181–208.
——, 'The kingless kingdom: the Scottish guardianships of 1286–1306', in *SHR* 61 (1982), 105–29.
Reid, N.H. and Barrow, G.W.S. (eds), *The sheriffs of Scotland: an interim list to 1360* (St Andrews, 2002).
*Reliquae Celticae, ed. A. Macbain and J. Kennedy (2 vols, Inverness, 1892–4).
*Rental book of the Cistercian abbey of Cupar-Angus, ed. C. Rogers (2 vols, Grampian Club, 1879–80).
Reynolds, S., *Fiefs and vassals: the medieval evidence reinterpreted* (Oxford, 1994).
——, 'Fiefs and vassals in Scotland: a view from outside', in *SHR* 82 (2003), 176–193.
——, *Kingdoms and communities in Western Europe, 900–1300* (Oxford, 1984).
Richardson, H.G. and Sayles, G., 'The Scottish parliaments of Edward I', in *SHR* 25 (1925), 300–17.
Ritchie, R.L.G., *The Normans in Scotland* (Edinburgh, 1954).
Robertson, W., *An index, drawn up about the year 1629, of many records of charters, granted by the different sovereigns of Scotland between the years 1309 and 1413* (Edinburgh, 1798).
Rogers, J.M., 'The formation of the parish unit and community in Perthshire' (PhD thesis, University of Edinburgh, 1992).
*Rotuli Scotiae in turri Londoniensi et in domo capitulari Westmonasteriensi asservati, ed. D. MacPherson et al. (2 vols, London, 1814–19).
*Royal Commission on Historical Manuscripts Commission, third report (London, 1872).

*Royal Commission on Historical Manuscripts Commission, seventh report (2 vols, 1879). 1902).
*Scalacronica by Sir Thomas Gray of Heton, knight, ed. J. Stevenson (Edinburgh, 1836).
Scott, W.W., Syllabus of Scottish cartularies: Paisley (privately published, 1996).
*Scottish verses from the Book of the Dean of Lismore, ed. W.J. Watson (Scottish Gaelic Text Soc., 1937).
*Select Scottish cases of the thirteenth century, ed. T.M. Cooper (Edinburgh, 1944).
Sellar, W.D.H., 'Celtic law and Scots law: survival and integration', in Scottish Studies 29 (1989), 1–27.
—, 'Custom in Scots law', in La Coutume/Custom II: Europe occidentale médiévale et moderne/Medieval and modern western Europe (Brussels, 1990), 411–19.
—, 'Highland family origins – pedigree making and pedigree faking', in The Middle Ages in the highlands (Inverness, 1981), 103–16.
—, 'Marriage, divorce and concubinage in Gaelic Scotland', in Transactions of the Gaelic Soc. of Inverness 51 (1978–80), 464–93.
—, 'William Forbes Skene (1909–92): historian of Celtic Scotland', in PSAS 131 (2001), 3–21: 17.
Seymour, S.J.D., 'The coarb in the medieval Irish church (c.1200–1500)', in Proceedings of the Royal Irish Academy 91C (1933), 219–31.
Shahar, S., Childhood in the Middle Ages (New York, 1990).
Shaw, J., Water power in Scotland 1550–1870 (Edinburgh, 1984).
Shead, N.F., 'The administration of the diocese of Glasgow in the twelfth and thirteenth centuries', in SHR 55 (1976), 127–50.
—, 'Benefactions to the medieval cathedral and see of Glasgow', in Innes Review 21 (1970), 3–16.
Shearer, J., Antiquities of Strathearn (4th edn, Crieff, 1891).
*The sheriff court book of Fife 1515–1522, ed. W.C. Dickinson (SHS, 1928).
Simms, K., 'Guesting and feasting in Gaelic Ireland', in Journal of the Royal Soc. of Antiquaries of Ireland 100 (1978–9), 67–100.
—, 'Frontiers in the Irish church – regional and cultural', in T.B. Barry, R. Frame and K. Simms (eds), Colony and frontier in medieval Ireland: essays presented to J.F. Lydon (London, 1995), 177–200.
Simpson, G.G., 'An Anglo-Scottish baron of the thirteenth century: the acts of Roger de Quincy, earl of Winchester and constable of Scotland' (PhD thesis, University of Edinburgh, 1965).
—, 'The familia of Roger de Quincy, earl of Winchester and constable of Scotland', in K.J. Stringer (ed.), Essays on the nobility of medieval Scotland (Edinburgh, 1985), 102–29.
— and Webster, B., 'Charter evidence and the distribution of mottes in Scotland', in K.J. Stinger (ed.), Essays on the nobility of medieval Scotland (Edinburgh, 1985), 1–24.
Simpson, W.D., 'The Augustinian priory and parish church of Monymusk, Aberdeenshire', in PSAS 59 (1925), 34–71.
—, The province of Mar (Aberdeen, 1943).
Skene, W.F., The highlanders of Scotland (Stirling, 1902).
—, Celtic Scotland: a history of ancient Alban (3 vols, Edinburgh, 1886–90).
Smith, B. (ed.), Britain and Ireland 900–1300: insular responses to medieval European change (Cambridge, 1999).
Smith, J.G., The parish of Strathblane and its inhabitants from early times: a chapter of Lennox history (Glasgow, 1886).
—, Strathendrick and its inhabitants from early times (Glasgow, 1896).
Smout, C., 'Woodland history before 1850', in T.C. Smout (ed.), Scotland since prehistory (Aberdeen, 1993), 40–9.
Smout, T.C., A history of the Scottish people, 1560–1830 (Glasgow, 1969).
Smyth, A.P., Warlords and holy men: Scotland, AD 80–1000 (Edinburgh, 1994).
Society of Antiquaries of Scotland, Archaeological Field Survey, The archaeological sites and monuments of Clackmannan District and Falkirk District, Central Region (Edinburgh, 1999).
—, The archaeological sites and monuments of Dumbarton District, Clydebank District, Bearsden and Milngavie District, Strathclyde Region (Edinburgh, 1978).
—, The archaeological sites and monuments of Stirling District, Central Region (Edinburgh, 1979).
Squatriti, P., Water and society in early medieval Italy, AD 400–1000 (Cambridge, 1998).

★*Statutes of the Scottish church*, ed. D. Patrick (SHS, 1907).
Steer, K.A. and Bannerman, J.W.M., *Late medieval monumental sculpture in the west highlands* (Edinburgh, 1977).
Stevenson, J.F., 'How ancient is the woodland of Mugdock?' in *Scottish Forestry* 44 (1990), 161–72.
Stevenson, J.H., *Heraldry in Scotland* (2 vols., Glasgow, 1914).
—— and Wood, M., *Scottish heraldic seals* (3 vols, Glasgow, 1940).
Stock, B., 'Medieval literacy, linguistic theory, and social organization', in *New Literary History* 16 (1984–5), 13–29.
Stringer, K., 'Reform monasticism and Celtic Scotland: Galloway *c.*1140–*c.*1240', in E.J. Cowan and R.A. McDonald (eds), *Alba: Celtic Scotland in the medieval era* (East Linton, 2000), 127–65.
——, 'State-building in twelfth-century Britain: David I, king of Scots, and northern England', in J.C. Appleby and P. Dutton (eds), *Government, religion and society in northern England 1000–1700* (Stroud, 1997), 40–62.
—— and Grant, A. 'Scottish foundations', in A. Grant and K.J. Stringer (eds), *Uniting the kingdom? The making of British history* (New York, 1995), 85–108.
Stringer, K.J., 'Acts of lordship: the records of the lords of Galloway to 1234', in T. Brotherstone and D. Ditchburn (eds), *Freedom and authority: Scotland, c.1050–c.1650* (East Linton, 2000), 203–34.
——, 'The charters of David earl of Huntingdon and lord of Garioch: a study in Anglo-Scottish diplomatic', in idem (ed.), *Essays on the nobility of medieval Scotland* (Edinburgh, 1985), 72–101.
——, *Earl David of Huntingdon 1152–1219: a study in Anglo-Scottish history* (Edinburgh, 1985).
——, 'Periphery and core in thirteenth-century Scotland: Alan, son of Roland, lord of Galloway and constable of Scotland', in A. Grant and K.J. Stringer (eds), *Medieval Scotland: crown, lordship and community* (Edinburgh, 1993), 82–113.
Stuart, J., 'Notices of a group of artificial islands in the Loch of Dowalton, Wigtonshire, and of other artificial islands or 'crannogs' throughout Scotland', in *PSAS* 6 (1865), 114–78.
★*Symeonis monachi opera onmia*, ed. T. Arnold (2 vols, London, 1882–5).
Tanner, R., *The late medieval Scottish parliament: politics and the three estates, 1424–1488* (East Linton, 2001).Thomas, N., 'The Old French *Roman de Fergus*: Scottish mise-en-scène and political implications', in *Parergon*, new ser. 11 (1993), 91–101.
Thomson, D. 'Gaelic literature [Scotland]', in P.H. Scott (ed.), *Scotland: a concise cultural history* (Edinburgh, 1993), 127–44.
Thomson, D.S., 'Gaelic learned orders and *literati* in medieval Scotland', in *Scottish Studies* 12 (1968), 57–78.
——, 'Influences of medieval thinking on the Gaelic world in Scotland in the sixteenth century and later', in M.-F. Alamichel and D. Brewer (eds), *The Middle Ages after the Middle Ages in the English speaking world* (Woodbridge, 1997), 17–26.
——, 'The Mac Mhuirich bardic family', in *Trans. of the Gaelic Soc. of Inverness* 43 (1960–3), 276–304.
——, 'Three seventeenth-century bardic poets: Niall Mór, Cathal and Niall MacMhuirich', in A.J. Aitken, M.P. McDiarmid and D.S. Thomson (eds), *Bards and makers: Scottish language and literature, medieval and renaissance* (Glasgow, 1977), 221–46
Tittensor, R.M., 'History of the Loch Lomond oakwoods', in *Scottish Forestry* 24 (1970), 100–18.
Todd, J., 'Pre-reformation cure of souls in Dunblane diocese', in *Innes Review* 26 (1975), 27–42.
Toorians, L., 'Twelfth-century Flemish settlements in Scotland', in G.G. Simpson (ed.), *Scotland and the Low Countries, 1124–1994* (East Linton, 1996), 1–14.
★*The triumph tree: Scotland's earliest poetry, 550–1350*, ed. T.O. Clancy (Edinburgh, 1988).
★*Vetera monumenta Hibernorum et Scotorum illustrantia*, ed. A. Theiner (Rome, 1864).
Walker, J.R., 'Holy wells in Scotland', in *PSAS* 17 (1892–83), 152–210.
Watson, F., 'The enigmatic lion: Scotland, kingship and national identity in the wars of independence', in F. Broun and M. Lynch (eds), *Image and identity: the making and re-making of Scotland through the ages* (Edinburgh, 1998), 18–37
——, 'The expression of power in a medieval kingdom: thirteenth-century Scottish castles', in S.M. Foster, A. Macinnes and R. MacInnes (eds), *Scottish power centres from the early Middle Ages to the twentieth century* (Glasgow, 1998 59–78.

Watson, W.J., *The Celtic placenames of Scotland* (Edinburgh, 1929, repr. 1986).
Watt, D.E.R., *A biographical dictionary of Scottish graduates to A.D. 1410* (Oxford, 1977).
——, *Fasti ecclesiae Scoticanae medii aevi ad annum 1638* (2nd edn, Edinburgh, 1969).
——, 'The minority of Alexander III of Scotland', in *TRHS*, 5th ser. 21 (1971), 1–23.
Watt, J., *The church in medieval Ireland* (Dublin, 1972).
Watts, V.E., 'Medieval fisheries in the Wear, Tyne and Tweed: the place-name evidence', in *Nomina* 7 (1983), 35–45.
Webster, B., *Scotland from the eleventh century to 1603* (London, 1975)
White, S.D., *Custom, kinship, and gifts to saints: the* laudatio parentum *in western France, 1050–1150* (Chapel Hill, 1988).
Whittington, G., 'Field systems of Scotland', in A.R.H. Baker and R.A. Butlin (eds), *Studies of field systems in the British Isles* (Cambridge, 1973), 530–79.
—— and Soulsby, J.A., 'A preliminary report on an investigation into *Pit* place-names', in *Scottish Geographical Magazine* 84 (1968), 117–25.
Whyte, I.D., *Scotland before the industrial revolution: an economic and social history* (London, 1995).
Wickham-Jones, C.R., *The landscape of Scotland: a hidden history* (Stroud, 2001).
Wightman, W.E., *The Lacy family in England and Normandy 1066–1194* (Oxford, 1966).
Willelmi Rishanger ... chronica et annales, ed. H.T. Riley (London, 1865).
Willock, I. D., *The origins and development of the jury in Scotland* (Stair Soc., Edinburgh, 1966).
Winchester, A.L., 'The distribution and significance of the place-name "bordland" in medieval Britain', in *Agricultural History Review* 34 (1986), 129–39.
Winchester, A.J.L., 'The multiple estate: a framework for the evolution of settlement in Anglo-Saxon and Scandinavian Cumbria', in J.R. Baldwin and I.D. Whyte (eds), *The Scandinavians in Cumbria* (Edinburgh, 1985), 89–101.
Wormald, F., 'A fragment of a thirteenth-century calendar from Holyrood abbey', in *PSAS* 69 (1934–5), 471–9.
Wormald, P., 'Charters, Law and the Settlement of Disputes in Anglo-Saxon England', in W. Davies and P. Fouracre (eds), *The settlement of disputes in early medieval Europe* (Cambridge, 1986), 149–68.
Young, A., 'The earls and earldom of Buchan in the thirteenth century', in A. Grant and K.J. Stringer (eds), *Medieval Scotland: crown, lordship and community* (Edinburgh, 1993), 174–202.
——, 'Noble families and political factions in the reign of Alexander III', in N. Reid (ed.), *Scotland in the reign of Alexander III* (Edinburgh, 1990), 1–30.
——, *Robert the Bruce's rivals: the Comyns, 1212–1314* (East Linton, 1997).

Index

Place names followed by (S) are located in the earldom of **Strathearn**, and by (L) in the earldom of **Lennox**.

Aber (L), 170
Abercairney (S), 48, 62, 110, 136
Aberdeen
  bishops of, 153n
  cathedral chapter of, 180
Aberdeenshire, 76, 188
Abernethy (S)
  church of, 134
  lands of, 47
Aberuchill (S), 83
Aberuthven (S)
  church of, 132, 135, 152, 165
  lands of, 151, 152, 165
Abraham, bishop of Dunblane, 144, 145, 150 and n, 151, 155
  his son Arthur, 150n
Abraham the chaplain, 64, 65 *See also* Abraham bishop of Dunblane
Absolon, son of Macbeatha, 56n, 58
Absolon of Lennox, 58n, 61
Absolon the chaplain, 65, 66
ach- place names, 81, 101
Adam the chaplain, 65, 66
Adam, son of Edolf, 56n
advowsons, 136, 137, 140, 142
affray, 114, 126
aids, 32n, 108, 138, 147
airigh, 81
Alan, abbot of Inchaffray, 45
Alan, master of the scholars of Ayr, 146
Alba, 29, 38
Aldie (S), 79, 93, 97, 98
Alexander I, king of Scotland, 28, 29, 169
Alexander II, king of Scotland, 8, 20–9 passim, 42, 47, 50, 56n, 58, 85, 90, 114, 120, 125, 139n, 140n, 146, 170, 185, 222
Alexander III, king of Scotland, 2, 23–32 passim, 56n, 72, 73, 79, 85, 87, 88, 104, 120, 148, 187, 213, 222
  his wife, Margaret, 24
Alexander IV, pope, 155
alms, 54, 67, 144, 200

almshouses, 136, 174
Alpin, prior of Inchaffray, 136 and n
amercements, 107 *See also* fines
Anecol, thane of Dunning, 51, 224 *See also* Dunning
Angus
  earldom of, 6, 181
  earls of, 14, 16, 27, 28, 139
  Gilbert earl of, 126
Annandale, lordship of, 40
Antermony (L), church of 42, 138, 157
'Appeal of the Seven Earls', 28
appropriation, 142–4, 148, 151, 152, 154, 159
arachors, 57, 99–100, 101–2, 103
arbitration, 202
Arbroath
  abbey, 131, 138 and n, 139, 160, 161, 166, 167, 180, 206
  abbots of, 154n
archdeaconries, 171–2, 182
ard- place names, 101, 102
Ardchattan, 180
Ardoch (L), 59
Ardoch (S)
  lands of, 49, 102
  parish of, 96
Ardrossan
  Brice of, 75
  family, 75
Argyll
  bishops and see of, 179
  lordship of, 7, 26, 122, 179 and n, 181, 222
  Somhairle of, 5, 7, 15, 131, 161
  his sons, 161 *See also* Raonall
Arkill, 13
Arrochar (L)
  lordship of, 58
  parish of, 122, 172n, 193
  superiority of, 86
Arrochymore (L), 122
'Aschend' (L), 94, 105
assarting, 83n, 98–9, 100–1

241

assault, 107, 126 and n
Atholl
  earldom of, 1, 22, 72
  earls of, 14, 16, 27, 28, 34
  Mael Coluim earl of, 180
Auchencloich (L), 59
Auchentoshan (L), 59
Auchinreoch (L), 57
Auchterarder (S)
  church of, 134
  Maurice de, 78
  parish of, 75
  sheriff of, 125
  thanage of, 52
Auchtermuthill (S), 128
Augustinian order and rule, 21, 44, 45, 80, 103, 133 and n, 134, 136, 178, 181, 200, 205, 214, 216
Avicia the Breton, 144
Ayr
  church of, 39
  scholars of, 146
Ayrshire, 53, 75

'Bagimond's Roll', 128
Badenoch, lordship of, 180, 181, 183
baile– place names, 81
bailies, 121, 137, 216
Baldernock (L), parish of, 55, 157n
Balfron, (L), parish of, 157n
Ballagan (L), 121
Balliol
  Edward, king of Scotland, 35, 37
  family, 1, 5, 7, 31, 34, 35, 37, 225
  John, king of Scotland, 32, 34, 77
Balloch (L), 58, 77, 94, 101, 105, 117, 121
Balmaha (L), 122
Balquhidder (S)
  church of, 120
  parsons of, 120
Ban, Domnall, 26
Banchory-Ternan, 183
Banffshire, 36, 37n
Bannockburn, battle of, 34, 36
Barbour, John, 36
Bardenock (L), 59
Bardrill (S), 50n
Bede Ferdan, 62, 147, 169
  his son Cristin, 147, 169
Beg
  Mael Coluim, 39, 56, 58, 61, 147
  Rotheric, 29
Bellyclone (S), 94, 95, 96, 135
Belnello (S), 75, 128, 136, 138

ben place names, 102
Benedictine monasticism, 204
Bennie (S), 44, 50, 138n, 144, 167n
Berkeley
  Roger de, 96
  Walter de, 40
Bernham, David de, bishop of St Andrews, 184
Berwick, 32, 180
Blackford (S), parish of, 46
blair– place names, 102
Blane River, 81, 94, 102, 105, 121
Blantyre
  lands of, 71
  Stephen of, 56, 57, 59, 74 and n, 156n
  his son Patrick, 74 and n
Blar, 102
Blarefad (L), 100, 102
blench ferme, 79, 109, 110, 111
bloodwite, 107, 126
Bondington, William de, 146
Bonhill (L)
  lands of, 59, 83, 87n, 141
  parish of, 58, 64, 100, 102, 157n, 172n
Bordland (S), 97 and n, 169n
bovates, 96, 102
Bower, Walter, 134, 136n, 149, 151, 160, 213
'Bracton', 198, 203
Brechin, 137
  bishops of, 181
  church of, 134
  family, 88
  Sir William de, 77
breitheamh, office of, 52, 61, 62, 112, 114, 115, 216 See also *judex*
Brewland (S), 81, 97n
Brice, *judex* of Strathearn, 62
Brice, parson of Crieff, 166
Brice, thane of Dunning, 51, 61, 217 See also Dunning
Broich (S), 117
Bruce See also Robert I
  cause and family, 1, 2, 5, 7, 28, 31, 32, 34, 37, 73, 75, 78, 88, 117, 187, 225
  William, 208
    his wife Christina, 208
Buchan
  Alexander, earl of, 203
  earldom of, 1, 16, 34, 41, 52, 72, 129, 164, 176, 180, 189, 197, 206
  earls of, 16, 22, 25, 27, 28, 134, 177, 214
  Feargus, earl of, 22
  heiress of, 180–1

Index

Buchanan (L)
  family, 58n, 74, 75, 84
  lands of, 122
  Malcolm, 78
  Maurice de, 93, 101
  parish of, 122, 157n, 172n
  Walter of, 170n
Buchanty (S), 119
butler, office of, 40, 68 See also Causantin; pincerna

cain, 44, 92, 59, 67, 103, 104–5, 132, 134, 137, 144, 200
calp, 108
Caithness
  bishops and see of, 178, 179
  earldom of, 34, 35, 177, 181, 225
  earls of, 14, 16, 20, 27, 120, 130, 137
Caithness and Orkney, Gille Brigter, earl of, 137
  his daughter Maud, 137
Callendar (L)
  family, 58
  lands of, 58
  thanes and thanage of, 56 and n, 58, 60, 192 See also Donnchad; Mael Coluim
Cambinch (S), 45
Cambuskenneth
  abbey of, 48, 151
  abbots of, 133, 151, 154n
Cameron, Robert de, 77
Campbell, Sir Neil, 118
Campsie (L)
  church of, 42, 63n, 79, 138, 139, 140, 155, 157
  lands of, 102
  parish of, 100
Canmore kings, 13, 20, 25, 27, 131, 134, 185, 189
Caputh (S), 125
Carbeth (L), 55
Cardross (L)
  church of, 156, 165
  lands of, 37, 83
Carlisle, 32
Carrick
  dean of, 146, 158 See also Lawrence
  Donnchad, earl of, 68n
  earldom of, 39, 108, 139
  earls of, 73, 161
  family, 73n
  Gille Brigte, earl of, 100, 156
  Niall, earl of, 108, 126
carucates, 95–6, 99, 100, 101, 102, 129

castles, 8, 53, 116–24, 223
Castleton (S), 118, 119
cathair, 95, 120, 125
Cathcart, Gille Brigte de, 55
cathedra, 120
Catherlavenach (S), 50, 53, 95
Cathermothel (S), 50, 53, 95, 98, 138n
Catter (L), 95, 117, 121, 125
Causantin the *pincerna*, 68
Causantin, *judex* of Strathearn, 62
Céli Dé brethren, 80, 132, 133, 134, 139, 143, 151, 152, 162, 164, 166, 169, 170, 180, 182, 188, 205, 217
Cenél Fergusa, 185
Chamberlain, office of, 40, 47, 60, 66, 67, 70
chaplains, household, 40, 65, 66 and n, 76, 136, 140, 144, 150, 170, 175
charter writing, 43–4, 70, 188–95, 223
chattels, 107, 127, 135, 136
cheese, 26, 57, 68, 75, 83, 93, 102, 103, 104, 108, 110, 122, 129, 132, 135
Christian, mair of Dunning, 127, 128
church, reform of, 131–56 passim, 158, 159, 161–84, 225
Cistercian order, 133, 134, 138, 162, 180
Clarinch (L), 58
Clement, bishop of Dunblane, 64, 144, 145, 150–5, 159, 181
Clerk, Christian, 52
clerks, household, 64–5, 76
Cloan (S), 50n
Clova, 180
Cluny, order of, 83, 138, 140, 141, 146, 166, 168, 179, 184, 218
Clyde River, 14, 55, 81, 83, 105, 146, 187, 211
Clydesdale, 182, 211
coarb, office of, 172–4
Cochno (L), 62, 101
Colquhoun (L)
  family of, 59, 73 and n, 75, 224
  lands of, 59
common army, 20, 44, 57, 93, 104, 110
common law, 63, 92, 111, 113, 196–7, 199, 206, 214, 222
Comrie (S), 46
Comyn
  Agnes, 25, 31, 34, 35
  Alexander, 25, 203
  family, 7, 22, 31, 32, 33, 34, 72, 88, 171, 206
  John, 32, 24
  Walter, 41, 180–1
  William, 22, 40, 41, 134, 180

Conall Corc, 210
Concraig (S), 138n, 144, 167n
Conghal son of Donnchad, 50, 125
constable, office of, 40
conveth, 51, 52, 59, 67, 103n *See also fretellis*;
    frithelagium; wayting
Corbet family, 208
Cortachy (S), 137
'Cotken' (S), 98
Coul (S), 50n
Coulgask (S), 49
Coupar Angus abbey, 116, 131, 138, 180
courts of law, 29, 62–3, 88, 89, 92, 95, 107
    and n, 112–19, 125–6, 134, 145, 146–8,
    160, 176, 189, 191, 192, 196, 198, 199, 216,
    223 *See also* suit of court
craig– place names, 101
crannogs, 82, 90, 118, 120, 122, 123
Cremannan
    Thomas de, 73, 74, 83
        his daughters, 74, 83
Cressingham, Hugh de, 127
Crieff (S)
    church of, 47, 143
    lands of, 87, 117, 118, 119, 125, 127
    parson of, 30, 118, 143, 166 *See also* Brice
    'stayt' of, 117, 125
Cristin, *judex* of Lennox, 56, 62, 101, 146, 168
    his son Dùghall, 56, 62, 101, 146, 147, 168
Cristin the chaplain, 64
Croc
    family, 88, 192, 214
    Robert de, 64
        his son Simon, 55, 56, 190, 224
    Thomas, 63n
Cromdale, 183
Croy (L), 101, 105
cuit, 108
Culthill (S), 125
Cumbria, 29
cumelache, 225 *See also* serfs
cumherba, 225 *See also* serfs
Cungi the chaplain, 65
Cunningham
    dean of, 146, 158 *See also* Richard
    lordship of, 40
'Curelundyn' (S), 87

D'Aubigny
    Maud, countess of Strateahrn, 23, 44, 45,
        46, 67, 69n, 134, 161, 165, 175, 205, 208,
        209, 210, 214, 216
    Sir William, 175, 208, 216
Dalmanno (L), 64, 156

Dalnotter (L), 58
Dalpatrick (S)
    lands of, 44, 45 and n, 50, 96, 97, 168
    Nigel de, 44
    Richard de, 45 and n
Dalquhurn (L), 88
dapifer, office of, 60–1, 68 *See also* Causantin;
    Lennox, steward of; Strathearn,
    steward of
davachs, 47, 95–6, 103
David, earl of Huntingdon; *see* Huntingdon
David I, king of Scotland, 3, 4, 5, 6, 9, 14–19,
    29, 40, 41, 72, 142, 149, 163, 164, 181, 189,
    196, 213, 219, 223
David II, king of Scotland, 1, 9, 35, 37, 47,
    127
De situ Albanie, 28, 212
Deer
    abbey, 134, 164, 180, 188, 198
    Book of, 108, 214
    brethren of, 180
demesne lands, 42, 51, 60, 97, 98, 117, 135,
    137, 157
demspter, office of; *see Breitheamh*; *Judex*
dispenser, office of, 63, 67
Dominican order, 144, 151, 174
Donald, son of Anecol, steward of Lennox,
    61n, 74
Donegal, 185
Donnchad, son of Adam, 39
Donnchad, thane of Callendar, 56 and n, 58
    his son Mael Coluim, 56n
Donnchad, thane of Strowan, 51
Douglas Water, 122
Douglas, William, 203
Dower, 48, 64
drum– place names, 101
Drumdowan (S), 96
Drummond
    family, 73, 75
    Malcolm de, 75
Drumsagard (S), 48, 76, 79, 92, 110
Drymen (L)
    parish of, 59, 77, 95, 102, 122, 157n
    toun of, 100
Duibhne son of Croscrach, 66n, 70
Dumbarton
    burgesses of, 74
    burgh of, 36, 90, 160
    castle of, 26, 27, 36, 42, 120, 121, 123, 125
    sheriff of, 26, 36, 37, 114, 120, 125, 129,
    130
Dumbarton Muir, 101
Dumbartonshire, 83

Index

Dunbar
  earls of, 17, 27, 161
  Patrick, earl of, 180, 208
Dunbarney (S), 98
Dunblane
  archdeaconry of, 171
  bishops of, 64, 94, 131, 132, 133 and n, 142, 143 and n, 144, 145, 149, 150–89 passim, 191n, 206 *See also* Abraham; Clement; Jonathan, Lawrence; Robert de Prebenda, Simon; William
  cathedral church and see of, 66, 149, 150–5, 159, 160, 163n, 169, 171, 181
  chapter of, 151, 153, 154, 159
  precentor of, 151
Dundaff (S), 56, 82
Dundurn (S), 118
Dunfallin (S), 94, 105, 119, 125, 135, 136
Dunfermline, 20, 180
Dunkeld
  bishops and see of, 143, 151, 169, 181, 189, 206 *See also* John
Dunknock (S), 119
Dunning (S)
  church of, 135
  lands of, 51, 52, 103, 119
  mair of, 127, 128
  parish of, 46
  shire of, 53, 127
  thanes and thanage of, 51, 61, 79, 118, 119, 127, 192, 224
  vicarage of, 52
Duntiglennan (L), 140
Duntocher (L), 140
Durward, Alan, 25, 47
Duthil, 47

Earn
  Bridge of, 98
  islands of, 90, 118, 120 *See also* Kenmore, Neish
  Loch, 82, 83, 97, 118, 120, 127, 170
  River, 44, 48, 49, 54, 80, 81, 94, 118, 119, 162
earthworks, 117, 120, 123
'Edardoennech' (S), 45, 81
Edinample (S), 120
Edinburgh, 41, 123
Edintaggart (L), 122, 170
Edward I, king of England, 8, 29, 32, 33, 36, 78, 79, 103, 114, 124, 127, 129, 188
Edward II, king of England, 33
Edward III, king of England, 35
Elan Rossdhu (L), 122

Elgin, 41, 180
Endrick River, 81, 102, 105, 121
England, kingdom of, 24, 27, 30, 116, 118, 189, 196–204 passim, 216, 219, 220
escheats, 88, 107
Espec, Walter, 18
estate management, 47, 48, 53, 60, 66–7, 71, 86, 87, 91, 93–5, 111, 127
Ethne, wife of Fearchar of Strathearn, 209
'Europeanization', 1–2, 4–6, 8, 9–10, 25, 29, 78, 132, 133–4, 161–2, 177n, 186, 188–9, 206, 208, 219–21, 222, 223, 226
Exmagirdle (S), 96, 103

Falaise, 20, 41, 53
Farbhlaidh de Monorgrund, 168
Farbhlaidh, daughter of Kerald, 56n, 157n
Faslane (L)
  lands of, 124
  Walter of, lord of Lennox, 37 and n, 60, 68, 89, 91, 116, 124, 129, 160, 226
fealty, 5, 32, 55, 78, 109–10
Feargus, son of Cunningham, 56n, 140, 146
  his son Mael Coluim, 56n
Fearn, 180
Fedale (S), 87, 98, 144, 167n
feu and heritage, 111, 119
'feudalism', 3–6, 22, 28, 55, 57, 71–2, 95, 108, 109–11, 116, 125, 179, 196, 199, 225
Fife
  Donnchad III, earl of, 7, 40, 208
  Donnchad IV, earl of, 7, 48, 208
  earldom of, 1, 16, 40, 59, 105, 112, 124, 139, 154, 176, 181, 183, 206
  earls of, 7, 10, 14, 16, 17, 21, 22, 27, 28, 34, 49, 72, 107, 113, 126, 139, 161, 177, 179
  Ela of, 214
  Isobel of, 34
  Mael Coluim I, earl of, 7, 43n, 48, 49, 64, 98, 100, 116, 164, 179, 180, 201
  Mael Clouim II, earl of, 179
Findony (S), 120
fines, 88, 106–7, 110, 126, 129, 135, 136, 160
Finnick (L), 101
Fintry (L)
  lands of, 117, 121
  Michael de, 157, 158, 173
    his son Luke, 157, 173
  parish of, 56, 82, 157n
'Fitheleres Flat' (S), 50, 97
Fleming, William, 74
Fordun, John of, 18, 19, 27, 165
forest, 29, 57–8, 58n, 73, 83–9, 91–3, 101, 105, 120–1, 122, 137, 195 *See also* woodlands

forest law, 84–8, 91–2
forester, office of, 59–60, 88–9, 92
forfeiture, 106–7
forinsec service, 42, 54, 57n, 78, 96, 100, 102
  See also Scottish service
Forteviot (S), 51, 53
fortir, 81
Fortriu, 14, 95
Fossoway (S), 49
fosterage, 48, 70 and nn, 213–14
Foswell (S), 50n
Fowlis Wester (S)
  church of, 135
  lands of, 96, 105, 117, 118, 119, 127, 132, 138
  parish of, 50, 79
  parson of, 166 See also Maol Iosa
  shire of, 53, 95, 119
France, kingdom of, 18, 32, 219
Franciscan order, 174
fretellis, 51 See also conveth
frithelagium, 103 and n See also conveth
Fruin Water, 124
fustum et baculum, 192

Gaelic language, 3, 7, 66, 67, 166, 177, 185–6, 187, 215–18, 224, 226
Gàidhealtachd, 27, 28, 30, 38, 176, 179, 185, 210, 215, 219, 221
Galbraith
  Arthur, 56n, 59, 126, 156n, 202, 211
    his son William, 56n, 59, 156n, 192, 203
  Donald, 78
  family, 59 and n, 73, 74, 75, 126, 211, 212, 224
  Gilleasbuig, 55, 70, 202
    his son Mael Coluim, 55, 56n
  Maurice de, 56n, 74, 202
  Patrick de, 61n, 74, 92
Galloway
  Alan of, 219
  Feargus of, 5, 7, 150, 161, 164, 165
  lords of, 6, 72, 113, 123, 131, 139, 150, 161, 165, 180, 185
  lordship of, 6, 7, 10, 21, 22, 34, 53, 62, 71, 72n, 95, 114, 116, 122, 139, 161, 162, 163, 176, 178, 181, 183, 199, 206, 220, 222
  Thomas of, 26
gallows, 95, 115–16, 125–6
Gallowshill (L), 125 See also Moathill
Galwegians, 5, 18, 175, 182
Garchell (L), 77, 103, 122
Gare Loch, 58, 90, 124, 141, 166

Gargunnock (L), 102, 122
Garioch, 183
gart- place names, 81, 101
Gartbeg (L), 102
Gartconnel (L), 57, 59, 102
Gartfarren (L), 102, 122
Gask (S)
  church of, 135, 143 See also Trinity Gask
  Geoffrey of, 48
  Germanus the chaplain of, 66n
  lands of, 48n, 79
  parson of, 143, 175 See also Walter
Gilbert, the earl's 'fellow', 70
Gille-Aldan, bishop of Whithorn, 150
Gille Brigte the chaplain, 65
Gille Brigte, *judex* of Lennox, 62
Gille Brigte, son of Samuel, 56n, 146, 147, 192
Gille Criosd Gall, 70n
Gille Criosd the chaplain, 65
Gille Criosd, *judex* of Lennox, 62
Gille Criosd, son of Bede, 62
Gille M'Aodhán, parson of Rosneath, 167
Gille Mícheil, 56n
  his sons, 56n
Gille Moire the dean, 166–7
Gille Moire, dean of Lennox, 157, 172, 173
  See also Luss; Lennox
Gille Moire, son of Maol Iosa Bane, 73n
Gille Moire, tenant of Lennox, 54
Gille Naomh, steward of Strathearn, 60, 61
Gillecolman, son of Domnall 'MacBref', *judex* of Lennox, 62
Glanvill, 196
Glasgow
  archdeaconry of, 157, 171
  bishops of, 42, 79, 86, 100, 104, 131, 138–83 passim, 206
  burgh of, 82, 118, 129, 174, 187
  chapter and see of, 54, 63n, 66, 106, 128, 138, 141, 153, 155, 156, 157, 165, 168, 171, 181, 183–4, 190
  dean of, 157n See also Mortimer
  fair of, 187
  precentor of, 184
  treasurer of, 157n
Glen Douglas (L), 73
Glen Finglas (L), 102n
Glen Lednock (S), 83, 98
Glen Luss (L), 170
Glencarnie
  family of, 46, 75
  Gilbert of 34
  lands of, 46, 47

Index

Glendevon (S)
  lands of, 83
  parish of, 49
Glenfruin (L), 58, 102
Glenlichorn (S), 87
Gortachorrans (L), 102
Gorthy (S)
  family, 45, 75, 167
  Henry son of Tristram de, 45, 96
  lands of, 44, 45, 94, 105
  Tristram of, 44, 45, 167, 224
    his son Tristram, 45
  Tristram III of, 45
Graham
  David de, of Dundaff (d.c. 1282), 9, 56 and n, 57, 58, 64, 76, 87, 100, 101, 108, 110, 112, 123, 124, 187, 190, 192, 193, 200, 201-2, 203, 224
  David de, 129
  family, 59, 73, 74, 76, 78, 84, 88, 101, 124
  Malise, 38
  Patrick de, 74n, 76
Great Cause, 28, 31
Gregory IX, pope, 146, 147, 152, 153 and n, 154
Gregory X, pope, 136
Guardians of Scotland, 31

Hakon IV, king of Norway, 30
Halidon Hill, battle of, 1, 35, 37, 92, 225
Hay
  David de la, 49
  family, 75, 76
  Gilbert de la, 36, 200
Henry I, king of England, 213
Henry II, king of England, 18, 20, 221
Henry III, king of England, 24, 77
heriot, 106, 107, 225
hermits, 34, 45, 91, 132, 139, 168-70
Hertford, Robert de, 64, 156
hill forts, 123
Holyrood, 35
homage, 5, 55, 110-11, 118
Honorius III, pope, 150n
hospitals, 160 and n, 174
hostiarius, office of, 68
household knights, 70 and n
Hugh, abbot of Inchaffray, 138
Hugh, son of Simon, 63n
hunting reserves and rights *See* forest
Huntingdon
  David, earl of, 15, 25, 27, 40, 42, 44, 54, 64, 68, 69, 71, 138 and n, 144, 147, 167, 197, 210

  his daughter Ada, 23, 208
  earldom of, 26, 197, 208
hybridity, 2, 6, 8, 10, 73, 77, 92, 112, 163, 195-207

Inchaffray (S)
  abbots of, 65, 106, 136, 138, 151, 152, 154n
    See also Alan; Hugh;
    Innocent
  canons of, 51ff, 60, 62, 65, 81, 82, 85-107 passim, 130-8, 149, 151ff, 159, 162, 167, 168, 169, 189, 198, 200, 201, 205, 217, 225
  cartulary of, 217
  hermit priests of, 132, 133, 152, 165, 169, 200, 205, 216 *see also* J; Maol Iosa
  lands of, 80, 81, 82n, 97, 135, 137, 162, 205
  priors of, 46, 136, 200 *See also* Alpin; Innocent; Maol Iosa
  priory, later abbey of, 9n, 21, 31, 39, 43, 44, 45, 46, 48, 52, 61, 63, 69n, 71, 77, 79, 80, 82, 84, 93, 96-107 passim, 112, 115, 119, 128, 131-8 passim, 140, 149, 151, 152, 154, 155, 159, 161-78 passim, 180, 183, 189, 200, 201, 205, 206, 214, 217
  servants of, 67, 86, 135
Inchcailloch (L), 83, 129, 169
Inchcolm, 169
Inchconnachan (L), 58
Inchcruin (L), 58
Inchfad (L), 129
Inchmahome, 181
Inchmoan (L), 58
Inchmurrin (L), 58, 117, 120, 121, 122, 124, 129, 169
Inchtavannach (L), 58, 170
Inglis, 215, 218
Innerpeffray (S), 117, 119
Innocent, abbot of Inchaffray, 152
Innocent, canon of Scone, 136 and n
Innocent III, pope, 64, 133
Insula Missarum; *see* Inchaffray
Iona, 180, 183
Ireland, 3, 4, 16, 26, 172, 173, 179, 185, 189, 204, 206, 208, 210, 212, 216
Irish Sea, 15, 185
Irvine, 39
Iseulte, countess of Strathearn; *see* Kinbuck
Isle of Masses; *see* Inchaffray

J., hermit of Inchaffray, 133
James I, king of Scotland, 226
Jocelyn, bishop of Glasgow, 145

John the chaplain, 65
John, bishop of Dunkeld, 169
Johnstone, Sir John of, 200
Jonathan, bishop of Dunblane, 132, 133, 151
judex, office of, 39, 52, 56, 61, 62, 63, 69, 112, 125 See also *Breitheamh*; Brice; Cristin; Lennox, *judex* of; Macbeatha; Strathearn, *judex* of

Kelso
   abbey, 42, 44, 63n, 66, 79, 138 and n, 155, 190
   abbots of, 79, 155
Keltie Water, 58
kenkynnol, 108
Kenmore (S), 33, 117, 118, 120, 124
Kenneth III, king of Scotland, 28
Kerald, *judex* of Lennox
   his daughter, 168
Kerald, steward of Lennox, 61
ketheres, 104, 108
Kilbride (L), rector of, 166 See also Maol Iosa
Killearn (L)
   lands of, 74n, 101
   parish of, 56, 157n
Killermont (L), 56
Killin (S), 170
Kilmahew (L), 58, 74n
Kilmarnock (L), 157n, 170
Kilpatrick (L)
   church of, 39, 54, 80, 140 and n, 143, 145, 146 and n, 147, 148, 158, 160, 162, 166, 168, 169, 174, 183, 191
   hospital at, 174
   Humphrey de, 56n
   lands of, 39, 58, 62, 63, 70, 80, 113, 114, 139, 140, 145, 146, 147, 148, 158, 160, 168, 169, 174, 183, 203 See also Cochno; Monachkenneran
Kilsyth (L), 102, 157n
Kinbuck (S)
   family, 75, 76
   Iseulte of, countess of Strathearn, 48, 62, 71, 136, 166, 168, 175, 194, 209
   Joachim of, 48, 194
   lands of, 48
   Malcolm of, 78
Kincardine (S), 50n
Kinkell (S), 134
Kinross-shire, 98
Kintocher (S)
   Alan de, 45
   lands of 45, 68, 96
Kintyre, 26, 139

Kinveachy (S), 23, 47
Kirkintilloch (L), 55
Kirkmabrech, 183
Knaik Water, 50
knight service, 15, 18, 22, 42, 44, 46, 48, 55, 56–7, 76, 77–8, 109–11, 131
Knighton, Henry, 35
Knock (L), 101, 168
Kyle, lordship of, 40

Lanark, 41
Lanarkshire, 55, 76
'Langflath' (S), 97
Lasceles, Ralph de, 77
laudatio parentum, 194
Lawrence, bishop of Dunblane, 149
Lawrence, dean of Carrick, 146
Laws of the Bretts and Scots, 114
Leamhain (L), 218
Leamhain, daughter of Fearadhach, 210
Legerwood, 182
Lennox
   Adam of, 171n
   Ailin I, earl of, 15, 185
   Ailin II, earl of (d. *c*.1217), 8, 15, 17, 25, 26, 27, 29, 42, 54 and n, 55, 58, 59, 60, 65, 66n, 69, 70, 74, 100, 101, 113, 121, 138, 140, 141, 145, 147, 148, 155 and n, 156, 157 and n9, 166, 169, 185, 186, 189, 192, 194, 209, 210, 211, 212, 226
   Amhlaibh, son of Ailin II, 8, 25, 37n, 74, 78, 90, 124, 139, 141, 161, 166, 168, 185, 194
   army of, 223
   cartulary of, 190
   clergy of, 156
   Corc, son of Earl Ailin II, 56, 210
      his son Muireadhach, 74
   Cristin, son of Earl Ailin II, 78
   David, lord of; *see* Huntingdon
   deanery of, 157 and n 173 See also Luss; Gille Moire, Maoldomhnaich
   Donald, earl of (d. *c*.1365), 1, 37, 60, 80, 88, 89, 90, 93, 106, 116, 125, 129 and n, 60, 209, 226
   Donnchad, son of Earl Ailin II, 78
   Donnchad, son of Earl Maoldomhnaich, 58
   Dùghall, son of earl Ailin II, 39, 55, 56, 58, 74, 101, 113, 143, 145, 146, 147, 148, 156, 166, 168, 169, 183, 192
      his heirs, 74, 113, 148, 183
   Duncan, earl of (d. 1425), 38, 160n, 226
   earls of, 1–15 passim, 25–40 passim, 43, 55, 59, 63, 66, 69, 70–131 passim, 138, 140,

Lennox (contd)
    141, 142, 155–68 passim, 172, 175, 178, 179, 181, 186, 188–226 passim
  chamberlains of, 66, 67, 70 *See also* Duibhne
  chaplains of, 64, 65, 66n *See also* Absolon; Adam; Carrick, Thomas de; Germanus; Gille Brigte; Gille Crìosd; Hertford, Robert de; Muireadhach
  clerks of, 64
  hostiarius of, 68 *See also* Maol Iosa
  marshal of, 68
  Eva, daughter of Earl Ailin II, 43n, 58, 100, 210n
  free forest of, 87
  Isabella, countess of, 160n, 174
  judex of, 56, 62, 101, 146, 168 *See also* Cristin; Gille Brigte; Gille Crìosd; Gillecolman; Kerald
  Gille Crìosd, son of Earl Ailin II, 56, 58, 86, 193
    his son Donnchad, 57, 86
  kindred, 1, 3, 9, 29, 31, 32, 36, 56, 69, 78, 86, 88, 90, 91, 107, 108, 120, 123, 130–48 passim, 157–68 passim, 175, 179, 192, 193, 194, 195, 202, 204, 209–10, 211, 221, 224, 226
  Mael Coluim, son of Earl Ailin II, 74
    his granddaughters, 74
  Mael Coluim, son of Earl Maoldomhnaich, 10, 27, 29, 56 and n, 58, 63, 68, 78, 110, 112, 187, 189, 202, 209
  Malcolm I, earl of (d. *c*.1303), 9, 27–32 passim, 36, 39, 61, 67, 71, 73, 74, 75, 79, 83, 85, 87, 88, 89, 104, 107, 110–16 passim, 126, 139, 140, 141, 148, 157, 160, 166, 179, 187, 201, 203
    his wife Marjorie, 32, 33, 36
  Malcolm II, earl of (d. 1333), 1, 27, 33, 34, 36, 37, 59, 60, 73, 74, 75, 77, 88, 92, 93, 109, 113, 116, 124, 128, 129, 130, 160, 170, 179, 188, 209
    his son Murdoch, 90
  Maoldomhnaich, earl of (d. *c*.1250), 8, 9, 25, 26, 27, 29, 39, 42, 43 and n, 54–93 passim, 100 and n, 101, 104, 107, 108, 109, 110, 112, 114–32 passim, 138, 139 and n, 140–48 passim, 155 and n, 156, 157, 160, 161, 165, 166, 168 and n, 169, 175, 179–216 passim, 224, 225
    brothers of, 25, 191, 193, 209
    Elizabeth Stewart, countess of; *see* Stewart
  Margaret, daughter and heiress of Earl Donald, 37, 61, 68, 129

Lennox (contd)
  Muireadhach, son of Earl Ailin II, 56, 185
  stewards of, 56, 58, 61, 74 *See also* Absolon of Lennox; Beg, Mael Coluim; Donald son of Anecol; Fleming, William; Galbraith, Maurice de and Patrick; Kerald; Sproull, Walter
  tenants of, 104, 110, 111, 112, 114, 126, 140, 142, 156, 157, 168, 169, 170, 174, 186, 190, 191, 192, 193, 194, 197, 198, 199, 202, 203, 204, 205, 214, 219 *See also* Feargus; Luke; Mael Muire; Maoldomhnaich
  waters of, 26
  Walter of Faslane, lord of; *see* Faslane
Leny
  Alan de, 74
  family, 88
Letter (L), 56
Leven River, 81, 90, 91, 102, 105, 121, 140, 156, 166
Lindores
  abbey, 46, 96, 98, 131, 138 and n, 143, 144, 145, 149, 151n, 167, 180, 198, 200, 201
  abbots of, 154n
  monks of, 82, 98–9, 145, 151, 153, 198, 201
Lindsay
  family, 78
  David de, 40, 203
  John de, 89
  Patrick de, 59, 60, 73, 88, 89
Loch Leven, 134, 188
Loch Lomond, 30, 54, 58 and n, 59, 81, 82, 83, 84, 100, 101, 120, 121, 122, 139, 169, 203
  islands of, 30, 57, 83, 90, 101, 120, 121, 122, 124, 129, 169 *See also* Clarinch; Elan Rossdhu; Inchcailloch; Inchconnachan; Inchcruin; Inchfad; Inchmoan; Inchmurrin; Inchtavannach
Loch Long, 56, 58
Lochearnhead (S), 170
Logie (S)
  family, 78
  John de, 34
  Malise de, 110, 112
  parish of, 170n
  Walter de, 118
lords of the Isles; *see* western isles
Lothian, 50, 182
  justiciar of, 203 *See also* Lindsay, David de
Louth, 173
Luguen, 47, 48
  Richard son of, 48 *See also* Kinbuck

Luke, deean of Lennox, 56n
Luke, tenant of Lennox, 56, 202
Luss (L)
  church of, 172, 173, 174
  deanery of, 128, 157, 167, 171, 172, 173, 175
  family of, 54–5, 56n, 58, 73 and n, 74, 100, 110, 172, 173, 191
  Gille Moire of, 56n, 107, 110, 172, 173
  John de, 170, 172n
  lands of, 157, 172, 173, 203
  lordship of, 54, 58
  Malcolm of, 109, 110, 168
  Maoldomhnaich of, 56n, 107, 157n, 172, 173, 175
  Maurice de, 86, 92, 167
  parish of, 56, 83, 122, 157n, 170, 172 and n, 182, 193
  sanctuary at, 172
Luvetot
  family, 44 and n, 75, 76, 167–8, 192, 203, 224
  Nigel de, 44, 45, 96
  Roger de, 44, 50
  Soliva de, 50

Maddadsson, Harold, 20
Madderty (S)
  abthane of, 132, 169 and n
  church of, 96, 132, 135, 151
  lands of, 23, 151
Mael Coluim the clerk, 166
Mael Coluim III, king of Scotland, 2, 7, 13, 14, 16, 20, 55, 164, 165, 188, 211
  his queen, Margaret; see St Margaret
Mael Coluim, thane of Callendar, 58
Mael Muire, son of Niall, tenant of Lennox, 58, 59 and n
mair, office of, 67, 127, 128 See also Christian
Malcolm IV, king of Scotland, 3, 4, 5, 6, 14, 15, 16, 17, 18, 19, 182, 190, 208, 211, 212, 221
Malediction, 204, 205, 206, 207
'Malgegill', hermit of Muthill, 133 and n, 166
Malherbe, Gilbert de, 110
Malvoisin, William, bishop of St Andrews, 150
Mambeg (L), 57, 79
Mamore (L), 59
Man
  isle of, 26
  king of, 130
Maol Iosa the *hostiarius*, 68
Maol Iosa, parson of Fowlis, 166

Maol Iosa, prior and hermit of Inchaffray, 45, 132, 133, 134, 169, 200
Maol Iosa, rector of Kilbride, 166
Maol Iosa, son of Brice parson of Crieff, 39
Maol Iosa, steward of Strathearn, 39, 60, 61, 75
Maoldomhnaich, dean of Lennox, 157, 172, 173, 175 See also Luss
  his son Gille Moire, 157, 172, 173
Maoldomhnaich, tenant of Lennox, 54 See also Luss
Mar
  earldom of, 6, 21, 22, 47, 72, 139, 154, 181, 183, 189
  earls of, 16, 71, 113, 139, 161, 164
  Gille Crìosd, earl of, 180
  Morgrund, earl of, 180
Margaret, Maid of Norway, 31
marshal, office of, 68
Meikleour (S), 49, 167 and n
Melrose
  abbey, 15, 55
  chronicler of, 18, 19, 221
mendicant orders, 174
Menteith
  earldom of, 16, 21, 22, 41, 154, 171, 180, 197, 199
  earls of, 14, 16, 27, 28, 29, 34, 161
  Joanna of, countess of Strathearn, 35
  John, 35, 36
  Muireadhach, earl of, 182
merchet, 106, 107, 225
merklands, 99, 129
Methven (S)
  battle of, 36
  family, 167
  lands of, 87
  Michael, son of Edulf de, 73n
  Robert de, 50, 97
Mid Cambushhinnie (S), 48
mills, 45, 94, 100, 103, 105–6, 119, 135, 167
Milton (S), 94
Moathill (L), 125
Monachkenneran (L), 101, 146, 147, 192
Monifieth, 134
Monkcroft (S), 136
Monorgrund, Norrinus de, 168
  his wife, 168
Monymusk
  brethren of, 180
  church of, 134, 164
  Thomas de, 75
Monzie (S), 64
Monzievaird (S), 135

Index

Moravia
  family, 76, 78
  John de, of Drumsagard, 48, 76, 79, 92, 110
  Malcolm de, 75
  Maurice de, earl of Strathearn, 36
  William de, 32n, 75, 77, 79, 96, 98, 125
Moray
  bishops and see of, 179, 181, 183, 222
  earldom of, 5, 16, 21, 47, 59, 170, 180, 199
  earls of, 7, 14, 16
More, Reginald, 76, 92
Moreville family, 7
mormaers, 6, 13, 14, 17, 52, 53, 57, 108, 114, 130, 186, 223, 226
Mortimer, Walter de, dean of Glasgow, 157n
mottes, 116–18, 120, 121, 123, 125
Mugdock (L), 56, 59, 84, 101, 102, 123, 124
Muireadhach Albanach Ó Dálaigh, 121, 185, 210, 211, 212, 214
Muireadhach the chaplain, 65
multiple estates, 94–5
multures, 94, 103, 104, 105–6, 135, 136, 137
Murray, Andrew, 32, 33
Murroch Burn (L), 90
Muschamp, Marjorie de, countess of Strathearn, 128, 130
  her daughters, 130
Muthill (S)
  archdeaconry of, 171
  church of, 95, 132, 133n, 143, 144 and n, 145, 148, 151 and n, 152, 154, 162, 167, 169
  hermit of, 133
  lands of, 143, 151
  Mael Coluim of, 143n
  Mael Pol of, 143n
  parish of, 46, 182
  Sitech of, 143n
Mac Aeda
  Cinaed, 26
  kindred, 26
Mac Alpin, Monach, 78
Mac Duib, Cinaed, king of Scotland, 28
Mac Elibarn, Isaac, tenant of Strathearn, 77
Mac Gille Crìosd, Gilleasbuig, 56n
Mac Gille Mhartainn, Farquhar, 56 and n, 82, 193, 202
Mac Uilleim
  kindred, 5, 7, 26, 185
  Domnall, 22, 47
MacAulay
  Duncan, 78
  family, 73n, 74 and n
Macbeatha, *judex* of Starthearn, 39, 62

Macbeatha, son of Fearchar, tenant of Strathearn, 77
MacCessán
  Eòghann, 77
  family, 73n, 75
  Michael, 77
Mac Cessóc, Cessóc, 56n
MacDuff, 32
MacDùghall, Donnchad, 180
MacGilchrist's Land (L), 193
MacQueen, Hector, 197
Mac Yvel, Domnall, 56n

Napier
  Duncan, 73
  family, 74 and n
  John, 73, 92
nativi, neyfs, 77, 183
Neish Island (S), 118
Nether Cambushinnie (S), 48
Nethergask (S), 97, 105, 106, 119, 136
Nicholas IV, pope, 159
Nithsdale, lordship of, 40
Norham, 31, 32, 77, 188
Norman conquest, 16, 196, 215, 219
Normandy, 4, 41, 44, 196
Northallerton, 17, 19
Norway, 30, 83, 101, 211

Ó Dálaigh; *see* Muireadhach
Ochill Hills (S), 49, 105
oes dána, 215–16, 220
Ogilvie, 79, 124
Oliphant
  family, 48, 76, 78
  Walter, 208
ollamh, office of, 185
Orchill Muir of (S), 82, 94, 98, 128, 167n
Orkney
  earldom of, 35, 225
  earls of, 20, 27, 130, 137
Orkney and Caithness, Maud of, countess of Strathearn, 137
outer isles, 34

Pairney (S), 50n,
Paisley
  abbey, 9, 25, 58n, 61, 62, 63, 80, 83, 84, 86, 90, 100, 101, 131–49 passim, 160, 166, 168, 169, 174, 179, 180, 190, 192, 203, 205, 206, 214, 217, 218
  abbots of, 39, 63 and n, 64, 65, 101, 141, 146, 148, 192, 203 *See also* William

cartulary of, 218
monks of, 65, 70, 85, 86, 87, 90, 91, 100, 108, 140, 141, 160, 184, 192, 205, 206, 218
parishes, formation of, 26, 133, 142–3
parliament, 31, 32, 33, 35, 36
Patrick's Seat (L), 169
Pecham, John, archbishop of Canterbury, 165
perambulation, 62, 71, 99, 193, 224
Perth, 1, 18, 20, 33, 41, 82, 129, 174, 187
Perthshire, 35, 171
Pettincleroch (S), 95
Picts, Pictland, 81, 95, 210, 212
pincerna, office of, 68 *See also* butler; Causantin
pit and gallows, 42, 116, 126
Pitcairns (S), 51, 95
Pitlandy (S)
  family, 75 *See also* Theobald
  lands of, 45, 50, 68, 95, 97
Pitmeadow (S), 95
'Pitvar' (S), 96
pleas of the crown, 114
poinds, 135
Polmadie (L), 130, 160 and n, 174
Pow Burn, 44, 81, 90, 94, 105, 119, 134, 135, 162, 167
Premonstratensian order, 133
profits of justice, 88, 107

Quenching, 198
Quincy, Roger de, 40, 69, 126 *See also* Winchester

Rahallo (S), 136
Raith (S), 96
rannaire, office of, 63, 67, 68 *See also rechtaire*
ransellis, 126
Raonall, son of Somhairle of Argyll, 131, 164, 180 *See also* Argyll
rechtaire, office of, 67
Reddehow, Robert de, 146, 147
Redgorton (S), 167
Regiam Majestatem, 196
relics, 111, 172, 173–4
relief, 108–10, 128, 129
Renfrew
  lands of, 59, 202, 218
  lordship of, 40
Renfrewshire, 55, 224
rents and renders, 44, 51–9 passim, 67, 68, 75, 78, 79, 81, 82–3, 88, 92–117 passim, 120–3, 126–30, 131, 134, 136, 137–8, 144, 145, 148, 151–2, 155, 156, 162, 167n, 168, 187, 195, 200, 202

res nullius, 85, 86, 88, 89
Richard the chaplain, 65
Richard, dean of Cunningham, 146
Riddel, Gervase, 40
Rievaulx, Aelred of, 17, 18, 175
righe, 101
Robert de Prebenda, bishop of Dunblane, 155, 159
Robert I, king of Scotland, 1, 2, 30, 31, 32, 33 and n, 34, 35, 36, 37, 73, 75, 76, 83, 118, 130, 174, 188, 209, 213
Rollo family, 120
Roman de Fergus, 219–20
romance literature, 219–20
Rome, 98, 145, 150, 177, 178
Ros, Walter de, 73
Rosneath (L)
  church of, 141
  parish of, 56, 69, 167 *See also* Gille M'Aodhán
  peninsula, 124
Ross
  earldom of, 22
  earls of, 14, 16
  Fearchar, earl of, 180
Ross (S), 83
Rossie (S), 47
'Rossmadidrdyn' (S), 87
Rottearns (S), 96
ruighe, 81, 101
rural deaneries, 94, 128, 157, 171–2, 181–2
Ruthven famly, 76
Ryedale, Walter of, 196

St Andrews
  bishops and see of, 150n, 153, 174, 179, 181, 183, 184 *See also* Bernham; Malvoisin; Turgot; Wishart
  church of, 33, 36, 134
  priory of, 44, 180
St Bean, 171
St Blane's (S), 170
St Fillans (S), 118
St John the Evangelist, 149
St Kessog, 157, 170, 171, 172, 173, 182
St Patrick, 143, 145, 147, 169, 173
St Margaret, queen of Scotland, 16, 133, 163, 164, 168–9, 174, 182
St Mirren, 83, 121
St Serf, 120, 171
Saddell, 164, 180
Sallochy (L), 101, 122
sanctuary, 172 and n, 17–4
scoloc, 225

Index

Scone
  abbey, 17, 20, 24, 27, 28, 31, 34, 36, 131, 134, 136n, 189, 217
  canons of, 136
Scotia
  province of, 28, 71, 189, 199
  justiciar of, 20, 41, 63n, 114, 147, 216
seals, 2, 54, 64, 76, 91, 151, 189, 190, 191, 192, 194, 200, 201, 202, 203, 217, 219, 223, 224
seanchaidh, 211, 213
serjeanty service, 156n See also *ketheres*
Senlis, Maud de, 208
serfs, 82, 136, 183, 224–5 See also *nativi*
sheriffs and sheriffdoms, 25, 26, 36–7, 52, 113–15, 120, 124–5, 129, 130
shires, 52–3, 94–5, 103, 181–2 See also thanes, thanages
shrines, 25, 139, 170, 181–2, 183, 191
silver, 78, 79, 98, 111, 137
Simon, bishop of Dunblane, 132, 133 and n, 143n, 151, 169
Simon, son of Bertolf, 55, 56, 63n, 190, 224
Sligo, 185
Somhairle the parson, 167
Somhairle of Argyll; *see* Argyll
Soules conspiracy, 19 and n
Soules, Ranulph de, 40
Soulseat, 164
Sproull
  family, 74, 88
  Walter, 61n, 73, 74, 88
Standard, battle of the, 17
Stephen, king of England, 18, 19 and n
steward, office of, 60–1, 61n, 69 *See also* dapifer, office of
Stewart
  David, earl palatine of Strathearn, 115, 127, 226
  Elizabeth, countess of Lennox, 29, 55, 59, 65, 130, 139, 140, 166n, 175, 209, 211, 214, 216
  earls of Menteith, 29
  Euphemia, countess palatine of Strathearn, 38
  family, 5, 7, 25, 32, 49, 57, 86, 88, 128, 140, 168, 179, 226
  kings, 78
  lordship, 55, 56, 59, 63, 113, 130, 182, 202
  Robert, earl of Strathearn, 36, 37, 52, 120, 125, 127, 226
  tenants, 69n, 73
  Walter; *see* Walter II
Stirling, 20, 32, 26, 52, 123, 129

Stirling Bridge, battle of, 33
Stirlingshire, 58, 83, 110, 122
Strageath (S)
  church of, 39, 63, 95, 134, 138
  lands of, 49
  priest of, 176
Strathblane (L)
  church of, 100
  lands of, 56 and n, 58, 82, 100, 101, 110, 193
  parish of, 56, 59, 84, 121, 157n, 202
Strathcashell (L), 122
Strathclyde, 14, 57, 211
Strathearn
  Annabelle, daughter of Earl Robert, 50 and n
  archdeaconry of, 171
  army of, 20, 223
  Cecilia, daughter of Earl Gille bRrigte, 43, 49, 201
  Christian, daughter of Earl Fearchar, 208
  David Stewart, earl palatine of; *see* Stewart
  earls of, 1, 2, 6, 7, 8, 9, 10, 13, 16, 17, 23, 24, 32, 33, 38–53 passim, 66, 69, 71, 72, 73, 77, 78, 84–127 passim, 130, 131, 136–45 passim, 150–222 passim, 223, 225, 226
  chamberlains of, 66
  chaplains of, 64, 65, 76 *See also* Abraham; Cungi; John; Richard
  clerks of, 64, 76 *See also* Cristin
  dispensarius of, 67
  marshal of, 68
  pincerna of, 68 *See also* Causantin
  rannaire of, 67, 68
  scribes of, 76
  servants of, 70
  tenants of, 111, 112, 114, 120, 136, 167, 168, 170, 174, 175, 186, 192, 194, 197, 198, 199, 204, 205, 219 *See also* Macbeatha; Mac Elibarn
  Ethne, daughter of Earl Gille Brigte, 49, 210
  Ethne, wife of Earl Fearchar of Strathearn, 132, 151, 153, 189, 209, 210
  Euphemia Stewart, countess palatine of; *see* Stewart
  Fearchar, earl of, 8, 14, 17, 18, 19, 22, 47, 49, 57, 58, 132, 133, 134, 143, 149, 151, 153, 165, 178, 209, 210, 221, 226
  Fergus, son of Earl Gille Brigte, 10, 44, 46, 47 and n, 50, 78, 82, 98, 99, 103, 107n, 115, 116, 123, 126, 138n, 144, 145, 167, 194, 198, 201

Strathearn (contd)
  Gilbert, son of Earl Robert, 75, 138
  Gille Brigte, earl of (d. 1223), 8, 9, 19–27
    passim, 39, 41–107 passim, 114, 115, 123,
    126, 129–217 passim, 224
  Gille Brigte, son of Earl Gille Brigte, 46, 47
    See also Glencarnie
  Gille Criosd, son of Earl Gille Brigte, 47
    and n, 134, 165
  John de Warenne, earl of; see Warenne
  Iseulte, countess of Strathearn; see Kinbuck
  judex of, 61, 62, 63n, 125 See also
    breitheamh; Brice; Causantin; Macbeatha
  kindred, 1, 3, 9, 32, 32, 34, 46, 69, 78, 86,
    108, 123, 130, 132, 134–61 passim, 164,
    166 and n, 167, 168, 175, 178, 183, 185,
    193, 194, 195, 201, 204, 209–10, 211,
    212–13, 216, 221, 224, 226
  mair of; see Christian
  Malise, son of Earl Gille Brigte, 46, 47, 78,
    143, 167, 173, 175, 194
    his son Nicholas, 47, 143, 173
  Malise II, earl of (d. 1271), 9, 20, 23, 24,
    28, 31, 39, 41, 45, 47, 51, 60, 62, 66, 67,
    73, 75, 76, 77, 82, 97, 99, 105, 106, 107,
    110, 117, 118, 126, 128, 129, 130, 132,
    136, 137, 152, 155, 158, 159, 174, 183,
    187, 199, 202, 204, 209, 210, 213, 217,
    225
    his daughters, 130
  Malise III, earl of (d. *c*.1317), 23, 25, 28, 31,
    32 and n, 33 and n, 34, 36, 39, 52, 61,
    62, 73, 75, 76, 77, 79, 86, 93, 112, 118,
    120, 124, 125, 127, 128, 130, 136, 137,
    138, 142, 159, 188, 210
    sons of, 32, 210
  Malise IV, earl of (d. *c*.1329), 23, 33 and n,
    34, 76, 93, 106, 110, 127, 159
    his wife Joanna; see Menteith
  Malise V, earl of (d. *c*.1350), 1, 23, 25, 36n,
    76, 80, 83, 92, 106, 127, 159, 225, 226
    his daughters, 36n
  Manach of, 92
  Maria, daughter of Earl Malise IV, 48
  Maria, daughter of Earl Robert, 50 and n
  Marjorie de Muschamp, countess of
    Strathearn
  Maol Iosa, son of Earl Fearchar, 23, 46 and
    n, 47, 49, 57, 78, 115, 123, 126, 138n,
    143, 144, 155, 167 and n, 194, 201, 208
  Maol Iosa I, earl of, 8, 14, 17, 18, 19
  Maud, daughter of Earl Gille Brigte, 48, 49,
    83, 98, 201, 214
  Maria, daughter of Earl Robert, 75

Strathearn (contd)
  Maud, daughter of Earl Malise III, 128, 130
  Maud D'Aubigny, countess of Strathearn;
    see D'Aubigny
  Maurice de Moravia, earl of; see Moravia
  Robert, earl of (d. 1245), 8, 23, 24, 39–58
    passim, 61 and n, 63, 64, 65, 67, 69, 75,
    76, 86, 112, 117, 132, 136, 137, 138n,
    142, 150, 152, 155, 158, 167, 179, 186,
    187, 189, 198, 200, 201, 209, 210, 217
  Robert, son of Earl Malise II, 210
  Robert, son of Earl Malise III, 210
  Robert Stewart, earl of; see Stewart
  steward of, 50, 53, 60, 61, 66, 75, 125 See
    also Conghal; Dapifer; Gille Naomh;
    Maol Iosa
  thanes in; see Dunning; Strowan
  women of, 79, 104, 214
Strathgryfe, 55
Strathspey, 181, 183
Strathtay, 47, 49, 123, 167 and n
Strathy (S), 50n, 75
Strowan (S)
  church of, 136, 142
  lands of, 118
  thanes and thanage of, 51, 53, 103, 117, 192
Struc a' Chabeil (S), 170
suit of court, 112, 125
Sutherland, earls of, 16 , 27

Tambowie (L), 59
Tarbert (L), 83
teinds, 51, 67, 85, 90, 94, 99, 104, 105, 107,
  128, 132–45 passim, 151–2, 154–6, 163,
  165, 167n
thanes, thanages, 50, 51, 52, 58, 59, 60, 69,
  79, 103, 117, 118, 119, 125, 181, 192, 217,
  224 See also Auchterarder; Callendar;
  Dunning; Forteviot; Strowan; *toísech*
Theobald, son of William son of Clement, 45,
  50, 97, 168
  his son Luke, 45, 168 See also Pitlandy
Thony, Sir Robert de, 128, 130
timber, 81, 85, 86–7, 88–9, 116, 122–3, 124,
  135, 137, 147, 169
Tironensian order, 133, 138, 139, 167, 200,
  201
tocher, 48–9, 50 and n, 58, 83, 130, 166, 186,
  201
toísech, office of, 52, 59, 60, 74, 89, 92, 95 See
  also thanes, thanages
tolls, 88, 106
Tom-na-Chaisteal (S), 119
Tom-na-Clog, 170

Index

transhumance, 81, 102
Trinity Gask (S), 96, 127 *See also* Gask
Tristram; *see* Gorthy
Tullibardine (S), 50, 125
Tullieden (S), 151
Turgot, bishop of St Andrews, 133, 163, 168, 174
Turret Water, 81
Turriff, 180

Vikings, 212

Walenus, 13
Wales, 3, 4, 16, 189, 204, 206, 208
Walkinshaw (L), 168
Wallace, William, 32, 33
Walter I, son of Alan, 140, 200, 218
Walter II, son of Alan, 43, 49, 55, 69, 71, 86, 114, 130, 166, 182, 201, 209, 211
Walter, bishop of Glasgow, 42, 139, 155, 156, 157
wappinshaws, 114
wardship, 29, 34, 108, 109, 110, 112
Warenne
  earls of, 72
  family, 208
  John de, earl of Strathearn, 33, 35
warrandice in Scotland, 147, 195–207

warranty in England, 195–9, 202, 207
wars of independence, 1, 30, 31, 32, 33, 34, 35, 36, 37, 188
wayting, 103 *See also* conveth
Wester Cambushinnie (S), 48
western isles, 15, 25, 26, 30, 161, 164, 176, 178, 179, 183, 185, 187
Whithorn
  bishops of, 150 *See also* Gille-Aldan
  church of, 153n, 170n
William I, king of England, 220
William I, king of Scotland, 3, 5, 6, 8, 14, 15, 16, 20, 22, 23, 25, 26, 28, 41, 46n, 47, 53, 114, 135n, 167, 180, 208, 213, 216, 221
William, abbot of Paisley, 63n, 70, 71, 146, 148
William, bishop of Dunblane, 159
Winchester, earl of, 68 *See also* Quincy
Wishart, William, bishop of St Andrews, 184
witness lists, 14, 15, 19, 23, 24, 39, 40, 42, 45 and n, 48, 50, 61–77 passim, 93, 152, 157n, 166, 183, 193, 203, 207, 213
woodlands, 81, 82–4, 85–9, 90, 91, 92, 93, 101, 103, 105, 135, 140, 141 *See also* forest

York
  burgh, 20, 23
  Treaty of, 23 and n